OLD FUTURES

POSTMILLENNIAL POP

General Editors: Karen Tongson and Henry Jenkins

Old Futures

Speculative Fiction and Queer Possibility

Alexis Lothian

NEW YORK UNIVERSITY PRESS

New York

NEW YORK UNIVERSITY PRESS
New York
www.nyupress.org

References to Internet websites (URLs) were accurate at the time of writing. Neither the author nor New York University Press is responsible for URLs that may have expired or changed since the manuscript was prepared.

Library of Congress Cataloging-in-Publication Data
Names: Lothian, Alexis, author.
Title: Old futures : speculative fiction and queer possibility / Alexis Lothian.
Description: New York : New York University Press, [2018] | Series: Postmillennial pop |
Includes bibliographical references and index.
Identifiers: LCCN 2017060983| ISBN 9781479811748 (cl : alk. paper) |
ISBN 9781479825851 (pb : alk. paper)
Subjects: LCSH: Speculative fiction—Women authors—History and criticism. | Speculative fiction—Black authors—History and criticism. | Speculative fiction—20th century—History and criticism. | Future, The, in literature. | Gender identity in literature. | Race in literature.
Classification: LCC PN3448.S64 L68 2018 | DDC 809/.93353—dc23
LC record available at https://lccn.loc.gov/2017060983

New York University Press books are printed on acid-free paper, and their binding materials are chosen for strength and durability. We strive to use environmentally responsible suppliers and materials to the greatest extent possible in publishing our books.

Manufactured in the United States of America

10 9 8 7 6 5 4 3 2 1

Also available as an ebook

For Alan Lothian (1947–2010)

and Ellen Brush (1953–2011)

It is not that I have no future. Rather it continually fragments on the insubstantial and indistinct ephemera of then.
—Samuel R. Delany, *Dhalgren* (1974)

The future is already here. It just isn't very evenly distributed.
—William Gibson (sometime in the 1980s)

We can't know in advance, but only retrospectively, what is queer and what is not.
—Elizabeth Freeman, *Time Binds* (2011)

CONTENTS

Introduction

The Future's Queer Histories

Futurity Now and Then

We are living in the future. At least, we often say we are. A Google search for the phrase at any point in the 2010s would bring up technologies that exist in the present, from wearable computers to 3D printing. The act of internet searching itself invokes the runaway pace of technological change; futuristic technologies from a few years ago look dated and old-fashioned now. And the projected social futures of dystopian fiction have become everyday touchstones for current political events and ongoing technocultural transformations alike. What do we gain and what do we lose when we call our present the future? What does the language of futurity make possible, what does it exclude, and what are the histories that have brought us to this point? And what happens to the futures we have imagined once they have been superseded by real-world events? This book asks what it has meant to conjure alternative futures, including no-futures, from the standpoint of a potentially apocalyptic present. Recognizing that our present moment, the second decade of the twenty-first century, is not the only one that has experienced an obsession with futurity, it delves into the archive of futures that have been imagined and that failed to come to pass, identifying a queer tradition of critical speculation in the twentieth century that continues to make itself felt in the twenty-first.

Searching online for "the future" brings up not only real-world technologies and political thinkpieces but also the iconic spaceships and flying saucers of popular science fiction. Narratives of possible futures have given us languages through which to understand our present. But the discourse of "the" future has never been a singular one. Living in the future for some may mean that the twentieth century's technological utopias are playing out in continual wireless connectivity and media availability. For others, it means laboring to build that future amid violent, dystopian realities. In the language of capital, the future is a matter of financial speculation: traders gamble on possibilities for the sake of profit, rarely attending to other long-term consequences. Meanwhile, the spectacle of speculative destruction converges intimately with the unpredictable yet repetitive events of catastrophic climate change; science fiction imagery becomes indistinguishable from news reports. The end of the world as we know it seems continually imminent. Yet we live in the debris of many ended worlds, whose inhabitants continue to live on.

The history of the imagined future has been written before. Scholars have shown how the idea of the future was central to the creation and maintenance of imperial domination and technological modernity, shaping the tropes of what we now call "science fiction" as it arose in the United Kingdom and United States.[1] *Old Futures* focuses on works that counter these narratives even as they are part of them—the possible and impossible futures speculated by and for oppressed populations and deviant individuals, who have been marked as futureless or simply left out by dominant imaginaries. Feminist science fiction, Afrofuturism, and new media studies are three areas in which futurist imaginaries have been extensively studied; this book participates in the scholarly conversations in all three fields even as it pursues an idiosyncratic archive for each. The texts and moments I explore bring marginalized futures into conversation with the radical reconceptualizations of temporality offered by recent scholarship in queer studies. My goal is to better understand the social, political, and cultural forces we invoke when we practice the art of living in the future, of imagining the consequences of the present as we seek to change it. Grappling with the dense futurities of the present and the past, the project adds new dimensions to the scholarly frames of queer theory, to studies of temporality in narrative and media, and to existing critical discourses on speculative narrative genres and the publics that surround them.

The cultural politics of the imagined future follow some familiar trajectories. Humanity's continuation seems to demand the privileging of heterosexual procreation; technological capital seems to define the possibility of advancing toward a desirable technoscientific future, leaving those who cannot access it behind in the past. Movements against racial and imperial domination also rely on a future toward which adherents can work, even as scholars in postcolonial and black studies have highlighted the influence of empire on ideas of historical time.[2] Queer temporal theory has insisted on a nonlinear approach to the production and reproduction of futures. It asks what worlds are made and what pleasures found when time is not a relentless onslaught of future generations angled toward progress, degeneration, or some combination of the two. Scholarship on queer temporality has highlighted ways in which political and social orientations to futurity often reproduce conservative norms, suggesting backwardness or ephemerality as alternative formations.[3] Yet the narrative act of imagining the future has received little concern in queer scholarship. Meanwhile, in the most influential literary and cultural studies of the speculative genres, the gendered and sexualized underpinnings of futurity itself remain relatively uncomplicated.[4] In recent years, scholarly attention to the radical potentialities of imagined futures and speculative or science fictions has been growing exponentially. Throughout its gestation, this book has been in conversation with thinkers both inside and outside the academy who are attending to the politics of speculation.[5] Its major contributions to that conversation are twofold: to think through the queer cultural politics of speculative narrative with a breadth and depth not yet attempted; and to offer a historical grounding to show one possible genealogy for the act of queer world-making through speculative imagining. *Old Futures: Speculative Fiction and Queer Possibility* is simultaneously a partial shadow history of speculative fictions, centering on oppositional and marginal works that tend to appear as footnotes at most in genre histories and taxonomies, and an intervention in contemporary queer theories of temporality and futurity.

Since the publication of Lee Edelman's *No Future: Queer Theory and the Death Drive* well over a decade ago, something of a consensus on the relationship between queerness and the future has emerged. Queer time signifies breaking with straight and narrow paths toward the future laid out for the reproductive family, the law-abiding citizen, the believer in markets. Instead it lingers or refuses, flashing up in moments of ephemeral utopia or doubling back to reanimate the pleasurable and/or painful past. Queer theory offers creative and fertile ways to think about time. Yet so far it has rarely considered the possibility that vital queer alternatives may lie at the end of linearly projected, even reproductive, futurist imaginaries. What if, instead of a queer present reshaping the ways we relate to past and future, turning to the futures imagined in the past can lead us to queer the present?

At the same time as the fashion for *no future* arose in queer theory, narratives of apocalyptic conditions in a world pushed seemingly to its end by speculative capital and environmental destruction have become dominant in transatlantic cultural commentary, leading both to techno-logical solutionism and to expressions of the abandonment of hope.[6] *Old Futures* turns to often-forgotten insights and narratives to find ap-proaches that take up the future as a transformative possibility without either idealizing or demonizing the past. The queer possibilities invoked are not always hopeful, desirable, or even livable. To open up a future for speculative contemplation is not the same as to demand it be brought into reality. But old futures cast unexpected light into the present. If we attend to them closely enough, we might find that queer futures' histories underwrite our present efforts to imagine possibilities for the future, to enact transformations in the present, and to think critically about time.

This introduction unpacks what is at stake in my identification of a queer cultural politics for speculative fiction, in terms of both queer stud-ies' relationship to the speculative and scholarship on science fiction as a genre. It also explicates the archive that I have brought together, whose three sections each address one queered formation of speculative futu-rity. Centering on feminist utopian/dystopian reproductive futures, on futures of racialized gender as imagined in black science fiction, and on images of speculative possibility that queer the temporalities of moving-image media, *Old Futures* gathers an archive of feminists, queers, and people of color who insist that the future can and must deviate from dominant narratives of global annihilation or highly restrictive hopes for redemption. By broadening the ways we think about speculation in the mode of the political, I seek to better account for the roles of gender, race, and sexuality in the production and destruction of futures both real and imagined.

In the epigraph, I cite a famous remark from William Gibson, the sci-ence fiction writer whose coinage of the term *cyberspace* has immortalized him in media history: "The future is already here, it just isn't evenly dis-tributed."[7] The project of this book is to ask what imagined futures mean for those *away from whom* futurity is distributed: oppressed populations and deviant individuals, who are denied access to the future by dominant imaginaries, but who work against oppression by dreaming of new possibility. Each chapter chronicles some of the myriad means by which uneven distributions of discursive and material futures takes place: through eugenics, utopia, empire, fascism, dystopia, race, capitalism, femininity, masculinity, and many kinds of queerness, reproduction, and sex. In each case, I try to show what we can learn from negotiations and transformations enacted by speculative fictions' engagements with and critiques of the future's discursive creation—to highlight cultural producers' efforts to imaginatively redistribute the future.

A Brief History of Queer Time

The history of queer scholarship is a history of futures. As a politicized anti-discipline growing out of a longer history of gay and lesbian studies, queer theory emerged in the early 1990s from the convergence of activist energies with the US academy at what Janet Halley and Andrew Parker describe as "the riveting nexus of the feminist sex wars with the crescendo—which at the time we did not know would diminish—in AIDS-related death among United States gay men."[8] Judith Butler, Eve Sedgwick, and other instigators wrote criticism and theory that was motivated by a compulsion to change the world in such a way that gay people's futures would no longer be curtailed, whether through death from AIDS or via the policing and delegitimization of deviant desires. Their work built on Michel Foucault's epistemological histories, which had foregrounded the intersections of gender and desire with power and ideology—showing the imbrication of power and resistance yet also opening spaces for a future when those relationships could look different than they had in the past.[9] Queer theory and activism pushed against structures that seemed immutable, insisting on the contingent past and unpredictable future of masculinity, femininity, kinship, and desire. How could attempts to envisage possibilities outside heteronormative structures not involve a certain futurity? There is a powerful speculative element in the move from deconstructing existing binaries to visualizing—one might even say fictionalizing—how the world might be changed by those binaries' subversion or destruction.

In one of the first uses of the phrase "queer theory," in 1992, Teresa de Lauretis asks whether "our theory could construct another discursive horizon, another way of living the racial and the sexual."[10] A queer future is held up as hopeful prospect at the end of 1990's *Gender Trouble*, too, when Butler writes that "if identities were no longer fixed . . . a new configuration of politics would surely emerge from the ruins of the old."[11] Queer theorizing has been, in Lauren Berlant and Michael Warner's 1995 description, "radically anticipatory, trying to bring a world into being."[12] Radical queer politics has been seen as a potential way out of the normativities imposed by the capitalist, neoliberal political economy of dominant Western (particularly American) culture. Queer theory began as a way to imaginatively activate new or emergent ways of life through intellectual work, through writing or teaching as well as philosophizing. Even as queer studies becomes part of academic disciplinarity, this speculative intensity has continued. Donald E. Hall's 2003 primer in queer theory, for example, explicitly invites its undergraduate readers to become queer critics, joining "a volunteer organisation devoted to working very hard to queer our *future*."[13]

The queer worlds and new horizons to which early queer theorists allude tend to be located in subcultural ways of living, buried in the insufficiently documented past or between the lines of existing texts. Yet recurrent theoretical emphasis on the *newness* of queer perspectives suggests—as José Muñoz would later make explicit—that the queerest space and time was viewed as one that had not yet come into being. Figurative futures in queer scholarship have invariably been *invoked*, but rarely imagined in the literally representational terms I explore. To precisely name what a queer future might look like would seem to go against queerness's refusal of binding normative constraints, tying things down to an overly predictable future. I argue throughout the book that this is not, or at least not simply, the case.

Propositions like Hall's suggest that an ahistorical future will remain perpetually ripe for queering. But the actual political future that US-based queer activists had a hand in creating did not resemble early queer scholarship's implicit utopias. Instead, a politics of what Lisa Duggan named in 2003 as "homonormativity" emerged, and the most privileged of those formerly excluded from heteronormative life—often well-off, white gay men—consolidated "a privatized, depoliticized gay culture anchored in domesticity and consumption."[14] Same-sex marriage activism, in which working towards equality becomes synonymous with participating in the couple form and politicizing the consumption of wedding-related commodities, has become a primary signifier of homonormativity.

At the same time, critics of queer theory's relative lack of attention to class and race were calling for an understanding of queer possibility untethered from genealogies of gay assimilation. In a field-defining 1997 essay, Cathy Cohen argues that the "transformational" potential of queer politics could be realized only through a "radical intersectional left analysis" that would attend closely to the ways that "heteronormativity interacts with institutional racism, patriarchy, and class assimilation" and acknowledge that racialized heteronormativity is oppressive to more than just individuals who hold LGBTQ identifications.[15] Even as liberal gay and lesbian activists have succeeded in campaigns for marriage, military inclusion, and hate crimes legislation, radical thinkers and activists refuse to be satisfied with a politics based on assimilation into conservative nationalist timelines, restrictive racialized gender norms, and the reproductive family home.[16] They focus instead on queerer possibilities, such as the social and political transformations required to challenge the continuing curtailment of marginalized queer and trans people's futures. In his 2011 book *Normal Life*, Dean Spade describes a radical transgender politics as necessitating "a shared imagination of a world without imprisonment, colonialism, immigration enforcement, sexual violence, or wealth disparity."[17]

In his *In a Queer Time and Place* (2005), Jack Halberstam writes that queerness should be considered less as a question of gender's interface with desire and more as the site of "strange temporalities, imaginative life schedules, and eccentric economic practices" that open up "queer relationships to time and space."[18] From this branch of queer politics has emerged a definition of queerness as a site where the lines between past and future created by heteronormative structures of social and biological reproduction can be diverted or broken off. In this context, the proposition of a queer future requires new ways of thinking about temporality itself.

Perhaps the single most influential work on queer time has been Edelman's flamboyantly argued *No Future* (2004). *Old Futures* came into being as a search for alternatives to the relationships between queerness and futurity that have come to seem like common sense in the wake of Edel-man's work, and I engage with specific elements of his critique in some depth as part of the "History of No Future" that I trace in part 1. Arguing that to be queer is to oppose futurity, Edelman coined the term *reproductive futurism* to describe the overwhelming tendency for political value to be defined in terms of a future *for the children*. He insists that the power of queer critique inheres in its opposition to this narrative and therefore to politics as such. Working within Lacanian theory to create a psychoanalytic response to the assimilation of queer difference into conventional modes of familial time, Edelman insists that invocations of a better social reality for future generations are inextricably entangled with a straight ideology that narrows the terms of debate to those that ensure the protection of a symbolically innocent "Child" and the dream of a clean, new future it symbolizes.[19] Political futures are "kid stuff"; forward-looking temporalities are by definition part of a normative model that grinds out the same social relations over and over again while pretending to advocate progressive change and obscure the horrifying fact that "the future is mere repetition and just as lethal as the past."[20] There is little room for speculative futures of queer possibility when queers are assigned to embody the "death drive" that unmakes subjectivity, the "grave" that "gapes from within . . . reality's gossamer web" and exposes its fragility and falsehood.[21] The oppositions between queerness, negativity, and futurity are never as straightforward as Edelman lets them appear, however. Among the old futures of feminist and queer speculative fiction I explore in this book, there are moments in which the anti-futurist negativity he names as queer is used for multiple political ends.

My work rebounds from Edelman's to attempt an intersectional understanding of queer anti-futurism by broadening and deepening the archive of futures on which an analysis of reproductive futurism can draw, attending particularly to the articulation of fictional futures with nation, empire, race, and gender. One way that I do this is to think intensely about reproduction itself. In a rare discussion of gendered embodiment that takes place in a footnote, Edelman argues that queer anti-futurism is most often embodied by male figures because of "a gender bias that continues to view women as 'naturally' bound more closely to sociality, reproduction, and domesticating emotion."[22] This gendering of futurity and sociality, to which Edelman briefly alludes, will be a consistent theme throughout *Old Futures*, especially though not exclusively in part 1, which focuses on the reproductive politics of feminist speculation. The historical and political presence of reproductivity shapes the gender politics of the future: if children are the future, someone must bear and parent them, and the significance of that biological and social reproduction cannot be written off as a byproduct of patriarchy.

Feminist theory has long challenged women's relegation to a reproductive position subordinate to men's productivity. Shulamith Firestone's 1970 polemic *The Dialectic of Sex* is an important example: not only does Firestone call for the abolition of gestation and its replacement with cybernetic wombs, but she also insists that childhood itself is an oppressive dystopian structure that ought to be abolished. Childhood for Firestone is the imposition of adult fantasies of innocence on individuals who should be acknowledged for their existence, not only for their potential.[23] When Firestone talks about reproduction, she is as much concerned with the perpetuation of means of production and ways of life through reproductive labor, as understood in the Marxist sense, as she is with baby-making. She insists that the only way to reproduce a future that would not continually oppress women would be to separate the former from the latter senses of the term. And, because "the heart of woman's oppression is her child-bearing and child-rearing role," biological reproduction must be ended in order to stop women being dehumanized by their role as incubators for the future of the human race.[24] Few feminists have seriously contemplated demands as revolutionary as Firestone's call to abolish children and mothers, but they have often imagined what it might mean to reconfigure the gendered politics of reproduction.[25] Queer scholarship and activism, by contrast, has tended either to elide feminist critiques of reproductive labor or to take them as a given, moving immediately to the ways reproduction can be resisted and alternative temporalities and futurities explored. Queer worlds seem self-evidently not to include reproductive futures. Yet reproduction and heterofuturity are not always easily equated.

This book devotes considerable space to recounting historical aspects of the critique of reproductive futurism and developing new ways to think reproduction and futurity together without, hopefully, submitting to the clichés of a singular reproductive futurism. My arguments assume and assert that same-sex orientations and queer political critiques do not straightforwardly map onto one another, and that this disjuncture is not purely a product of the homonormative present but extends into the past. I consider the imaginative production of multiple reproductive futurisms at specific historical moments and ask how they are differentiated by gender, desire, colonialism, capitalism, nation, and race. What looks normative and oppressive through one lens may appear differently through another, and we will better understand the complexities of queer political possibility in the present if we angle our analysis through multiplex frames. In devoting a substantial part of this queer studies project to the cultural workings of reproductive bodies, I hope to show that it is necessary to pay attention to the deviances within what appears normative, as well as the normativities within what is, ostensibly, utterly queer. I look at the historical reproduction of bodies, races, nations, and social relations in white British feminist utopias (chapter 1), in white English women writers' uses of futuristic fiction to engage with European fascism (chapter 2), and in African American figurations of reproductive futurisms that insist on the differential meanings of sex and reproduction across racial lines (chapter 3). In each case, "the future of the race" and the idea of "no future" or "the end of the world" are central fictional tropes that I unpack to show their exposition of historical contradictions and deviances and their resonances with queer thinking in the present.

The idea of queerness as oppositional to futurity emerged in critical response to queer theory's more utopian emphases on hope and transformation, and to assumptions that sexual and political radicalism could naturally align to create fabulous avant-garde socialities. From a different angle, other queer theorists of time have emphasized the pull of the past on the present. In *Feeling Backward* (2007), Heather Love writes that "advances such as gay marriage and increasing media visibility of well-heeled gays and lesbians threaten to obscure the continuing denigration and dismissal of queer existence," and draws on fictional depictions of queer subjects in the past whose self-articulation demands that they be seen as more than "the abject multitude against whose experience we define our own liberation."[26] Love insists that to let go of the past's problems and discomforts in the hope of a better future is to give up on the misfit elements that have most shaped the meanings of queer existence. She challenges the optimism of future-focused thinking as well as its temporal flow. Elizabeth Freeman's 2011 *Time Binds* begins with a brief personal narrative that resonates with Love's work. Freeman writes that she once "thought the point of queer was to be always ahead of actually existing social possibilities," but now accepts that "the point may be to trail behind actually existing social possibilities: to be interested in the tail end of things, willing to be bathed in the fading light of whatever has been declared useless."[27] Among the useless things she cites, with their "ways of living aslant to dominant forms of object-choice, coupledom, family, marriage, sociability, and self-preservation," are "embarrassing utopias," the futuristic emissions of outdated modes of being.[28] Many of the oldest futures I discuss feel embarrassing to approach if we are looking for historical precursors for radical queer thought. Freeman's and Love's generosity toward the uncomfortable, ugly, and often violent past is a necessary tool for entering into what I argue is a necessary engagement with these works, without obscuring either problems or potentialities.

Time is not only a linear movement from past into present and on to the future, although this progressive or developmental model is predominant in much speculative fiction. It is also lived in the rhythms of the body. Freeman coins the term "chrononormativity" to talk about the bodily rhythms of normative time. Drawing from Dana Luciano's writings on "chronobiopolitics," she describes the way that temporal norms embed the rhythms of economic production into the body, shaping individuals' lives into forms that enable them to participate in dominant histories and socialities. Chrononormativity is "the use of time to organize individual human bodies toward maximum productivity"; through it, "institutional forces come to feel like somatic facts," as "manipulations of time convert historically specific regimes of asymmetrical power into seemingly ordinary bodily tempos and routines, which in turn organize the value and meaning of time."[29] The somatic and embodied aspects of temporality and futurity that chrononormativity describes come especially to the fore in part 3, where I engage the technological reproduction of imagined futures as experienced in the bodily tempos and routines produced by our interaction with the analog and digital screens on which imagined futures are displayed.

Chrononormativity weaves all who can follow its tempo into the fabric of dominant culture, making them part of the production and reproduction of social life and of capital. It leaves out or leaves behind those who are out of step, who cannot keep up—often due to poverty, disability, race, or sexuality. To think against chrononormativity is to acknowledge that "within the lost moments of official history, queer time generates a discontinuous history of its own," which is best told through the erotic entanglements of past, present and future.[30] Freeman shows how dominant cultures exert power by naturalizing the temporal narratives they impose, leaving those who cannot or will not follow their schedules in a limbo of asynchrony. The official time line she describes is based on a state-recognized life narrative that follows marriage with reproduction and the creation of nuclear families to engage with capital as good producers and consumers. These privatized reproductive futures converge toward an ever-expanding future, a colonizing global modernity in which alternative modes of being will have been wiped out. Old futures are the traces that remain to show that the official narrative is never the whole story.

Chrononormativity and chronobiopolitics also mark the ways that gender and sexuality are racialized and classed. Thinking race, coloniality, and capital along with gender and sexuality is necessary to thinking queerly about histories, futures, and histories of futures, as will be evident in each formation of futurity analyzed in the book. Queers are most easily identified as those who evade the "straight" timelines of normalized heterosexual, reproductive life narratives. But matters of race, location, gender, and economics also affect the straightness of those timelines. Sara Ahmed unpacks this idea in the spatialized version of queerness she develops in *Queer Phenomenology* (2006), where to be queer is to deviate from the expected social and structural "line." Focusing on the "orientation" in "sexual orientation," she insists that queer deviations can produce their own coercive directions:

> If the compulsion to deviate from the straight line was to become "a line" in queer politics, then this itself could have a straightening effect. . . . Not all queers can be "out" in their deviation. For queers of other colors, being "out" already means something different, given that what is "out and about" is oriented around whiteness.[31]

Ahmed reminds us to "avoid assuming that 'deviation' is always on the side of the progressive."[32] Even as this book seeks to highlight the speculative production of queer possibility, it remains attentive to the co-production of possibilities and impossibilities along lines that histories of empire, race, nation, and global capitalism set in place.[33]

We are queered by more than the directions of our sexual desires. It is possible to deviate along one angle while holding the line and enforcing it for others in a different direction. Cohen, Roderick Ferguson, and other queer of color critics have highlighted the simultaneous exclusion of nonheteronormative subjects from the radical narratives of racial futures produced by movements against white supremacy, while race- and class-specific exclusions from heteronormativity (named by Cohen as "punks," "bulldaggers," and "welfare queens," and figured by Ferguson as the black drag queen sex worker) are illegible to mainstream queer politics.[34] Siobhan Somerville shows in *Queering the Color Line* (2000) that racial and gendered deviances have been co-produced in American history through the commingling of anti-black racism and gender normativity. Sexually deviant white bodies have been imagined as racially other and bodies of color marked as sexually deviant, with both understood to be out of time with relation to dominant culture.[35] Valerie Rohy writes about the shared "anachronism" of black and queer subjects in US discourse, where they have been mutually implicated in the white supremacist, heteronormative, eugenic ideal that the best future would come from "assigning both homosexuality and blackness to the place of the past."[36] Black and queer temporalities would seem to differ in that to be heir to slavery is to have had one's native sense of time ripped away, to have been forced into the past as other to European modernity alongside though not identically to other colonized and racialized populations, while to commit to a politics of queerness implies a rejection of the temporality foisted upon one—whether that is defiantly to refuse any futurity at all or to take on a form of subjectivity that can be fully realized only in the future. But these modes are neither separate nor separable, as I discuss in part 2, which is dedicated to the futures that arise at the intersection of black and queer speculative thought.

Kara Keeling uses Marx's invocation of "poetry from the future" to assert that the *when* of those lost to imperial and reproductive timelines could have its own rhythms, worlds, and poetries, though these may not be available to the scholarly seeker whose institutional perch is always to some degree contained by normative time.[37] This book seeks to understand how speculative fiction writers, media producers, and audiences have depicted and transformed these dynamics.

The Cultural Politics of Speculative Fiction

The practice of imagining the future has been polished to a fine art in the genre and cultural field of science fiction, in which debates over terms and categories are fierce and ongoing. Many scholars have been invested in erecting clear boundaries between science fiction, speculative fiction, and fantasy. In the 1970s, Darko Suvin (whose work I discuss further in chapter 4) defined science fiction through a structuralist notion of cognitive estrangement, in which both the estranging act of thinking things otherwise and the use of a cognitive, rational practice to do so were necessary for a text to be worthy of the formal designation.[38] Fredric Jameson stringently distinguishes science fiction from fantasy, arguing that science fiction maintains a rigorous material focus while fantasy, as "the other side of the coin," speculates with a greater and more idealistic freedom.[39] Roger Luckhurst writes that science fiction is a fictional engagement with "Mechanism," by which he means the permeation of technology into everyday life. He asserts that the conception of time that allows the future to be a primary focus of speculative cultural production is "associated with modernity" in the way it "orients perceptions towards the future rather than the past or the cyclical sense of time ascribed to traditional societies."[40] This connection with technological modernity has also been central to genre analyses of science fiction film, where it filters through Susan Sontag's 1965 contrast between the "intellectual workout" provided by science fiction novels and the "sensuous elaboration" of films (discussed further in chapter 5).[41] In a popular guidebook to science fiction film published in 2009, Steven Jay Schneider asserts that "cinema itself is science fiction" because its technologies and special effects make the impossible seem possible.[42] Spectacular visions of advancement, disaster, and adventure on a planetary or galactic scale showcase cinematic technology, seducing audiences to pay for what Garrett Stewart described in 1985 as "the fictional or fictive science of the cinema itself, the future feats it may achieve scanned in line with the technical feat that conceives them right now and before our eyes."[43]

All these definitions highlight important cultural and historical realities. Yet they also limit the extent of the cultural politics that the genre can be seen to engage. Feminized concerns about gender, sexuality, and emotional life are likely to slip into the margins, to be viewed as insufficiently cognitive, materialist, technological, or spectacular. Works that are about the future yet not overtly concerned with technological modernity (like Katharine Burdekin's 1937 *Swastika Night*, a key text in chapter 2) or that speculate visually without the aid of special effects (like the films I discuss in chapter 5) may not seem to count as science fiction at all.

The search for a taxonomy of science fiction invariably overlaps with Damon Knight's 1967 assertion that genre is defined by the communities who gather around it, so that "science fiction is what we point to when we say 'science fiction.'"[44] Concerned with an orientation toward futurity that crosses many genre lines, I prefer not to make such definitional gestures of my own, even as I engage queered visions of fictional futures that demonstrate the multiplicity of spaces and times within the Anglo-American modern period from which the genealogy of science fiction emerged. I have settled on "speculative fiction" as a term that is roomier, more evocative, and also more specific. This book centers on the act of *speculation*: of imagining things otherwise than they are, and of creating stories from that impulse. Understanding the terminologies and taxonomies of science fiction to refer to specific cultures and moments that have produced particular kinds of speculative narrative, I draw upon them as appropriate within individual chapters.

As a literary and media genre, science fiction has entered the archive of critical cultural theory in some well-defined ways. Politically engaged science fiction, utopia, and dystopia have often provided fictional evidence for Marxist theoretical models, as in Jameson's use of the left-leaning speculative tradition to develop his theory of capitalism, utopia, and social change, or Carl Freedman's assertion that "of all genres, science fiction is . . . the one most devoted to the historical concreteness and historical self-reflectiveness of critical theory."[45] Since the 1980s, feminist theorists have drawn on the well-developed, intertextual literature and culture of feminist science fiction to help them demonstrate the cross-fertilization between fiction and social movements.[46] Feminist science and technology studies has also long seen speculative and science fiction as a vital theoretical force, viewing it as creating fictional worlds where feminist ideologies can play out in greater complexity than theoretical writing will allow, or opening literary and visual spaces within which new formations of gendered technological embodiment can be imagined. Donna Haraway's 1991 "Cyborg Manifesto," whose influential theory of technocultural subjectivity is built in part from analyses of Anne McCaffrey's 1961 "The Ship Who Sang" and Joanna Russ's 1975 *The Female Man*, is a powerful example of how speculative fiction and speculative theory can converge.[47] While feminist science fiction studies has been centered more on literature than on media, it has also had much to say about the sensuous elaborations of gendered embodiment that science fiction films invoke, uncovering the possibilities for reconfiguring gender and sexuality in the reproductive weirdness of the *Alien* movies or in the technological performances of *The Matrix*.[48] This book does not engage in great depth with the texts and contexts most discussed by feminist science fiction studies scholars, but it stands on their shoulders as it reaches for less well-trodden sites of speculative gender and sexuality.

Sustained scholarly engagement with the interrelationships between queer theory and science fiction studies has been surprisingly rare, given the speculative force of queer theory and activism and the highly active queer world-making that takes place both in science fiction and fantasy writing and in its active fan cultures (the latter of which I discuss in the second wormhole and chapter 6). Literary science fiction's tendency to concern itself with changing societies' effects on subjectivities resonates strongly with queer critics' articulations of nonheteronormative time and space, as Wendy Pearson's important 1999 article "Alien Cryptographies: The View From Queer" demonstrates. The 2008 anthology *Queer Universes: Sexualities in Science Fiction* showcases the predominant conversations between queer studies and science fiction that have shaped queer science fiction studies as a small disciplinary subfield. In these essays, science fiction is articulated as a form of utopian writing that makes the queer future imaginable;[49] as a signifier of sexual subjectification through technology;[50] and as a politicized co-producer of queer realities.[51] If queer theory deconstructs binary logics of identity and imagines how the world might be changed by their subversion or destruction in collaboration with activist political and sexual practice, here it naturally seems to converge with science fiction's imaginative production of sometimes-utopian futurities. This queer science fiction theory occupies the temporality of a promise, in which science fiction will offer an endpoint to queer theory's anticipatory trajectories. But the relationship between queerness, science fiction, and futurity is far from self-evident, for one of the things that both queer theory and fictional speculation can do is question the structures around which we base our valuations of what progress signifies, who benefits from which forms of demand for social change, and what it means to "have" a future or be denied one. The convergence of queerness and science fiction requires that neither one be defined in advance. The expansive, emergent language of the speculative fosters such radical openness.

The choice of "speculative fiction" to refer to cultural production that imagines futures calls forth significant critiques. Science fiction writer Samuel R. Delany stated in a 1990 interview that "'speculative fiction' was a term that had a currency for about three years—from 1966 through 1969," when it "meant anything that was experimental, anything that was science-fictional, or anything that was fantastic" and "was a conjunctive, inclusive term, which encompassed everything in all three areas—before it began to signify only experimental works that included science fiction elements, and eventually became a term used by non-science-fiction-oriented academic literature scholars, who used it to legitimate the science fiction that they liked."[52] Is "speculative fiction" simply a name used to increase intellectual capital by papering over the pop-culture connotations of science fiction? It is true that I initially settled on "speculative" over "science" fiction in some part because I hoped that it might encourage those not already enamored of the genre to pick up the book. Yet the cultural landscape, popular and otherwise, has changed greatly since 1990 and even more since 1966–1969. These days, "speculative fiction" is widely accepted in scholarly and fannish circles alike as a capacious term that "covers practically the entire fantastic end of the sliding scale of realistic vs fantastic," including "science fiction, fantasy, alternate history, and everything in between."[53] And, while the scientific and technological elements of traditional science fiction narratives are praised by some members of science fiction fan communities, these are often the most socially and politically conservative elements, while science fiction publishers and organizations who encourage queer, feminist, and decolonial narratives draw from broader definitions.[54] It is true that the majority of the works on which this book focuses could be categorized as science fiction according to many of the definitions cited above. Yet my elaborations of the cultural logics of speculative fiction could as easily be drawn from other fields and genres, and I hope that this project will prove to have relevance in contexts well beyond genre studies.

The speculative fiction whose cultural politics and queer possibilities *Old Futures* explores is a varied mode of cultural and critical production. I am interested in one particular practice within it: the process by which cultural producers reconfigure their historical present in order to speculate about what a possible future might be like. Those futures may be (and are) optimistic, pessimistic, and/or critical of the concept of linear progressive time. The practice of speculating futures not only is enacted in fiction but also forms an approach to the world at large—hence my assertion in the previous pages that queer theory is itself often a practice of speculative fiction.

As I discuss above, queer scholarship does more than contribute to envisioning and activating possibilities for living queer lives in the future; it unpacks the significance of sexual norms and deviations to cultural constructions of futurity itself. Speculative and science fiction have rarely been associated with the currents in queer theorizing that emphasize queerness as countering assimilationist, normalizing politics through emphases on refusals, debasements, and impossibilities (although I will make such an association in chapter 2 and revisit it in chapter 5). They seem to have little to do with the genealogy of antisocial or negative queer theory that is most vividly associated with Leo Bersani's work on the value of *un*making rather than creating coherent selves and worlds.[55] A fictional representation of an alternative future does feature as an exemplary text in Edelman's *No Future*; I discuss his use of P. D. James's 1992 *The Children of Men* further in the wormhole that links parts 1 and 2. In his infinitely more hopeful 1999 book *Disidentifications*, Jose Muñoz writes movingly of Osa Hidalgo's 1996 short speculative film *Marginal Eyes*, which seeks to "imagine the future" as "a queer world as brown as it is bent."[56] Yet, making the same move Edelman does in the service of a quite different argument, the rest of his book moves away from this speculative representation of a literal future in order to root his queer temporality of performance firmly in the present. Muñoz's stellar 2009 book on queer futurity, *Cruising Utopia*, does not mention speculative cultural production at all.

It is not difficult to understand why speculative and science fiction futures seem antithetical to queer understandings of temporality that question the self-evident value of progress. Linear, literal articulations of utopian visions, dystopian fears, and futuristic extrapolations are inextricably entangled with the reproduction of racialized heteronormativity, with spatial and cultural colonization, and—especially in science fiction film's emphasis on special effects—with capital's fetishization of commodified newness. Science fiction's frequent voyages of interstellar discovery trace their lineage to early modern narratives of European encounters with "alien" indigenous peoples, as John Rieder demonstrates.[57] The notion of traveling into space, colonizing what *Star Trek* called the "final frontier," has often served conservative national political interests. And the genre's focus on technological innovation has fostered a dynamic in which, as Kodwo Eshun writes, "Science fiction is now a research and development department within a futures industry that dreams of the prediction and control of tomorrow."[58] This is sometimes literally true, as in the case of technologists' use of what Brian David Johnson of Intel Corporation calls "science fiction prototypes," fictions "based on real science and technology" that are used "explicitly as a step or input in the development process" in order to "imagine and envision the future."[59] Speculative imaginaries and science-fictional representations can both lead capitalist and colonial temporalities to appear inevitable.

But just as some speculative fictions may be prototypes for the prediction of a future more or less like the present, others may preemptively imagine its collapse or transformation. Space travel has been imagined not only as a continuation of settler colonialism but as the opening of a space where black, indigenous, and other colonized people could create worlds that would not leave the earth behind so much as reimagine the possibility of relating to it.[60] Science fiction prototyping could describe the imaginative work of speculating political possibility as much as marketable commodities.[61] The cultural politics of speculative fiction are never not gendered and never not racial, any more than they can be independent of national and socioeconomic location. This is no less true for queer and feminist theory. But while futuristic fictions are reliant on the violent and gendered progress narratives of technological modernity, capitalism and colonization, they are not coextensive with them. Linear models of temporality give fictions of imagined futures shape and structure; yet an extrapolative orientation toward alternative futurities can also demonstrate the complex and contradictory ways such modes can be employed.

Constituted by and constitutive of scientific dynamics built with assumptions that Western European man signified the most advanced, most adult, and most human of subjects, fictional futures have also provided experimental sites for working out other ways of being. As a scan through literary anthologies devoted to science fiction's queer,[62] feminist,[63] postcolonial,[64] and indigenous[65] versions will show, speculative fiction has cherished uses for those whose embodiments situate them at a deviant angle to techno-utopian futurities. Modernist discourses of technological development are never sufficient to understand the speculative practices of creators committed to envisioning futures for the nonproductive and nonreproductive, queer bodies, and bodies of color that colonizing and developmental discourses relegate to a "savage" and genocidally obliterated past. Fictional speculation often opens up alternative potentialities only to close them down into futures that are all too predictable according to dominant logics. A central argument throughout this book is that the failures of speculative fictions' radical possibilities do not invalidate their meaning, their interest, or their capacity to make a difference.

Futures imagined through engagements with history's structural exclusions tell us much both about dominant ways of thinking about time and about how we might create alternatives. Speculative imaginings that have not been encoded into the everyday realities of the science fiction present help to demonstrate that the future need not be closed down into familiar, straight lines. The lingering presences and possibilities of past futures open possibilities for thinking and living the present in different, deviant ways. If a forward-oriented narrative of historical development signifies the time of capitalism and colonialism, then the time of the colonized, excluded, and othered is most frequently to be found in the past.[66] The temporalities of ghosts, the supernatural, and myth are those that discourses of European Enlightenment seek to associate with childhood, alterity, unseriousness, times gone by. Bliss Cua Lim writes about how the cinematic fantastic "translates" between what Walter Benjamin called homogeneous, empty time and other temporalities that are supposed to have been wiped out but that surface as ghosts;[67] Avery Gordon's sociology of haunting similarly describes the perpetuation of the past in the present and the impossibility of ever leaving it behind.[68] The old futures this project follows suggest that technological, scientific, and reproductive futurisms can exceed the homogenization of time. Appearing in modes both desirable and discomfiting, these are futures for sexual, gendered, racialized ways of being that dominant temporal politics have tried and failed to eradicate. They deviate both from the conventional timelines of familial norms and from the successes and failures associated with life under capitalism.

During the time between this project's beginnings and its completion, the logics and politics of speculative fiction have become more central to the worlds of critical theory. This has not so much changed the relationship between theory and genre studies as it has begun to suggest new ways of thinking *speculation*, a term that applies to finance capital as much as to possibilities and alternatives.[69] Speculative theory is work that grapples with the dense futurity of the present, altering concepts of reality even as the real itself is continually cast into question. In 2012, Jayna Brown and I gathered a dossier for *Social Text's* online *Periscope* on a theme of "Speculative Life." Our introduction expresses this mode:

> To speculate, the act of speculation, is also to play, to invent, to engage in the practice of imagining. And, as Ernst Bloch said, it may be in our imaginative worlds that we catch glimpses of utopian possibility beyond our present paradigm. At a moment when so many have been struggling to enact alternatives to the depressing world produced by Wall Street's speculative failures, we need to practice imagining now more than ever.[70]

Speculation in this modality is both the prospect of temporal elsewheres and a logic that enforces capitalism's here and now, through the dominance of financial speculation.

Speculative critique, as Brown and I articulated it and as I seek to extend here, embraces the potentiality of utopias, forward-looking timelines, and possibilities of radically different and better elsewheres. It also acknowledges the embeddedness of such imagination in the often dismal logics of the present's inequalities. This structure underlies the queer possibility inherent in the cultural politics of speculative fiction, which provides tools for vernacular theorizing about the politics of the future. In their production of alternatives and deviations from and/or within predetermined progress narratives, returning to the possibilities embedded in old futures may allow such narratives to be occupied differently. Old futures insist that we acknowledge the extent to which temporal norms are not easy to repudiate; they force us to linger over processes of articulating what other ways of being in the world, anti-futurist lives, or non-normative temporalities might feel like.

In writing scholarship that seeks to be in dialogue with its political, cultural, or technological moment, it is difficult to resist the pressures, the inspirations and disappointments, of trying to keep up with a rapidly moving target. One begins a project focused on what is happening *now*, galvanized by the possible futures it portends, then finds that social and technological shifts have rendered one's insights out of date before the first draft of writing is completed. This book's emphasis on *old* futures offers, I hope, a way to sidestep such anxieties, lingering instead with the futures of the past and their effects in multiple presents. Attending to old futures might suggest some ways to redistribute the future in the present.

A Map of the Book

When I began to conceptualize a project that would conjoin queer critique and radical speculative fiction, I imagined I would find myself awash in worlds of marvelously desirable sexual and social possibilities, where space, time, economics, gender, race, and ability would be brought into new queer forms. This has occasionally been the case, but more often I have found myself recounting the limitations of works that aim to escape but are inevitably determined by the cultural conditions out of which they emerge, following the same logics of assimilation that have brought queer critique face to face with its own imperialisms and normativities. Certainly, queer sex is far from absent in speculative fiction, within the science fiction canon and elsewhere. But, as Candas Jane

Dorsey writes in a 2009 essay, most of the time "queer isn't queer enough in sf."[71] As I have come to realize, this may not be the end of the world.

If queer science fiction and queer speculative theory seem to be located at a permanently receding utopian horizon, there is still much to learn from the conditions of possibility for coming closer to that horizon and slipping away from it. Rather than wading through the margins of the contemporary to assemble an archive that would reflect the way I wanted to think of queer worlds being built, I found myself on a quest to understand where such an archive of possibilities might emerge from—and why it does not materialize as often as some of us might wish. This led me to construct an archive of my own that works to supplement the most widespread genealogies of queer theory and science fiction studies, by looking to speculative creativity produced in the margins of times and places where dominant futures were being constructed through colonial, capitalist, white supremacist, heteronormative temporalities. This book brings together works whose interconnection is rarely acknowledged: white feminist utopias and dystopias of the nineteenth and twentieth centuries; Afrofuturist narratives that turn the dehumanization of black lives into visions of transformation; and queer artistic adoptions and appropriations of science fiction media. In each case I explore how queer possibilities are constructed and deconstructed through speculative narrative, through extrapolative projections from the present and the past, and through excesses and margins that invite affective engagements with alternative temporalities.

Old Futures is structured in three parts, each addressing one particular convergence of political economy, theoretical framework, and narrative form that has given rise to a formation of speculative futurity. Two shorter sections, named "Wormholes" in homage to the science fiction genre trope of a time-space distortion that connects distant locations, draw in more recent examples to highlight continuing resonances of the old futures under discussion. Throughout the book, I draw on my archive of old futures to craft an alternative discourse around what Edelman named *reproductive futurism*. In queer studies, this has been a concept whose role is consistently that of an object of critique, a thing to be avoided, even when Edelman's arguments are rejected. In contrast, I argue that there are many reproductive futurisms, often in conflict and contradiction with one another: reproductive Afrofuturisms, futurisms of technological and biotechnological reproduction, futurisms that reproduce political activism, queer reproductive futurisms that are not simply a matter of new populations stepping onto a singular normative path.

Although this book is invested in resisting and challenging the logics of progressive and developmental time, it also acknowledges the impossibility of letting go of them entirely. And it invests in a progression of its own, spiraling gradually from imagined futures that do queer work within the bends and twists of normative temporalities—often reproducing them even while calling them into question—toward the production of futures out of time that take the raw material of dominant futurities and transport it to entirely different affective terrain. The book itself is a speculative work in many ways, often reaching out from interpretation and analysis to imagine, or at least gesture toward, alternate possibilities. I do not assume that readers will have encountered all or even any of the texts I discuss—even the best known are not routinely read or viewed outside of specialized audiences. Because I am interested in the theoretical and cultural work done by details of the worlds these texts create, a certain amount of summary is unavoidable. While I have tried not to include more than is necessary to make my arguments, I hope that some readers will find moments of pleasure in the moments of description, as I experienced pleasure in writing them.

In common with many of the works I engage, I follow a largely linear path while at the same time unfolding webs of entangled arguments. Though the book is intended as a cohesive monograph, its breadth and scope mean that readers will often be interested only in particular sections. Bearing this in mind, chapters and parts are written with the intention that they may be read separately as well as together, though references to the many connections among different texts and arguments encourage readers to pick up the book as a whole. I also aim to offer sufficient direction, in the form of footnotes and citations, so that readers will be able to pick up and pursue strands that particularly interest them. The structure is broadly chronological and thematic but also proceeds through associative logics that are unpacked at length in the final chapter, where I discuss my practice of video remix and the effect it has had on my critical methodology. This approach resonates with Yên Lê Espiritu's methodology of "critical juxtaposing": the "bringing together of seemingly different and disconnected events, communities, histories" such that, rather than viewing different elements as "already-constituted and discrete entities," we come to appreciate "that they are fluid rather than static and need to be understood in relation to each other and within the context of a flexible field of political discourses."[72]

In part 1, "A History of No Future: Feminism, Eugenics, and Reproductive Imaginaries," I argue that "no future" is a more capacious notion than Edelman has allowed, and that it need not necessarily be defined against the reproductive. Indeed, the notion of no future often becomes meaningful through various ideas of reproductivity (apportioning it to some, denying it to others). "No future" is also itself a concept that must be and has been reproduced. I historicize the idea of "no future" through both utopian and dystopian imaginaries: utopia as a vision of perfection that is also an end, and dystopia as a negative imaginary that participates in the creation of worlds. Chapter 1, "Utopian Interventions to the Reproduction of Empire," engages the work of marginal middle-class women writers in late nineteenth- and early twentieth-century Britain. Situated at the heart of a metropole whose outward expansion had slowed or stopped, they used speculative fiction to reckon with what it meant to be charged with reproducing Englishness, empire, and the notion of a white race. Feminists have reclaimed, and later disavowed, the racially purist utopias of white American feminists Charlotte Perkins Gilman and Mary Bradley Lane; their transatlantic contemporaries also have much to tell us about how feminist politics of reproduction and gendered embodiment function at the intersection of gender, sexuality, and race with mechanisms of white supremacy and state power. Chapter 2, "Dystopian Impulses, Feminist Negativity, and the Fascism of the Baby's Face," extends this analysis to show how feminist dystopian fiction of the 1920s and 1930s enacts the speculative production of futurelessness—which signifies not just an undesirable world for some, but the notion that the future could end altogether.

I sought out archives of early twentieth-century feminist speculation because I hoped to find imagined futures that would predict the radically, critically queer speculative projects of the more recent past. In the history of feminist speculation, I did not find works that severed the connection between white feminist politics and the reproduction of empire. But I did find narratives in which ambiguously utopian and dystopian gender politics intersect with imperial speculation in complicated and disturbing ways. In the work of Elizabeth Burgoyne Corbett and Susan Ertz, whose ambiguous utopias feature in the first chapter, and of Charlotte Haldane and Katharine Burdekin, whose dystopias are the subject of the second, genres of feminist debate, romance, and scientific speculation intersect to create visions of gendered futures that undermine and reproduce imperial dominance at the same time. Their articulations of anxieties surrounding the reproduction of the human race persist in the ways national futures are projected and reproduced in later media and fiction. In the first wormhole, I use a speculative engagement with Alfonso Cuarón's 2006 film *Children of Men* to highlight the insights that the previous chapters' archive of old futures can bring to questions of racialization, sexuality, and reproduction in contemporary transnational popular culture.

Crossing the Atlantic into part 2, "A Now that Can Breed Futures: Queerness and Pleasure in Black Science Fiction" offers a different set of perspectives on reproduction. Here I turn to histories of African diasporic speculation that have received significant media attention in the past few years and have been termed *Afrofuturism*, which Ytasha Womack describes as "the world of black sci-fi and fantasy culture."[73] Building on Afrofuturism's focus on black diasporic speculative imagining as a way of creating futures for those rendered futureless by global white supremacy, I focus on the figuration of gender and queerness in black imagined futures as they have interfaced with the genre frameworks of science fiction narrative—including the persistence of reproductive Afrofuturisms that have sometimes overlapped with eugenic discourses. Chapter 3, "Afrofuturist Entanglements of Gender, Eugenics, and Queer Possibility," introduces pleasure as a central term, tracing figurations of black women's sexual futures that emerge from narrative foreclosures in W. E. B. Du Bois's "The Comet" (1920) and following their trail into Jewelle Gomez's *The Gilda Stories* (1991) and Octavia E. Butler's *Fledgling* (2005), which demand we think reproductive futures outside the logics of heteronormativity and white supremacy. Chapter 4, "Science Fiction Worlding and Speculative Sex," extends my analysis of queered and gendered black futurities to the realm of racialized queer masculinity. Linking the discourse of "world-making" developed in utopian theories of queer performance with the idea of "world-building" common in science fiction theory, I analyze Samuel R. Delany's science fiction iterations of 1970s and 1980s public sex cultures, which use genre tropes to initiate a process for reimagining sexual and racial temporalities in response to both the histories of enslavement and the beginning of the AIDS epidemic.

The second wormhole, "Try This at Home: Networked Public Sexual Fantasy," connects the chapters on black queer science fiction with the media cultures the last part of the book analyzes by exploring sexual fantasy as a speculative world-making practice. This short, somewhat personal chapter reads a particularly queer and sexy scene from the science fiction TV show *Sense8* (2015–2018) to map correspondences between the depictions of gendered spectatorship in Delany's writings about male public sex cultures and the mostly female fan communities whose erotic fiction-writing practices form a speculative kind of sexual public.

In part 3: "It's the Future, but It Looks like the Present: Queer Speculations on Media Time," I turn to the cultural and technological reproduction of speculative futures in audiovisual form. Chapter 5, "Queer Deviations from the Future on Screen," argues that the popular understanding of science fiction film as the genre of spectacular special effects has obscured the work done by queer speculative independent films that map a politicized imagined future onto the people and locations of a present whose shifting temporal location refuses progressive teleologies. I engage Derek Jarman's 1978 *Jubilee* and Lizzie Borden's 1983 *Born in Flames* as old futures whose narratives, aesthetics, and structures have sprouted unforeseen resonances in emerging political landscapes of the late 2010s. Sharing an intense focus on media and communication, the films offer contrasting strategies for building futures out of a present moment saturated with representations of the end of the world. Finally, chapter 6, "How to Remix the Future," moves from futures depicted on screen to the audiences who take them up and respond to them, connecting my research on speculative fictions' histories with grassroots cultures of video remix that have flourished in the digital age. Focusing on the critical and creative practices of science fiction television fans, I draw on an artistic community of which I am a member in order to complicate the promise of digital media as the democratization of media production. The chapter centers on the affective and political temporalities of fan-made music videos that reimagine the racialized and gendered economies of digital media production and consumption, with the most extended analysis pertaining to the television series *Battlestar Galactica* (2003–2009). I discuss my own video remix practice as a way to incorporate the insights of this form into scholarly production, coming full circle to reflect on the practice of remix as a methodological force in the composition of this book. *Old Futures* ends with a short epilogue that considers how the role of speculative futures in political discourse and popular culture have shifted over the period of research and writing, from approximately 2007 to 2017.

This book does not, and does not seek to, exhaust all possible iterations of old futures and their queer politics. As I have developed its analyses of transatlantic futurities in and immediately after the twentieth century, I have contemplated many other archives of old futures whose analysis I can only hope others might take up, joining the scholars and artists already engaged in the labor of speculative transformation and critique. The work of Grace Dillon on indigenous futurisms; of Aimee Bahng on transnational Asian futures and speculative capital; of Curtis Marez on the "farm worker futurism" of migrant laborers in California; of micha cárdenas on trans of color futures; of André Carrington on speculative blackness; of Shelley Streeby on speculative archives; and of Alison Kafer on disability and futurity—these are just a few possible approaches in a transdisciplinary network engaged in the production and critique of critical speculative world-making.[74] The future and its queer potentialities mean differently across each of these contexts, and it is my aspiration that the work done here will add possibilities to the already multiple ways of seeing, analyzing, and enacting speculative futures, old and new.

A line from Delany's *Dhalgren* animates the project's frame: "*It is not that I have no future. Rather it fragments on the insubstantial and indistinct ephemera of now.*"[75] The speaker, a queer, working-class, half-Native poet living with mental illness, knows that living without a future is not an uncommon mode of being. Delany's protagonist is among those who fail to inherit. Yet "*it is not that [he has] no future.*" The double negative insists that futurity is not denied so much as dissipated among moments of joy, pain, sex, love, oppression, and resistance—whether in the immediate present or a stubbornly persisting past. Through processes similar to the logics of remix I explore in the final chapter, insubstantial and indistinct moments reconfigure themselves into new kinds of possibilities and impossibilities—as Delany's line does, repeated multiple times in slightly different form both in his novel and in this book. The future need not be figured as a straight line, but neither must any lines that may form be repudiated for the sake of implicit present potentialities. *Old Futures: Speculative Fiction and Queer Possibility* takes this insight as its starting point.

PART I

A History of No Future

Feminism, Eugenics, and Reproductive Imaginaries

Who *would*, after all, come out *for* abortion or stand *against* reproduction, *against* futurity, and so against *life*?
—Lee Edelman, *No Future* (2004)

Let the world end. Let it end.
—Susan Ertz, *Woman Alive* (1936)

1

Utopian Interventions to the Reproduction of Empire

Queering Futurity, Reproducing History

What has it meant to reroute the generational lines between past and future created when heterosexual procreation structures social and biological reproduction? One definition of queerness is the embodiment of such a break. In what Sara Ahmed calls a "failure to inherit the family line," straight teleologies can be dislodged by those whose desires and practices are not contained by and do not continue heteronormativity.[1] Yet distinctions between queer and straight time are not always uncomplicated or obvious. The white feminist utopian archive I analyze in this chapter demonstrates how breaks and bends in normative time have been articulated through the intersection of class, colonial, and racial imaginaries with questions of gender and desire.

The temporalities of the fictions I discuss below are conceptualized as *lines*—as chronological trajectories from past to future focused through a present in which writing and thinking take place. While futurity, especially when approached through a rubric of queerness, can equally be thought as a gesture, an eruption, or a rhythm reaching backward and/or forward from the present, we cannot avoid experiencing the irrevocable forward flow of time. Narrative temporalities centering on that flow dominate Anglo-American cultural common sense. Turning to the future's histories allows me to ask whether the linear temporalities of "normal" life narratives (from birth to childhood through adolescence, reproductive adulthood, and old age to death), and the notions of development and progress that Euro-American philosophies have often associated with them, are necessarily straight.[2]

Since his 2004 monograph *No Future: Queer Theory and the Death Drive*, Lee Edelman has become the avatar for a position that queer desiring bodies, constituted by their implicit challenge to the dominant sexual order's devotion to procreation, signify opposition to the powerful normative force of *reproductive futurism*. Edelman argues that political struggle for any cause, whether radical, liberal, or conservative, is defined by the idea of creating a better future and as such is necessarily constituted by normative appeals to the "extrapolitical" value of "fighting for the future" by "fighting for the children." In other words, it is through structural *form* that futurity and all its associations belong to heteronormativity. Differences between children, families, representations, images, and projections are far less relevant than the hymn to the "Futurch," the sacrifice of present pleasures for the sake of posterity, which they all have in common.[3] The queer, in this model, becomes that which figures the end of the future.

It is difficult to counter Edelman's anti-futurist argument on the figurative level at which it unfolds. Unsullied by political materiality's complicities and ambiguities, the anti-future position is also seemingly unmarked by the compromising messiness of racialized, gendered embodiment. Nor do I precisely want to counter it. The figure of the innocent child certainly does set limits on what is speakable in political discourse—limits that are as dangerous to nonfigurative children as to adults. However, taking the *content* of Edelman's formalism as a starting point can lead us in new directions.

Fantasies of futurity, both figurative and literal, are never not connected to material and political projects. Edelman's "queer" is a figure of destructive negativity whose racial and gendered embodiments and global locations are not specified. Nevertheless, this figure emerges from a British, French, and American archive of white gay masculinity and arises in a context where the Christian Right dominates US politics.[4] Affiliating his queer critique with feminism via the political issue of abortion in the United States, Edelman critiques the pro-life/pro-choice binary when he describes himself feeling interpellated by a billboard remonstrating against abortion rights, called out as a negation of its "biblical mandate" to "'Be fruitful and multiply.'"[5] "Who *would* . . . stand *against* reproduction, *against* futurity, and so against *life*?" he asks, before insisting that it is the role of queers to do so.[6] And yet this pro-life logic is not as universal as it seems once we look away from the billboard toward more complicated contexts.

The connection between heterosexual sex and procreation is the backbone of oppositions between queerness and futurity; queerness is what makes visible the drive for pure, self-shattering pleasure that is a potential in all sexual acts. Neither Edelman nor many of his critics attend closely to the gendered politics of procreation that ground his argument, relegating physically reproducing bodies to the realm of normativity.[7] But to take mainstream American culture's pro-natalism at its universalizing face value is to elide much. The figurative child may be the sign of futurity on which most if not all politics rely, but analyzing the intersecting gendered, racial, and national investments that create narratives of reproductive futurism shows that this child does not come without a figurative family that is also politically, and unevenly, deployed. This chapter and the next are about the mothers in that family.

To jump from futurity to children to mothers is certainly on some level to participate in a heterosexual logic of (re)generation in which the future is indeed kid stuff and kids' only meaningful connections are to the presumed-to-be female, presumed-to-be heterosexual bodies from which they emerged. Yet to ignore the bodies from which queer and other subjects literally emerge is to risk participating in racialized and classed dynamics that elide the question of who disproportionately carries out reproductive labor.[8] The history of population control has involved plenty of "coming out . . . against reproduction," in the form of forced sterilizations of disabled, poor, and racialized women, as well as the demonization of the inappropriately reproductive. Historically, the politics of birth control as feminist autonomy have been closely connected with ideas about shaping the reproductive future of the human race.[9] Predictions and projections of the future of the human race have never been innocent of racialized and nationalistic understandings that seek to determine which kinds of humanity ought to be most desirable. And we should be able to look at those projections in a way that takes this into account, while remaining attentive to a queer critique of reproductive futurism.

While Edelman's work shapes recent queer thinking about futurity, Walter Benjamin's 1940 "Theses on the Philosophy of History" is a foundational reading for thinkers focused on the past and committed to theorizing temporality in a way that does justice to those absent from or oppressed by dominant tellings of history. Benjamin demands that the dominant narrative of progress be broken, calling for a counter-evolutionary temporality that would "brush history against the grain" and grant priority to those who did not survive—a call that has been heeded by generations of historians, particularly those who seek to recover the queer past.[10] Benjamin describes the brutality of a model of history structured as a progress narrative in which the fittest survive to tell stories of past struggle in ways that justify their victory. His critique of this "historicist" model demands a nonlinear understanding of temporality that does not obfuscate the perpetuation of historical violence's pain. "A present . . . in which time stands still and has come to a stop" is necessary to critique the assumption of a homogenous progress through generations, in which history's subjects climb over the bodies of the oppressed to reach a future useful only for a victorious few.[11] This stoppage in time demands a relationship with the past wherein history's victors would no longer be heroes. It means that linearity and development are insufficient structures for thinking about time politically.

Female bodies, as desiring and as reproductive, hold a complicated position in the metaphoric language Benjamin uses to articulate the project of historical materialism. He wants to "stop" time in a moment whose potentiality has been translated into English as "pregnant with tensions," refusing to capitulate to normative historicist temporality by birthing generational progress.[12] Benjamin, in the translation whose phrasing has resonated with generations of scholars, writes:

> The historical materialist leaves it to others to be drained by the whore called "Once upon a time" in historicism's bordello. He remains in control of his powers, man enough to blast open the continuum of history.[13]

The seductive, obfuscating utopia of progress is a "bordello" for Benjamin, conjuring the image of a debauched female body laid out for the use of men who will be corrupted by her touch.[14] In Benjamin, "the whore called 'Once upon a time'" sucks masculine energy from the historical materialist who would heroically counter historicism's erasures. Routed through the economic, female sexuality figures linear, conservative, straight time; through that figuration, it does the work of the oppressor. Benjamin's insistence on thinking history through "oppressed ancestors" rather than "liberated grandchildren" challenges the dominance of reproductive futurism with its insistence that we give the past its due and not give up on changing the present for a vague dream that the future might be better.[15]

But if the historical materialist "blasts" a stop in a "pregnant" moment before it can birth a new generation of progressive history, we must wonder what it means that women's work of reproduction (giving birth, keeping things rolling) is so easily dismissed as counter-revolutionary.

Benjamin's "blast" out of the continuum of historical time has not been restricted to those who shared his radical politics. As a method, it connects to many writers and artists whose critical engagement with modernity was primarily aesthetic, including Wyndham Lewis's *Blast* magazine, Ezra Pound's proclamation to "make it new," and the Italian futurists.[16] In Benjamin, the blast's connection with oppositional politics is intended to cast light on overshadowed and overpowered participants in the past, rather than to celebrate the aesthetics of the break itself. Benjamin critiques the presumption that history has ever been or can ever be a stable continuum, but he does not refuse or turn away from history itself. And yet that vital critique performs an overshadowing of its own, pushing aside the labor that has underwritten history's continua and the erased subjects whose contributions may not have been either politically or aesthetically radical enough to reflect in the flashes from the blast furnace.

I seek to account for the ways the future looks from the perspective of the bodies that are pregnant (the English translation of Benjamin's formulation suggests they may be so perpetually): the employees in historicism's bordello who may not *blast* through history or seek to break its continuum, but who nevertheless imagine how the future could be *bent* in different directions. We might be reminded of Julia Kristeva's influential 1981 essay "Women's Time," in which woman as figure stands as a constitutive outside to time as linear history and is associated with "repetition and eternity" through reproductive cycles, on the one hand, and the iconography of the sacred, on the other.[17] The female figures in the fictions I examine in the rest of this chapter do not demand such radical departures from patriarchal or colonial time, but there is still much to learn from their struggle to imagine alternate possibilities within the temporal structures that define them.

Deviant Futures at the Turn of the Twentieth Century

As the twentieth century dawned in Britain and the United States, the imagined future was a critically important rhetorical site for thinking about the present. The onset of modernity with its rapid, uneven social and technological upheavals meant that the present seemed like something very different from a seamless continuation of the past. New modes of production and communication, from photography and radio to machinery for manufacture, were altering the ways many people lived and worked; new scientific discoveries and the idea of evolution were popular topics of conversation; and radical political ideas were in ferment on both sides of the Atlantic. Speculation about the future as a point of completion, within which the complications of the present could be resolved, gave rise to visions of future civilizations and gleaming technological futures that would later become the stuff of science fiction cliché.[18] Not all representations of technological futurity were hopeful ones. E. M. Forster used a vision of the future to critique what he saw as the alienating dangers of modernity in "The Machine Stops" (1907), and much anxiety was produced by the galloping changes in modern temporality instilled by the growing ubiquity of mechanical technology.[19] Nevertheless, the dominant story told about the future was a positive, hopeful one of human ingenuity's triumph in a changing world—where "human" implies white, male, and heterosexual.

Representations of utopian futures were used to firm up progress narratives that understood scientific development as a route away from the backwardness associated with non-Western cultures, over which Europe reigned, and towards a perfectible rationalism. The immense popularity of Edward Bellamy's 1888 American utopia, *Looking Backward 2000–1887*, which Phillip Wegner describes as "the single most influential narrative utopia of the nineteenth century," exemplifies this trend.[20] Dohra Ahmad writes that turn-of-the-century US utopian futurists viewed history as a linear journey to overcome a "hopelessly primitive" past— "an imperialist model that predicts and even predicates a world arrayed in various stages along a preset, hierarchical line of civilizational progress—in other words, what we would now call 'uneven development.'"[21] Bellamy's faith in this model is explicit, defining history as a relentless forward march of "progress that shall be made, ever onward and upward" toward the human race's "ineffable destiny."[22] His imagined future portrays a gleaming Boston, empty of racial, ethnic, and economic conflict, where citizens listen daily to telephonic orchestras and sermons.[23] Bellamy hoped for a liberal destiny in which social progress would diminish inequality; he even declared, predicting the liberal colorblind racism of the twenty-first century, that "the people referred to . . . so far as we remember, might have been black, brown, or yellow as well as white."[24] He reaches for this supposedly multicultural destiny by mapping Darwinian ideas of evolution onto imperial expansion and white supremacy via the commonplace idea that true progress would mean the global dominance of European or Euro-American civilization. Utopian imaginings were not exclusively devoted to such imperial chronologies.[25] But this chapter is primarily concerned with what was articulated through, rather than in evasion or contestation of, the temporality of empire.

Situated at the metropole of a still-powerful empire, many late-nineteenth-century British progressives used the idea of racial destiny to naturalize a temporal order whose pinnacle was their society. Women's place in such a future—even when the women were white and economically privileged, part of the civilized and civilizing elite—was less clear. Bellamy's utopia exemplifies a dominant late-nineteenth-century way of understanding history, which Patricia Murphy describes as structured by "progress, Christianity, and evolution" unfolding in a "masculine," linear, goal-oriented time, while women are relegated to the private sphere's subordinate temporality of reproduction and family.[26] Describing his postcapitalist utopia as liberating for both genders, Bellamy nevertheless creates an archetypically gendered space in which men "permit" women to work only because it increases their "beauty and grace" and makes family life more amenable.[27] Women give birth to those who, Bellamy imagines, will inherit a better future, and they are also love objects for men engaged in building the new society, but it is men alone who are capable of forward progress, whether that be political engagement in the present or the capacity to imagine a different future. Grappling with the contradictions of this position led some feminist utopians to create future visions in which cracks in the genre's "perfect faith in developmentalism" become apparent.[28]

In debates over gender within the late-nineteenth-century middle-class public sphere, challenges to the place of women's embodiment and sexuality centered on the figure of an independent and dangerous "New Woman." Sally Ledger describes the New Woman as a utopian figure "committed to change and to the values of a projected future" that might include universal suffrage, less restrictive expectations for feminine dress, and changes to the legislation that banned married women from property ownership in Britain.[29] If the New Woman was a modern figure who belonged to the future, her insistence on stepping out of the space and time of the home might mean that she was making irresponsible demands for power in the present at the expense of future generations. Murphy writes that "in contesting her ordained gender role, detractors claimed, the New Woman . . . imperiled . . . the future development of the human species," because her "agenda countered the natural progression of civilization and hampered the female's primary reproductive function."[30] Utopian fiction, in which an improved "progression" could be depicted as happening because rather than in spite of women's changing position, was an obvious avenue for women writers to register protest.

More than a hundred utopian texts by women were published in Britain and America between the years 1869 and 1920.[31] Each of these fictions makes its own engagement with ideas of advancement, evolution, and civilization, which are part and parcel of imperial and settler colonial enterprises. Yet, overwhelmingly, reproductive futurism is the engine through which these ambiguously utopian and dystopian feminist futures are imagined. Using the apparently unquestionable necessity of procreation as part of a discursive arsenal in activism directed toward women's rights as mothers, utopian formations of reproductive futurism are imbricated with speculative ideas about "the future of the race." In unpacking the history of feminist reproductive futurisms, I do not seek to idealize or recuperate their narratives. Rather, I want to explore the complex ways they perpetuate, and occasionally complicate, the idea that humanity's caliber could be improved by eugenic discourses that mark some bodies as more worthy of reproduction than others.

Eugenics itself is inherently speculative and utopian. Charles Darwin's cousin, Francis Galton, coined the term to situate the contingency of Darwinian selection within a future-oriented framework where the improvement and purification of the human race could become a utopian breeding project, improving "the stock" to eliminate more "animal" strata. Galton understood eugenics to be crucial in order to maintain the human race's quality against a danger that natural selection could become a downward spiral:

The race gradually deteriorates, becoming in each successive generation less fitted for a high civilization . . . until the time comes when the whole political and social fabric caves in, and a greater or less relapse to barbarism takes place.[32]

Galton's barbarians are those who have been left behind by temporal logics of scientific progress and evolution, which in his model demand pressure from the most advanced human actors in order to create a future worthy of the name. Founding texts of eugenic discourse figured the poor, the so-called feeble-minded, the colonized, and the sexually deviant as dangers to the future of humanity. Such figures risked provoking a descent from civilized man into barbarian alterity, a collapse from progress into chaos. Freud's description of a "similarity between the process of civilization and the libidinal development of the individual" in his *Civilization and Its Discontents* (1930) would later offer a psychoanalytic justification for the positioning of non-European subjects as temporally backward.[33]

An idea that the worthiest human beings were those with visionary access to futurity was written into the "civilized" personality by Galton, for whom an ability to "keep before his mind the claims of the morrow as clearly as those of the passing minute" marked a proper subject for evolutionary perpetuation.[34] For the eugenic activists who followed him, undesirables were likewise marked by their inability to plan for the future. Eugenics meant controlling the population of the "residuum," racially imagined as "a degenerate subspecies" who "live only in the present" and were far too likely to reproduce without proper consideration for their contribution to evolutionary futurity.[35] Beyond reproductively focused eugenic discourse, the imbrication of evolutionary, colonial, and sexual logics in the late nineteenth century is evident from Max Nordau's 1892 *Degeneration*, which figures the sexual excesses of the "over-cultured decadent pervert" as a resurgence of the "primitive" that could endanger the future of civilization.[36]

Foucault describes the shift in the status of sexual discourse from personal practice to public issue bearing on racial futurity as part of the development of state-led systemic analyses of population.[37] When sexuality comes into its own as a vector of power, there are regulations that "favor or discourage" increasing birthrates according to "exigencies of the moment."[38] In shaping the future through the discursive disciplining of bodies, emergent biopower combined ideas of "hygiene," "evolutionist myths," and "moral cleanliness" as it "promised to eliminate defective individuals, degenerate and bastardized populations"[39] Part of the logic of elimination was that "sexual perversion resulted in the depletion of one's line of descent—rickets in the children, the sterility of future generations."[40] If progressive temporalities were to be maintained, the lines of posterity from deviant bodies had to be cut.

Foucault briefly mentions the "racisms of the state" when he brings the question of population control into his analysis of sexuality and power, implying that the encouragement of reproductivity for Western desirable subjects is accompanied by anxiety about encroaching others.[41] Ann Laura Stoler unpacks Foucault's theory to show colonial taxonomies for class and race working through reproductive circuits. She writes that the management of sexuality was also the management of empire, with both operating through racialized discourses of class and gender: "The colonial order coupled sexuality, class and racial essence in defining what it meant to be a productive—and therefore successfully reproductive—member of the nation and its respectable citizenry."[42] Sexual deviants, colonial subjects, and the lower classes were brought together as undesirable populations—as people who had, according to various connected logics, no future. The fictional production of speculative futures lets us see how the idea of the futureless population was invoked, reproduced, and questioned among a group often presumed to share an unequivocal commitment to futurity.

Feminist Utopias and Eugenic Ambiguities

In the remainder of this chapter, I turn to the details and complexities of fictional feminist futures that negotiate the temporal, political, racial, and imperial discourses of the late nineteenth and early twentieth century through utopian writing. Created by white professional-class women authors who were struggling to redefine their relationship to state, nation, and empire, this genre of popular futurist cultural production is often explicitly racist in its language and narrative. It may well seem deservedly forgotten. Yet elements from its portrayals of gender, sexuality, race, and queer possibility persist in the twenty-first century. Now as then, sexuality and gender intersect with imperial speculation in contradictory and disturbing ways.

Charlotte Perkins Gilman is the best-remembered of the early feminist writers who deployed speculative ideas in pursuit of gender equity, but archival recovery work has shown that American women were creating utopian narratives on feminist themes as early as Mary Griffith's 1836 "Three Hundred Years Hence."[43] Gilman's 1915 *Herland* imagined a manless utopia; it captured feminist imaginations when it was republished in 1979, by which time the idea of women-only societies had become a popular trope in both feminist and nonfeminist science fiction writing.[44] An earlier utopia by Mary Bradley Lane, *Mizora* (1880, republished in 1999) depicts another women-only country, in which an aristocratic Russian woman discovers a perfected society buried underground in Antarctica. For these writers, utopian speculation was a means of proving that (white) women's liberation would advance national governance in both public and private spheres, especially if technology could be developed to free women from the burden of domestic labor.

Refusing the confines of gender, and even reproducing without the heterosexual family, has had a central place in feminist utopias' reconfigurations of national futures. In Gilman's *Herland* and its 1916 sequel *With Her in Ourland*, populations deemed futureless when women are given total control of posterity include men. Herland is not situated in the future, but is a hidden land in which Gilman constructs a parthenogenetic female space that feels retrospectively queer in its absence of compulsory heterosexuality. Nevertheless, as Alys Eve Weinbaum shows, "national familialism" remains a "normativizing mechanism through which the nation's 'Aryan,' female citizenry imagines its relationship to 'futurity.'"[45] Refusing Galton's worldview of evolution as a violent "struggle for existence" among "an everlasting writhing mass of underbred people," which includes the "hopeless sub-stratum of paupers and degenerates," Gilman proffers a model of the nation as a female-headed household, practicing eugenics with love.[46] Herland's parthenogenetic "Mothers" are described as "Conscious Makers of People," and those who are not mothers are likewise conscious of their reproductive duty. Gilman describes some women's willingness to give up procreation for "the sake of the race" as "negative Eugenics," undertaken by choice.[47]

Disability and antisocial behavior alike would, Gilman implies, be eliminated through this strict eugenic control of reproduction. Her writing offers no outside to a eugenic model. The male visitor to utopia must learn to accept the righteousness of the Herlanders' ideals before he can contribute his much-desired diversity to their gene pool and receive the reward bestowed on the final page: "In due time, a son was born."[48]

A vision of race that places white femininity at the peak of development is central to the achievement of utopia for both Gilman and her less-remembered contemporaries in the United States and the United Kingdom. Mizorans, located at the South Pole, have developed a eugenic technology that enables "dark complexions" to be eliminated.[49] Herlanders are white and blond, despite a South American location that allows Gilman to contrast them with indigenous populations of color. Herland's origin point is the overthrow of a slave revolt by virginal mistresses, leading Ahmad to describe the novel as "a feminist version of *Birth of a Nation*" and to point out that D. W. Griffith's film about the Ku Klux Klan was "released in the same year that Gilman serialized *Herland*."[50] Celebratory feminist reclamations of racially purist utopias have, in recent years, been rightly replaced by analyses of the persistent presence of eugenics and empire in feminist thought.[51] I linger with these texts because of the ways they make the presumptions and prejudices of their feminist moments acutely visible, forcing us to remember how easily critiques of gendered norms can coexist with the imperialism, racism, class hierarchy, and ableism that have justified eugenic reproductive practices.

Gilman's utopian predecessors used feminist futurisms to suggest a range of variations on the idea that a world inhabited only by women would be a better one. Evading the awkward need to speculate on biological alternatives to heterosexual procreation, many works argue that it is women's *governance* that has the potential to solve the problems of patriarchy, rather than women's bodies. Utopian writers who shared this idea include the English aristocrat Lady Florence Dixie, whose 1890 *Gloriana, or the Revolution of 1900* features an aristocratic woman who dresses as a man in order to incrementally revolutionize British gender relations through parliamentary reform. A more radical case for women's governance is made by Bengali essayist and educator Rokeya Sakhawat Hossain, who published "Sultana's Dream" in 1905. Hossain's short story describes a "purdahnishin" Muslim woman who falls asleep and wakes to a world where her timidity in walking around unveiled is regarded as "mannish" by inhabitants of "Ladyland," who keep their men behind closed doors and who have used education and scientific advancement to surpass male society.[52] Hossain's utopia is notable for the absence of reproductive questions from its imagined future: rather than focusing on women's capacity to reproduce a nation, "Sultana's Dream" turns on the distinction between domestic and public space, highlighting what could be gained by granting Muslim women access to the latter.[53]

When utopian arguments for women's governance operate in conjunction with imperial formations, they have much to tell us about how feminist politics of reproduction and gendered embodiment function at the intersection of gender, sexuality, and race with mechanisms of white supremacy and state power. The 1889 novel *New Amazonia: A Foretaste of the Future* by Elizabeth Burgoyne Corbett, an English suffragist who published as Mrs. George Corbett, is a powerful and intriguing example of the ambiguous means by which feminist futurists both opposed and reproduced imperial civilization. Corbett's work illustrates the convergences of science, imperialism, and eugenics, displaying period and genre tropes in a sometimes awkward, sometimes humorous tone. As I discuss in my introduction to the 2013 reissue from feminist science fiction publisher Aqueduct Press, one can never quite tell whether Corbett wishes her narrator's voice to be taken at face value.[54] In an entry for a playful feminist speculative encyclopedia, L. Timmel Duchamp brings this tonal uncertainty to the fore, imagining Corbett's narrative as a critique addressed to the utopian society by a radical citizen who borrows the voice of a woman from the past in order to criticize retrograde political movements in her country.[55]

New Amazonia opens with a scene from the working desk of a New Woman writer who has just read an open letter denouncing the idea that the franchise should be extended to women, signed by an array of upper-class ladies. She falls asleep in fury at the betrayal, only to awake five hundred years later in a world where women have not only garnered the vote but have taken on all politically powerful roles. For both *New Amazonia*'s sleeper and the state in which she wakes, biology is not quite destiny; female power does not necessarily lead to a utopian polity. It is women who deny the possibility of votes, leading Corbett to make a distinction between "ladies" with aristocratic class interests and "women," like herself, who prefer independence.[56] This distinction in turn shapes the utopia: New Amazonians' greatest horror is reserved for nineteenth-century women's gender conservatism, as Corbett's protagonist learns during the obligatory tour of utopian institutions on which she is taken before mysteriously returning to her office to awaken with renewed political vigor.

In her opening tirade against anti-suffrage campaigners, Corbett makes a surprisingly fierce critique of her own country: she announces that "British Civilization" is "Corrupt, Degraded," and "Rotten to the core."[57] Projecting five hundred years ahead, she gets rid of Britain altogether—though not of the legacy of empire. In the protagonist's questions to the first New Amazonians she meets, she learns that "England" and the "English" no longer exist and that the country of New Amazonia was once Ireland.[58] The protagonist and reader learn how this came about by reading a partisan history book, which describes the influence of Germany on the English monarchy and Queen Victoria's love for Scotland coming together in a United Kingdom that is no longer synonymous with England but is rather tantamount to "Teuto-Scotland." Age-old hostilities between Britain and France return to create an imagined twentieth century quite as bloody as the real thing: France goes to war with Britain and Germany, which are allied; Ireland allies itself with France against its colonizers; and the result is a massacre of the Irish that leaves the island empty of all its men.[59] The women of Teuto-Scotland, who have been left vastly outnumbering men after years of war and who have recently achieved universal suffrage, volunteer to step in and create a new colonial state.

Corbett imagines the womanly nation of New Amazonia as a tightly controlled state. This is not just a country of women, with a few men allowed (only those descended from sons brought along by colonizers). It is a nation of women who are defined as "fit" in multiple ways. Yet New Amazonia's reproductive ideologies are not easy to sum up. The New Amazonian state is called the Mother, but those who hold positions of power within it and shape the future of the polity are banned from marriage and procreation. Because its "laws and social economy hold out wonderful premiums for chastity," the "most intellectual compatriots, especially the women, prefer honour and advancement to the more animal pleasures of marriage and re-production of species."[60] In common with writing by many New Women, Corbett seems to offer "little or no conception of female sexual desire" save as a signal of failing self-control from a rampaging, oversexed underclass perceived as less than human because of their capitulation to animal instincts.[61] If non-procreative pleasures take place in the homosocial, scientifically enabled environment of the Mother's bosom, they are invisible and therefore un-denounced, because sexuality is strictly linked to population control. The only result of indulgence in "carnal propensities" Corbett mentions is illegitimate offspring, whose risk of social deviation can be quickly, if unpleasantly, eliminated: "The offspring of vice is not permitted to live."[62] Sexual continence is a condition of being allowed access to posterity via either political or reproductive futurity.

The mistress race in *New Amazonia* breeds itself through strict im-migration controls and a regime by which "each new-born child was subjected to examination, and no crippled or malformed infants were permitted to live."[63] Each colonist must have had enough money to pass a stringent economic test, their "health" proven free from all disability, disease, or deformity, and their ancestry without "taint" of illegitimacy or "vice."[64] It goes without saying for Corbett that the settlers who pass such tests will be white, as the superiority of European races did for Galton and his contemporaries. Some scholars have understood women's eugenic rhetoric as being capable of making eugenics more than "rac-ist" ideology insofar as they place it in the service of a "constructive" feminist project.[65] If women were conventionally expected to give up their own right to futurity for the sake of their children's, then for them to insist that their status as productive and reproductive actors in their own right was essential to the evolution of a better race could support the improvement of women's lives in the here and now. This argument was effectively debunked by one of Corbett's contemporaries. In an 1899 essay, self-described New Woman Mona Caird mounted a "Defense of the 'Wild Woman'" who would not give up autonomy for the sake of her children or the future they would embody. In a passage prescient of twen-tieth- and twenty-first-century feminist and queer politics, she writes:

> I would suggest what appears to be a new idea (strange as this may seem), namely, that the rights of the existing race are at least as great as those of the coming one. There is something pathetically absurd, in the sacrifice

> to their children, of generation after generation of grown people. . . .
> I protest against this insane waste of human energy, this perpetual renun-
> ciation for a race that never comes.[66]

Caird challenges the imperial logic of racial futurity by insisting that the present deserves consideration as more than a rung on an evolutionary ladder. Instead, she embraces *no* future in an ethical commitment to those who are alive here and now. This is a position toward which Corbett's concerns about whether the colonial feminist utopia is worth the bodies it leaves in its wake also, eventually, drives her.

Corbett's protagonist responds to New Amazonian eugenics with some anxiety even though, as a woman writer, it is her posterity that will be assured. Awe and wonder at her trip through utopian marvels are halted briefly when she learns that the population of New Amazonia is kept at its progressive height by the practice of eliminating those who would bring it down: the physically or mentally disabled, the sick, and those whose desires or actions run in directions contrary to the uplift of the state. Given the likely unexceptionality of Galton-style discourse to Corbett's reading public, it is interesting that the shock contemporary feminist readers feel at the New Amazonians' explicit dehumanizing of those who deviate in body, mind, or desire is at all mirrored in the text. While in the rhetorics of uplift and degeneration that many feminist utopians use, eugenic population control is figured in an abstract sense, Corbett makes a concrete and direct link to the loss of children's lives. When the narrator learns that New Amazonian children born disabled or outside of matrimony (itself a eugenic contract requiring "a medical certificate of soundness") are euthanized, she responds with an "involuntary shudder."[67] If readers had been nodding along, confident in the desirability of this utopia with politically minded women on top, here they might be liable to pause. And perhaps, at least for anachronistic readers engaging with old futures out of their time, imaginations might wander into the realm of the condemned child, the unpermitted life, the dark side of a utopia unavailable to all.

Ambivalence deepens with a figure in Corbett's narrative who stands for an aspect of Victorian social life that has, in her opinion, no future. For what brings the protagonist back to the nineteenth century—and brings the narrative to some small implication that the nineteenth century might have advantages over the twenty-fifth—is her sympathy for a eugenically unfit subject whom she personally hates. Corbett's narrator arrives in New Amazonia accompanied by a pseudo-aristocratic poseur named Fitz-Musicus, the embodiment of effete masculine heterosexual decadence, who somehow arrived in her dream by taking "hasheesh."[68] Fitz-Musicus is unable to conform to the mores of the future and spends his time there aggrandizing himself and trying to seduce women, to the point where they declare him feeble-minded and decide to euthanize him because he constitutes a force "more likely to promote retrogression than progression."[69] The narrator's "blood [runs] cold" at such a clear example of New Amazonia's negative eugenic policies, and she decides to warn him that his "life . . . was in danger"—upon which act her utopian dream is brought to an abrupt close.[70] Despite its hegemonic take on racial, imperial, eugenic temporalities, *New Amazonia* hints in the end that pastness, immaturity, and even degenerate pleasures may be preferable to the violent purity of an immaculately evolved future.

New Amazonia presents a seamless vision of futurity in which ruling-class women have used eugenics to dominate the temporality of evolution, building their world off the backs of lower classes, colonized subjects, and profligate ruling-class men. It is only with a closer reading that cracks and ambiguities in this narrative appear, revealing that the exclusions and violences on which visions of utopian futurity as fully achieved progress rest are not wholly uncontested. Later representations of the future in the twentieth century keep their cracks closer to the surface. One more example from the archive of women's popular utopian fiction will show how such ambiguities further play out.

Race and the Future as Violent Romance

It is commonplace to view the First World War as a cataclysmic break when Europeans' predominantly optimistic approach to modernity and the future was replaced by fear and anxiety. Matthew Beaumont writes that after 1918 "the new machines and new societies of the late nineteenth-century prophets and predictors suddenly appeared in an obscene light, like a form of technological or sociological pornography" because "social development was dramatically interrupted, collapsing the supports on which the troubled late-Victorian dream of progressive evolution had rested" and turning the dominant mindset from utopian to dystopian.[71] Before turning to dystopian feminisms in the next chapter, though, I want to highlight some continuities in the ways that optimistic futures for progressive evolution were imagined before and after this seemingly radical break. The "obscenity" of looking head on at hopes for orderly utopian perfection should not obscure the work still done by those dreams, even in the wake of their destruction. Perhaps utopian images of progress are described as pornographic by Beaumont because they are what many dare not admit they desire. Just as violence was always inherent to utopias of Victorian social progress, eugenic utopias continue to seduce after their supposed collapse as a dominant imaginary. The remainder of this chapter analyzes a narrative that draws upon a feminist, progressive reproductive futurism to lay claim to eugenic utopianism in an age of no future.

Susan Ertz's 1936 futuristic romance *Woman Alive* was published at a moment remembered best in speculative fiction studies for the dystopian critiques of rising European fascism I discuss in the following chapter.

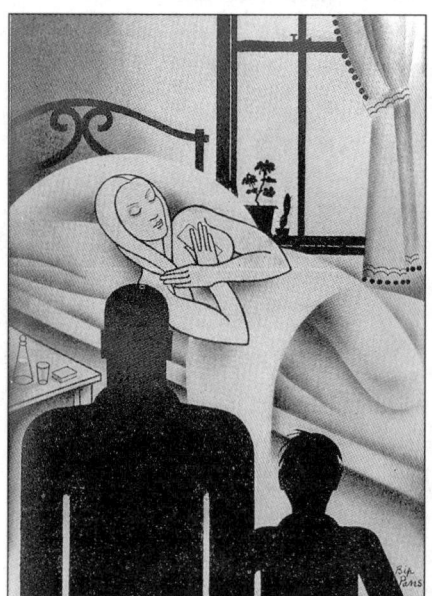 

Figures 1.1 and 1.2. Femininity idealized in Bip Pares's illustrations for Susan Ertz's 1936 novel *Woman Alive*.

Ertz's novel's ostensible faith in the "proud and progressive" English nation makes it seem more appropriate to the Victorian era than to the moment of uncertainty at which it was written.[72] Its untimeliness may be part of why it has scarcely been discussed in studies of 1930s literature, though Ertz—"dismissively categorized" as a writer of domestic fiction—is left out of even most feminist histories.[73] In her one speculative work amid a career focused on narratives of genteel popular femininity, Ertz maps sexuality and the future of the race through an ostensibly pacifist feminist project. The novel's illustrations, by prolific woman illustrator Bip Pares, highlight its contradictions: stylized images of female figures, geometric cities, and anonymous crowds situate it within a combination of romance and propagandistic futurism (figures 1.1–1.4).[74]

Woman Alive, like *New Amazonia*, narrates a dream vision of the future in the first person. A psychic grants a male doctor the perception of his own old age, and this turns into a vision of a post-apocalyptic landscape in which biological warfare has killed off all women. The doctor discovers the last woman alive, Stella Morrow, and with some difficulty persuades her to take up the task of regenerating the human race by marrying his widowed son-in-law and having children. Appearing in Pares's drawing as a passive, pallid figure under a multigenerational male gaze (figure 1.1), Stella is a conflicted character who at first defiantly repudiates her gendered relationship to reproductive futurity, wishing to "let the world end" by accepting the destruction of male civilization.[75] Only later does her role shift into regal maternity, as she accepts a reproductive role in order to guide the future history of the human race through the eugenic choice of its ancestors and the archival work of selecting knowledge for the utopia her descendants will build. Through Stella's struggle with the gendered burden of reproductive responsibility, Ertz shows English women in a liminal position: ineluctably wedded to national and imperial futurity, but also critical of the violent masculinity that has made the nation what it is.

The futuristic England that Ertz represents mingles imagery of utopian technological progress with social democratic visions of a welfare state. London is a city of chrome and glass towers, the Thames is fit for swimming, and "all those who could not be absorbed by the trades made parks and beautiful England instead of living idly and miserably on the dole."[76] But this future appears in the background, parenthetical to the primary plot. The scale of importance is delineated in the illustration of Stella's wedding (figure 1.2), where the woman all in white towers above small, silhouetted, androgynous men who hold her veil, a crowd of dark figures cheers behind her, and the futuristic landscape—star of most utopias—is merely a set of geometric shapes on which barely visible human figures perch. We are here not for a treatise on social possibility, but for the ways in which one woman can be shown to inhabit and make a personal future from well-established utopian and dystopian tropes.

Within this frame, *Woman Alive* presents a progressive future whose history has come to a stop with the "amputation" through women's death of "man's mystical dependence on a future."[77] From this standpoint, the narrator contemplatively reflects that "national prejudices, factional hatreds, jealousy, cruelty, bigotry" would regardless have led to humanity's "end."[78] Even as human nature is blamed for the slide of utopian progress into violence, Europe and the West are depicted as clinging more tightly to the disappearing future. Women, Ertz writes, "went quickest in the hot countries," while the "inertia" of "fatalism" in "Eastern countries" meant "the dead lay in the streets and the living merely awaited their turn to die."[79] Orientalist visions of racialized alterity as futurelessness are also articulated in sexual terms:

> In some countries men were trying to outdo the vice and libertinism of Rome in its worst days, and making a parade of it. In England and America . . . such behaviour was severely punished, as indeed it was discouraged and frowned upon in most of the European countries. It was an offence here for men to masquerade as women. . . . In those countries where it was permitted or ignored, order and discipline of any sort were soon overthrown.[80]

Even in a futureless world, deviance from an Anglo-American norm of gendered behavior appears as a danger. Though nonreproductive sexual behavior is not directly blamed for the end of the human race, the "parade" of "libertinism" here stands diametrically against any prospect for renewal of the old social order. The "order and discipline" of English and American men, who "go down with the ship with . . . flags waving" rather than seeking pleasure with one another at the world's end, is evidently rewarded by appearance of the world's last woman in their ranks.[81]

What has drawn me to spend time with this old future is Stella's response to her position of responsibility for future generations: she views the end of human civilization as a not undesirable possibility. A former girls' gym teacher, Stella is at first horrified by the idea that she will be forced to mother an entire species. When first rescued, she seeks to evade her responsibility through gender transgression, dressing in men's clothes and declaring that she means "to live as a man and die as a man."[82] When the British prime minister implores her to remember that she is "the only woman in the world," she replaces this literal truth with a reminder of perfidious masculinities, snapping "'No one's ever said that to me before.'"[83] The text suggests that Stella's anti-male prejudice results from having been jilted—yet her nihilistic insistence that "men . . . [deserve] to die" is met as a proposition containing "a good deal of truth" by the logical male narrator.[84] His response positions Stella's desire to join with the English men in their disciplined fatalism as being completely different from the "vice" of men who masquerade as women: rather than

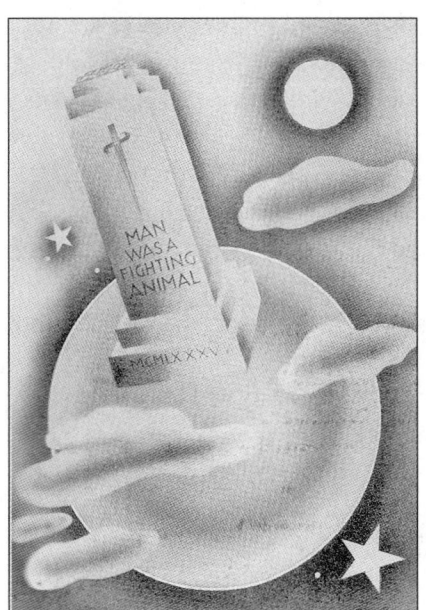 

Figures 1.3 and 1.4. Monuments to futures lost and found in Bip Pares's illustrations for Susan Ertz's 1936 novel *Woman Alive*.

queer degeneration, it signals good sense and English grit, even as it does nothing to avert the future's end.[85]

Stella embodies the future in the most literal sense, her ovaries being the last prospect for human reproduction. Yet she insists on defining futurity as something beyond herself. In defiant repudiation of her gendered relationship to hetero-eugenic reproductive futurity, she makes a vow to "let the world end." She demands that the men who want to breed her "let it end"; yet the world that will be ending is only "the old world" of patriarchal human civilization. Even if there is no future for any human being, there may be one for the planet. For Alan, the man Stella eventually submits to marrying, the "monstrous joke" of humanity's "absurd failure" is that "it took several million years . . . to evolve out of the slime" in order to "commit suicide."[86] Stella takes a less humanist view and suggests that "man" might "give way to other animals" as part of an evolutionary process.[87] She imagines "a vast grave for all the men left in the world," marked by a "towering monument" engraved with the line "Man was a fighting animal" to highlight the opposition between species-futurity and gendered violence.[88] In Pares's illustration (figure 1.3), the planet is dwarfed by the phallic memory of humanity, making visual the end of men as the end of all futures. Stella more optimistically embraces a Darwinian decentering of human beings in relation to nature, declaring: "Let's make way for . . . sensible lions and tigers and bears."[89] From this perspective, her refusal to bear humanity's future is not only a demand for masculine autonomy but also an attempt to escape naturalized femininity by refusing the future altogether. Denied full humanity by her gender, she calls for an understanding of futurity in which the continuation of "the world" is not automatically a national or even a human project.[90]

The post-human future and female masculinity of *Woman Alive* are only tantalizing glimpses. Ertz sets both aside for a plot driven by romantic love and eugenic futurity; Stella's nonreproductive autonomy disappears when she falls in love with a genetically fit man. Yet, even as she accepts her status as bearer of the future, she continues to challenge masculinist nationalism by "threatening to remain single" in order to shape the future as she wishes it.[91] As men fight over whose genes will combine with Stella's, she points out the contradictions in their insistence that they would "rather the world had no future at all than that [theirs] shouldn't be the predominant race in it."[92] No longer committed to the end of humanity, Stella develops her own eugenic project, announcing that "each of [her] daughters" will marry "a member of a different race or nation" deemed "worthy of preservation . . . because of their value to the world and to civilization, or because of some peculiar racial genius."[93] Racial hierarchy will be reinscribed in the form of multicultural biodiversity, with the white Englishwoman deciding how humanity will be defined.

Stella plans to use the power of her gender to control not only biological but also textual reproduction: war and violence will be elided from her children's future. Her goal is a nonviolent "pleasantly homogeneous world"—a "colony" reminiscent of Corbett's New Amazonia, where everyone is carefully chosen, related, and fundamentally English though they may have diverse heritage.[94] In other words, her post-national feminist peace is a neo-imperial future of cultural hegemony for the English colonizing class, where undesirable bodies will at last have no future in literal as well as figurative terms. A nonhuman future will develop in the parts of the world Stella's family does not reach, but we are apparently expected to hope that they will eventually overrun it.

Stella's conflictedness pushes *Woman Alive* against the grain of its conventional narrative, offering moments of queered temporality that undermine its reduction of global futurity to one heterosexual, Anglo-American family. Pares's images enhance the book's queer possibilities. In figures 1.2 and 1.4, Stella stands alone amid crowds of stylized men whose adoration invokes 1930s fascist imagery. Even when Pares portrays her marriage, Stella's is the only face visible in a cheering throng, a bride dwarfing the nation she will renew. In the last illustration (figure 1.4), she stands forth as an androgynous figure cheered by anonymous hands. Stepping into her heterosexual destiny, Stella takes her place as the body of a dominant progress that will reproduce a racial future even as it guards against the reproduction of inappropriate knowledge. Yet the unfulfilled moments of speculation toward a different future linger, hinting at queerer paths through a reader's present.

* * *

Nothing gets outdated as quickly as the future. This chapter has focused on utopian dreams of the imperial past that can be unnerving to unearth, with their visions proclaiming futures filled with hope and peace even as they calmly glorify gendered, racialized, and colonial violence. Yet even these murderous utopian visions are born from a longing to live history differently, to create a future that will not wholly reiterate the past.

Utopian thinking and writing have long formed a site in which the temporal politics of racialized and gendered bodies, and of sexual acts, have been thrashed out. This chapter has explored ideas about gender and the future expressed in feminist utopian fictions at points in the late nineteenth and early twentieth century when projections of imagined futures constituted a burgeoning mode for thinking about a recently modern present. These old futures showcase anxieties about the reproduction and definition of the so-called human race, demonstrating an operation of gendered and racialized deviance that has persisted in the ways national futures are projected and reproduced in media and fiction up to and including the twenty-first century. Grounding my exploration of queer temporality in feminist discourse by tracing the ways reproductive futurisms are produced, invoked, challenged, and negated in women's writings about the future, these texts have allowed me to explore how critiques of reproductive futurism that have shaped more than a decade of queer analysis were rehearsed in earlier contexts.

Though I have been focusing on how feminist utopian imaginaries create futures open for colonial speculation, my goal in working with these texts has never been only to demonstrate their racist complicity. Instead I have tried to stay with their transient alterities, to highlight speculative feminisms' capacity to briefly halt and divert the imperial imaginaries they participate in reproducing. Glimpsing speculative narratives of feminist resistance and queer possibility as they slip in and out of imperial and eugenic discourses, this chapter aspires to provide background against which to set other old futures whose deviations from the present may feel more satisfactorily queer and decolonial. The next chapter continues this tack, further examining how white British feminists used speculative popular fiction to imagine the end of the world as they knew it. In chapter 2, I move from utopian flirtations with the political mobilization of *no future* to dystopian narratives that confront the absence of futurity head on.

2

Dystopian Impulses, Feminist Negativity, and the Fascism of the Baby's Face

Destroying the Future

"If you want a picture of the future, imagine a boot stamping on a human face. Forever."[1] George Orwell, in this memorable line from the canonical 1949 dystopia *Nineteen Eighty-Four*, envisions the worst-case scenario of a futureless future. A boot stamps forever; a single moment of violence eliminates the possibility of futures, since the lively potentiality of each human face will be continually, repetitively obliterated. Orwell's speculative image, his "picture of the future," crystalizes the affective force that representations of unpleasant futures can carry when they invoke the impossible possibility that there might be no future at all. This chapter is concerned with the cultural, political, and aesthetic work that speculating about the nonexistence of the future can do.

Orwell's boot belongs to a figure responsible for enforcing systemic oppression of minoritarian futures in the twentieth century and beyond: the cop, soldier, fascist in uniform. Around this figure, speculative and realistic images of the violent negation of choice, potential, and futurity flower into narratives about dystopian futures, pasts, and presents. The fascist boot also appears in theoretical writings about futurity and negation by queer theorists focused on the relationships among sexuality, negativity, and politics. Here I explore that nexus of sexuality, violence, and futurity through a history of dystopian fiction that predates yet has been overshadowed by more canonical works. Between the First and Second World Wars, antifascist British women writers used speculative fiction to explore complex ideas about gender, sexuality, race, and violence.

The dystopian fiction of Charlotte Haldane (1894–1969) and Katharine Burdekin (1896–1963) was written in dialogue with the rise of twentieth-century European fascism and is alert both to its seductions and to its horrors. Their work routes anxieties about science, gender, and fascism through images of desire, sexuality, and reproduction in ways that often present the fascist boot in the face as coexisting with representations of queer sexuality and sociality that would not be out of place in twenty-first-century sex-positive media. While imagining futures devastated by genocidal violence, Haldane and Burdekin depict societies where same-gender desire is a healthy part of male sexuality; sex workers are as respected as artists and musicians; and consensual sex is a source of guilt-free pleasure. To present sexual pleasure within a negative future might simply serve to underline the immorality of such behavior, as it does in Aldous Huxley's 1932 *Brave New World*.[2] Yet the presence of queer desires' fulfillment in the past's negative futures can also demand that we recalibrate the ways we think about queer politics, reproduction, and sociality in the present. Feminist dystopias offer much material for such calibration. Haldane's 1926 *Man's World* and Burdekin's 1937 *Swastika Night* use divergent strategies to route modernity's futures through reproductive bodies in ways that trouble oppositions twenty-first-century critical theory tends to naturalize: between heteronormativity and its others, queer and straight time, futurity and negativity, deviant and normative pleasures.

The violent unfuture of *Nineteen Eighty-Four*, together with Huxley's pseudo-utopia of technological false consciousness in *Brave New World*, has set the terms for dystopia's meanings in academic criticism and popular culture. In these terms, dystopia signifies oppression, state surveillance, the seductions of technocracy, and, often, the need to preserve the world as it is in the face of frightening changes. Orwell and Huxley will appear as reference points below, but this chapter focuses on precursors that have not entered the popular imagination in order to insist that there are different, and differently gendered, ways to think about dystopian futurity. *Man's World* depicts reproductive anxieties similar to those in the utopian texts I discussed in the previous chapter, creating an ambiguous and discomfiting dystopian future that shares elements of its biological and ideological critique with the later *Brave New World*.[3] *Swastika Night*, which has been slowly growing in influence since its 1985 reissue by the Feminist Press, portrays a devastatingly negative future whose resemblance to Orwell's vision has often been remarked.[4] I am less interested in these novels' relationship to canonical texts than I am in the shapes they give to gender, violence, and futurity in and of themselves—shapes that have the power to intervene in the intellectual reproduction of twenty-first century ideas. As fascist populisms rise again in the United States and Europe and those who seek to resist them turn to fiction as a way to understand current events, this seems an urgent undertaking.[5]

In everyday conversation as in speculative fiction, to say that a given idea, institution, or social structure has no future is to mean that things are looking grim and ought to be replaced with something else. Though we may not see the way there, we assume and assert that another future lies, existentially unthreatened, in a new direction toward which we should turn. Yet both popular dystopias and offhand references to the absence of the future center on a core of negativity: the idea that the future, as it is possible for us to know it, could be destroyed. In Haldane and Burdekin's novels, the production of futurelessness—not just an undesirable world for some, but the notion that the future could end altogether—is a powerful element in depictions of gender, power, and especially biological reproduction. This negative speculation resonates with the queer project of articulating a politics that might not rely on reproduction: a futureless politics. At the same time, both Haldane and Burdekin insist that same-sex desire can all too easily appear as one of the various interlocking forces that set in place politically horrifying futures. This convergence of reproductive oppression with homoerotic nationalism calls forth concerns and conflicts in queer studies over the ways nonheterosexual bodies, communities, and politics have participated in the perpetuation of racial and colonial violence.[6]

The chapter begins by laying out some ways that futurelessness interweaves with fascistic ideas and images in the politics and aesthetics of modernity, dystopian theory, and queer studies. I identify a dystopian impulse whose appearance in feminist dystopias of queer reproduction connects negative strains in queer and Marxist thought with the centrality of images and histories of fascism to dystopian imaginaries. From there, I unpack the ways that *Man's World* and *Swastika Night* route anxieties about power, violence, and sex through images of male homoerotic desire and speculative modes of biological and social reproduction. Haldane creates a "homosexual" understanding of futurity in which cultural and biological reproduction are separated in order to best serve the future of "the white race"; brief images of female rebellion suggest ways this could be unmade.[7] Burdekin's depiction of Nazi futurity is also aided by a homosocial view of cultural reproduction in which she creates images of female-gendered futurelessness in order to critique not only German Nazism but also British imperial and English nationalist politics. In the history of speculative anti-futurism this chapter brings to the fore, to have no future can mean to be taking the human race in the wrong direction; to be out of time; to occupy a space of political negativity; or to be in a state of hopelessness and despair. Refusing to either embrace or repudiate negativity, Burdekin's and Haldane's novels connect absent futures to sexual pleasure, eugenics, reproductivity, race, and nation—in complex and unpredictable ways.

Queer Dystopia and "the Fascism of the Baby's Face"

What compels writers and artists to imagine futures unbearably worse than their present? Gregory Claeys describes dystopia as a twentieth-century literature about fears of future annihilation, writing that after the "grotesque slaughter of the First World War," "Enlightenment optimism respecting the progress of reason and science was . . . displaced by a sense of the incapacity of humanity to restrain its newly created destructive powers."[8] If *the future* stands for an imagined endpoint to Enlightenment progress narratives, *no future* is what we are left with when those narratives break down. Yet Claeys's account does not acknowledge the uneven distribution of "progress" itself.[9]

The "optimism" of Enlightenment creates dystopias by relying on what Walter Benjamin calls "homogeneous, empty time" to frame the story of history's winners as an uplifting timeline for human development.[10] To see the present as the triumphant culmination of evolution, where the fittest have survived to tell stories that justify their victory, is profoundly dystopian for those who have been defeated. Benjamin speaks of the "working class" oppressed by capital, but Enlightenment models of humanity and history have had most power as justifications of empire.[11] Denise Ferreira da Silva shows how the Enlightenment model of humanity and history was co-produced with racial formation. The developmental temporality on which colonial hierarchies rely enables white, European subjects to perceive themselves as autonomous and self-determining because colonized people of color have become the material upon which enlightened, civilized subjects act, rendering them racialized others "without a future" in and of themselves.[12] The loss of Enlightenment optimism that Claeys associates with the First World War is also, then, an effect of the realization that white, Western subjects can be dehumanized in ways that seem natural for the nonwhite and non-Western, especially those marked by blackness.[13] In the quotation with which I opened, for example, Orwell's boot stamping on the human face was portrayed as a future to fear. Yet, as it directs us to contemplate the horrors of the future, it directs our attention away from real faces that may already be ground into oblivion in the present and in the past.

Dystopian fictions may invoke or challenge Enlightenment progress narratives, but the purpose of imagining the end of the world has often been to set the stage for political transformation—or at least to make transformation more imaginable. Raffaella Baccolini and Tom Moylan, writing about feminist science fiction, describe "critical dystopia" as fiction that enables "a space of contestation and opposition for . . . subjects whose class, gender, race, sexuality, and other positions are not empowered by hegemonic rule."[14] If utopian hope develops through plans for and impulses toward better things, Baccolini and Moylan suggest that dystopia's value can come through the same impulse: one might imagine things getting worse in order to believe they can become better. To paraphrase the villain from Duncan Jones's 2011 film *Source Code*: if new hopes and possibilities are to arise from the rubble of what we call civilization, there will have to first be rubble.

Dystopias here become outgrowths of what Marxist philosopher Ernst Bloch called the "utopian impulse"—a kind of active "longing" that can be mobilized to change the world.[15] Yet this fails to account for the affective power of dystopian negativity—our response to the violence of the boot on the face. Building on the notion that *no future* can be an important starting point for thinking the politics of history from the perspective of those excluded from dominant narratives, I instead ask what a *dystopian impulse* might produce. Can negative futures be imagined without either a redemptive kernel of hope or an implicit acceptance of the way things are? What pleasures and politics grow from dystopian speculation?

The perverse pleasures of negative imagination are explored by queer theorists who critique assimilationist, normalizing politics by homing in on refusals, debasements, and impossibilities. Filled with dystopian impulses, queer anti-futurist critique appears in the writing of French socialist gay liberationist Guy Hocquenghem in the 1970s, before being taken up by US queer theorists Leo Bersani in the 1980s and 1990s and Lee Edelman in the 2000s.[16] Hocquenghem wrote in 1978 that "the gay movement is . . . not the signifier of what might become a new form of 'social organisation,' a new stage of civilised humanity," but instead "demonstrates that civilisation is the trap into which desire keeps falling."[17] Drawing from psychoanalysis, Hocquenghem argues that straight society sees gay sex as a danger to humanity's future because sexuality without reproductivity signals "a fear that the succession of generations, on which civilisation is based, may stop."[18] Hocquenghem embraces this seemingly homophobic perspective rather than refuting it to demand gay inclusion within dominant culture. He places queer sex's disruptive force in the service of revolution, arguing that the end of "civilisation" homosexual desire portends would break down capitalist oppression and exploitation—the basis of which is the consumerist family. Hocquenghem's dystopian impulse destroys in order to build: he insists that a new order is possible, though it must be structured so differently from the old that it will no longer be understandable as "civilisation."

Like Hocquenghem, Bersani understands gay male sexuality as exemplifying sexual desire's capacity to unmake the social. His 1987 "Is the Rectum a Grave?" was written at the height of the AIDS epidemic, when many gay men were dying and all were viewed by the straight public sphere as contaminant sources of illness and death. The essay focuses on anal sex as the vector by which gay men become demonized, casting the "rectum" as a zone of waste and shame whose association with pleasure and death has the potential to shatter idealized understandings of the relationship between sex, power, and subjectivity held not only by the homophobic public sphere but also within liberal gay and lesbian activism.[19] Both Hocquenghem and Bersani revel in metaphorical ends of the future by insisting that sexual pleasure can constitute a dystopian impulse on the level of the body—underlined by gay sexual refusal of female-sexed anatomy's connotations of fecundity and life.

Gay male antisocial critique is not without its glimmers of utopian possibility, however. Hocquenghem's dystopian impulse finds destruction in pleasure, insisting that any possible new order will be so different from the old that it cannot be imagined within existing terms. Yet his work is also predicated on the notion that it is imperative to imagine such a new world. Bersani, too, gestures towards the possibility that acts of debasement and refusal could participate in the creation of futures and worlds that do more than reproduce homogeneous time. He closes *Homos* (1995) by suggesting that "in a society where oppression is structural, constitutive of sociality itself, only what that society throws off—its mistakes or its pariahs—can serve the future."[20] The future he imagines sociality's underside to be serving is not explicated in detail but stands as a moment of flash utopianism, a gestural merging of negativity and hope.

The most expansive queer critique of futurity has been Lee Edelman's. Edelman extends Hocquenghem and Bersani's framework from the sexually specific into a universalizing critique of reproduction itself, disavowing utopia, politics, and hope entirely for their positivist futural visions. His analysis of political futurity names the way in which an image of "the Child" functions as a guarantor for political projects through a universal temporal politics he names *reproductive futurism*.[21] Heterosexual reproductive sex becomes the alibi for a re-production of political and social structures, ensuring a conservative propagation of things as they are. To be queer is to refuse that reproduction (a dystopian impulse); not to refuse it is to become part of conservative futurism. I do not intend my analysis of dystopian anti-futurism as a confrontation with Edelman, yet the specific examples and connotations through which his dystopian impulse is elaborated are important if we want to understand the history of no future on which his work implicitly builds.

Naming and shaming the forces that reproduce politics as *heterofuturity*, Edelman uses a 1938 conversation between Bertolt Brecht and Walter Benjamin to explicate his memorable phrase "the fascism of the baby's face."[22] Brecht wrote to Benjamin in 1938 that futurity was fundamental to both fascism and its opposition because "[the Nazis] are planning for the next thirty thousand years."[23] Benjamin remembered Brecht as invoking reproduction to denounce a fascist futurism that wished to "deform the baby in the mother's womb," in a struggle against which "we must under no circumstances leave out the children."[24] For Edelman,

Benjamin's description of "a power that has its source no less deep in history than fascism" shows the flattening universality that comes from emphasizing children, and threats to children, as justification for political futures. Invoking fascism for the figure of reproductive futurism adds an emotive rhetoric to Edelman's insistence that "whatever the face a particular politics gives that baby to wear—Aryan or multicultural, that of the thirty-thousand-year Reich or of an ever expanding horizon of democratic inclusivity," all "political programs" are defined by reproductive futurism and thus "are programmed to reify difference and thus to secure, in the form of the future, the order of the same."[25] If the worst imaginable thing is always the deformation of childhood, then the same images define both fascist and antifascist politics.

Neither fascism nor antifascism are easy to define outside the specific historical referents from which Edelman abstracts them. In twenty-first-century Anglo-American popular culture, to describe a political project as "fascist" has long been to insist that it has no future—or that any future to which it is liable to lead should be avoided at any cost.[26] Edelman's analysis can help us see why: if all political programs are characterized by authoritarian enforcement of the forms of social reproduction they wish to fulfill, then elements of the fascistic can be identified, and denounced, at will. Similarly, Edelman's conception of the queer as anti-reproductive force becomes that which opposes fascistic politics by refusing the baby's face, even if queerness in and of itself has no political content. Yet Edelman's image of queer negativity as that which would shatter "the fascism of the baby's face" unsettlingly mirrors Orwell's depiction of fascist futurity as a "boot stamping on a human face." This proximity should remind us that Edelman's analysis of social-psychic structures of futurity offers an upheaval and a challenge to conceptions of politics rather than a contribution to political discourses themselves. It is a commentary about the chilling effects exerted by baby-faced iconography on what can be legitimated as political, not a discourse on either fascism or procreation as such.

The impossible ends of reproduction that inspire Edelman's theorizing are represented by figures who absolutely refuse to think about the children or to act in coherently political ways. These are invariably men who defy normative sociality (from Scrooge to various Hitchcock protagonists). Edelman understands this masculine dominance to be due to "a gender bias that continues to view women as 'naturally' bound more closely to sociality, reproduction, and domesticating emotion."[27] Yet, in feminist hands, the fascism of the baby's face has the potential to become a force no less violent than the fascism of militarized nationalist rhetoric.

Gender and the Science of Racial Futurity

The work of Marie Stopes, a British feminist best known for advocating birth control and sexual pleasure, demonstrates how eugenics, empire, fascism, and feminism can work together to create a reproductive futurism in which straight familiality, nationalism, and colonial time all line up.[28] In her 1921 *Radiant Motherhood*, Stopes asserts that women's poverty and oppression can be alleviated through projects of reproductive improvement involving family planning, better hygiene, and access to sexual pleasure. She writes: "We at present in the flesh may link hands with grandchildren belonging to a generation so wonderful, so endowed and so improved out of recognition, that the miseries and the depravity of human nature to-day so wide-spread, may appear like a black and hideous memory of the past, as incredible to them as the habits of cannibals are to us."[29] Stopes's rhetoric serves as a reminder that her argument operates through the temporality of colonization. She contrasts races and places on the globe that are already associated with the "cannibal," the "black and hideous," with the civilized bodies, radiant with light, that ought to inherit the earth. Only a few will link hands with grandchildren in the "wonderful" renewed nation; other bodies must be left only to memory lest a vast and ever increasing stock of the "degenerate" (that is, eugenically unappealing, futureless, excessively reproductive) endanger the future of the human race altogether. With this risk at hand, Stopes writes, it is "in the hands of the mothers" to redeem the reproductive future of the nation and the world.[30] This maternalism was a strategic historical intervention: after gaining many rights due to their work for the nation in the First World War, women in Britain as elsewhere in Europe were losing jobs to returning men, and a significantly larger population of women than men raised questions about the fate of the "surplus."[31] Stopes mobilized traditional gender roles to reassure women that marriage and childbearing could bring as much value to the nation as industrial employment. Linked to national and racial futurity through a eugenic feminist reproductive futurism, the fascism of the baby's face gains the potential to become a genocidal force.

The eugenic maternal future that Stopes invokes is imagined and examined in writings by her contemporary, journalist and popular fiction writer Charlotte Haldane. Haldane, born Charlotte Franken, was the child of a German Jewish immigrant, whose status as an enemy alien during World War I brought her into a difficult relationship with British nationalist fervor.[32] A prolific journalist, she supported her first husband and son through her writing before marrying her second husband, the celebrated scientist J. B. S. Haldane, in 1926. Neither Charlotte Haldane's writing nor her politics is easy to categorize. In 1927 she published *Motherhood and Its Enemies*, a screed whose promotion of maternity above all else and dismissal of "unfeminine" ambition lead Susan Squier to describe it as a classic of antifeminism.[33] Among other claims, Haldane identifies non-mothering women as a "female intersex" best suited to "subordinate positions that do not call for great emotional development."[34] *Motherhood and Its Enemies* was, however, rushed into print so that Haldane could sell it at a conference on population control where the "dangerous" profession of "human geneticist" was being mapped out.[35] Haldane had elsewhere been critical of eugenics because of its potential for race- and class-based abuses, and this focus colors *Motherhood*'s view of gender.[36] In insisting on motherhood as womanly fulfilment, she perhaps sought to highlight what might be lost amid celebrations of reproductive control and eugenic science, each of which would restrict motherhood only to progenitors of what Stopes rhapsodically called the "new and irradiated race."[37] Haldane's 1926 *Man's World* shares this concern, speculating about a future in which evolution has been taken firmly in hand by an authoritarian State for whom white supremacy, practical eugenics, and prenatal sex determination are tripartite ingredients for the triumph of science.

In the future *Man's World* dreams up, a coterie of übermen takes over the world after a cataclysm that resembles the First World War, and they set out to craft a scientific society—regardless of the body count. Haldane's novel, unlike those of better remembered futurists from the early twentieth century, makes the racial status of this dystopian utopia explicit.[38] Her post-national "world" of scientific perfection is reserved for "the white race," while bodies of color appear exclusively as part of the material on which scientific experimentation is carried out.[39] "Artificially created desert tracts" have been created to mark "the boundary lines between the white and adjoining races"; even the need for colonial labor has been eradicated by science, since "oil, cotton, quinine, and other vegetable products" have been "abandoned in these synthetic days" to the apparent "disorder" of a premodern past.[40] Most chillingly, *Man's World* depicts the scientific dehumanization and mass murder of racialized people through a process that literally targets skin color as a vector of death: "Thanatil" is "a deadly poison" that targets the "enzyme which produces the black pigment" in skin, causing the death of all darkskinned individuals.[41]

Haldane's speculative poison, engineered by one of the leaders of the scientific dictatorship, is a pure technology of genocide, figuring skin pigmentation as a biological determinant of death. To mark racialized others for death in this way might have been a utopian dream for Nazi scientists and US white supremacists alike. Its presence calls to mind Achille Mbembe's reminder that "the gas chambers and the ovens" of the Nazis "were the culmination of a long process of dehumanizing and industrializing death, one of the original features of which was to integrate instrumental rationality with the productive and administrative rationality of the modern Western world (the factory, the bureaucracy, the prison, the army)." Mbembe writes that the industrialization of death was "aided in part by racist stereotypes and the nourishing of a class-based racism that, in translating the social convicts of the industrial world in racial terms, ended up comparing the working classes and 'stateless people' of the industrial world to the 'savages' of the colonial world."[42] This integration of race and class also takes place in Haldane's novel, most visibly in the fate of less elevated ethnicities within the "white race," who are also portrayed as evolutionarily undesirable and dealt with accordingly. A settlement of "Celts" whose "decadence was incorrigible" in that they refused to abandon relatives infected with disease, for example, is exterminated.[43]

Characters in the novel, even those who are critical of the State under which they live, speak of racialized mass murder in a matter-of-fact manner that would be easy to interpret as the author's acceptance of a bureaucratic rationality demanding that sacrifices must be made for the triumph of science. Haldane's biography suggests that there may be more at stake here than what Sarah Gamble describes as an "apparently uncritical foreshadowing of many of the policies advocated by Nazism," however.[44] Herself Jewish, and having experienced antisemitism in Germany and in Britain, Haldane would become an active antifascist in the 1930s.[45] I interpret *Man's World* as seeking, though not always succeeding, to offer a disturbing vision of the way scientific progress can dehumanize through racialization. The novel's dystopian impulse imagines a depth and power of ideology that would make critique almost impossible, since the likeliest critics' lives will have been extinguished before its beginning.

While race in *Man's World* signals the realistic dystopia of necropolitics, in the form of a scientific imperialism that shades seamlessly into protofascism, the novel's gender politics—ostensibly its primary focus and the main area on which discussion of the novel as an early work of feminist science fiction has centered—are less easy to define. Elizabeth Russell considers the novel's thesis to be that "the future of women in a man's world is grim."[46] But white women are portrayed, on the whole, as happier in this future than they might have been elsewhere. Faced with Haldane's speculative technocracy, as Gamble remarks, it can be difficult to tell whether what we are reading was intended as "a utopia or a dystopia."[47]

Women's position in *Man's World* centers on reproduction, but is not reduced to childbearing. Some women are defined as "Mothers," venerated as "vessels singled out for the propagation of [their] race."[48] Haldane seems to have found the idea of a maternal vocation appealing, although she herself worked as a journalist while raising children; her feminism was influenced by an unfulfilled longing for the economic capacity to care for her children full-time.[49] Her Mothers insist that "by giving [them]selves wholly to motherhood [they] do not surrender [their] own chances of development" and view themselves as having escaped from the "employee" role of nuclear-family wife.[50] They are trained from adolescence in a discipline that lets them give birth to boys by focusing intensely on masculinity while they are pregnant, and they live in "breeding grounds" at the "most exquisite spots" on the ethnically cleansed "North American, Australasian, and European continents," where they submit "to the stringent discipline of hygiene, striving to attain physical and mental perfection . . . and to transmit it to those born to the high wonder of scientifically directed living."[51]

Women not drafted for Motherhood are sterilized and become "Neuters": among their ranks are "dancers, actors, singers, poets, novelists, essayists, painters, sculptors, architects."[52] Neuter life in *Man's World* seems something like a bluestocking utopia in its own right. Haldane writes that the Neuters' "interests were wide and entirely communal; they led calm and beautiful lives; their friendships were lifelong and many, and between those of all communities there was constant interchange of visits, and stimulating contact. . . . Beauty was their cult; they were perfectly trained and fashioned to bring beauty to the world. . . . In art they found their supreme satisfaction. They smiled perpetually."[53] Of course, "trained to bring beauty to the world" implies that the Neuters' own communities are not part of a world defined by reproduction; "perpetual" smiling implies intensive and exhausting emotional labor going on below the surface, which accompanies the expectation that Neuters will be sexually available to men. Nevertheless, Haldane's descriptions of their community, with its "constant interchange" of "stimulating contact," are rife with possibilities for queerly speculating readers. She evidently perceived some ways in which a proto-fascist scientifically reproductive state could open up marginal spaces for the nonreproductive to create different futures.

The plot of *Man's World* focuses not on its women, reproductive or otherwise, but on a man whose gender fails to align with the eugenic dystopia. The sexually "intermediate" protagonist, Christopher, embodies a failure of reproductive femininity: he turns out queer because his mother wanted a girl. (Stopes believed that a similar maternal failure could explain the queerness of Oscar Wilde, whom she describes as a "racial loss."[54]) Christopher, whom we first meet as he earnestly explains the eugenic common sense of his society to his younger sister, Nicolette, grows up to tempt her away from her vocation as a Mother. His queerness becomes a threat to the reproduction of his society's future. Nicolette is drawn back from rebellion by falling in love with a suitable man and recommitting to maternity,[55] while Christopher's deviant relationship to gender is punished when the governing elite decide his tendencies must be expiated for the sake of the "virility" of the "white race."[56]

Christopher chooses to die rather than to attempt to conform, exiting with a suicidal monologue that describes his society's fear of a nonreproductive queer futurity: "It was not the homosexual body they dreaded, but the homosexual soul; the soul in which the seeds of 'love' were doomed to infertility, the soul that was sufficient unto itself."[57] Shortly after, Nicolette's partner—one of the governing scientific elite— makes a similar analysis while assuring Nicolette that her brother's death was for the best, since the eradication of the abnormal is necessary in order to maintain the scientific state. He declares that "the men and women of the governing class . . . have no use for sterility, for above all things [they] aim to keep the race going until each individual shall have achieved complete self-consciousness."[58] Christopher's "homosexual soul," his embrace of "sterility," is a danger to the dystopia's hegemony— but it also, being "sufficient unto itself," draws close to the "individual . . . self-consciousness" that the scientific elite are seeking for everyone. He is a threat to the future of the race, these two passages suggest, because he embodies its possibilities; he has come too early. His role is to suffer for the sake of the future, and so his futureless existence opens on to the prospect of an as yet unimaginable queer futurity.

Christopher's death gives him a future by aligning him with the transcendent teleology of the governing class. This sublimated mode of reproduction is unavailable to women, as we learn through the fate of the minor character Morgana, a Neuter who also rebels against her assigned gender role. Morgana comes to resent the Neuter/Mother division; having chosen to be a Neuter because she was interested in science, she now wants to have a baby because it will be an interesting "experiment."[59] Denied permission to give birth, she complains that women are "pushed into [men's] beastly rigid castes and divided off into breeders and nonbreeders to serve the race."[60] Rebelling against this division, she is inspired by Christopher, and perhaps hopes for the kind of immortality he attains when she follows his suicide with her own.[61] But her rebellion is restricted to women's realms—she cannot achieve his kind of premature futurity, only a petulant demand to have it all. A woman resisting her embodied role in reproducing the future (whether by procreation or other forms of reproductive labor) can make even a suicidal protest only when routing it through a heterosexual relationship to masculinity. Haldane's novel holds no space for a female queerness that could break the eugenic stranglehold of racial production, even as the inchoate possibility of such a position is indicated by Morgana's mournful insistence that she "does not care about the race."[62]

If elements of Haldane's narrative seem familiar, that might be because of their resemblances to 1932's *Brave New World*, the classic dystopia by her cousin-by-marriage Aldous Huxley. *Man's World*'s status as a source for Huxley is one of few contexts in which Haldane gets mentioned in studies of dystopia and science fiction.[63] The two novels have much in common: the creation of a third gender of nonfertile women (Neuters or freemartins); a new world emerging when scientists take the reins of society after a catastrophic war; scientifically organized utopias full of seemingly happy inhabitants. Huxley's dystopian society does not specify, as Haldane's does, that it is restricted to white people. Yet the only bodies of color in his novel come in the form of a reference to the high production rate of a "negro ovary," deemed more responsive to genetic modification than the "European" equivalent, and the "Savage" Native Americans who stay out of the way of modernity on their "Reservation."[64] In the light of *Man's World*'s explicit racial eugenics, *Brave New World* aligns with Huxley's 1958 *Brave New World Revisited*, in which he makes sweeping critiques of overpopulation, worries about the fate of the world when "teeming illiterates" cannot be trusted to use birth control, and suggests that the future of *Brave New World* may be neither as dystopian nor as avoidable as his earlier novel implied.[65]

Brave New World also reminds us that nonheteronormative means can reproduce conservative futures. It refuses the association of female bodies with biological reproduction on which Haldane concentrates. Indeed, Edelman reads Huxley's pontificating scientist-politician, Mustapha Mond, as a figure exemplifying what it means to "stand outside the natural order of sexual reproduction," in opposition to reproductive futurism and the fascism of the baby's face.[66] Yet Huxley's text focuses intensively on reproductive futures. Childbearing becomes obsolete, replaced with the precision engineering of embryos whose intelligence is calibrated to an exact degree as they are churned out along production lines. In the place of the family, industrial capitalism has run riot; babies are decanted at the "Hatchery" in order to ensure homogenous production as Mond oversees embryos being prepared for their role as satisfied, promiscuous, genetically predetermined citizens. But this is still a future organized around children.[67] The disgust that serves Edelman's argument is reserved for reproduction in the confines of the family, and for motherhood in particular, such as when Mond describes old-fashioned babyhood through misogynist use of animal sexual metaphors: the mother is "a cat that could talk," "brooding" over the child at the breast with "unspeakable agonizing pleasure."[68] His vision may be figured by the embryo on the production line, many workers produced from a single egg and sperm through the "Bokanovsky" process of splitting,[69] rather than the singular babe in arms, but Mond remains the architect of an industrial-reproductive futurism keen to reproduce itself through the fascism of many identical babies' faces. Where cultural reproduction of oppressive futurity takes place through such anti-heteronormative practices, the neatness of oppositions between queerness and reproductive futurism collapses.

If Edelman's queer theory sees "no future" as what queer negativity reproduces, historical dystopian fictions depict queer kinds of sexual, social, and cultural practice as reproducing both oppressive futures and revolutionary no-futures. To understand their complexities requires a queer feminist analytic attentive to histories of empire and racialization. Sara Ahmed describes this mode in her writings about the "feminist killjoy," whose constant reminders of gendered power refuse to accept a complacent present or an unproblematized future.[70] Writing about "shadow feminisms," Jack Halberstam argues that queer theory's history of negative critique has been oriented around masculinity and seeks to rethink it through a radical embrace of the associations of femininity—such as the passivity and self-abnegation displayed by artists whose work subjects their own bodies to harm.[71] In the rest of this chapter, I build on these analyses of a feminist dystopian impulse through the contribution to popular dystopian narrative made by Katharine Burdekin's 1937 *Swastika Night*, which prefigures negative or shadow feminisms as it unmakes the eugenic timelines of reproductive and fascist temporalities. The path I chart through Burdekin's novel is a killjoy's one, evading narratives of heroism and redemption in favor of a relentlessly, queerly dystopian take on reproductive futurism.

Katharine Burdekin's Futureless Feminism

In 1934, the novel *Proud Man* by Murray Constantine used the speculative conceit of a visitor from the far future to criticize Huxley's recent *Brave New World* for its inability to imagine that altering social and familial norms might lead men and women to "change" their nature.[72] Constantine's protagonist was a "person" without gender, who looked with sympathy and confusion on the antics of men and women in the twentieth century. When turning to futuristic prediction to learn about society in a less "dogmatic" way, the "person" discovers that Huxley's effort at futurism has "no imagination."[73] By implication, Constantine's own imagination offers superior methods for thinking futurity. "Murray Constantine" was a male pseudonym for English author Katharine Burdekin, who published three of her ten novels under that name; Daphne Patai made the connection between the two identities and brought some of Burdekin's work back into print in the 1980s.[74]

Burdekin lived for much of her life with a woman companion in rural England, preferring to remain outside social, literary, and cultural centers.[75] She cared little for stylistic experimentation, writing to express ideas and rarely revising her drafts extensively. Much of her work was unpublished during her life and remains so; many of her later novels were never submitted to presses. Though her work remains obscure, much of Burdekin's writing articulates futures for gender and reproduction with greater "imagination" than Huxley in that it does not assume meanings or politics will remain historically stable.

Burdekin wrote several novels that use a futuristic perspective and long historical scope to look critically at gender relations, including same-sex erotic relationships. Her work in the 1920s and early 1930s was engaged with many of the same scientific, technological, and historical themes as Huxley and later Orwell, but in a more utopian than dystopian vein. Her 1929 novel, *The Rebel Passion* (published under the name Kay Burdekin), depicts a gay medieval monk who is taken on a time-traveling tour by an angel and shown the inevitable upswing of European progress, whose traumatic break in the First World War will be healed by the then-prominent League of Nations.[76] In *The Rebel Passion*, as in *Proud Man* (1934) and *The End of This Day's Business* (written in 1935 and posthumously published in 1989), scientific endeavor is portrayed as part of an evolutionary progression that will lead to a better future. *The Rebel Passion* takes its place among the visions of utopia I have already discussed, whose racial and colonial elements showcase the violence of developmental temporality. *Proud Man* and *The End of This Day's Business* both represent the future as a more complicated set of possibilities, in which changing gender norms brings its own problems: structural discrimination against men in *Business*, the loss of modern gender's pleasures with its difficulties in *Proud Man*.[77] The most widely read Burdekin novel, however, is the one whose orientation is dystopian rather than utopian. In its intense negativity and its response to specific and urgent political events, *Swastika Night* (1937) was a significant departure from Burdekin's earlier speculative fiction.

After the Second World War, "What if Hitler won?" dystopian alternate-history scenarios became commonplace.[78] Yet *Swastika Night*, written before war between Britain and Germany became certain, remains one of the most complex. For Andy Croft, Burdekin's is "undoubtedly the most sophisticated and original of all the many anti-fascist dystopias of the late 1930s and 1940s."[79] That sophistication lies primarily in the novel's engagement with ideas about femininity and reproduction. Like *Brave New World*, *Swastika Night* imagines a future in which alternatives to marital heterosexuality are mandated in order to guarantee a future for an all-powerful state. But *Swastika Night* is little concerned with the futuristic tropes of techno-capitalist modernity around which Huxley's dystopian impulses are oriented. Its industrialization of motherhood takes place not through technology but because of the enslavement and debasement of women.

The texture of life in Burdekin's dystopia is more medieval than modern, with only an occasional plane to remind us that we are long past the twentieth century. The biggest change, seven hundred years into the future, is that women's nature has altered so much that they are no longer considered—by men or, it appears, by themselves—to be human. And this is not because the human race has evolutionarily degenerated, punished for its racial or sexual sins, but for specific political reasons: the global ascendance of Nazism. While Orwell, Huxley, and Haldane were concerned, through their different emphases, that modern life might possess generalized fascistic tendencies threatening to the future of British society, Burdekin sees the immediate threat of Nazism as a potential annihilation of scientific, technological, and all other hopeful futures.

Swastika Night, whose action takes place almost entirely among men, enacts a direct link between masculine domination and the rise of fascist political movements. Burdekin depicts what Keith Williams describes as the "logical conclusions" of "the Fascist 'cult of masculinity.'"[80] Across the

German empire that rules the Europe in which the novel is set (and, we are given to assume, the Japanese empire that controls the rest of the world), Nazi power is maintained through a pseudo-religious cult that insists "women [are] not part of the human race at all."[81] Other non-Aryan subjects viewed as less than human have been obliterated. Nazi mythology idealizes an image of Hitler as "exploded" rather than of woman born, and so women are not even respected for their role in incubating future generations.[82] They are allowed to exist only because Burdekin's Nazis lack the scientific knowledge to develop a viable technique for reproduction without women.[83] Instead, female bodies become reproductive conduits with no hope or future of their own. Kept in cages, their sole function is to be raped when men want children. The closest they come to humanity, for a powerful German we see indoctrinating a "herd" of women into their lowly position, is when they mourn for the sons who are taken from them at a young age to learn to be men: the only "human feeling allowed to them" is "the leave to be . . . passionately proud of a male child."[84] Inarticulately, the no longer human women want access to the future whose bodies they birth, even though it is one that excludes them.

Swastika Night's speculative misogyny may seem excessive, but it has clear sources in twentieth-century proto-fascist thought. Burdekin's understanding of fascist misogyny draws on the Austrian Otto Weininger's 1903 work *Sex and Character*, which was admired by Hitler and by many intellectuals sympathetic to fascist movements. Weininger's book draws the reader through carefully constructed logical formulations to lead us, apparently inexorably, to the conclusion that women are not human.[85] "Woman," whose existence is defined only by a sexuality Weininger finds repulsive, embodies utter negation and meaninglessness; he sees femininity as a "demure outward self" created to be "a simulacrum constructed in keeping with male expectations and assumed in order to win male esteem."[86] This echoes the opinion of a high-status Nazi in *Swastika Night*, who declares that "women will always be exactly what men want them to be. They have no will, no character and no souls; they are only a reflection of men."[87] Weininger associates womanhood with a lack of capacity to engage with history or even with the rhythms of social life, since "woman" is a purely sexual force that gathers men to her and away from productive autonomy either in order to push into an undifferentiated reproductive future (if she is a woman of the type "mother") or into a futureless and narcissistic zone of sexual pleasure (if she is of the type "prostitute").[88] Women's reproductive capacity, and the families that are built around it, becomes a prop to the real reproduction of social and political life, which is transmitted nonbiologically from men to men.

Some feminists have shared Weininger's analysis of power's masculine lineages and women's position outside of nation and politics. Virginia Woolf's 1938 *Three Guineas*, for example, calls for women to oppose war through an "Outsiders' Society" that embraces the notion that women "have no country," "want no country," and may therefore belong to "the whole world."[89] While Woolf's critique of the patriarchy of fascism found the utopian possibility of an alternative, transnational humanism in the idea that women were excluded from the production and reproduction of the nation, Burdekin's dystopia unpacks the purely negative side of this conceit.[90] Literalizing the idea of women as outside nation and history, she refuses humanism altogether through her disturbing depictions of female figures who appear to lack any consciousness at all.

For all that Burdekin draws clear connections between masculinity and Nazism, she does not exonerate women from complicity with the politics that inspire her dystopian impulses. *Swastika Night*'s plot revolves around a book of secret history that documents the reduction of women. This history, written by an appalled male observer, describes women as "throwing themselves into" the negation of their own personhood with "conscious enthusiasm."[91] Burdekin does not suggest reasons for women's complicity in their own subjugation, other than a misogynistic false-consciousness theory asserting that women believed "if they did all that men told them to do cheerfully and willingly, the men would some-how . . . love them still more."[92] But the real history of Nazi feminin-ity offers some suggestions. Claudia Koonz's work shows the extent of women's complicity with male supremacist ideology, demonstrating how "the blatantly male-chauvinist Nazi Party" was supported by the repro-ductive labor of its Women's Bureau, "the largest women's organization in history."[93] Koonz draws from speculative fiction rhetoric to describe Nazi women's organizing as "the nineteenth-century feminists' vision of the future in nightmare form."[94]

Burdekin's harsh portrayal of femininity is a sharp rejoinder to Stopes's and Haldane's suggestions that women's single-minded devotion to procreation could occupy dominant temporalities in a way that would prove empowering, or that dedication to reproduction in the service of a racial project for improved heredity could be potentially good even for white, dominant-class women. In *Swastika Night*, capitulating to a solely reproductive role leads women not to a separate sphere of feminine power but to obliteration. In a future that becomes wholly male, they are not even significant enough to be a threat. Burdekin lingers with the ugly consequences of that possibility. She creates a futuristic politics of feminist negativity by asking what would happen if women acceded wholesale to their figuration as bodies on which male visions of futurity could be engendered.

Burdekin's nightmare of Nazi patriarchy relies on a social world that reproduces itself through relations between men. Both in Burdekin and in many historical analyses of fascism, that homosocial misogyny shades into homoeroticism. The antisociality of fascistic violence connects to the antisociality of homosexuality for thinkers who imagine both as rejecting the positive forces of life and reproduction signified by the female body: Wilhelm Reich has written that "the most brutal . . . types were those . . . . who were either latently or manifestly homosexual," and Adorno has declared that "totalitarianism and homosexuality go together."[95] William Spurlin describes this kind of thinking as "the discursive reduction of homosexuality to fascism, or to the location of homosexuality as fascism's source," which he critiques for its "conflation of sexual with political deviance, whereby homosexuality is pathologized as a fascistic fascination with the erotics of power, and fascism is reduced to a psychosexual manifestation of homosexual narcissism."[96] The sexual deviance of homosexuality, Spurlin implies, is a benign variation; the political deviance of Nazism is genocidal, and it is horrifying to think that the two could be in any way connected. Erik N. Jensen calls the idea that "homosexuals . . . formed the backbone of the Nazi movement" a "pernicious myth" that disregards the persecution and murder of gay people under Nazism.[97] The pink triangle, concrete marker of that murder, has been an important symbol for AIDS activism because it stood for homosexuality denied a future, a denial repeated in the criminal neglect of gay men and others with HIV/AIDS. Nevertheless, Stuart Marshall's 1991 essay on the problematic nature of the pink triangle as a logo for AIDS activism is an important reminder that the homoerotic imagery of fascism has been both a site of murderous homophobia and a means by which hegemonic state and patriarchal power is maintained.[98] Homosexuality does not consist of a pathological fascination with the erotics of power, but such fascinations exist there as surely as they do within heterosexualities. Fascisms may have sought to destroy homosexuality, yet homoeroticism may have been involved in their reproduction.

The erotics of fascist violence are confronted head on in Bersani's antisocial queer theory. Describing Jean Genet's homoerotic "fascination with what he outrageously calls the beauty of Nazism" in *Funeral Rites* (1948), Bersani argues that the depiction of Nazi soldiers as erotic objects is "in no way a plea for the specific goals pursued by Nazi Germany" but rather "insists on the continuity between the sexual and the political."[99] While this "superficially glorifies Nazism as the system most congenial to a cult of male power justified by . . . male beauty," he argues, it also "transforms the historical reality of Nazism into a mythic metaphor for a revolutionary destructiveness which would surely dissolve the rigidly defined sociality of Nazism itself."[100] When the Nazi and collaborator Erik and Riton fuck, Bersani reads the twinned virtues of Genet's anality and amorality as negatively transformative, nonreproductively bringing forth a future born of society's leavings that will refuse "to accept a relation with any given social arrangement."[101] These are the impulses of queer negativity: eroticizing and anally fucking the Nazi breaks down the rigidity on which Nazism's violently hierarchical structure relies, and by extension breaks down the rest of society's close-to-fascistic underpinnings. Though anti-Nazi politics are rejected, the idea that disgusting sex among those considered disgusting could be revolutionary and transformative provides grounding for the suggestive, near-utopian call to "rethink what we mean and what we expect from communication, and from community" with which *Homos* ends.[102]

Although its relationship to fascism, sex, and sociality differ wildly from Genet's, *Swastika Night* develops a feminist version of this antisocial politics. Bersani remarks parenthetically that "the metaphoric suitability of Hitler's regime" for Genet's project of revolutionary destruction "can hardly be untroubling"; Burdekin places the trouble front and center.[103] While Bersani's reading of Genet breaks down Nazi, and all other, socialities through the destructive power of desire, in Burdekin the destructive force of Nazi masculinity produces, through the antisocial practices of its dehumanized others, the seeds of its own annihilation.

The contradictions through which homoeroticism and fascism interweave become clear in Erin Carlson's analysis of homosexuality's significance within the antifascism of W. H. Auden and his generation, who were "alienated by the hypocrisy of the ruling-class values that permitted almost any degree of exploitation, deception, or brutality within the confines of institutionalized heterosexuality, but punished love between men."[104] Carlson quotes Christopher Isherwood's recollections of male homosexuality and homosociality under Nazi ultra-nationalism, which describe the prospect of an alignment between the two as a tragic misrecognition:

> [Christopher] knew only one pair of homosexual lovers who declared proudly that they were Nazis. Misled by their own erotic vision of a New Sparta, they fondly supposed that Germany was entering an era of military man-love, with all women excluded. They were aware, of course, that Christopher thought them crazy, but they dismissed him with a shrug. How could he understand? This wasn't his homeland. . . . No, indeed it wasn't. Christopher had realized that for some time already. But this tragic pair of self-deceivers didn't realize—and wouldn't, until it was too late—that this wasn't their homeland, either.[105]

Eventually, it was "too late" for the "era of military man-love" to materialize; same-sex love was dangerous enough to the fabric of Nazi society that it was punished in the same way as other forms of deviance. But Burdekin, writing about what it might mean to live in a world organized around German masculinity from the perspective of an English woman living outside a heterosexual family structure, could not know how that story would end. Her imagined future creates a world of nationalist homoeroticism that offers precisely that "New Sparta," with its exclusion of women, and takes it to its extreme. Both in Burdekin's fiction and in the realities that coexisted with and followed it, the dream of homo-Nazism creates a nightmare. Burdekin attempts to represent the gendered elements of a fascist homoerotic nightmare without falling victim to the homophobic blaming of fascism on that homoeroticism—and, in so doing, evades standard views of homosexuality and fascism that members of later gay movements have held. *Swastika Night* cuts through the tangles by imagining a Nazi homosexuality that is not antisocial.

The Nazi empire of *Swastika Night* is suffused with homoeroticism. "Men . . . love boys, nearly all of them, at one time or another, in one way or another."[106] That love is not demonized, but it is not idealized either. One man's "love" of a boy, for example, leads to the boy being battered to death for sullying his pure flesh with the body of an unclean girl.[107] Though visiting the "Women's Quarters" is a reproductive duty, "no stigma attaches" to men who avoid it or to whose "whole sexual and emotional life [is] lived among men."[108] Male love is a site of pleasant feeling in the extraordinarily ugly world Burdekin creates. As Maroula Joannou writes, men's love of men in *Swastika Night* even has the capacity to "destabilize the established boundaries of race and class."[109] German Hermann abandons his fatherland and eventually dies for the love of English Alfred, whom the national hierarchies of Nazi ideology have trained him to despise. But male love is also, through the erotics of the uniform and an idealized virility that abhors the feminine, the vector along which fascist power is transmitted. Eve Sedgwick's influential queer scholarship identifies male homosocial desire as a vector of patriarchal power's transmission in European culture; Burdekin shows a homosocial future in which female debasement is the corollary of male love.[110] She separates a homoerotic masculinity that slots neatly into existing power structures from any kind of gender deviance that might lead men to identify with women's concerns. And she imagines a world where the former has become so powerful that the latter is no longer possible.

In *Swastika Night*, male love reproduces the Nazi future, while motherhood and biological reproduction become sites of abjection. Burdekin's dystopian impulse is to take Weininger's notion of women's exclusion from subjectivity to its logical extreme. Associating femininity with the antisocial, anti-relational force that Bersani finds amid the parts of queer sex deemed most politically and physically repulsive in dominant culture, she places their degradation center stage and offers little prospect that it might be heroically overthrown. Caged women are portrayed as "living their stupid lives in little groups of two or three women with their daughters and very tiny sons," but of what those "groups" might do among themselves, we are told nothing.[111] A glimmer of possible resistance appears in the figure of Marta, a woman "so old she was no longer a woman at all, and therefore out of reach of all womanly feelings of shame and humility," who while "not free . . . perhaps by mere age had passed out of reach of psychic subjection."[112] But she appears only on one page, and thereafter leaves the novel to go about her cynical life without spearheading a community in resistance.[113]

The true protest of the women does not take place through a positive, heroic politics but in a negativity played out on the ground of reproduction—for the *female* birth rate is steadily and catastrophically declining. High-ranking Nazi von Hess thinks this is "the tragedy of the human race": that women have "destroyed [men] by doing what we told them," birthing boys without reproducing their subhuman selves.[114] Now "the race is coming to extinction" because of the "unconscious" "discouragement" of the women; and the men cannot admit to this because "if a woman could rejoice publicly in the birth of a girl, Hitlerdom would start to crumble."[115] Even as they inchoately mourn their own erasure from the future their sons will build, the women's very biology protests. Through excess of submission, they commit themselves to the end of the world.

George McKay finds this depiction problematic for its "biologic essentialism," which reduces women to "bodily functions, the sole aspect for which they are valued."[116] I am more inclined to read it as a commentary on the ways ideology shapes material reality than as an inscription of women as mindless bodies. Even as Burdekin decries the reduction of women to breeders, she insists that the most thorough denial of selfhood and subjectivity cannot render human flesh fully pliable, wholly without volition. Denied the opportunity to refuse, the women's very submission to reproductive dehumanization becomes their resistance. Rather than create more of their debased and unwanted selves, they continue the male master race, and in so doing bring it closer to its end. By following an evolutionary timeline in which the rewarding of masculinity leads to the production of more men, which in turn leads to the failure of human reproduction, the women demonstrate a contradiction Burdekin understands to be at the heart of fascism. It can perpetuate itself only by producing more of those it claims to want to eradicate.

In *Swastika Night*, women's futurelessness contains a seed of protest against oppression, but it is one that is routed through impossibility, silence, and a refusal to even exist. Given this negativity, it is interesting that Burdekin's work—which by 2010 could be described as "the best known" of dystopian "fictional satires" written in response to the rise of fascism—has been taken up by critics as a barely ambiguous narrative of feminist positivity.[117] Patai contrasts Burdekin to Orwell and other male dystopians because of her narrative of "hope" rather than despair.[118] Similarly, in a 1987 review, Robert Crossley wrote that the text "should appear on anyone's short list of the essential works of dystopian imagination, as a novel with as much critical energy and point as either Huxley's or Orwell's more celebrated warnings, but built on a substructure more . . . inspiriting than theirs."[119] Yet, on the novel's publication under a male pen name, a major concern seems to have been whether its pessimism made Hitler's victory seem too likely. Publisher Victor Gollancz found it necessary to add a note to the frontispiece of the 1940 reissue, insisting that the author has "changed his mind" and now takes a more encouraging and nationalistic view:

> While the author has not in the least changed his opinion that the Nazi idea is evil, and that we must fight the Nazis on land, on sea, in the air and in ourselves, he has changed his mind about the Nazi power to make the *world* evil. He feels that, while the material destruction and misery they can and have brought about are immense, they cannot do spiritual harm even in the short run: for they can communicate the disease only to anyone who has the tendency to take it. He further feels that Nazism is too bad to be permanent, and that the appalling upheaval through which the world is passing is a symbol of birth, and that out of it will emerge a higher stage of humanity.[120]

Swastika Night's negative depiction of a Nazi future in the throes of imminent extinction was too close to a future that the publisher could not risk suggesting as possible—it would have been unpatriotic to imply that Hitler was likely to win the war. And so readers were invited to reinterpret the futureless dystopia as a "symbol of birth," a route toward better possibilities. But it did not seem so to readers on its first publication, at least according to a 1937 reviewer in the *Guardian*, who describes the book as not a "novel" but a "nightmare."[121]

Hope that dystopia can mature into utopia is located by most critics in the fact that amidst all the death and misery, our protagonist—Alfred, an Englishman oppressed by Nazism—tries to change things. From the German von Hess, he learns how pre-Nazi history was erased by the new world order; he is astonished to see an image of a beautiful, evidently intelligent woman who was once granted the honor of standing next to Hitler. When von Hess gives Alfred a book to share with others in order to reconnect the future with the past, reproducing a new kind of futurity and halting the dominant time of Nazism become the work of an archive that passes from eccentric German knight to English rebel to the care of oppressed Christians who live on the margins of Nazi society. Alfred aims to deploy this archive to "destroy" the German "Empire."[122] He learns that he must do this by teaching gender history and showing men that women used to be, and could again become, so desirable they could be mistaken for boys.[123] He plans also to teach the English how their past was stolen from them, including the beauty of women and—crucially— the fact that they once possessed a great empire.[124] Once this process continues for "hundreds of years," gender equality and heterosexuality may be rediscovered and the Germans conquered.[125] Whether an English conquest of Germany would truly vanquish the cult of Nazi masculinity remains open for the reader to decide.

Burdekin describes England as a burgeoning site of potential resistance to Nazism. Yet she also makes a direct connection between British imperial dominance and the future Nazi empire, even as she mobilizes English nationalism to enable Alfred's hope for change. Burdekin informs us that "one of the motive forces of German imperialism" was "jealousy of the British Empire"; one of Alfred's motive forces is a powerful nostalgia for it.[126] Alfred has developed his own theory of selfhood, which comes to him because he realizes he is not "inferior" to the Germans who oppress him. He thinks that to be truly oneself (which for him means to be a man) one must "know [one] is superior to everything else."[127] For an oppressed subject, this may be a radical conception; attributed to a British man in the twentieth century, it is impossible to separate from a colonizing mentality. On this note, it is necessary to point out again that, like the other futures I have so far examined, the devastated future Europe of *Swastika Night* is wholly white. Jews have long since been eradicated, the role of despised other taken by non-Germans and Christians; Asian and African people persist, but are located outside Europe. The novel's protagonist is a colonized English subject whose rebellion against his subject state is encouraged by a dissident German aristocrat. Alfred wants England to be the future, to take the place of Germany. And though he dreams and plans to create a different world, his hope is rooted in a perpetuation of preexisting hierarchies.

The conjunction of Alfred's efforts to change the future with the women's resistance through refusal distinguishes Burdekin's queerly feminist dystopian impulse from better-known dystopian narratives. Alfred recognizes what has been lost in the reduction of women. His longing for something different is reminiscent of the male heterosexual desire that drives narrative plots in dystopian fiction and elsewhere.[128] Instead of either the fascinations of femininity or a strong female character's critique, Burdekin presses a bleak denial of subjectivity on her readers. Whatever relationships, desires, and philosophies the women of *Swastika Night* may have among themselves, the male perspectives that govern the narration will never know.

At the end of the novel, looking at the daughter born to the woman he habitually fucks, Alfred tries to imagine a situation in which she might rise to his level. Such a future is unimaginable to him. Women are too mired in oppression to feel the requisite superiority in Alfred's worldview, he is sure, and so their position as the negative reflection of man seems to be set. Loretta Stec finds a "utopian impulse" in Alfred's attentiveness to his daughter, drawing from it a reading of the novel as "a hopeful, feminist" suggestion that "when women are more respected a better world will result."[129] Yet what Alfred discovers in picking up his daughter is also that the hope the baby represents, as an embodiment of a possible future that may be different from the present, cannot coexist with a gender that marks a total absence of futurity. Alfred thinks,

> If I took this baby away . . . from all other women and never let her see a man or a boy and brought her up by myself, . . . I could make a new kind of human being, one there's never been before. . . . Even now, though he liked to hold the baby, he was feeling restless about being so long in the same room with Ethel. A man could sit with a dog quite indefinitely, but he could not stay with a woman except to satisfy his natural needs. . . . Once you've started to think about women, it's intolerable. It has the atmosphere of a stinking bog, heavy and evil and sickening. . . . Edith must live all her life [in the women's quarters]. I hope she'll die.[130]

From hope for a life after gender, Alfred is distracted into disgust. Baby Edith is "his," which suggests the beginning of a patriarchal lineage; but she is also of Ethel, her mother, and like her mother, which bans her from the world he occupies. The contradiction is "intolerable," and transforms his initial utopian impulse into a dystopian one. Alfred ends his soliloquy by hoping for his daughter's death, since if he does not think of the baby as equivalent to a "dog," like her mother, he cannot conscionably relegate her to the "bog" of femininity. He is forced to realize that a baby does not contain all the hope and potential of a new world when its prospects for life are curtailed from birth. He turns instead to his sons to pass on his new knowledge in what becomes, on the eve of the Second World War, a project for an English nationalist future. The futureless politics of the women offer a dystopian critique more incisive than the politics of hope contained in narratives of masculine rebellion.

* * *

It is comparatively straightforward to assert that *no future* is a concept that has a history. This chapter has tried to unpack some of the complications involved in taking seriously what that history has been. Both Haldane and Burdekin manipulate the politics of their historical moments into hidden histories of no future where the speculative reimagining of gender leads—always ambiguously—into critiques of nationalism and empire that resonate into the twenty-first century. Reading them, we are forced to confront and acknowledge the ease with which ostensibly progressive frameworks of sexuality and gender become complicit with fascist racial nationalisms.

Burdekin's prescient feminist critique of Nazi genocide develops gendered ways of thinking about reproduction and futurity that challenge these concepts' most common associations, and this has given the novel an interesting contemporaneity in queer studies. In particular, Burdekin's narrative of fascism's homosocial reproduction has resonated with queer scholars' efforts to come to terms with the growing capacity for race- and class-privileged nonheterosexual subjects to be assimilated into neoliberal capitalism and the conservative marital timelines of the reproductive family home. In a 2002 article, Heidi Nast invokes the novel's "postmarriage, postfamily state" as a worst-case scenario extrapolated from her analysis of gay transnational adoption as contributing to a globalized segregation of reproductive labor in the early twenty-first century. She asks: "If children are increasingly commoditized . . . and privileged white heterosexual and gay men hold a competitive edge in their purchase, what sorts of politics will emerge in future around poor women's bodies and ownership over their reproductive products? Will a queerly patriarchal scenario similar to that depicted by Burdekin ([1937] 1985) obtain hundreds of years hence?"[131]

Burdekin's queer afterlife shows how the constructions of reproductive futurism and futurelessness produced in early twentieth-century dystopias map onto contemporary discourses at a global scale. In Nast's model, children are idealized, longed for, and claimed in the global North while they are overproduced in the global South, whose women are imagined as in danger of becoming like Burdekin's: producers of raw human material to reproduce a future that will not be their own. Like any speculative fiction, Burdekin's future was a commentary on the immediate political concerns of her present. Yet, when Nast borrows the predictive logic of Burdekin's vision, the historical future gives her a framework to comment critically on the developing shape of a new present. Spending time with imagined futures that stand for roads not taken out of the past provides a lens through which we might come to better see that queer sociality and antisociality are as capable of perpetuating political horrors as heterosexual reproductivity.

The histories of no future I have traced in part 1 force us to recognize that we cannot easily discard or reclaim the ways of living and thinking futurity that we inherit, however committed we may be to challenging the logics of generational transmission. Visions of the ends of temporalities of domination become affirmative reproductions all too easily. The feminist, eugenic, imperial history of no future serves as a reminder that political and artistic efforts to imagine and enact an alternative future must reckon with these complicities and ambiguities.

To attend to the feminist negativity hinted at by Haldane and made explicit by Burdekin is not to refuse the validity of other imaginaries—of positive futures, hopes for change, and the perhaps more easily articulated political projects of more recent experiments in feminist speculation. The futureless politics outlined here show negative possibilities opening out of the foreclosure of futures, cautioning us to recognize when such foreclosures take place and to attend to their complications.

The most crucial of these is that the commonplace opposition between queerness, whether understood as homoerotic desire or as deviant gendered subjectivity, and reproductivity, does not hold across multiple times and spaces. Queer dystopian impulses matter not because they hold kernels of hope that might make it possible to reclaim negative futures, but because they disrupt too-easy narratives of hope and progress, highlighting their complicities and disappointments. In shining a light on the negativity of the present, the obsolete future endures.

The Future Stops Here

Countering the Human Project

Taken from a science fiction film, the image in figure W.1 is a picture of an imagined future. It is also an image about futures. Graffiti on a wall insists that "THE HUMAN PROJECT LIVES": somebody wants to insist, against the odds, that something called the human project will have a future, while the military presence of an armed soldier suggests that this future may be strongly contested. The shot centers on a white man (Clive Owen), who strolls along with a latte in hand. The dystopian future in which he lives has not denuded him of creature comforts. He is, in fact, the protagonist of the film. Yet the promise of the graffiti is not, his distant gaze and stride toward the edge of the frame imply, for him. In fact, this film is the story of a reproductive future that both reiterates and complicates the eugenic feminist histories part 1 discusses. Like the oppressed women in Burdekin's narrative, the population in Alfonso Cuarón's 2006 film *Children of Men* has unconsciously rejected procreation. The major studio film—adapted from P. D. James's 1992 novel and filmed in London by the Mexican director—highlights the presence in twenty-first-century popular culture of tropes from the old fictional feminist futures unearthed in the previous pages.

What kinds of human projects are most likely to live, and what futures arise from those that die? The stenciled slogan makes a claim about the future, placing hope in something called "the human project." Yet the text is not the only thing in the image. Faces and lines surround it, filled with significance we could only know by speculatively immersing ourselves in the film's real and imagined contexts. Settled at the edge of the frame and staring out at an angle, the soldier may also have thoughts, feelings, and interpretations of his own. These narratives are not obviously central to the primary cinematic project in which Cuarón is engaging. But my interest lies with the audiences and creators who would ask and answer

Figure W.1. Still from the opening sequence of *Children of Men* (directed by Alfonso Cuarón, 2006).

such questions—who would take an image such as this one, and all it connotes, as a resource from which to craft a different future. This section's speculations function as a bridge connecting the historical and reproductively oriented analyses of part 1, with their focus on the nuanced possibilities of "no future," with the more affirmative alternative futures produced and reproduced by queer of color speculative imaginaries I will go on to discuss in part 2. In science fiction terms, *Children of Men* creates a wormhole linking the disparate times and spaces that part 1 and part 2 of *Old Futures* address: the history of no future shown by feminist, eugenic, imperial narratives addressed above and the affirmative prospects for queer of color futures examined below.

The DVD release of *Children of Men* came packaged with a short documentary titled *The Possibility of Hope*. The phrase implies that the film's dystopian intensification of present-day state violence is intended to have a positive social value. For who could argue against the significance of hope? Against possibility, a category open to infinite expansion? Judith Butler writes that "possibility is not a luxury. It is as crucial as bread."[1] Yet the very breadth of possibility's possibilities demands we think about what might be obscured by universal insistence on the necessity of hopes for better futures. The historical analyses part 1 has worked through highlight a tradition of science-fictional wrestling with eugenic futures from which *Children of Men* emerges.[2] The film, the 1992 novel by P. D. James on which it is based, and their many precursors underline the uneven distribution of possibilities for hope along lines of race, gender, sexuality, capital, and globalization.

James's 1992 *The Children of Men* is the textual example that kickstarts Lee Edelman's 2004 *No Future*, whose excoriation of the rhetorics of normative possibility I discuss at length in part 1. James's quiet apocalypse born of universal infertility is an easy target. It ends, in Edelman's words, "as anyone not born yesterday surely expects from the start, with the renewal of our barren and dying race through the miracle of birth."[3] The impossibility of refuting the redemptive logic of procreation, and the novel's attribution of this to excessive sex and desire, neatly maps out Edelman's critique of the anti-sex, anti-pleasure logic of reproductive futurism: "If there is *no baby* and in consequence *no future*, then the blame must fall on the fatal lure of sterilized, narcissistic enjoyments understood as inherently destructive of meaning and therefore as responsible for the undoing of social organization, collective reality, and, inevitably, life itself."[4] But the blame cannot only fall there, for, as I have already shown, *no baby* and *no future* do not mean the same thing to every gendered and racialized body.

Envisioning a self-induced evolutionary dead end, James depicts the human race's future as ended altogether; the last bastion of civilization, Britain, is beset on all sides by those who cannot cope with the end of days. The specters of eugenic histories that view the poor, the disabled, the racialized, and the sexually deviant as dangers to the future of humanity are alive and well.[5] James frames the end of reproduction as a direct result of a moral failure to engage with the future. She suggests this has been brought about by past generations' eugenic insufficiencies: "Pornography and sexual violence . . . increased and became more and more explicit but *less and less in the West* we made love and bred children."[6] Making love and breeding children have become something only the non-Western do, and the absence of reproductive futures "in the West" seems to have brought all of humanity to an end. The distance between Western and human races is evidently a negligible leap for James; non-Westerners may have continued to have children, but they do not appear in the book.

Cuarón places the elisions of James's profoundly conservative novel at the heart of his adapted story, updating its messianic narrative for contemporary transnational anxieties. Inspired by the events of 9/11 and the idea that "the future isn't some place ahead of us; we're living in the future at this moment," *Children of Men* widens its politics of re/production beyond James's demonization of sterile pleasures.[7] In an early scene, the camera pans across a news collage that collects speculative archival materials to depict the end of hope, linking a worldwide failure of human reproduction to global political crises. Infertility (the headline "NO BABY HOPE") is depicted as a root cause of massive social unrest and forced migration, as shown in newspaper pictures of crowds of panicked faces and screaming headlines. In transferring events from James's nostalgic middle England to a contemporary landscape of hypermediated propaganda, high-tech decay, and immigration paranoia, Cuarón shifts focus from individual to global modes of reproduction and the apocalyptic narratives that accompany them. In a video screened on a bus in the film, images of collapsed and burning cities around the world are followed by the slogan "ONLY BRITAIN SOLDIERS ON." These images call forth multiple scenes of endangered national futures, showing how hyperbolic media discourses surrounding immigration are underwritten by the vision of a militaristic yet civilized imperial nation holding out against ravening barbarian hordes. The possibility of a future becomes explicitly national and racial.

Both novel and film seek the redemption of futurity through the reclamation of those the state marks as futureless, but they do so by incorporating them into preexisting political temporalities. In the novel, the baby who will regenerate a moribund humanity evades state recognition because it is born of two people whose disabilities exclude them from the list of fit parents for a potential new humanity and who therefore have avoided compulsory fertility tests.[8] James makes occasional mention of shadowy "Sojourners" who are "import[ed] from less affluent countries" to do the "dirty work," but the affairs and future of British citizens are the novel's only real concern.[9] The film carries the idea of a redemptive futurity built from rejected bodies further, bringing front and center the illegal others whose subjugation enables Britain's pretense that it has a future. Given Cuarón's status as a Mexican director working transnationally between the United States, the United Kingdom, and Latin America, we must also see connections to the stigma attaching to those who have crossed the US border from the South and worked to sustain a country increasingly hostile to their presence even as it relies on their labor.[10] As Clive Owen's Theo walks obliviously through London, flashing his passport, noncitizens are imprisoned and policed beside and behind him while they continue to die on TV.[11] Even when no one has a future, some futures are still more desirable than others.

The future in *Children of Men*, as in *Woman Alive*, is held by one woman. Kee is a young black refugee of undisclosed national origin, and she does not know who fathered the baby she carries.[12] Her pregnancy might save all of humanity's future, yet she, a person without citizenship, lacks human rights and is marked by the dystopian British state as a polluting force. She gives birth to the future in a refugee camp. Yet, as her daughter's birth signals moments of transcendent hope onscreen, any prospect of visual or narrative autonomy for Kee is erased as she is handed from her white male protagonist protector into the hands of anonymous scientists on a mission to save humanity. As Aimee Bahng has shown, Cuarón's film critiques many of global capitalism's models for futurity while technologically reproducing reproductive futurism in the form of "a narrative arc that writes a man's hopes and visions for the future across the body of a woman of color."[13]

The film's open ending offers no suggestion that Kee's fate at the hands of the Human Project scientists will be a pleasant one. The uses that scientific humanisms make of the bodies of the excluded are well documented. Hortense Spillers names "captive flesh" of black people as having provided a "living laboratory" for the curing of white captors, in the history of slavery and after.[14] Looking at the film through Kee's perspective demonstrates the extent to which childbearing bodies may be excluded from the larger implications of reproductive futurism. A double meaning here inheres in the association between children and the future. A future *for* the children (born and unborn) of some may be built *from*— off the backs, at the expense, on the labor, and out of the bodies of—the children of others. Kee's possible fate as the brood mare for a future in which nothing but her loins are given a stake was prefigured by representations of women who bore forth futures without having the ability to live in them. She has helped me see the extent to which gendered and racialized histories of futurisms haunt contemporary queer theory, and the processes by which critical speculative fictions try and fail to counter dominating temporalities.

In *The Possibility of Hope*, environmentalist James Lovelock—initiator of the Gaia hypothesis that personifies Earth—epitomizes how ecological discourses have inherited the eugenic content of reproductive futurisms. He speaks of his grandchildren's anxiety about perpetuating a world on the brink of collapse. As the screen shows the elderly white man playing with some beautiful pale-skinned children, he declares that they are the ones who should be reproducing. These children, it appears, can recognize the problems of the world and therefore exert some control over it. Elsewhere, the documentary intercuts archive footage of teeming dark-skinned bodies in a postcolonial metropolis with mountains of decomposing garbage, suggesting a connection between the mounds of trash and the presumptive others on the screen who lack the capacity to think about the future, unlike the beautiful white children. The racializing, imperial future with which the white feminist speculative fiction writers of my first two chapters wrestled is uncritically reproduced in this supposedly progressive environmental narrative—an odd choice given the critical lens that *Children of Men* itself casts on the racialization of futurity. It is difficult, it seems, to gain significant distance from visions of humanity's future that mark some human bodies as futureless, or to give up relying on the colonially inflected temporalities of progress and development that reduce disparate historical realities into a linear frame.

The scientists who save Kee belong to "the human project"; the histories I discuss in part 1 show how little innocence projects of human futurity have had. Yet it is the disenfranchised, the futureless, who write desperately on walls that "THE HUMAN PROJECT LIVES." They will not go gently into the end of the future and they will not allow the official designation of futurelessness to bar them from the pleasures of existence. Kee bears the future of the whole human race yet has no official home or state-recognized identity. Cuarón's decision to cast a young black woman in the role of the last and first reproductive subject, along with his constant attention to the violence of borders, makes room for this narrative. Black British actor Clare-Hope Ashitey's presence as Kee combines the conservative narrative of reproductivity that undergirds the film—children are our future, and if adults do not take due responsibility for producing them, then human relationships with the world and one another will collapse—with a body few viewers will be accustomed to seeing signify a future to be desired. Still, as Jayna Brown points out, it is not uncommon in science fiction film for black characters to hold symbolic or visionary power even as they are rarely narrative protagonists.[15]

As a poor, pregnant, black teenager and undocumented immigrant ignorant of the father of her child's identity, Kee fits every eugenic, colonial narrative of the person whose excessive reproduction ought to be curbed. Yet, in the closing shot of *Children of Men*, she sits amid the wreckage of the world, in a boat with her daughter, Dylan, and the corpse of a white man who has just died to save them. Patiently, they wait for a crew of scientists who will nurture mother and child in their role as the origin point for a renewed humanity. In their role as humanity's hope, Kee and her daughter might conceivably signify the prospect of a future where the dominance of whiteness, nationalism, empire, and borders will be made irrelevant.[16] But her position, in the boat awaiting rescue, signals something less utopian: the triumph of procreation, in which a nonwhite, noncitizen future will be made the best of, assimilated into the human project in the absence of a better option, but in which Kee's own life experience and knowledge will be subordinated to the scientists who rescue her.

Yet there is something about the figure of Kee that eludes her apparent role in the reproduction of futurity as subtly as Corbett's and Ertz's protagonists did theirs in this book's first chapter. The lines from Kee to the white racial mothers discussed there are broken, mediated by the discarded bodies of those deemed unwelcome or unacceptable in eugenic genealogies. She appears constantly surrounded by white women, black men, or white men, never alone from her first appearance in the back of a crowded car to her elevation from a small boat containing one white man to a larger boat containing many. It is as if each representative of each possible future is afraid of what might happen if she were to slip out of their sight. Kee is not explicitly queer-identified, but there is something queer about the way she fails to synchronize with the narrative in which she is situated. She carries a singular, straight future in the most normative reading of Cuarón's film, but when placed in the context of her affinities with other similar figures, other laborers in the reproduction of futurity, she embodies uncertainties and excesses to which we should pay attention.

Around the edges and against the grain of the primary narrative *Children of Men* employs, the film offers visual cues for alternative, negative, perhaps impossible models of presents and futures that work in spite of and against reproductive futurity, colonial reality, normative hope. Though we follow a conventional story in the foreground, background images in *Children of Men* suggest stories to tell about futures and possibilities that run against, alongside, and underneath the story of redemptive reproductive possibility the film promotes. It suggests that there might be unknown quests and pleasures buried in and hidden by violence—futures unforeseen and unforeseeable, which we could access through viewing, reading, or inhabiting the film in a different way. In one background scene, nameless refugees rise up against the state; as our protagonists march past, in a shot that ends on a shot of a woman in hijab with her fist raised, we see people standing up to a regime that has declared their lives impossible even as they lived them.

In another brief yet iconic background moment, a quieter crowd stands around demanding the end of possibility, holding a sign that declares "THE FUTURE STOPS HERE." The film tells us that the future does not have to stop here, if we have faith in the hopeful science of the human project. But it also invites us to ask whether the people in this shot are campaigning in favor of the apocalypse, perversely hoping to avert it by acknowledging it, or just trying to force their way into the main plot of the film. The image with which I began marks these prospects. While Theo strides past, we might look to the graffiti, whose demands that we pay attention hint at the existence of oppositional media networks and perhaps at significations of the images we could only know by context. We might also wonder whether the hopes of the person who painted the slogan can be satisfied with the way things are turning out.

What might Kee know about the people who drew the graffiti—the slogan writer the human project failed as a source of hope when it carried Kee away from all the other futureless subjects—or about the artists who made the other drawings? The soldier, a man of color whose position in retrenched anti-immigrant Britain cannot be secure, may have more in common with the painters than with the citizen subjects he is tasked to project. Within the narrative strictures that make *Children of Men* saleable to its global distributors, these are impossible stories. But the film, like any speculative narrative, opens up to possibilities beyond the ones it depicts directly, allowing audience members to enter at multiple points. In conjunction with Kee's story, these background glimmers point to alternative temporalities and possibilities—those created by people who are Kee's ancestors and heirs according to different systems of reproduction.

Kee's heirs in this sense might be other representations of black women's futures, but they might equally be versions of herself that traffic outside the legitimated purposes of studio profit. I have been responsible for one of these, creating a critical remix video by re-editing scenes from *Children of Men* together with other futuristic films to bring her and other marginal figures to the center.[17] Creative science fiction fans active in feminist and antiracist critique have written stories that provide her with a truculent, rebellious, or contemplative internal voice.[18] Looking closely at figures like Kee, who do not quite line up with the narratives they are supposed to reproduce, shows the potential of such figures to remake or unmake the world in different ways. That may mean occupying the timelines and hierarchies they inherit without being legitimated by them, as the narratives I discussed in part 1 have tended to do. Parts 2 and 3 highlight demands for those lines to flow in different directions. The remaining chapters focus on works that (re)produce futures radically different than the ones they inherited—on projected breaks in historical continuity that suggest more than the merest glimmers of alterity for the oppressed. From here on out, the future becomes a different kind of place.

PART II

A Now That Can Breed Futures

Queerness and Pleasure in Black Science Fiction

seeking a now that can breed
futures
like bread in our children's mouths
so their dreams will not reflect
the death of ours
—Audre Lorde (1978)

Can the future stop being a fantasy of heterosexual
reproduction?
—José Muñoz (2009)

3

Afrofuturist Entanglements of Gender, Eugenics, and Queer Possibility

Breeding (Afro)Futures

In her 1978 poem "A Litany for Survival," Audre Lorde gives voice to a conversation about possibilities and impossibilities often drowned out by dominant futurologies.

> for those of us who cannot indulge
> the passing dreams of choice
> who love in doorways coming and going
> in the hours between dawns
> looking inward and outward
> at once before and after
> seeking a now that can breed
> futures
> like bread in our children's mouths
> so their dreams will not reflect
> the death of ours:
>
> For those of us
> who were imprinted with fear
> like a faint line in the center of our foreheads
> learning to be afraid with our mother's milk
> for by this weapon
> the illusion of some safety to be found
> the heavy-footed hoped to silence us
> For all of us
> this instance and this triumph
> We were never meant to survive.[1]

Her words articulate the power that discursive articulations of possible futures can have when immediate, personal futures are profoundly uncertain. Calling on those who "were never meant to survive," Lorde invokes the historical and present struggles of black diasporic subjects who are heirs to the social death of slavery: laborers who created the edifices of modernity but would not be permitted to live in them.[2] The "we" of the poem is made up of bodies who will not or cannot be disciplined as proper subjects for the progressive futures encouraged by liberal individualist politics. Yet, even as Lorde's poem gives voice to the everyday experience of exclusion, it insists that to be made an object in this way is also to resist.[3]

To speak as one "never meant to survive" is to acknowledge yet shrug off the figurative weight of structural futurelessness. The precarity of this status forces Lorde's speaker to perceive space and time beyond their linear surfaces: "looking inward and outward / at once before and after," because they are denied the privilege that lets futures seem foreseeable. "The illusion of some safety to be found" is too likely to be a trap—to restrict possibilities even as it seems to open them up. Yet the poem refuses to conflate oppression and misery. All this risk becomes worthwhile due to the pleasures that happen while out of dominant time and space: "in the hours between dawns," "in doorways coming and going." Without a program or a set of predictions, in the allusive language of poetry, Lorde envisages the "now" of oppression and pleasure converging to bring forth futures in all directions. Here, the imagined future is not only a far-off image that casts its light into the present and the past and limits what we can see there. It is also a resource out of which dreams and worlds can be built. And that resource has meant most for those whose access to material resources in the present has been most limited.

Speculative fictions by radical people of color have grown in popularity in recent years among readers who see them as hopeful articulations of radical political possibility.[4] The possibility of alternate futures matters urgently at a moment in US history when movements galvanized by the deaths of Trayvon Martin, Michael Brown, and Eric Garner have forced dominant culture to attend to the fact that, despite liberal allegations of progress toward multicultural diversity, racialization in general and blackness in particular continue to define who is meant and not meant to survive.[5] Sharing Lorde's commitment to the notion that imagined futures are central to the work of survival, part 2 looks to old futures that predate—sometimes contradicting, sometimes inspiring, always queering—the upsurge of interest in race and speculation in the second decade of the twenty-first century.

Black American cultural producers, reckoning with histories of exclusion from a dominating dream, have long labored to imagine queer kinds of futures for race and gender. In the twentieth century, their visions have accompanied the emerging dominance of the United States as a global and imperial power, calling attention to and widening the cracks in exceptionalist visions of the US state as founded on and exporting freedom.[6] Building on my analyses of gender and eugenics in white feminist futurisms, this chapter traces how discourses of technological and reproductive futurity have been adapted, adopted, and resignified in fictional visions of black futures, beginning in 1920 with W. E. B. Du Bois and stopping in 2005 with Octavia E. Butler.

Lorde uses the language of procreation to describe how possible futures emerge from the present when she hopes for "a now that can breed / futures." "Breeding," more often than not, has been a word used to animalize human reproduction, whether in queers' desultory references to heterosexuals or in owners' views of enslaved women as less than human, capable of being "bred" like livestock. The word links back to histories of eugenics considered in part 1, wherein desirable racializations for the future of humanity were imagined to be planned and predicted by "breeding" in and out particular strains of deviance, ability, and gender. Lorde, however, reclaims and reframes the notion of "breeding" to conjure a reproductive futurity that would not mean only the recreation of heteronormative, white-centered families and the exclusion of othered bodies. Her futures will not be for children and childishness at the expense of adults, but will keep the "dreams" of ancestors constant in existences to come. These are futures that matter as much for their power in the present as for the concrete ways they may or may not be brought into being—yet the futures they invoke and create are real.[7] The way Lorde invokes "breeding," transforming it from a term antithetical to queerness and offensive to blackness into a nexus of hope and possibility for the black, queer, feminist subjectivity she articulates, guides me through the complexes of race, reproduction, sexuality, and pleasure that I consider in this chapter.

In fellowship with Alexis Pauline Gumbs's project to interweave the "two rhetorically impossible claims "'Black maternity' and 'queer inter-generationality'" and to perpetuate their co-creation of a "rival model of production, interrupting a developmental timeline with the possibility for a radically transformed society," this chapter engages the reproductive practices by which black cultural producers have labored to imagine futures different from and challenging to the "now" in which they spoke.[8] I focus on how speculative fiction, racialized reproduction, and queer possibility converge around the processes that *breed* futures, and how these connections underlie the emergence in the 2000s of a canon of literary black science fiction. The idea of "breeding," with all its problematic entanglements, has continually been invoked in speculative imaginings of black futures. Part 1 explored how imagined futures functioned as interventions into the dominant order for cultural producers (white, middle-class, British women) whose positions within dominant futurity were assured, if marginal. This chapter details some disruptions and continuities to the eugenic narratives that appear when we contemplate how futurity has operated as a resource for those who, in Lorde's words, "were never meant to survive."

This aspect of the cultural politics of speculative fiction has been most widely explored, in the past two decades, under the sign of Afrofuturism, which has emphasized the particular relationship that Afro-diasporic subjects (often but not exclusively black Americans) have to history and futurity. The term is generally attributed to a 1994 interview Mark Dery carried out with Samuel R. Delany, Greg Tate, and Tricia Rose, in which Dery asked whether "a community whose past has been deliberately rubbed out, and whose energies have subsequently been consumed by the search for legible traces of its history" can "imagine possible futures."[9] Dery has been justifiably critiqued for the sometimes disingenuous framing of his article, which opens with a question—"Why do so few African Americans write science fiction?"—whose premise relies on a reductive interpretation of speculative narrative genres.[10] Yet the framework of Afrofuturism has flourished and expanded as both a popular and a scholarly movement, taken up by African diasporic thinkers, musicians, writers, and filmmakers to describe the vitality of speculative futures created in opposition to official, colonial, normatively white timelines.[11]

Afrofuturist theorizing deals with music, everyday uses of technology by black people, and a wide range of works of speculative fiction, ranging from Sun Ra's aural vistas of Egyptian space travel to Robin Kelley's invocation of surrealism as the heart of the "emancipation of thought" that black political radicalisms demand.[12] Alternative figurations of time and space come together, growing transformative politics from the memory of racialized horror or, as in Rasheedah Phillips's concept of "Black Quantum Futurism," calling forth the overlap between ancient African temporal theory and quantum physics in order to "seize upon a vision of a future and collapse it into your existing reality."[13] Drawing from many modes other than narrative, Afrofuturistic thought often figures disruptions to the dominant time line as rhythmic rather than directional. An exemplary moment is the passage in Ralph Ellison's 1951 *Invisible Man* where the protagonist listens to jazz and finds that the invisibility of racial exclusion allows him aural access to "those points where time stands still or from which it leaps ahead."[14]

Afrofuturistic analyses call forth cross-time touches and nonteleological histories that resonate with evocations of queer temporality. As Lorde's linkage of wayward modalities of "love" with the "fear" of racial oppression demonstrates, when positionalities of blackness and queerness converge, being forced outside the regulations and protections of dominant temporality can open up alternative futures, worlds, selves, and relationalities. Kara Keeling describes both blackness and queerness as sites of unpredictability and risk within the capitalist markets that compete to sell foreseeable futures.[15] Within the logic of capitalism, we are used to thinking about the future as a resource—one that is bought and sold to the highest bidder, as in the case of futures markets where investments in possibility are bought and sold; or one that is about to run out, as with the ecological futurity that is transmuted into capital by carbon trading. In capitalism's mobilization of the logics of heteronormativity, children become the ultimate site of futurity, to be saved, saved up for, given expensive commodities, and idealized at the expense of adult needs, pleasures, and desires. At the same time, racialization and colonization render marked populations, regardless of their sexuality, family status, or age, as queer and deny them access to normative frameworks of futurity.[16]

Lorde's "futures / like bread in our children's mouths / so their dreams will not reflect / the death of ours" insist that futurity can be a different kind of resource—a nonpredictive mode of possibility that keeps oppressed people going in a world where, hostile as it may be, adult pleasures and children's interests need not be at odds. Yet I do want to home in on the *predictive* narratives in which those who were never meant to survive engage—the concrete and rationalized attempts to imagine futures different than oppressive presents. To what extent might these futures participate in the logics of capitalism, risk, and the reproduction of oppressive social norms? Many of the literary texts claimed for the emergent canon of Afrofuturism are entangled with techno-futurist temporalities of science fiction and gendered systems of reproductive futurism. It is these works that I contemplate in this chapter.

I begin by historicizing black futurity, looking in some detail at one of the earliest texts claimed for Afrofuturism: W. E. B. Du Bois's 1920 "The Comet," which carries out an intense critique of the racial and colonial politics of modernity while producing a literal, melodramatic vision of what "breeding" a future to challenge racism could mean. I show how reproductive futurism and eugenic discourse operate to underline Du Bois's critiques of racialized temporality, moving from the general themes he employs to the way they play out in the barely visible figure of a black mother in the background of the story. What kind of future can she breed, and what would a narrative of black futurity look like from her perspective?

In the last section of this chapter, I explore the ways that Jewelle Gomez and Octavia Butler join science fiction futures with vampire mythology to create a speculative breeding ground for Afrofuturist visions and queer futurities, bringing forth eternal life from histories that were "meant to be" dead ends. By providing a mode of reproduction that is not (hetero)sexual and does not revolve around children, the convergence of vampire stories with science fiction futures allows Butler and Gomez to do queer and decolonial work with received discourses of black female futurity, reconfiguring the history and future of racialization by imagining how it would look according to a different set of norms. Altering the meanings of birth, death, and consumption through their re-production of a figure commonly associated with whiteness and wealth, Octavia Butler's last and queerest protagonist—the black vampire child, Shori—and Jewelle Gomez's eternal lesbian-feminist vampire, Gilda, stretch reproductive time and unbalance history by refusing the double binds of racialized and gendered reproductivity.

Modernity, Science Fiction, and Black Futurity

As a genre, science fiction has tended to look very white. This is true both of the historical demographics of its self-proclaimed writers and fans and of the cultural politics that underlie its dominant themes.[17] Istvan Csicsery-Ronay Jr. describes science fiction as an outgrowth of the temporality of European Enlightenment thought and the technological developments of modernity: it is "an expression of the political-cultural transformation that originated in European imperialism and was inspired by the ideal of a single global technological regime."[18] The imperial projects of the Enlightenment and the transformations that followed were, as Denise Ferreira da Silva shows, reliant on the production of blackness as a constitutive outside.[19] If the timelines that structure futuristic fiction map an Enlightenment vision of history onto the past, present, and future of the globe, according to a colonial taxonomy of human development that places male, Western European whiteness in the privileged position, then stepping forward in this timeline may be less than appealing for those who are not its official subjects. Yet the act of speculating a future has never been restricted to those for whom the future seems to be created. Paul Gilroy's influential work on the black Atlantic describes the longstanding presence of a transatlantic Afro-modernity that challenges the racism and nationalism of Anglo-American narratives about modernity's technological and social forward march.[20] Gilroy insists on black peoples' material understanding of a modernity that relied on their labor but excluded them from subjectivity. For the descendants of black people enslaved in the Americas, seeking a future in spite of being denied one has long been a matter of life and death.

In her influential 2000 anthology *Dark Matter: A Century of Speculative Fiction from the African Diaspora*, Sheree R. Thomas brings together the discourses of science fiction, Afrofuturism, and the black critique of modernity to argue for the consistent presence of black speculation in the twentieth century. Her introduction figures black writing as an unrecognized shaping force—like the "dark matter" physicists know is there because of its effects but cannot perceive directly—in the history of modernity and of literary futures.[21] She argues that the established genre of science fiction in literature, film, and television has been a vital resource for black people thinking about their individual and collective futures in the twentieth century. This has been true, Thomas implies, even though the practice of projecting futures out of the present and imagining them to be inevitable has given power to the temporalities of modernity and empire. Gregory Rutledge makes this part of Thomas's argument explicit, writing that "Africans and their descendants have been marked as the primitive for centuries" and therefore objectified within "a protracted science fiction, or insidious fantasy"—in other words, white modernity—"against which the slave narratives were some of the first counter-briefs."[22] In a critical contribution to *Dark Matter*, novelist Walter Mosley draws from this context to insist that for black Americans who have been "cut off from their African ancestry by the scythe of slavery and from an American heritage by being excluded from history . . . science fiction offers an alternative where that which deviates from the norm is the norm."[23]

These accounts of Afrofuturism as an alternate history and future for science fiction let us see how a genre often associated with political or spectacular extrapolations from the large-scale changes of modernity can also be crucial to re-envisioning and changing the "norms" that govern racialized power structures. In relating science fiction to racial history, Mosley finds that imagining other futures is a way to suggest that the failures of the present and the past need not be permanent ones. Black uses of science fiction tropes emerge less as extrapolations asking where scientific and technological teleologies might lead, and more as meditations on what the possibility of such extrapolation might mean. Counter-futures must continually be imagined without the colonizing mindset that a singular future could overtake every incipient possibility. But to what extent is it possible to rewrite the hegemonic futurisms that operate to produce and maintain the uneven, unequal world as we know it?

Among the earliest works included in the *Dark Matter* anthology is Du Bois's "The Comet," which was originally published in *Darkwater* (1920), a collection of his fiction, nonfiction, and poetry.[24] Thomas uses Du Bois, a perhaps surprising addition to the roster of science fiction writers, to add weight and depth to her construction of a genealogy of "black writers . . . offering distinctive speculative visions of the world."[25] The distinctive speculative vision of "The Comet" transferred smoothly from *Darkwater* to *Dark Matter* thanks to its activation of tropes that would become intensely familiar to aficionados of twentieth-century science fiction. The story's focus on the production and reproduction of black futurity make it foundational both to Afrofuturism's retroactive canon and to the history of critical futurism this book explores. "The Comet" draws an African diasporic critique of colonial modernity together with interventions into US discourses of racialized gender, interracial coupling, eugenics, and miscegenation.

The story's premise is a catastrophic one: New York has passed through the tail of a comet that emits deadly asphyxiating gas. Only those breathing air away from the surface of the earth are saved, and for them it seems as if the entire world has been destroyed. Our protagonist is Jim, a young black bank messenger sent by his employers on an errand into the "fetid slime" of the bank's underground "lower vaults," where he escapes the destruction of the city.[26] Eventually, he meets another survivor, a young white woman named Julia who had been developing photographs in a darkroom when the comet hit. After confronting racial prejudice and despair, the two of them prepare to come together—ready to breed a new, post-racial humanity in the ruins of the old world. Their consummation of an interracial future for the human race is aborted, however, when Julia's father and fiancé arrive. Jim narrowly escapes lynching. As he leaves to return to his marginal position, a black woman who seems to be his wife emerges, holding the corpse of their child.

Like many European writers at this historical moment, Du Bois draws on the experience of the First World War to present apocalyptic violence as a cataclysmic break in forward-looking temporalities of progress and modernity. But, unlike the white European writers I discuss in part 1, he places the cataclysm into the context of the long-lasting trauma and apocalyptic loss brought upon people of color by the colonization and enslavement that underwrote white modernity.[27] In "The Souls of White Folk," which also appeared in *Darkwater*, Du Bois connected the violence of the First World War in Europe with the oppression to which Europeans had not ceased to subject those of African descent: "As we saw the dead dimly through rifts of battle-smoke and heard faintly the cursings and accusations of blood brothers, we darker men said: this is not Europe gone mad; this is not aberration nor insanity; this is Europe; this seeming Terrible is the real soul of white culture."[28] The killing fields of the First World War here turn into the violence of empire brought home.

"The Comet" imagines a similar fate for white America through a fictional vision of New York's destruction. The comet's passage transforms a "human river" of New York working people into the "stillness of death," where "a hundred men and women and children" are "crushed and twisted and jammed . . . like refuse in a can."[29] They resemble those felled by the guns of the Western Front. But Du Bois's consciousness of black history demands we also see the transformation of people into "refuse" on which slavery depended.[30] The trail of bodies outside the New York bank remind us that slavery is the apocalypse whose legacy keeps global capitalism in motion, providing bodies whose labor creates value while their lives are held cheap.[31]

Jim's position in the New York of "The Comet" is that of a life that can easily be spared. He is sent into the vault because the danger to a "more valuable" white man would not be worth the risk.[32] As Amy Kaplan writes, "In his descent into the bowels of the earth, the black working man from Harlem evokes the work of colonial laborers and links them to the financial center of New York."[33] His race denies him access to the accumulation of resources through which the bank that employs him will capitalize on the future. Banned from access to full humanity, Jim is "outside the world," and so the world's end—talk of whose imminence he overhears from white people who address him directly only to assign him a task—does not end him.[34]

Du Bois suggests that although black futurity has not been considered a good investment, its capacity to survive in the face of outrageous risk may lead it to inherit the earth. And so Jim sets out to capitalize on the death of the white future in order to repair damages caused by the white past's ownership of him and his. He roams the ruins of New York, sole participant in a post-human future, satisfying his hunger on the high-class cookery of "ghost-haunted halls" that "yesterday, would not have served [him]."[35] Alone in the world, Jim can at least taste the fruits of the labor that he, standing in for masses of transnational colonized workers, represents. Holding out the future to a black living subject in the midst of death, Du Bois transforms white modernity's relentless insistence on forward motion into a death march, turning the experience of historical apocalypse into a source of strength and bringing about a transcendent culmination of black history through Jim's ascension to effective ownership of the city.[36]

After the destruction of the world as he knew it, the consolidation of black futurity requires that Jim be provided with descendants. Du Bois invokes a utopian act of interracial heterosexual intercourse to set that future in motion. Jim will, the story implies, move from standing outside the world to creating a new world through sexual congress with Julia, on whose white female body a new breed of interracial reproductive futurism will be engendered. In this narrative move, "The Comet" works simultaneously with and against the official timelines of modernity, combining its radical critique of white culture not only with Jim's pleasure in finally enjoying that culture's advantages but also with a glorification of reproductive heterosexuality.[37]

Julia's devotion to a maternal future enables Jim to experience an empowered masculinity that contains a connection to his racial history: "She looked upon the man beside her and forgot all else but his manhood—his sorrow and sacrifice. She saw him glorified. . . . In fascinated silence the man gazed at the heavens. . . . The shackles seemed to rattle and fall from his soul. Up from the crass and crushing and cringing of his caste leapt the lone majesty of kings long dead. He arose within the shadows, tall, straight, and stern, with power in his eyes and ghostly sceptres hovering to his grasp."[38] Du Bois refigures the racial past here so that, instead of being defined by literal and figurative "shackles," Jim will contain African majesty in his status as the new Adam, no longer forced into the "crass and crushing and cringing" place we saw him take up at the story's beginning. Through transcendent union with the white woman, his "sceptre" of phallic patriarchy will be "ghostly" no more.

Gazing toward Jim, Julia sees herself in turn as "primal woman; mighty mother of all men to come and Bride of Life."[39] Without the surround of a society to enforce them, race- and class-based divisions fall away so that Jim is "no longer a thing apart, a creature below, a strange outcast of another clime and blood, but her Brother Humanity incarnate . . . great All-Father of the race to be."[40] Having grieved and accepted the end of the world, here the white woman embraces her position as transcendental breeder, last and first woman in the "race to be." This conception of a post-racial state, in which humanity will no longer be granted to whites at the expense of colonized and racialized people because racial politics will have been bred out, relies on the inscription of "primal" gender divisions through which the future can be reproduced. Like the imperial mothers of the feminist utopian fictions I analyzed in chapter 1, this white woman understands herself to be the source material from which a new and better future will emerge. Out of her body will come the personification of an improved human race.

The utopian future Du Bois evokes in "The Comet" is an unashamedly eugenic one—biologically shaping the races that could inherit the earth by claiming Jim and Julia as the fittest survivors—for all that it does not participate in the white supremacy that has categorized most eugenic projects. As part 1 has shown, a white future and a heteronormative future were often close to the same thing in the ideas about improving the human race that trafficked through both popular and scientific discourses in the wake of Francis Galton. For sexual reformists and feminist birth control advocates, as well as the architects of American immigration law, desirable reproducers were primarily those who would bring America's racial mix closer to a universal whiteness.[41] However, as Daylanne English demonstrates in her work on eugenic discourses in the Harlem Renaissance, eugenic calls for "interventions in individual reproductive lives in the name of collective (racial or national) progress" were "not necessarily accompanied by a platform of white supremacy, or, for that matter, even racial purity."[42] African American projects for racial uplift and improvement have also followed the strategy of encouraging better breeding, leveraging heterosexual intercourse to improve the material and social conditions of black Americans rather than to maintain a white supremacist status quo. In addition to "The Comet," Du Bois's 1928 novel *Dark Princess* also highlights "racial uplift through selective breeding."[43] In that novel, a half-Indian, half-African American baby is declared by "'The Great Central Committee of Yellow, Black, and Brown' . . . to be the 'Messenger and Messiah to all the Darker Worlds!'"[44] Like Jim, this boy is set to inherit the earth when the reign of whiteness fails.

"The Comet" proposes interracial hetero-futurity as a potential eugenic utopia made possible by the literal destruction of a racially unequal world. But Jim and Julia's vision of glorious prospects for a new racial future does not hold; the arresting power of the racial present intervenes. As the exalted couple moves toward consummation, they are interrupted by the real world in the body of Julia's fiancé and father, wealthy white men who have the real power to control Julia's reproductive capacities and define a eugenic national future. It turns out that the comet has not destroyed the world at all; it has destroyed only New York, and the world rushes in. Jim, his life threatened by the white men's terror of miscegenation, steps "outside the world" again, "shrinking" as he goes.[45] Interracial heterosexuality cannot conquer racism after all.

When a black woman appears at the end of "The Comet," we might expect a suggestion that Du Bois's real eugenic hope for a post-apocalyptic future lies in intraracial heterosexuality, in a baby uncontaminated by whiteness's corruption. Yet the mother of Jim's child does not lead him back behind the veil to repopulate Harlem as a site of hopeful pan-African futurity. Instead, she appears alongside death: "A woman mounted to the platform and looked about, shading her eyes. She was brown, small, and toil-worn, and in one hand lay the corpse of a dark baby. The crowd parted and her eyes fell on the colored man; with a cry she tottered toward him."[46] From a queer speculative perspective, the most important figures in the story are this tragic couple, mother and child. The dead baby is a visceral reminder that, even in the face of overpowering reproductive rhetorics, *breeding* for some is productive of death rather than birth. The genderless small body stands as evidence for the damage that the history of racial slavery has done to the future of blackness.

Jim's wife also demonstrates how the vision of post-racial, post-apocalyptic futurity that Jim and Julia experience—foreclosed though it may be—blinds both them and us with its light. For this woman has somehow survived without the transportational resources held by Julia's family, and therefore Jim and Julia were not the only New Yorkers who made it through the comet's transit. Du Bois does not offer us an explanation of this woman's survival. Did she get out of New York? Was she, too, underground? How did she slip through the gaps though her baby did not? Has a lifetime of oppression taught her secret ways to keep breathing in a poison atmosphere? The woman appears in the story as little more than a holder for her dead baby, proof that Jim's community will forgive him for wanting to father a new humanity with Julia. But even as this woman—who was never meant to survive, but who did—fails as a signifier for reproductive or eugenic futures, we can ask what meanings she carries in and of herself. If we look for the future as she might have imagined it, what might we find?

Motherless Futures, Futureless Mothers

"The Comet" gives Jim and his community two apparent options: an elevated future of post-racial reproductivity that looks disturbingly similar to colonial eugenic logics, or no future at all. Either way lies the end of the black cultural identity Du Bois fought to elevate and preserve. The survival of Jim's wife is the only moment in the story that allows a future to be imagined outside of that binary. In "The Damnation of Women," which also appeared in *Darkwater*, Du Bois invoked the reality of figures like hers, writing that he saw "more of future promise in the betrayed girl-mothers of the black belt than in the childless wives of the white North" and sought to ward off "[black] race suicide . . . by honoring motherhood" even outside marriage.[47] The mention of "race suicide" hearkens to Theodore Roosevelt's 1905 proclamation that the "willful sterility" of white women was endangering the glorious future of the white American race, leaving the nation susceptible both to queer nonreproductivity and to women of color's excessive production of nonwhite children.[48] Yet Du Bois reminds us that the association of properly heterosexual, marital reproductive behavior with a racially desirable future is not exclusive to whiteness. That the "honor" of marital motherhood might not be the path any black woman would prefer seems to have been an impossibility for him, since its voluntary avoidance is associated with white femininity and since only the "betrayed" would be mothers without marriage.

The negativity of the future Jim's wife and her baby represent undermines these hopeful representations of an African American reproductive future. She shares race and origin with Jim, her husband, but—inescapably attached to a baby that did not make it—she cannot capitalize on the empty world as Jim, for a brief moment, did. Jim's wife seems worthy of "honor," since she has done her duty to keep the black race going. But she is nevertheless betrayed by Jim's romance with post-racial heterofuturity. No thought of her arises in the hyperbolic internal monologue he is given as he rises above his ancestry to make the future with Julia. The racial dead end that Jim's wife and her baby embody suggests a different sort of "racial suicide." Its metaphoric negativity implies a critique of Jim's misplaced virility, his seduction by the prospect of inheriting a future structured by whiteness and shaped like an empire.

I come to this understanding of "The Comet" through black feminist writings about reproduction. Black feminist thought identifies the extent to which racialized exclusion from futurity has been lived in gender-specific ways and demonstrates why an Afrofuturism that does not adequately account for gendered and sexual difference is likely to breed heteropatriarchal futures. Anne Stavney writes that Du Bois and other black male writers of the Harlem Renaissance advocated for racial renewal by using the image of "the black mother" as a "symbol for primacy and rebirth" that would connect "the past" of "racial and geographical origins" with "the future in terms of coming generations."[49] "The Comet" depicts that narrative as a failure, but nevertheless relies on it. Stavney also remarks that such figurative uses of black maternity "rarely attend to the actual social and economic conditions encountered by most black women of their era."[50] Women's writings of the Harlem Renaissance, which address racial futurity as a matter of personal realism rather than extrapolative possibility, narrate those social and economic conditions and their consequences. In Nella Larsen's 1928 *Quicksand*, Helga Crane grasps after futurity of and for herself and ends up beaten down by the demands of others—whether they be exoticizing, insisting on a respectability that precludes desire, or keeping her in her place through religion. Becoming reproductive is for Helga an experience of sinking, an admission of or capitulation to the fact that she can have no autonomous future, that she can have only a kind of death. Neither breeding a eugenic future of upwardly mobile racial eugenics nor giving herself over to reproduction can save her.[51]

Hortense Spillers explicates this double bind by tracing the operations of racial gendering to the discursive structures of slavery, which framed black women not as people but as laboring commodities with the capacity to breed. Spillers shows how slavery's "ungendering" of "female flesh" has been and continues to be enacted as exclusion from the normative gender of the (white) nuclear family.[52] Using the grammar of psychoanalysis to show how African American women have been positioned in a negative relationship to femininity, Spillers demonstrates that the psychoanalytic language of subjectivity is undone when it is forced to describe a material history in which people were not only inscribed into the dominant social order in abject positions, but denied access to that social order's definitions of human subjectivity altogether. They are not meant to survive within that story, even while the story would not and could not exist without their presence and their labor. As Spillers puts it: "My country needs me, and if I were not here, I would have to be invented."[53]

To understand reproductive temporalities in the wake of slavery requires recognition of the intolerable dynamics by which black women's refusal to survive has, at times, been the only way to lay claim to a future not owned by someone else. Toni Morrison's 1988 *Beloved*, which draws from the story of Margaret Garner, who killed her daughter rather than let her endure slavery, has become a literary touchstone for the ways histories of slavery haunt. A mother separates the reproduction of the social relations that dehumanize her from the reproduction of her child, resisting by giving in to the lack of value placed on her body; refusing to breed a future for slavery is the only possible route to freedom she can perceive. Morrison tells us that *Beloved*'s is "not a story to pass on," because too many ghosts and too many pasts might render the present unlivable or unrecognizable.[54] For scholars working with this ghostly paradigm, that unrecognizability and its potential to change the present are essential. In *Ghostly Matters*, Avery Gordon transfigures Morrison's haunting prose into sociology and writes that the reader/scholar's task will be "to understand the conditions under which a memory was produced in the first place, toward a countermemory, for the future."[55] Gordon's book seeks to call back a future from the past that has made so many futures impossible; she does this through the operations of haunting and countermemory, with "the future" a marker of the things that must be done if the past can still be honored.

Following Lorde's invocation of the "now that can breed / futures," I take the futural gesture as a starting point. The remainder of this chapter focuses on the futures imagined and lived when countermemories arrive not only through reckoning with death and its after effects, but by cheating it when stories are passed on, futures are bred, and somehow something other than a recapitulation of preexisting social relations is created, even if just for a while. I have used Du Bois's 1920 story to lay out some of the norms and complexities of racially gendered futurity. To bring forth the mother and baby's potential to deviate from that narrative requires moving into her future—to dreams of different presents, alternate narratives, and a step out of the temporality of periodization. When might the time for such out-of-sync figures be, given their resistance to the convergence of straight reproductive and historicist temporalities?

The *when* of Jim's wife is not the secure insistence of maternal origin and futurity that both Julia and white feminist utopians at the turn of the twentieth century set forth. As Kara Keeling writes, "From within the logics of reproductive futurity and colonial reality, a black future looks like no future at all."[56] But, in an important intervention into studies of queer temporality that do not account for the dimension of race, Keeling also insists that the absence of futurity can be a starting point as well as an ending. Drawing on Franz Fanon's work, she connects the impossibility of incorporating blackness into the United States' white, heteronormative national time to the time and space of colonization, working within a transnational Afrofuturist paradigm to figure black political (im)possibility as decolonial futurity. Being without a future in this sense is not just a position of exclusion but also a point from which radical disruptions can be enacted. And the forces that corrode and disrupt time, so that the meanings of futurity and humanity themselves are brought into question, are as important as the concrete visions of better possibilities that activism for material improvements in the condition of oppressed people might bring about. The figure of the queer in Lee Edelman's work and Franz Fanon's image of the native as a "corrosive element" within colonialism are the two points from which Keeling triangulates this disruption.[57] Du Bois's childless black mother brings reproductivity into the conversation. If futures are not bred through modes that ensure the predictability of a straight time tied to the accumulation of resources gained through exploitation, they must have some other relationship to reproduction. What might that relationship be?

In the final section of this chapter, I answer this question by turning to works that breed black futures in Lorde's sense by severing the commonsense connection between heterosexuality and reproduction, replacing the logics of genealogical blood lines with deviant visions and building new kinds of pleasures. Black feminist speculative fictions offer some answers to the question Alex Weheliye, building on the foundation laid by Spillers, asks in his 2014 book *Habeas Viscus*: "What different modalities of the human come to light if we do not take the liberal humanist figure of Man as the master-subject but focus on how humanity has been imagined and lived by those subjects excluded from his domain?"[58] The imaginaries to which I now turn engage gendered dehumanization not by seeking a return to the human or a future for it, but by extending metaphoric nonhumanity into imaginative fiction and laying claim to the possibility of antihumanist pleasures alongside nonheterosexually reproductive sexualities and temporalities.

Deviant Blood Lines: Queer Black Feminist Modes of Reproduction

From a straight perspective, the importance of sexual pleasure to reproductive futurity is straightforward. Pleasure is useful but marginal: its presence within social relations encourages them to keep going, whether through sexual reproduction or the pleasures of consumption that make life within capitalism fun. By making physically enjoyable the sex acts that will lead to the production of new human beings, the commonsense logic goes, sexual pleasure has evolved to keep the human future going (in a straight line). By the same token, the absence of pleasure from many reproductive sexual acts, the possibility of reproduction that does not commence with hetero sex, and the spending of sexual pleasure in nonreproductive directions are marginal, irrelevant deviations—footnotes in the biology textbook of life.

For the reproduction of queer futures, however, pleasure is never just an alibi. Nonstraight modes of being perpetuate themselves by affinity rather than biology: queers reproduce our cultures and identities by recruiting, drawing in people who will come to recognize and name something emergent within themselves. Although the perpetuation of queerness relies on somebody doing the biological work of reproduction that will result in new potentially queer youth, queer sexual and nonsexual pleasures in and of themselves are what create relationalities and communities. For women and femmes of color especially, Juana María Rodríguez writes, the capacity to consider "pleasure both important and possible constitutes a refusal of all that has been used to define us as damaged and unworthy, perverse and undesirable."[59] Elizabeth Freeman writes that "queers survive through the ability to invent or seize pleasurable relations between bodies" and that "we do so . . . across time."[60] In the hands of cultural producers committed to the politics of survival against the odds, this connection of survival to pleasure—where "pleasurable relations between bodies" are what makes life possible—sets forth new common senses and new relationships to time, race, and reproduction.

Jewelle Gomez and Octavia E. Butler have turned queerly pleasurable relationships between racialized bodies into transformative reimaginings of gender, race, history, and futurity. Their decolonial uses of vampire mythology in black feminist speculative fiction repurpose the gendered figures whose histories and connotations I trace in the first half of this chapter. In complex and sometimes ambiguous ways that cannot be accounted for by a straightforward narrative of reclamation, they create alternative visions of racialized reproductive temporality. Butler and Gomez write at different moments, in different contexts; I engage them together to draw attention to the interconnections in their joint creation of vampiric reproductive futurisms.[61] *The Gilda Stories* (1991) and *Fledging* (2005) map out alternative relationships between production and reproduction, routed explicitly through pleasure in ways that challenge not only the common tropes of vampire mythology and science fiction but also the AIDS-related associations that link queer sharings of bodily fluids with the reproduction of viruses that carry death. As a figure in white queer studies, the vampire has often signified the opposite of reproduction and futurity: speculative figures of the bloodsucking undead have stood for seductively predatory figures of gay men and lesbians who endanger the reproduction of white, heteronormative family and home.[62] Reimagined through a queer black feminism in which to claim and defend family and home in a world where survival cannot be guaranteed is often itself a radical act, the affordances of the vampire offer a speculative mode in which reproductive and desiring bodies live on after death. Twisting the connections between blackness and technologies of futurity, between consumption and exploitation and reproduction, Gomez and Butler reconfigure the meanings of racialized gender and sexuality both in the American color line and amid contexts of globalized labor and histories of colonization.

Vampires have long been used as metaphors for a capitalist mode of production that perpetuates itself by appropriating the life-force of those it exploits. The undead who suck blood to prolong unlife signify fear, desire and exploitation. In 1867, Karl Marx wrote of the deadly monstrosity of capital's "vampire thirst for the living blood of labour" in an analogy that has been enthusiastically taken up ever since.[63] Donna

Haraway writes that "the vampire" in culture has become inseparable from "the marauding figure of unnaturally breeding capital, which permeates every whole being and sucks it dry in the lusty production and vastly unequal accumulation of wealth."[64] In a recent account of contemporary global capital by Kalindi Vora, the vampiric is barely a metaphor at all. She points out that biological and communication technology advances have "opened up the human body and subject as a greatly expanded site for annexation, harvest, dispossession, and production" and allowed not just the products of labor but life itself, in forms that include surrogate pregnancy and organ donation as well as life-sustaining reproductive labor, to flow from the poor to the rich.[65] Like the alluring vampires of fiction and film, vampire capital seduces; its beneficiaries accumulate wealth by siphoning life forces from people and places made tender by histories of enslavement, settler colonialism, and racialized and gendered exploitation.

The metaphor of capital as vampire reminds us that human resources are not renewable. Gomez and Butler's works highlight unresolved contradictions in the ways that race, gender, and sexuality are lived amid circuits of capital, labor, and what Vora calls "vital energy"; they glimmer with more and less desirable prospects for utopia and change.[66] The changed meanings of reproduction, consumption, and pleasure in these queer of color vampire stories also shift what the future stands for. In the classic vampire/capital analogy, the future is a commodity that is highly in demand; the vampire's immortality is maintained by a constant supply of blood, just as capital's demand for incessant growth requires ongoing exploitation and expropriation. Gomez and Butler alter the terms, connecting their vampires to ecological models of consumption without exploitation. They transform the future from an ever-receding goal into a comfortable place to live. Instead of accumulation and expansion carried forth at the cost of life for all those who do not profit from it, human blood and labor appear as renewable resources, re-produced through a transmission of blood that signifies not genetic transfer but an exchange of pleasure. These vampires refuse to alienate the blood they take from the people it belongs to. Vampiric exchange instead transforms and reframes, without seeking to wholly avoid, frameworks of predation, objectification, and exploitation. Immortality shifts its metaphorical significance: no longer standing for an access to futurity for some that will always come at a cost to others, it now marks the possibility for survival in the face of overwhelming odds.

In each novel, vampire immortality and reproductive consumption mediate between African American women's histories and presents, pointing toward new futures that emerge over the course of the narratives. Published in 1991, *The Gilda Stories* situates Gomez's eponymous vampire in US black history, narrating vignettes that begin during slavery and end with a dystopian future reminiscent of Du Bois's post-comet landscape. Gomez works within an explicitly lesbian subcultural and political framework, describing the character of Gilda as embodying "a feminist perspective that [challenges] the traditional narratives about women of color and about lesbians."[67] Building a model of black and indigenous vampire futurism that owes much to Audre Lorde's writings on the erotic as a source of power and connection for women of color, she creates a larger canvas on which to engage the utopian prospects of a 1980s lesbian feminism that has often been dismissed by later queer theorists.[68]

Gomez cites Octavia E. Butler, whose novels of the 1980s and 1990s made her by far the best known black woman writer of science fiction and who was also a powerful speculative critic of US and global politics, as one of *The Gilda Stories*' greatest influences.[69] Butler's work often emphasizes the impossibility of getting away from gendered biologies of reproduction, where black women's bodies bear the weight of reproducing futures to which they rarely uncomplicatedly consent. Nisi Shawl writes that Butler saw *Fledgling* (2005), which would be the last book she published before her sudden death in 2006, as an "escapist fantasy" less embedded in social and political critique than many of her other works.[70] Yet the novel has much to say about racialized and gendered pasts, presents, and futures. It crafts a narrative of biological speculation on the scale of a single character's body—a mutation of vampire mythology that is also a queer rendition of racialized reproduction. In her version of the vampire, Butler invokes an alternative reproductive futurity whose structures draw from troubling histories of genetics and eugenics as well as colonial metaphors in ways that complicate Gomez's utopian tendencies.

Both novels open with scenes of bloodletting that are emblematic of the refigured futures to come, reversing the gendered and racialized power relations to which black women are subjected. Vulnerable figures—a young runaway slave girl, a child injured to the point of death—show their teeth and set alternative narratives in motion. When *Gilda* begins, it is 1850 in Louisiana. An unnamed "Girl," who will later become the vampire named Gilda, has escaped from slavery and is hiding in a cellar. A white man comes upon her hiding place and tries to rape her, and the book's first blood is spilled:

> He bent forward on his knees, stiff for conquest, already counting the bounty fee. . . . He started to enter her, but before his hand finished pulling her open, while it still tingled with the softness of her insides, she entered him with her heart which was now a wood-handled knife. . . . She felt the blood draining from him, comfortably warm against her now cool skin.
>
> It was like the first time her mother had been able to give her a real bath . . . a cleansing. . . . Looking down at the blood soaking her shirt and trousers she felt no disgust. It was the blood signaling the death of a beast and her continued life.[71]

Gomez portrays Gilda/Girl's death-blow in shockingly intimate terms. As her body is violated, it transforms into a weapon, the knife of her heart a necessary means to claiming what the slaveholder would alienate from her. He expects her to be nothing but "bounty," a personal "conquest" to match the cultural one he believes has already been completed with the theft of indigenous land and the enslavement of Gilda/Girl's people to work on it. But she turns back to "enter" him instead and prove the resilience of the objectified—even finding a sensual and reassuring pleasure in the violence, which rekindles a maternal connection slavery has broken for her. His blood flows over her, restoring the life energy he and his have expropriated and setting the conditions of possibility for her future and the world the novel will create.

Traditional vampires instrumentalize human lives as means to their own perpetuation, killing with indiscriminate ease. Where Dracula and his successors figure as sexual predators consuming feminized bodies, Gomez's victims bite back as she "turns the structures of racism, sexism, homophobia, and antisemitism in classical vampire narratives against themselves."[72] It is not the vampire but the human rapist who uses others for his own ends and the larger purpose of "conquest." Gilda/Girl identifies him immediately as one of "those whom her mother had sworn were not fully human," who "suck up the world and don't taste it."[73] Looking to consume and sell off a black female body he cannot perceive as unconsenting, he is an avatar for intersecting systems of white supremacy, patriarchy, and capital. His is the vampirism of voracious consumption and colonial expansion that created a world that makes reproduction a terrifying double bind for those who are not meant to survive as human subjects. Bathing in this man's blood is a rebirth for the Girl: a "cleansing" that enables her "continued life" into the future of peaceful immortality she will eventually gain by leaving the human behind when she becomes Gilda. Neither the girl nor the vampire are innocent of death and violence. But Gomez creates a utopian bloodlust from the ways in which, having known dehumanization and rebellion, Gilda will come to show a respect for those whose life force she consumes beyond anything this man could attain. As a vampire, her feedings will not kill but bring pleasure.

Butler's *Fledgling* also opens with its protagonist's consumption of another's life force, but this scene is far more difficult to read as empowerment. The narrator, unnamed as yet, awakes amnesiac in darkness and pain. All she knows is hunger, and she satiates it:

> I heard something coming toward me, something large and noisy, some animal. . . . It came to me like a tame thing, and I lay almost out of control, trembling and gasping, and thinking only, food! . . . It touched my wrist, my face, my throat . . . making noises of its own. . . . I seized the animal . . . tasted its blood, smelled its terror. I tore at its throat with my teeth until it collapsed. Then, at last, I fed, gorged myself on the fresh meat that I needed.[74]

Soon enough we learn that the "animal" she killed was a member of Shori's extended family who came to rescue her from the wreckage of her home after its destruction by white supremacist vampires. For the first chapters, though, all we know of Shori is her appearance—that of a young black girl—her hunger, and the power this hunger lends to her determination to survive, no matter the cost. After her meal, the childlike figure is rescued by a white man in a car, whereupon she latches on to his neck and feasts. She seems to be bleeding him dry, but we learn that this connection—sexual like all vampire loves, and in this case offering a cross-age desire that is disarmingly queer for the grown man who finds in it an irresistible pleasure—has initiated a symbiotic relationship that will extend his life as well as hers.

Butler's vampires, who call themselves the Ina, are not undead or immortal but a long-lived parasitic species who exist in "mutualistic symbiosis" with the humans whose blood they drink.[75] They are vampires imagined through scientific rather than supernatural speculation. Their bite is potent because Ina saliva contains a "powerful hypnotic drug" that renders human "symbionts" "highly suggestible and deeply attached to the source of the substance."[76] In exchange for an addiction whose termination would end their lives, symbionts receive intense sexual pleasure when they are fed on; they grow "healthier, stronger, and harder to kill," and their lives "lengthen by several decades."[77] The Ina need their symbionts to live, the humans come to need their Ina, and yet humans are always more vulnerable.

Butler's Ina are slippery beings to read metaphorically. On the one hand, they colonize human territories and relationships, offering a pleasure to which symbionts cannot not consent. They make biological the seductions of assimilation to power. But just as Butler refuses to turn away from the darker sides of pleasure, she also bathes her readers in its possibilities, showing the joys of Ina life and leaving us to wonder whether it might not have advantages over human autonomy. Butler's exchanges of blood confuse easy correspondences of capital, eugenics, gender, and race. Their speculative intervention is best understood in the context of US racial and colonial histories that *Fledgling* does not address directly but that Gomez's *Gilda Stories* map out.

The Gilda Stories follows its vampires across two centuries, crafting a subaltern American history and future that brings to the fore those ostensibly rendered futureless by white supremacy and settler colonialism. Black feminist history is joined with indigenous knowledge. Gilda grows into vampire longevity alongside her Lakota lover, Bird, and they share their people's oral histories as they recall the "rhythm of life without bondage."[78] Bird invites Gilda into what Scott Lauria Morgensen calls "the queer temporality of Native modernity, wherein tradition is precisely not primordial but an articulation of memory and survival with life in a settler colonial situation."[79] It may have begun as an imported European mythos, but for Gomez, vampire longevity becomes a method for maintaining connections and collectivities among black and indigenous people in and beyond the United States, enabling both to know that, as Andrea Smith writes, "we lived differently before" colonization and enslavement and therefore "can live differently in the future."[80] Although taking blood invokes the logics of empire and capital for many of their peers, Gilda and Bird's vampirism always participates in a politics of collective struggle against racist domination, where their primary commitments are not to vampire kind but to networks of solidarity. Bird travels across the Americas to connect with indigenous peoples, "pulling together the strands of knowledge about her nation" to become a "living history."[81] Meanwhile, Gilda searches for a "link" to her people in "each new place" she lives, tying herself to black communities and taking on human obligations in a beauty parlor, at a women's church group, and amid black radical political and artistic movements.[82] Gomez takes the dead European conceit of eternal vampiric life and invests it with a temporal significance that emerges from different traditions, using the stretched-out life narratives of immortality to breed futures for communities whose past has been lost or stolen.

White patriarchal capitalist and queer of color decolonial vampires alike require blood on which to feed. Gomez imagines that act of consumption as a sharing of pleasure that reproduces interdependence rather than, or at least in addition to, exploitation. Gilda's vampire progenitor, a white woman hundreds of years old, tells her that "the real dream," the most important purpose for blood-sharing immortals, is "to make a world."[83] Gilda's stories tell how she made her own version of that world, structured by her need for queer love and racial community. Her queerness is, as Omise'eke Natasha Tinsley writes, an activation of pleasure relations between those who were never meant to survive. "A praxis of resistance," it is the need or desire "to love your own kind when your own kind is supposed to cease to exist."[84] This is the queer possibility that Gomez's vampirism speculatively activates: subjects who are supposed to be erased instead love others who are racialized and gendered as they are, who were not meant to survive either. Acts of pleasure flow between the consumer and consumed who are linked through race, community, sexuality, and desire. The speculative embodiment of vampire immortality makes the queer gesture endure for more than a moment, more than a memory.

Butler's version of vampire mythology is less utopian than Gomez's in its intervention into gendered and racialized futurity. Where the vampires of *The Gilda Stories* are embedded in racial and colonial histories by way of their human origins and affiliations, those in *Fledgling* are depicted as a separate species independent of and parasitic on *homo sapiens*. Like most vampires, the Ina are whiter than white, their pallor linked to their inability to tolerate sunlight. Race comes into play through constructed difference: *Fledgling*'s protagonist, Shori, is protected from the sun by dark skin she was given by genetic manipulation carried out in cooperation between her white Ina mothers and black human mother. Shori is a successful "experiment," an embodied possibility for a vampire future of color.[85] She provides a technological intervention of African humanity into this science fiction version of moribund European vampirism. By crafting Shori's blackness with reproductive technology, her mothers invent blackness *as* futurity, breeding it into their line in order to help them survive. That genealogy is not without its disturbing connections, for Shori is aged fifty-three in the early twenty-first century and is described as having been born shortly after her family left Europe.[86] Her vampire and human mothers were, we must assume, beginning their genetic research amid the genocidal triumphs of the 1930s and 1940s.[87] The symbiotic connection between these white and black, vampire and human women is underwritten by the trauma of racial and colonial histories.

Since she is the product of experimental breeding, Shori's breeders expect to breed her in return. In other words, the Ina plan for their much-heralded black future to be heterosexually reproduced once Shori—still a child by Ina reckoning—is old enough to "mate" with a group of brothers whose scent she finds irresistible.[88] Butler's linkage of vampire futurity to queer sexual pleasure seems here to fall back within the fold of straight reproduction. Yet, given the larger historical and structural context that marks blackness as an impediment to survival, the association of black life with the possibility of expanded futures in her vision of vampire eugenics is enough to render even this straight-seeming future queer. Shori's vampire family claim repeatedly that "human racism meant nothing to the Ina because human races meant nothing to them," but *Fledgling* insists that this is not and cannot ever be the case by embedding a critique of the racist discourse of colorblindness in its speculative premise.[89] Horrified at the interracial and interspecies miscegenation that produced Shori, several Ina plot to kill her and all who were involved in her creation; the novel's climax is a legal battle in which she challenges their racism and wins her own right to exist as a being neither fully Ina nor fully human.[90] Like Gilda and Bird in *The Gilda Stories*, Shori is more aware of her connections to the human than are her vampire peers because of her racial status. She sees race where her fellows refuse to recognize it, which means that she perceives human difference and the power relationships that structure it in ways her colorblind family cannot. For both Gomez and Butler, racially othered vampire figures blur boundaries between vampire and human, suggesting the possibility of a more or less utopian vampire politics that would be more concerned with collective longevity than with deathly consumption.

The Gilda Stories ends with an expansive projected future in which Gomez demonstrates the opposition between her version of vampirism and the bloodsucking accumulation and alienation into which it could all too easily be transformed. Amid a dystopian, apocalyptic earth of 2050, where excessive exploitation has brought the United States to a shadow of its former imperial might, "the existence of the Vampire" becomes widely known.[91] As "Hunters" are sent out to capture those who can give eternal life to the rich, the vampires have become the victims, and Gilda runs from men she recognizes as "essentially the same" as the bounty hunter who tried to rape her as a child.[92] In this dystopian future—which would not look amiss on primetime TV, twenty-five years after its publication—the vampires' life force becomes one more extractable resource, eaten up like the land, labor, and energy of every other oppressed and exploited population. The resistance to domination that Gilda and her people embodied could, it seems, function only in hiding, in the interstices of all-too-powerful social systems. And yet the vampire utopia is not entirely conquered. Even as she runs from those who persecute her, desperate to avoid becoming a part of vampire capital, Gilda brings hope to a suicidal woman by inviting her into her family and into the living history of African American consciousness that she represents. And, as the book comes to a close, Gilda and Bird meet at the ruins of Macchu Picchu. There, they resolve to continue living in the world where they and those like them have "lost land" and to bring it what life they can in the form of "stories and dancing again."[93] Gomez shows how the subaltern past can create a new kind of future when it is kept alive, even as it is continually faced with literal and figurative death.

Vampires constitute a kind of time travel, bringing the past into the present and signifying the oxymoronic prospect of an unchanging future. The prevalence of aristocrats and American Civil War veterans among the vampires of popular culture is a telling sign of the kind of memory they most often exist to perpetuate. Gomez's and Butler's vampire fictions transform the conventional and very white imagery of blood-sucking aristocrats, together with science fiction themes of possible futures and genetically modified organisms, into a breeding ground for queer reproductive possibilities. *The Gilda Stories* makes black and indigenous lesbian feminist relationality into an anticapitalist strategy for building a new world in the shell of the old; *Fledgling* gives us Shori, the embodiment of a eugenically bred future, who takes things into her own hands to fight racism and exploitation and create the world anew. Through immortal vampire sex and queer bloodsucking children, both novels create timelines that mingle the old and the new, while refusing to be coopted in the service of a future that will look just like the past. These timelines are not without their problems, for Gomez's lesbian feminism does at times slip toward nostalgic idealization of a lost indigenous world, and Butler continues to portray heterosexuality as an inevitable biological imperative. Their works are critical engagements with straight, capitalist, colonial temporalities, not negations of them. Their queered futures begin to be realized only when we read them with one another, alongside the histories they reframe, and through the nonlinear understanding of temporality that Lorde's poetry evokes.

* * *

I opened this chapter with Audre Lorde's poetic inscription of "a now that can breed futures." I have followed it through several more prosaic representations of what a black future bred out of the inequalities, complicities, and failures of assorted *now*s might look like. Of course, my own analysis emerges from a present itself bred out of the pasts these texts engaged. From images of Europe's apocalyptic wastelands during World War I and the consciousness of colonization and commodification, Du Bois bred a heteronormative future of post-racial, eugenic humanity that collapsed when punctured by the sharp image of a black reproductivity that was not meant to survive. Today, the post-racial future that was an ironic utopian dream for Du Bois has become a piece of increasingly threadbare nationalist propaganda. That a single heterosexual coupling cannot breed a shiny new future on its own was an obvious if not necessarily desirable conclusion for Du Bois, but it has often operated as a form of predictive common sense in US political culture. Tavia Nyong'o accounts for this narrative in the introduction to his 2009 history of American discourses of race amalgamation. He discusses how, in the stories told about President Barack Obama's interracial origins, "the long history of sex across the color line—a history utterly commingled with the history of Africans in America . . . was magically transmogrified into a simple story of redemption in which a single marriage across the color line redeemed a history of slavery."[94] Heteronormative reproductive futurism, inflected by a racial discourse that pretends to invoke history while obscuring its persistence in the present, is the narrative into which, from 2008–2016, the United States was somehow expected to buy as the price for an inspirational black first family.

In the first celebratory moments in the administration of a US president who was black, technologically enabled, and a science fiction fan, it seemed imaginable that the future forming the normative horizon of American politics might have become, in some ways, Afrofuturistic.[95] Yet the politically radical, transnational, anticapitalist content of Afrofuturistic imaginaries on which this chapter has focused remained resolutely marginal throughout the Obama era. After its end, to capture those imaginaries' ever-greater urgency requires an alliance with the world-making collectivities of Gomez's and Butler's queer vampire kin. If the face of American empire does not look as exclusively white as it once did, it is more important than ever to pay close attention to the radical critical uses to which racialized narratives of futurity have been put in the distant and not so distant past, and to pay attention to the futures dreamed up by those for whom economic and cultural precarity are nothing new. This is why we need to engage Afrofuturistic, queer, and feminist counterdiscourses through as many modes as possible—to understand how reproduction, futurity, and consumption need not always be put together in the same predictable ways.

The vampire narratives from which Gomez and Butler breed their queer feminist Afrofuturisms contain just a few possibilities for such deviant relationships between past, present, and future. There are many others. One, addressed in an earlier version of this chapter, is Butler's

1979 *Kindred*, which relies on heterosexual reproduction to power a narrative in which a black woman in the 1970s, married to a white man, goes back in time to ensure the occurrence of the interracial rape that will conceive her great-great-great-grandmother. Overdetermined, this ostensibly straight narrative catches on itself, bending backward into negative spirals and forward toward rhythms of possibility. In *Kindred*, Butler confronts us with the persistent logic of normative time, insisting that the logics of reproductive futurism are not easy to leave behind—yet *not easy* does not mean *not possible*. The circular temporal narrative *Kindred* employs is, in the end, very close to the science fiction conventions of time travel in which the logics of linear temporality are questioned only in order to set them more powerfully in place.[96] Butler's later work in *Fledgling* gives a stronger sense of how we might think the future queerly while doing justice to the historical intersections of race and reproduction and their power in the present, especially when put together with the queer activist project of Jewelle Gomez's lesbian vampire feminism of color. Both demonstrate that heteronormativity is not the only way to breed a future.

If the survival of Du Bois's anonymous black woman is unrecognizable within the tragically straight racial temporality of "The Comet," Butler and Gomez uncover some of the deviating lines we might follow in order to give her a future. And if factual and fictional historical depictions of black women's negotiation of reproduction and sexuality show how often they have been excluded from official timelines that were nevertheless erected on their backs, the extended life narratives of Gilda and Shori, and their empowered and queer relationship to reproduction, remind us of the persistent presence of the past within the future. In the larger scope of this book, these stories provide a middle ground between on the one hand, works that turn conventional reproductivities and temporalities against themselves, demonstrating the complications and ambiguities within seemingly straight temporalities, and on the other, the revolutionary temporalities of queer of color hope and desire that I go on to discuss in the next chapter. If Gomez and Butler imagine queer pleasure as a means to the end of a newly conceived biological economics, the black queer theorist and cultural producer I turn to next—Samuel R. Delany—engages pleasure as an end in itself, transforming its impulses and flows into queer speculative politics.

4

Science Fiction Worlding and Speculative Sex

Samuel R. Delany and the Queer Futures of Black Gay History

Samuel R. Delany, the prolific black gay writer of speculative fiction, memoir, literary pornography, and queer theory, planted a seed that would become this book with a recurrent phrase in his 1974 novel *Dhalgren*:

> It is not that I have no past. Rather, it continually fragments on the terrible and vivid ephemera of now.[1]

> *It is not that I have no future. Rather it continually fragments on the insubstantial and indistinct ephemera of now.*[2]

> It is not that I have no future. Rather it continually fragments on the insubstantial and indistinct ephemera of then.[3]

The speaker in these passages calls attention to twists and deviations in experiential and historical time. When humanity's continuation demands the privileging of heterosexual procreation, and when access to technological capital defines the possibility of advancing toward a livable future, certain individuals and populations are often rendered futureless. A queer, working-class man of color with a history of mental illness, Delany's protagonist is denied access to futurity by multiple intersecting axes of oppression. Yet "*it is not that [he has] no future.*" Each double negative highlights an instability that characterizes many of the old futures this book explores: What does it mean to refuse the oversimplifications of pure negativity, without taking up positivist visions of development and progress? To lose access to the past is to be denied a future. Yet this speaker has neither no past *nor* no future. Instead, he lives within the queerness of the present and its terrible, vivid, insubstantial, indistinct ephemera. This chapter explores how Delany's black, queer science fiction frames temporality not as a progressive timeline in which the future is a predictable tomorrow, but by conceiving futurity as it is known to *present* thought and feeling. When we approach futures queerly in this way, heterosexual reproduction, and the politics of sexual citizenship with which it is associated, slip into the margins. Delany's fiction shows how the narrative tactics of science fiction, a genre whose most popular literary and media versions have tended to proffer timelines reliant on unmitigated heterosexuality, can turn against assumptions that the future must be straight, or at least arrived at through heteronormative reproductive logics.

In works of queer scholarship that drive heterosexuality to the margins, some queer perspectives are more central than others. None of the archives of futures this book has so far explored—feminist utopianisms, dystopian representations of fascist homoerotics, Afrofuturistic renditions of women of color's sexuality—are the images most immediately associated with the word "queer." Within most genealogies of queer studies, that honor belongs to the histories and cultures of gay men's sexual activity. Ephemeral sexual contact between men has shaped thinking about queer times and spaces even among theorists for whom those are not the primary populations of focus; bathhouses, tearooms, and cruising grounds are at the center of radical theories on queer publics.[4] Where do the scenes that have inspired most critical writings on queer times and places fit in to the arguments I am unfolding?

Delany has been one of the most influential archivists of such spaces, while also offering a challenge to the frequently unmarked whiteness of gay male theory. His 1999 book *Times Square Red, Times Square Blue*, an elegy for a milieu lost to gentrification, lovingly describes sex among racially diverse, predominantly working-class men in New York porn theaters. There, Delany writes, men came together sexually to "fulfill needs that most of our society does not yet know how to acknowledge."[5] His "yet" suggests some possible future where the sexual needs met by the porn theaters would be at the heart of social organization. As a prolific science fiction writer, Delany has often contemplated what such a future could be like. I use his work to explore in depth what it means—what kinds of temporalities are created, what kinds of futures formed—when the science fiction mode engages with queer practices and histories, like those of the men in the Times Square theater, that are often left out of dominant futurities.

Recent critiques of queer urbanism have called attention to the limitations of thinking queer histories and potentialities primarily through metropolitan narratives and practices, arguing that queer lives in less central locations are equally necessary grounds from which to theorize. Scott Herring, in *Another Country* (2010), focuses on rural locations; Karen Tongson, in *Relocations* (2011), turns to Southern California suburbs occupied by communities of color. While Delany's work is grounded in New York and other urban locations, the imagined elsewheres of his science fictions have located vital queer world-making practices in what he calls *paraliterature*—which we might almost think of as the suburbs of literary production.[6] Delany's work stages a convergence of futurities that revolves around the idea of *making worlds*—of living and/or thinking in a manner that constructs potential alternative modes of being.

Scholars of queer public cultures discover, scrutinize, and validate worlds that already exist, feeling out possible futures from formations and practices of the present—like the sexual acts of men in darkened theaters. Science fiction writers imagine alternatives, crafting imaginative blueprints that envisage conditions of possibility for radically different lives. Delany's two most imposing science fiction novels, *Dhalgren* (1974) and *Stars in My Pocket like Grains of Sand* (1984), engage simultaneously in both projects, grounding futuristic imagination in queer and racialized affects and experiences. Both document futures imagined from times and spaces of cultural upheaval: urban social unrest in the late-1960s United States and male sexual communities on the cusp of the AIDS epidemic, respectively. The sexual worlds invoked in both center on Delany's life, well documented in memoir, as a black man moving through New York City's gay male sexual scenes. In both cases, class and race are at the heart of the ways queerness and futurity are imagined.

Delany's science fiction creates queer worlds that are both grounded in their historical moment of production and carried beyond it by the particularities of genre reading and writing. In the narratives and metanarratives his fictions unfold, he uses genre techniques to map futures that offer many readers paths into queer times, queer histories, queer spaces. Queer Caribbean-Canadian novelist Nalo Hopkinson states in a

2002 interview: "When I read Delany's novel *Dhalgren* at about twenty-two years old, it blew my brain apart and reassembled the bits"; it was so powerful to see, for the first time, a writer "use science fiction and fantasy to talk frankly and personally about the sexual and other lives of marginalized people."[7] In a different interview, Hopkinson further recalls: "When I discovered Delany was black, I wept."[8] His racial identity has not always been explicitly mentioned, especially in earlier work published while he was making his name in a white science fiction publishing world, but Delany's works examine racial histories and possibilities as acutely as they do sexuality and gender. His science fictions trace worlds and futures in which reproductive heterosexuality and white supremacy do not dominate constructions of sexuality and race, crafting alternative formations through speculative bodies, lives, cities, planets, and galaxies.

Delany's documentary and autobiographical works feature frequently on LGBT studies syllabi, where he stands as a spokesperson for the joys of cross-class public sex and the impact of AIDS on gay male sexual communities. In discussing work written before he took on this role, I resist nostalgically framing it as "pre-AIDS," for the importance of Delany's queer futurities goes beyond representational elegy for what might have been. As works that circulate in active communities of subcultural readers, his older writings have a role in the reproduction of queer presents after and beyond their originating moments. Exploring the extent to which a model of queer temporality as sexualized ephemera begins within and travels beyond specific historical gay male formations, this chapter shows how science fiction's narratives and associated cultures enable Delany's worldings to traffic widely. I first discuss convergences between discourses of world creation in queer theory and science fiction, then turn to the novels' textual production of queer times and spaces amid the terrible and vivid presences of black gay history.

Getting Better? Queer World-Making and the Uses of Science Fiction

In late 2010, US media began to show a surprising interest in queer futures—or, rather, in the absence of personal futures for young queers. A wave of reported queer suicides inspired a national focus on the hostile environment that high schools' social and institutional structures create for young people who are queer, trans, gender nonconforming, or otherwise marked as deviant. Sex columnist and gay nuclear-family memoirist Dan Savage began a viral video campaign to remind the young that "it gets better." Lamenting that "many LGBT youth . . . can't imagine a future for themselves," the "It Gets Better" project urged LGBTQ adults to "show" teens "what the future may hold in store for them."[9] While the range of videos was diverse and the project's intentions admirable, the insistence that growing up was all any queer kid needed to make things better promoted a dangerously narrow vision of LGBTQ futurity. If "it gets better," then everything will be okay when the teenagers being addressed come to embrace their destiny as a productive and happy member of American society. The possibility that such a state of "better" might never be achieved, given the structural oppression that differentially affects queer and trans people according to race, gender, class, and citizenship, was not on the menu. In response, politicized queer thinkers, including Eng-Beng Lim and Jasbir Puar, insisted that the narrative of "bullying" threatened to mark all queer youth as legible only in their susceptibility to self-inflicted death. They pointed out that righteous grief too easily transforms into a defense of liberal nationalism, ensuring "it" will get better for some only at the cost of worse fates for others.[10]

I bring up the campaign here because it showcases the ease with which LGBT activism can be folded into straight and narrow futures. This obscures not only the fact that things may not get better for any given individual, but also other prospects for what "better" could mean. What possibilities are there for thinking and living differently for even the most disenfranchised subjects within the world as it is? In "Queer and Now," published in 1994, Eve Sedgwick describes queer theory as a kind of "It Gets Better" project articulated for the collective rather than the individual. She writes that the work of theorizing is about keeping the "vividly remembered promises" queer adults have made to themselves in childhood; to "tell kids who are supposed never to learn this that, farther along, the road widens and the air brightens: that in the big world there are worlds where it's plausible, our demand to *get used to it*."[11] Savage seems to join his voice to this chorus when he says to his imagined former self that the world has gotten used to him. But the smiling faces he and his partner put forward on YouTube can offer hope only through norms that signify better futures only for those who can stick closely to what Sara Ahmed calls "happiness scripts": moving to a city, earning a middle-class wage, marrying and perhaps having children.[12] For queers seeking a different definition of a better or a livable life—one that certainly might include some or all of the elements just mentioned, but that is not defined by them—the idea of *making a queer world* broadens the meaning of Sedgwick's promises. The difference is between maybe, possibly, making individual LGBTQ lives better in the world as it is—or changing the world's orientation toward norms and bodies altogether.

In *Fear of a Queer Planet* (1994), Michael Warner declares that heteronormativity's "totalizing tendency" could only "be overcome by actively imagining a necessarily and desirably queer world."[13] Writing with Lauren Berlant four years later, Warner goes on to describe "queer culture" as "a world-making project, where world differs from group or community because it refers to more people than can be identified."[14] The world Berlant and Warner envisage queers making is a social life-world felt and shared by participants in communal practices (hanging out in bars, fucking in public space, messing around with drugs and gender) that are different from those straight society told them would make their lives better. Similarly, Ahmed closes *The Promise of Happiness* (2010) by suggesting that queer, feminist, and racialized subjects who "deviate from the paths of happiness" laid out by dominant culture might begin to "make a world . . . in which things can happen in alternative ways."[15] Ahmed's "things can happen" is a far more modest hope than Warner's "necessarily and desirably queer world," perhaps because the dominant structures of state and capital in the Anglo-American world took on many queer aspects between 1994 and 2010 without breaking the strangleholds of white supremacy in public culture. Nevertheless, these suggestive descriptions of possible queer worlds demonstrate that prospects of alternative futures have a powerful hold on queer imaginations. When things fail to get better is when the most interesting things might happen: transformations could occur, the world could be made to deviate because of deviant desires. If (as my preceding chapters on racializing futurities have discussed) only a rose-tinted, white-supremacist belief in Enlightenment progress could believe in things getting better without recognizing the logics of domination that shape understandings of what *better* is and can be, there are still worlds to make in practice.

The scholar whose work has most lyrically and expansively theorized queer life as the making of worlds is José Muñoz. His writing on queer futurity invokes counterintuitive temporal models that expand queer presents to counter the unmarked straightness that so often corresponds to invocations of the future. Muñoz initiated his practice of queer world-making in *Disidentifications* (1999), where he writes that "through the transformative powers of queer sex and sexuality . . . a queerworld is made."[16] This queer world-making is about the possibility of continued and unbowed existence for queers of color within a public sphere that oppresses them via far more vectors than just sexuality. In the form of performance by artists like Vaginal Creme Davis, it "offers a uto-pian blueprint for a possible future while, at the same time, staging a new political formation in the present."[17] In *Cruising Utopia* (2009) Muñoz further develops this idea that performative pleasures in the present can contain implicit "blueprints" for utopian worlds. In clubs, on dancefloors, and at art galleries, he finds "performances of queer citizenship" that contain "a sign of an actually existing queer reality, a kernel of political possibility within a stultifying heterosexual present" within which we can locate the "anticipatory illumination" of "social ac-tors performing a queer world."[18] Anticipatory illuminations of queer world-making can even be carried into profoundly negative situations, so that a "leap" to death or an experience of being beaten up can be as much a site of queer utopian (im)possibility as performance, sex, or other kinds of creative praxis.[19] Even when the future is impossible to imagine or is in the very process of being radically curtailed (as the fu-ture of queer world-making theory was with Muñoz's untimely death in 2013), the present still contains a promise that can leap across space and time to make and remake worlds.

For Muñoz, whose contributions enlivened discourses of queer pos-sibility at moments when antisocial and negative critique predominated, queer world-making was a utopian project that gathered glimpses and fragments of futurity without seeking to transform them into a coherent whole. The queer world makes itself felt through spectatorship at perfor-mances, through sexual comings together, and through the work of the-orizing itself. Muñoz draws on Jill Dolan's work for the category of the "utopian performative": it consists of momentary, affective utopias that can be created by the collective sensation of affective perfection audiences sometimes experience in the presence of a sublime performance. Dolan writes that such epiphanies have the capacity to "persuade us that beyond this 'now' of material oppression and unequal power relations lives a future that might be different, one whose potential we can feel as we're seared by the promise of a present that gestures toward a better later."[20] Such moments reproduce by leaping across time. When skin prickles in recognition at a sudden understanding, or a turn of phrase, an image, a touch brings tears to the eyes and shivers down a spine, a searing now reaches back and forward in flashes, breaking up the relevance of distinctions between now and later.

Muñoz's queer utopianism builds on the work of Ernst Bloch, who wrote *The Principle of Hope* (1951) to defend utopia against charges of naiveté and totalitarianism by insisting on the political power of longing. Bloch defines hope as the critically utopian impulse that motivates critique, separating longing from the violence its actualization may produce. That longing is the "Not-Yet-Conscious": an impulse of possibility that "wells up utopianly" from even the most untenable of positions and is both a psychic fundamental and the heart of revolutionary struggle.[21] This concept of utopia as a momentary and mobile negation of oppressions is what Muñoz activates as queer. Bloch argues that "everybody lives in the future," theorizing that hope for better possibilities to come is a central part of human consciousness and that such hopes manifest in utopian impulses through which people speculate futures in everything from daydreams to architecture to artistic production.[22] Muñoz showcases queer concretizations of such impulses, arguing that minoritarian and queer subjects have the greatest need to engage the Not-Yet-Conscious in order to enable survival, and indeed that queerness itself—the transformative ideal of a queer world—is located on a horizon we access through illuminatory glimpses that transcend the everyday. Bloch enables Muñoz to think futurity as an unfinishable project, a way of living difference from and in the present that creates intransitive queer possibility.

Muñoz's queer futurities are always ahead of the present, never expected to arrive. They are flashes of longing, epiphanies, and orgasmic moments, not goals to strive toward. Bloch's utopian theory is neither so firmly anchored in a present nor so hospitable to queer prioritizations of pleasure and desire. Bloch indeed praises the potentiality of dreaming, but prioritizes what he calls the "concrete" over the "abstract" utopia. The concrete dream is favorable because it "does not play around and get lost"; "the utopian function" that Bloch thinks will lead to revolutionary world-making is "only immaturely present" and "easily led astray" in the "abstract utopianizing" of individualist desires for better lives amid current social conditions, which may or may not develop into concrete, political hope.[23] Muñoz's queer version of Bloch, on the other hand, finds hope in forms of desire that play around and are rather likely to lead or be led astray from the realms of the normatively political. This is how he finds queer futurity in Andy Warhol's and Frank O'Hara's depictions of drinking Coke: in transmuting a poetic description of a quotidian capitalist practice into "feelings of fun and appreciation," he reimagines it not only "as a mode of utopian feeling but also as hope's methodology."[24] Pleasure here is the only necessary content for utopia, and utopianly pleasurable processes become the focus regardless of ostensible political relevance.

Bloch's take on pleasure is illuminated by his insistent critique of the psychoanalytic idea that sexuality is the central drive, in which he associates Freud with bourgeois ignorance of the importance of material existence in favor of the "spicy drives" of sex.[25] The dreams from which Bloch develops his ideas of the future are suspicious of sexual and other pleasures, while for Muñoz, pleasure is not something that can or should be separated from material needs. In a fascinating passage that underlines the difference between the original Bloch and Muñoz's version, Bloch writes:

> Hopelessness is itself . . . the most insupportable thing; downright intolerable to human needs. Which is why even deception, if it is to be effective, must work with flatteringly and corruptly aroused hope. . . . Even the latest miseries of Western philosophy are no longer able to present their philosophy of misery without loaning the idea of transcendence, venturing beyond, from the bank. All this means is that man is essentially determined by the future, but with the cynically self-interested inference, hypostasized from its own class position, that the future is the sign outside the No Future night club, and the destiny of man

> nothingness. Well: let the dead bury their dead. . . . The beginning day is listening to something other than the putridly stifling, hollowly nihilistic death-knell.[26]

Nihilistic, anti-Marxist, and anti-utopian forms of philosophy figure here as a dance party whose participants are having too much fun amid the pleasures of the present to attend to the future, thereby missing their chance to embody the redemptive power of radical hope. The image of the "No Future night club" prefigures Lee Edelman's *No Future*, the influential work of queer theory that *Cruising Utopia* is angled against.[27] The drive for pleasure that is not future-focused, that is presented as a drive toward death and annihilation, is understood by Bloch and Edelman in surprisingly similar terms, though Edelman embraces what Bloch rejects when he sets forth queerness as oppositional to the future. Muñoz demands a different formulation, within which even the most nihilistic pleasures of the No Future night club are sites where the politicized yearnings of queer futurity can be found. His queer futurity concretizes in flashes of pleasure that intimate the potentiality of a future whose arrival they do not expect: it is the work of performance, gesture, or orgasm more than of planning.

Queer theorists, from Warner to Muñoz, have made sense of their transformative project by describing queer practices as *world-making*, focusing on futurity and potentiality as they are sensed in pleasurable moments. Science fiction also revolves around the possible futures of possible worlds, but these tend to be described as works of design and planning— worlds that are *built*. World-building, as science fiction writers describe it, is about creating a plausible imaginary universe, one that will generally be contemplated from the outside by readers, rather than lived within. It focuses more on structures and institutions than on experiential and interpersonal realities, and would seem to hold few of the temporally fluid features of Muñoz's queer world-making. Yet scholars who claim science fiction's futures as structurally laden with radical possibility have also used Bloch's conceptions of utopia to make their case, focusing on how science fiction writers can craft imagined worlds to posit a future whose difference from the present can make a case for political change.

Darko Suvin, whose 1979 *Metamorphoses of Science Fiction* was a foundational work for the emerging subdiscipline of science fiction studies, draws on Bloch's idea of the Novum, the artistic construction of a Not-Yet-Conscious that lives inside the present.[28] Suvin defined science fiction as fiction *"distinguished by the narrative dominance or hegemony of a fictional 'novum' (novelty, innovation) validated by cognitive logic."*[29] The crucial feature of science fiction as the literature of "cognitive estrangement" is its ability to make readers think outside the obvious narratives of mundane existence.[30] Suvin's discussion of this estrangement relies on an economic understanding of the political that does not incorporate sexuality, gender, or race. Yet queer reconceptualizations of desire, identification, and reproduction also function as novums and cognitive estrangements for many who encounter them.

Connecting the concepts of utopian impulse and cognitive estrangement, Fredric Jameson writes that utopian fiction disrupts the narratives that assume the future's social structures will be much the same as the ones in the present. Whereas "discussions of temporality always bifurcate" into "two paths"—time as moment or "existential experience," and time as progression or "historical time"—the two modes are "seamlessly reunited" in literary utopias, which imagine the possibility of a timeline reaching from a problematic present into the experience of a better future.[31] Utopia envisages the moment-by-moment experience of a different kind of future, one that grows from impulses that do not take part in the capitalist futures market. Jameson's Marxist taxonomy of utopian form assumes gender, race, and sexuality to be peripheral concerns to the serious matter of global capitalist materiality. Nevertheless, he provides a tantalizing glimpse of co-production of the future with the present, of world-making moments with world-building extrapolations, of the orgasmic with the political.

If we bring these derivations of Bloch—Muñoz's affective moments, Suvin's novum, and Jameson's disruption—together, we might begin to envisage a queer science fiction that could do in the realm of the cognitive what Muñoz's momentary feelings of utopia do in the affective register: make new forms of futurity by thinking about, and from, moments of pleasure. We can read Delany's work since the 1960s as engaged in this project. For Suvin, the possibility of "deviating from the author's and implied reader's norm of reality" is what makes the cognitive estrangements of science fiction so important.[32] The capacity to make worlds that deviate from the norm is also Delany's major achievement. In a science fiction that centers queer and racialized speculation, though, imaginative deviation is less a matter of estranging perceptions than of finding ways other than realist representation to articulate lived experiences excluded from the implied norms that constitute dominant pictures of reality.

In the 1970s and 1980s, Delany published several essays theorizing the politics and poetics of the science fiction genre. He writes that "if science fiction has any use at all, it is that among all its various and variegated future landscapes it gives us images *for* our futures," while it also can "provide a tool for questioning those images, exploring their distinctions, their articulations, their play of differences."[33] For him, "science fiction does not try to represent the world" but instead "consciously misrepresents the world in an endless series of lucidly readable ways."[34] It tells of events that "*have not happened*" but, crucially, that *could*.[35] A 1978 description of a moment in his own youthful reading shows his personal investment in science fictions' ability to fruitfully misrepresent the world. In reading Robert Heinlein's 1959 *Starship Troopers*, Delany was astounded by a passing mention, well into the book, that its narrator was of Filipino descent. Delany was "dazzled and delighted" by this implication that in Heinlein's imagined future "the racial situation . . . had resolved itself to the point where a young soldier might tell you of his adventures for 200 pages out of a 300-page novel and not even have to mention his ethnic background—because it had, in his world, become that insignificant!"[36] This fleeting fictional description, within a novel scarcely noted for political progressivism, caused him to "realize that up until then, with all the efforts going on about [him] to 'improve the racial situation,' [he] really had had no image of what the 'improved racial situation' was actually going to look like." By writing his apparently race-blind future world, Heinlein inspired Delany to wonder what a post-race world would "smell like, feel like," to ask himself how he would "know it had actually come?"[37] Heinlein did not provide a utopian blueprint for that day, and in fact the precise moment Delany describes does not appear in that particular novel.[38] Nevertheless, the experience and the memory of reading showed Delany a fragment of possibility to grasp after—not so that the young Delany could imagine a race-blind utopian future, but so that the details, feelings, smells, pleasures, and pains of alternative racial possibilities could become more than the briefest intimation.[39]

Delany unpacks these conceptions in an account of science fiction's meaning-production at the level of the sentence that begins in his 1968 essay "About 5,750 Words" and is developed over years of later writing. Committed to the terminology of *science fiction* rather than a more expansive term like *speculative fiction* because he is invested in the origins of these reading protocols in American popular culture, Delany distinguishes science fiction from mundane or realist literature by its engagement in world-building on a linguistic level.[40] As readers move through the sentences of a science fiction novel, they must remain open to multiple threads of possible meaning. For example, in the phrase "he turned on his left side," the surface physical interpretation (lying down, the man or boy turned over) might, in a science fiction context, be superseded by a technological possibility submerged in mundane reading (the male cyborg or android switched on the sensors in his left side).[41] We might also think of a third meaning that would activate the erotic connotations of "turned on." Readers cannot take any interpretation for granted, cannot assume that familiar meanings are always in play, and therefore must come to recognize that the mundane reading of any sentence is as much defined by cultural assumptions as the science-fictional one is by the parameters of its imagined world. This speculative mode of reading, wherein social customs and sentences' meanings can be overturned at any moment by imaginary social change, calls attention to the arbitrariness of mundane realities' regimes of the normal. Thus, as Wendy Pearson argues, the cognitive estrangements of science fiction might render the genre's readers ready to be queered, preparing them for visions of widely varied social and sexual practices.[42]

The sense of expansive potentiality that Delany calls *reading as science fiction* is very similar to reading history or literature for queer presences in the past—to the erotics of queer textual searching, seeking the interpretation for which one longs and trying to resist the narrative and syntactic logics that would hide it, erase it, or shut it down in advance. Sedgwick's promises to queer children are tightly tied to these engagements with cultural production, where words and sounds and images are cathected to the point that they gift new shapes to inner worlds. Here words are feelings, and the suggestion that things might get better in the future is something to be experienced and lived for in the now.

Writings from the past still have the capacity to create and disrupt possibilities for queer worlding in a moment when the standard of mainstreamed LGBTQ political engagement often looks like a bland commitment to "it" getting "better." This is true even though—as I discuss in the introduction—queer-themed science fiction has sometimes had a tendency to restage the contemporary terms of LGBTQ political debates within futures that hold relatively narrow scopes. James Sallis writes that Delany has resisted this temptation by creating "entire societies in order to depict those at the society's margin."[43] His imagined worlds center on queer, racialized people, even as the meanings of queerness and racialization are radically shifted away from realist interpretations. Delany's characters never obscure what makes them queer beneath a veneer of respectability: his fictions, like his nonfictions, center on queer, weird sex, and that sex becomes central to our ideas of what a world is. Not because it is reproductive, at least not in the biological or procreative sense, although his nonprocreative sex is very often involved in the creation of structures that function like family. But because the acts and experiences, fantasies, and erotics of sex itself create socialities and worlds.

Bent Narrative, Perverted Reading, and Fiction as Queer Space/Time

"Once one abandons the hope of following all the rules and regulations of straight society, the future becomes an open *space* rather than the disciplinary, delayed *temporality* of generational, Oedipal succession."[44] Tavia Nyong'o writes this in an effort to make sense of a 1978 interview in which Patti Smith declares a surprisingly un-punk stake in reproductive futurism by announcing that "the future is children."[45] Nyong'o suggests that her approach to generationality allows a love for children to coexist with the embrace of adult deviance and perversity. This space of queered futurity, Nyong'o continues, "is not a disciplinary ideal . . . so much as it is that most queer of spatial tropes, an ambience."[46] Delany, who shared a temporal and spatial location with Smith in 1970s New York, has used fiction to make a queer futural ambience out of the disciplinary ideals of science fiction world-building. In the eight hundred pages of his best-known novel, *Dhalgren* (1974), a tangled narrative produces a space that is both the book itself and its setting and subject: the disintegrating metropolis of Bellona, where not only straight society's rules and regulations but the trustworthiness of cosmology, geography, even cause and effect have withered away. This section draws on *Dhalgren*, and on the ways that readers describe their experiences with the book, to contemplate the effects and affects of an ambient queer future.

Dhalgren's world is a city in which marginal desires and practices, often though not only sexual, structure a fictional vision of New York in the late 1960s and early 1970s. The plot, such as it is, involves a protagonist named variously Kidd, the Kid, and Kid. He enters an American city named Bellona, where an unnamed change has taken away all state and government structures, and encounters various inhabitants. Recalling the white flight, institutional abandonment, and gentrification that have shaped cities like Detroit in Bellona's image since *Dhalgren* was published, some characters—often though not exclusively white— have arrived there by choice, while others—often though not exclusively black—have simply been unable to leave.[47] But the complications of Bellona's social and physical world can never be reduced to an analogy.

For many readers, the book has been experienced as a space into which they, too, enter, sometimes finding in the process that they have been there all along. William Gibson's introduction to the 1996 edition tells of his transformative experiences in the "prose-city" and exhorts readers to "go inside" the book.[48] The spatialities of *Dhalgren* and Bellona influenced not only the personal lives of readers, but also the maps of antinormative desire that queer scholars and activists were creating in the 1990s. Patrick Califia's essay "The City of Desire," in the 1994 collection *Public Sex*, lists the novel as a source for the modeling of metropolitan sexual maps without giving an explanation for the reference.[49] Similarly, Gordon Brent Ingram cites *Dhalgren* when he coins the term *queerscape* in the 1997 anthology *Queers in Space*.[50] Invoking Bellona without explaining why, these oblique references invite the imaginary city to stand as a mysterious emblem of queered urban space.

Fragmentary, ambiguous narratives of the kind that *Dhalgren* both employs and inspires are a hallmark of queer literature. David Wojnarowicz's 1992 memoir *Close to the Knives* is one example of a literary ambience whose fragmented temporalities and queer activities bear multiple similarities to *Dhalgren*. What makes *Dhalgren* distinct is the speculative emphasis on worlding through which its form and content come together. If *Dhalgren*'s ambience is dislocating, this is not only because of the way its narrative formally represents subjectivity, but due to the weird materiality—imagined objects in imagined spaces—that the reader is invited to perceive. The novel, like all science fiction in Delany's articulation of the genre, builds a world different from the one that realism presumes we more or less share. This world can be inhabited by readers who are able to recognize its signs.

Despite challenges to its genre legitimacy on its publication, *Dhalgren* insistently and playfully participates in the cultural and genre logics of science fiction, offering clues to its futuristic temporality by playing on the age and date of birth of the protagonist.[51] Early on, as Kid approaches Bellona, he has a sexual encounter with a mysterious woman and the following exchange takes place:

> "How old are you?"
> "Twenty-seven."
> "You have the face of someone much younger. . . . You have the hands of someone much older."
> "What year were you born?"
> "Nineteen forty-eight." . . .
> "Well, if you were born in nineteen forty-eight, you've got to be older than twenty-seven . . . I was born in nineteen forty-seven. And I'm a good deal older than twenty-eight."[52]

The novel was published in 1974; someone born in 1948 was twenty-seven in 1975. We are, therefore, in the future, or at least the vicinity of Bellona. But this is not a future that can be identified through any predictable timeline, though the novel does contain science fiction tropes of as-yet-impossible technology (holographic projector necklaces) and astronomical irregularities (a second moon). A science fiction fan character (Tak, who also happens to be a gay leatherman and a former skinhead) describes Bellona as "science fiction" because it follows "conventions" of the world being malleable and hospitable when one lands on an alien planet.[53] *Dhalgren* operates much like that confusing, mysterious, yet hospitable planet.

As I explain above, Delany defines the praxis of science fiction as distinct from mundane literature at the level of the sentence because of the increased number of possible endings and meanings to any given proposition. In *Dhalgren*, those augmented possibilities are never closed down into one interpretation. The novel has the structure of an unfinished sentence—or perhaps of a computer game, where avatars follow quests that can be sent off track by errant user commands. (Indeed, *Dhalgren* gave its name to an early text-based multi-user online world in the 1990s.[54]) The novel's radical uncertainty pushes Delany's definition of science fiction's sentence-level world-building to its limits. As readers, our close attention is not rewarded with explanations and resolutions to the mysteries of life in Bellona. Despite tantalizing hints, we don't find out the "real" name that Kid has forgotten, why the novel is called *Dhalgren*, or what caused Bellona's change from a "normal" city to the always-already post-apocalyptic space in which the novel takes place.

The confusion that *Dhalgren*'s structure elicits is felt as much by the novel's characters as by its readers, and not only because of the unreliability of Kid's narration. Lacking a solid plot in which to participate, characters are hardly ever sure whether or when any described event has actually happened and what its effect may be. Delany troubles the linearity of not only plot but also time. Tak tells a story of his life in Bellona: "I go down a street; buildings are burning. I go down the same street the next day. They're still burning. Two weeks later, I go down the same street and nothing looks like it's been burned at all. Maybe time is just running backward here. Or sideways. But that's impossible too."[55] In *Dhalgren*, the impossible is a daily occurrence. Wondering *why* gets one nowhere; cause and effect cannot function when time is not straightforward. Recounted events never coalesce into a single story, and the stories told resist readerly expectations of narrative arcs and closures.

Time in *Dhalgren* is unpredictable, changeable, and liquid; it "leaks; sloshes backwards and forwards, turns up and shows what's on its . . . underside."[56] When we reach the end, we find an unfinished sentence ("I have come to"), which catapults us back to the first page for its possible completion ("to wound the autumnal city").[57] The temporal status of everything narrated between is thrown into confusion by this Möbius structure: Did the events told at the end occur before the novel's beginning? And lest we be seduced into believing that the book is structured as a simple circle, the final section is a collection of scattered, potentially connected, unfinished texts that date their own composition to numerous points within, before, and after events narrated elsewhere. Critics have charted various pathways around the novel, from rationalizing the protagonist's disorientation and loss of time as the worldview of "a multiple dyslexic with epilepsy" to reading the inconclusive structure as an unfulfilled quest narrative exemplifying the futility of the American dream.[58] *Dhalgren's* impossibilities remain open to many interpretations.

A lasting impression with which I emerged from my first reading of *Dhalgren* was of near-constant queer sexual activity throughout the book between men and in mixed-gender groups that the protagonist, Kid, encounters as he meanders through Bellona. On returning to the novel years later, I was astonished to see how small a proportion of the text is actually taken up with explicit sex description, and how very much of that sex is heterosexual. Andrew M. Butler finds the novel to be a poor response to the strides made by gay activism in the 1970s because most of the frequent graphic sexual depictions in the novel are straight ones.[59] But it is no accident that the novel leaves an impression of queerness despite the heterosexuality of its sex. Certainly, homoeroticism shows up frequently, graphically, and without fanfare. The city's main social center is a gay bar, Teddy's; Kid is introduced to this scene by Tak Loufer, a white gay man who makes it his business to "catch" new male entrants to Bellona (including Kid) and offer them a homoerotic sexual initiation, queering their experience of the city from the beginning.[60] When a member of the "scorpion" gang Kid leads calls him a "cocksucker," Kid responds calmly that he has "sucked [his] quota of dick. *And* enjoyed it," exposing the insult's homophobia and mocking a bystander who is thrown into panic by it.[61] Regardless of who is fucking whom, the novel works to imagine a social framework that is not based on heterosexual couples, nuclear families, or the state forms that privilege them.

Delany writes that his intention in *Dhalgren* was emphatically not to provide "a sympathetic portrayal of the social problems of those who deviate sexually from the social norm," but rather to "completely subvert . . . the entire subtext that informs a discourse of 'social problems/ sympathetic/sexual deviate/normal' in the first place."[62] In Bellona, the people who have and cause "social problems" are not the queered and/or racialized deviant subjects, but those who try to maintain some semblance of the previously hegemonic social norm—such as the Richards family, whose insistence on living out traditional white middle-class life in

Bellona is an extended delusion that eventually leads to the death of their son.[63] The novel does much more than insist that those who cannot fit themselves into the scripts of normative sex and sociality can be happy and functional despite their disadvantages. It rescripts the world entirely.

Sex in *Dhalgren* is a source of bodily pleasure that resists racialized gender ideologies in sometimes uncomfortable ways. In one scene set during Kid's sojourn with Bellona's "scorpion" gang, men of all races line up to have sex with Risa, a black woman who is one of few female members of the group. The extended description of this act takes up pornographic tropes, focusing on the men's competitiveness with one another; Kid's language dehumanizes the "dazed" Risa as he too steps up to "get a piece."[64] What should we make of this portrayal of something that one critic describes as "gang rape"?[65] Delany's depiction of Risa's responses makes it look like enthusiastic consent: she is described as reaching for and "grabbing" each man.[66] Even the visceral association of the men's turn-taking, the exertion of their power on a feminine body, is undermined by a casual remark that other scorpion women had participated.[67] Does the scene nevertheless reinforce tropes of the black woman as sexually ravenous, one who cannot not consent? It is certainly possible to read it that way. But to do so would require disregarding much of Delany's text. Feeling guilty the next morning and fearing that Risa may have been sexually exploited, Kid asks her whether she felt "forced" or "enjoyed" the experience. She responds vehemently, saying that (despite his participation) he "can't have any part of that"; it was "*mine . . . all mine,*" she says, and leaves Kid musing on whether he wants "to get gang-banged" himself.[68] Risa, then, is not the victim of a sexist, racist power dynamic but is rather pursuing, and finding, her version of the black feminist erotics that Jennifer Nash describes as opening up to "complex and sometimes unnerving pleasures."[69] Like Octavia Butler and Jewelle Gomez, discussed in the previous chapter, Delany insists that bodily autonomy and desire are not always clean, sanitary, or polite.

For those who are not dispelled by its formidable opacity, entering *Dhalgren* the novel is analogous to entering Bellona the city. "Once you have transgressed that boundary, every atom, the interior of every point of reality, has shifted its relation to every other you've left behind, shaken and jangled within the field of time, so that if you cross back, you'll return to a very different space from the one you left."[70] Once readers have been inside the novel, which is to say inside the city, they may never again entirely inhabit quite the same "field of time." Once again, *Dhalgren* extends a genre feature of science fiction to its limit. Dorothy Allison has written of childhood science fiction reading as accessing a "hidden message," the "secret" first intimation that sexuality "didn't have to be the way everybody said it was."[71] Images of different worlds can be transferred into life narratives more complex than "it gets better," to shape readers' queer futures as easily accessible books become portable queer worlds. The downmarket, juvenile reputation of science fiction may have helped to render such queer escapes (few of which will have been accessed through avant-garde works like Delany's) more accessible to isolated or young people than overtly gay, lesbian, or transgender subcultural activity and performance.[72]

In a 1999 review essay, Ann Weinstone uses an adolescent encounter with *Dhalgren* to describe how science fiction can become "a young person's first queer theory." Defining "queer literary studies" as a mode of "reading outside of established concepts and categories," which is rooted in queer readers' experiences of finding "transformative magic" in anti-heteronormative texts, Weinstone recalls reading *Dhalgren* at "a moment in queer adolescence when . . . having been sure that you were condemned to live alone among perpetual adults of perpetual resignation—a companion appears, a companion world."[73] Delany's novel drew her into "the relief and opportunity that flows from the lifting of the imperative to be socially, economically, and sexually coherent," into the speculative and material reality of incoherent alternatives.[74] The text's radical inconclusivity, "the pleasure of not making sense" it provided, enabled her to envisage a future in which making sense would not be required.

Weinstone's and Allison's stories are also my own. I first came across *Dhalgren* at an impressionable age, bowled over by passages like this one: "*Let* me ask the terrible question: Could it be that all those perfectly straight, content-with-their-sexual-orientation-in-the-world, exclusive-heterosexuals really are (in some ill-defined, psychological way that will ultimately garner a better world) more healthy than (gulp . . . !) us? Let me answer: No *way!*"[75] After days or weeks or months wading through a textual universe populated by social and sexual deviants whose connections and epiphanies and great sex I didn't entirely understand but didn't want to look away from, it occurred to me that this world might not be entirely separate from the one I inhabited when I looked up from my book. Delany pointed me toward an "us" out there neither straight nor contented with sexual orientations and their meanings in the world. At the same time, he offered a new view on how my surroundings already failed to live up to the straight rendering of what "a better world" might be. Disappointments transfigured to electric possibilities. For fans, readers, and scholars of whom I am only one, science fiction in general, and Delany's works in particular, provided initiation into realms of possibility we would later find articulated in queer theory and activism. They built worlds in our minds that we have been trying to make real ever since. This book is a product of that building and, though its final form strays far from those initial impulses, an effort to describe, theorize, and honor it.

After the End of the World: Speculating a Future for Slavery, Pleasure, and Black Queer Desire

Science fiction for Delany "is not about the future" because it "works by setting up a dialogue with the here-and-now, a dialogue as rich as the writer can make it."[76] His work has long used the figure of the imagined future to create rich dialogues with what Berlant and Warner describe as the "radical aspirations of queer culture building": the "changed possibilities of identity, intelligibility, publics, culture and sex that appear when the heterosexual couple is no longer the referent or the privileged example of sexual culture."[77] "Queer social practices like sex and theory" are the tools Berlant and Warner imagine as necessary for culture-building.[78] To these practices Delany adds science fiction, which shows readers how things might look, function, and feel if it were possible to give racialized bodies and queer sexual pleasures the centrality in world production that heterosexuality and whiteness have long held in dominant Anglo-American culture.

While *Dhalgren*'s mysterious city-world makes science fiction's temporal conventions spatial, *Stars in My Pocket like Grains of Sand* homes in on the future, setting up its dialogue with the present by projecting readers thousands of years forward in time. The novel (hereafter abbreviated to *Stars*) conceptualizes not just a world but thousands of planets—an entire galaxy structured around gay sex and queer world-making. Delany seeks to represent the intense complexity that might exist in a galactic civilization where millions of human and alien societies intersect, and his depiction of this "huge field of difference" has fascinated the text's scholarly readers.[79] Though this will not be the main focus of my reading, the universe of *Stars* also offers suggestive and intricate allegories for the computer-aided complexity of globalized finance capitalism.[80] The novel revolves around two protagonists, Rat Korga and Marq Dyeth, who are discovered by a presciently imagined all-pervasive computer surveillance operation to be one another's "perfect erotic objects."[81] Korga is a mentally mutilated former slave who escapes enslavement only through the destruction of his entire world, and Dyeth is an "Industrial Diplomat" who experiences the galaxy as an infinite cycle of heterogeneity among whose differences he is paid to negotiate.

Like *Dhalgren*, *Stars* stretches Delany's idea of science fiction's sentence-level cognitive estrangement to the limit of most readers' capacity to follow. In this novel, each sentence aims to create the texture of not just a world but a universe structured around assumptions radically different than any we can expect to find familiar. In the language used in the long second section of the novel, "the ancient, dimorphic 'he,' once used exclusively for the general indication of males (cf. the archaic term man, pl. *men*), [is] reserved for the general sexual object of 'she,' during the period of excitation, regardless of the gender of the woman speaking or the gender of the woman referred to."[82] Rather than human women and children being officially incorporated into the category of "man," "woman" has become a descriptive term that signifies nothing about gender, sex, or species but instead indicates legal personhood. As readers, we must constantly remind ourselves that "she" indicates neither female sex nor feminine gender, and that the use of "he" tells us nothing about the individual being described except that the speaker finds this person sexually desirable. We must constantly and consciously remember that a world is being built, with our collaboration, in every sentence that we read.

Alcena Madeline Davis Rogan finds the world encoded by *Stars*'s language to be exemplary of "feminist consciousness, since the default gender is female."[83] In some ways, it also anticipates the transgender activism of the decades following the novel's publication. At the end of *Sex Changes* (2003), Patrick Califia offers a brief utopian vision when he urges readers to imagine what it would be like "to walk down the street, go to work, or attend a party and take it for granted that the gender of the people you met would not be the first thing you ascertained about them."[84] The pronominal system in *Stars* forces the reader into this position, since we are rarely given enough information to identify how a character might be gendered in a society that tied gender to assumed genital sex.

Delany names this language Arachnia and explains its prevalence by the fact that his assemblage of diverse future cultures is linked by "web" implants worn by most galactic citizens, which connect them to a galactic system called General Information. This is a connection difficult not to link to the utopian and dystopian visions of digital connection that cyberpunk science fiction and the growth of internet studies would shortly make popular, or to the explorations of gender beyond reductive biological discourses that would become part of the language of digital media.[85] William Gibson's *Neuromancer*, which coined the term "cyberspace," was published in the same year as *Stars*. In an alternate universe where queer black science fiction writers are as popular as straight white ones, perhaps we are all speaking Arachnia.[86]

By sustained use of his Arachnia pronoun system, Delany suggests that the future of gender and sex will be the end of their existence as the primary characteristics that define any individual. Our narrator, Marq Dyeth, however, is "a strange human being . . . [whose] predilections run toward only one gender," meaning that we can rely upon the male identity and presentation of every character the narration calls "he."[87] Arachnia pronouns, then, fall surprisingly well into line with standard English "he" and "she": we are never presented with a female woman as "he" or object of desire, only male women. When Marq narrates one of his earliest sexualized memories, he recalls seeing a hand (bitten nails and calloused hands are his erotic fascinations) that he thinks belongs to a "human male" previously referred to as "she." The pronominal change to "he" in Marq's internal monologue enacts the recognition of desire: "the shift in pronoun coming . . . simply, with a warmth and pleasure flowering."[88] The eroticized hands, however, do not belong to the male but to a "muscular, human female"; as soon as Marq realizes that, the pronouns change again and he refers to "*her* big hand."[89] Merely to perceive a female body is enough to cancel out Marq's burgeoning desire, and to return the Arachnia pronoun to effective English usage. The conflation of grammatical masculinity and being the object of desire is exciting, even utopian, for a male-desiring male subject; as Robert Reid-Pharr writes, the novel creates complex, beautiful, and unsanitized representations of gay male identity and desire.[90] In the logic of the novel, when Marq loses desire at the realization that the body attached to the hands lacks a penis, it signals his realization of his own "strange" nature as a male-desiring male. Yet, when the "female" sex of the hands excludes them from masculinity, Marq's moment of desiring recognition also elicits an uncomfortable resonance with narratives that would follow the discovery of a trans person's assigned sex with exclusion from their lived gender. Such a reading, perhaps as anachronistic as it is unavoidable for a contemporary reader attuned to trans concerns, calls attention to the novel's less-than-utopian equation of both femininity and transgender possibility with the absence of desire.[91]

Delany insists that science fiction neither can nor should be utopian, because "utopia presupposes a pretty static, unchanging, and rather tyrannical world."[92] The failures of the Arachnia pronominal system serve to underline that critique of utopia, as well as to remind us of the focus on male embodiment that is present in all of Delany's queer worlds, built as they are out of the experience of a life lived amid gay male sexual cultures. All the same, castigations of utopia for their tyranny make sense only if we understand utopia and futurity to be reliant on outcomes rather than processes. They elide the more fluid utopian impulse and speculative act of which Arachnia is one possible outcome. What if we were constantly to mark our desire in language? In his 1988 memoir *The Motion of Light in Water*, Delany's "one piece of science fiction" was to hope for a "sexual revolution" that would "come precisely because of the infiltration of clear and articulate language into the marginal areas of human sexual exploration."[93] The encoding of desire into language in *Stars* seems to offer just such a possibility, especially when combined with the novel's lyrical and graphic sexual depictions. Where Delany's nonfiction writing articulated politicized longing for "new institutions" that might fulfil disregarded and marginal sexual needs, his science fiction had already crafted the plans for how such institutions might look, sound, smell, and feel.[94]

Stars crafts a future that institutionalizes queer sexual pleasures, most vividly through the integration of public sex into everyday society. In Marq Dyeth's home city on the planet Velm, anyone can enter a "run" that caters to their preferred type of sex—whether with humans, with the evelm native to the planet, or both—and enjoy a burst of pleasure as part of daily life. Runs are underground spaces that function as both public sex venues and art galleries "where you come for sex . . . and sculpture."[95] Delany's description of the protagonists' experience inside a run suggests a quasi-utopian potentiality for these communal pleasures:

> We walked off . . . between statues, where now there were three, now twelve, now two, some entwined with one another, some watching, now a hand, not his, lingering somewhere on his body or mine. Once we moved through nearly twenty, most in sexual contact with one another. . . . the many bodies centimeters away moving together, apart in the warmth, a moment of cool as contact broke, then warmth again, to hold, to handle, and, even though we only moved through, as supportive as if we'd stayed.[96]

The two protagonists do not join any of the sexual groups, yet the "contact" between bodies soothes and supports them, and the repetitive rhythms of Delany's prose give a sense of the "lingering" pleasures they encounter. In the "supportive" "warmth" of the sexual environment, individual identities break down to become components of a whole containing "many bodies." The scene offers readers a suggestive and enticing image of what it might be like to live in a world where sexual pleasure for all was embraced and supported.

In treating "institutions" as mediators and enablers of pleasure, Delany insists that a more liberated approach to sex would not be an escape from power. In the case of Velm, the liberating sexual scenes in which the narration takes such pleasure are rooted in the violence of empire. For the runs are indigenous institutions that predate humans' settler colonization of the planet: they were "integral" to Velmian culture "before humans came" and "moved right into them."[97] And while human colonization of Velm is covered over by the genteel appearance of equality in the south, where the book is set, it takes the form of open violence ("hunting parties" where humans kill evelm are mentioned) in the planet's north.[98]

Delany's "lovely sentences" are, as Reid-Pharr writes, "underwritten by a brutality and violence that are . . . world-shattering."[99] The diversity, difference, and desire on display in *Stars* showcase the ease with which queer possibility and colonial violence coexist, underlining Scott Lauria Morgensen's assertion that "nothing in the history of white-supremacist settler colonialism or the globalization of European capital and empire that it facilitates is separable from what is perceived as 'queer.'"[100] Marq and the evelm alike must come to terms with the reality that their connections facilitate both pleasure and oppression.

Stars was written at the same time as Delany's first forays into documenting what would become known as AIDS, and while he was part of public sexual cultures he would later extensively document in memoir. *The Motion of Light in Water* is punctuated with scenes that mirror those of Velm's runs, recollections of illicit spaces in New York where individuality broke down into a mass of sexual bodies and "cock passed from mouth to mouth to hand to ass to mouth without ever breaking contact with other flesh for more than seconds."[101] In nonfiction, Delany uses such scenes to call for sexual revolution at an urgent moment in queer history, highlighting the damage caused by AIDS and its attendant panics alongside the loss of working-class men's social and sexual life worlds to gentrification. Dianne Chisholm writes of Delany's public sex memoir that the "memory of mass sex . . . invokes the space of sexual revolution before the advent of gay militancy" as "shades of revolutionary prehistory bleed into the postrevolutionary present, where AIDS has decimated the village."[102] She situates Delany's revolutionary hopes for alterations in sexual discourse, and his suggestions that a future could emerge from utopian moments of sexual pleasure, in the context of the losses incurred by the epidemic.

We are used to thinking of queer futurity as curtailed by AIDS; the devastation the virus wreaked on the personal futures of gay men affected social and sexual landscapes in myriad ways. The specter of illness and premature death has shaped many narratives of queer temporality, creating a necessity for "rethinking the conventional emphasis on longevity and futurity . . . by making community in relation to risk, disease, infection and death."[103] Delany moved away from depicting large-scale futuristic societies as the epidemic and the gay political response to it burgeoned in the 1980s; a planned sequel to *Stars* was never finished, and

Delany has published little science fiction since.[104] While working on *Stars*, Delany was also beginning the work of merged fantasy and memoir that would later be acclaimed as among the first published works of fiction to deal with AIDS: "The Tale of Plagues and Carnivals" (1985), part of his *Neverÿon* series.[105] This novella is based on *"misinformation, rumor,* and *wholly untested guesses* at play through a limited social section of New York City during 1982 and 1983," and shows a city in which sexual contacts are permeated by fear.[106] Delany's expansively extrapolative queer futurities seem to grow more curtailed as the texture of gay life and gay worlds around him shifts, with sexual ebullience eventually to be replaced by narrower hopes that things might get better through a politics of respectability in which he has steadfastly refused to participate.[107] Yet his science fictions suggest ways to sustain alternate futures for what was in the process of being lost.

The world Delany builds in *Stars* maps systems that would allow queer social life to perpetuate itself through continuing generations. In the 1980s, the conservative strain of "family values" proved particularly virulent, with the protection of presumptively heterosexual children from gay male sexuality prioritized above the lives of people with HIV/AIDS.[108] Responding to this and other homophobic iterations of the project of "family," Valerie Lehr writes that "structural change" in "the family" is "necessary" for "guaranteeing freedom" for queer people, "since this institution is so powerfully implicated in the construction of identity."[109] Speculative fiction writers concerned with gender and sexuality have long sought to reimagine normative family structures, as even the most problematic feminist utopias discussed in this book demonstrate. Alternatives to child-raising structures based around heterosexual biological reproduction were common in the feminist science fiction of the 1970s; Delany's contributions to this archive include the communes of *Trouble on Triton* (1976). In the Velmian "nurture stream" that raised Marq Dyeth, *Stars* contains one of science fiction's most elaborately imagined models of a counterhegemonic reproductive structure. The Dyeth "stream"—which is never called a family—has existed for seven generations, merging human and evelm lives with "no direct egg-and-sperm relations between any ripple of parents and any ripple of children."[110] The lines between parent and child are blurred—hence the fluid and mobile metaphor of "ripples" in a "stream." The clearly delineated, gendered roles of a nuclear family are nowhere to be seen, and we are never clearly told how many parents or children there are in each "ripple." With the disappearance of sexual biology from the business of reproduction, the concept of a parent's power over or ownership of a child has also vanished: "the stream structure conceives of all children as gifts from society, as gifts to society" rather than as parents' possessions.[111] In breaking with the possessiveness of biological family and having kinship cross species as well as generational lines, the stream also aspires to decenter human settler supremacy on Velm. This element comes into sharp relief when human-supremacist visitors from the "Family" cult/religion/ideology, which idealizes patriarchal structures associated with long-lost Earth, insult the human Dyeths as "animals who copulate with animals, call animals their sisters and mothers."[112] Queer families of choice move from single-generation support network to multi-generational, decolonial modes of reproduction.

As a product of this reproductive mode, Marq is affirmed in a structure of desire that makes him unusual even in this broad universe. He takes pride in the sexual minority status afforded by his fetish for large hands with bitten nails, stating that the world in which he lives is "wondrous and the more exciting because no one has written plays and poems and built sculptures to indicate the structure of desire I negotiate every day as I move about in it."[113] He can revel in the absence of representation rather than lamenting it because all his various parental influences agreed that he "was a ripple that shored their stream."[114] The stream reproductive structure often feels like a utopian ideal, figuring the cultural reproduction of deviant desires as predictive of a future that extends to the novel's readers, who might be encouraged to find their own "structures of desire" to be "wondrous" and "exciting." Reid-Pharr cautions against such oversimplification, reminding us that, while the Dyeths "represent . . . precisely the kind of liberal, expansive family structure that would presumably have all of Delany's readers nodding their heads in self-satisfied affirmation," their story was nevertheless enabled to begin through the material legacy of a tyrannical ruler who bequeathed the real estate in which they make their home.[115] The vision of the Dyeth stream is an ultimate "It Gets Better" project for worlds as well as individuals—one that is not innocent of the privilege and exclusion attached to the individual story. Yet it is nevertheless a powerful and poignant vision of a future in which queerness could be respected and valued, imagined at a moment of mourning when things were about to get worse.

Delany's fictional worlds are fertile breeding grounds for queer speculative sex in all its messy glory. But his science-fictional dialogues with the present refuse to portray futures where things get *simply* better. Even as *Stars*'s speculative versions of grammar, sex, and reproduction suggest possibilities for joyous futures grown out of queer desire, they also call attention to gendered and colonial power structures. And the prospect that this future's possibilities will be curtailed looms continually large.

Stars opens with the literal loss of a world—the destruction of a planet, Rat Korga's homeworld of Rhyonon. It ends with the narrowly averted danger that Velm will also disappear through the mysterious forces of "Cultural Fugue," an ambiguous term describing apocalyptic conditions brought about through planetary and galactic processes of collective speculation that resemble the obscure causalities of stock market crashes.[116] The worlds we build through narrative and through living, the novel insists, are fragile; the future cannot be trusted. Reading the novel through the imminence of the AIDS epidemic offers one way to make sense of this elegiac quality, but not the only one. Delany also attends to the racialized and economic power structures that end worlds and foreclose futures through his invocations and representations of slavery.

The novel's first fifty-eight pages are taken up by a tale of a slave, Rat Korga, who loses his world in a narrative that is elided in some critics' focus on the queerly utopian aspects of *Stars*'s world-building. For Mary Kay Bray, Rat Korga's story functions as "an opening spectacle displaying a failed society, setting the stage for what follows."[117] Carl Freedman focuses his analysis on the "utopian moments" that emerge in Marq's narrative, describing Rat Korga's world of Rhyonon as a "counterutopic locus" whose repressiveness highlights the possibilities inherent in the "radically sexual and polymorphous utopia" Marq describes.[118] However, if we read the novel through Rat's subjection as well as Marq's pleasure, then the narrative temporality of the novel can no longer be experienced as a progress from worse to better, from the loss of a dreadful and oppressive world to the gaining of a gloriously queer one.

The science-fictional enslavement to which Delany subjects Rat Korga is both similar to and radically different from historical American slavery.

Saidiya Hartman's analysis of the subjectivity and subjection produced by the structures of slavery is helpful in understanding Delany's project. In *Scenes of Subjection*, Hartman describes the subjection of American slaves as a coercive rendering of "will . . . indistinguishable from submission," such that the choices available to individuals were systematically reduced to the point of erasure.[119] Delany uses science fiction to turn the discursive technology of enslavement Hartman describes into a literal, mechanical procedure that can delete personal autonomy. On the planet of Rhyonon (whose name, like Korga's own, we do not learn until we have moved out of the "Prologue" into Marq Dyeth's much longer narrative), slaves are those who have submitted to a treatment called "Radical Anxiety Termination"—the initials of which cause slaves to be called "rats," hence Rat Korga's name—which takes away the capacity to learn and to make choices. Rhyonon's model of slavery is considered by its culture to resemble suicide more than racialized oppression, since to become a slave requires consent. Yet Delany's description of Korga's induction into rat-hood make it clear that his consent, at least, is neither autonomous nor informed. He becomes a rat because his desires, physiology, and social status exclude him from any other personal or social future.

The novel's opening lines, in radical opposition to the discourses of queer utopianism it also contains, show us the end of Korga's official personhood. The state official who awaits his consent to the Radical Anxiety Termination process speaks to him:

> Of course . . . you will be a slave. . . . But you will be happy. . . . Certainly you will be happier than you are. . . . I mean, look at you, boy. You're ugly as mud and tall enough to scare children in the street. . . . You've been in trouble of one sort or another for as long as there are records on you: orphanages, foster homes, youth rehabilitation camps, adult detention units—and *you* haven't gotten along in any of them. Sexually . . . ? . . . In this part of the world your preferences in that area can't have done you any good. You're a burden to yourself, to your city, to your geosector. . . . But we can change all that.[120]

Here Korga is interpellated as a failed subject, a "boy" whose inability to live up to social norms fits him only to be a slave. Even his features are inscribed with the temporality of his subjection: "ignorance's determinant past, information's present impossibility, speculation's denied future."[121] These have been determined not only by his economic disadvantage, tendency to get in "trouble," apparent neuro-atypicality, and (homo)sexual minority status, but by physical traits (height) invested by his society with social significance. Korga's lack of place in Rhyonon society has, it seems, written future enslavement on his body. He is a ripple that shores no one's stream, a life that does not matter, a member of many groups vulnerable to premature death of the will if not the body.[122] He occupies, in other words, the structural position of blackness.[123] Speculative processes of racialization and gendering have pressed him into a position where physiological enslavement feels like the only available option—and that choiceless choice will destine him to a position of barely visible subordination, doing the work of a world to which he has no personal access and whose inhabitants seem scarcely to be aware of him.

Were there any doubt, the state-sponsored slaver's bad faith in promising "happiness" is made immediately evident by the abjection and maltreatment Korga suffers: rat existence offers none of the advantages with which the Institute try to dupe the marginalized and despairing. Nevertheless, degradation is not unremitting. As a rat, Korga is not happy, but he does manage to participate in world-making practices of sexual pleasure. Hartman's account of the formation of racialized subjectivities in postbellum America, where "the texture of freedom [was] laden with the vestiges of slavery," helps make clear how some of the most "utopian" moments, concepts, and pleasures in *Stars* rest on the legacy of Korga's captivity, on a loss of world and future that can never be relegated to the past.[124] The previous chapter discussed Afrofuturism as a speculative frame by which the erased histories of African diasporic subjects can be reimagined on the canvas of the future; Delany writes the losses of slavery and the continuing labor of enslaved and dehumanized individuals into even his most far-off future, yet refuses to separate them from experiences of pleasure.

Seeking to locate tactics of resistance among the everyday practices of the enslaved, Hartman writes that "on rare occasions the pleasures available within the confines of slavery indeed possessed glimmerings of insurgency and transformation."[125] In one long passage, for example, Korga is illegally purchased by a private individual. The unnamed woman who buys him is a self-described sexual "pervert" aroused by the unequal power relations of slave society. She would like to give Korga his freedom not for his sake but as a gift to herself; she has little interest in his needs and desires.[126] And yet, objectified in this way, Korga has more self-awareness and volition than at any other point in his narrative. The woman provides him with the major commodity that his life before and after the RAT process had denied him: information, in the form of a glove that connects to planetary communication networks. With the glove, he becomes aware not only of the history and geography of his planet but of horror at his own situation, of his "rage that welled through his body but, because of what they had done to him, connected with nothing."[127] He does not gain autonomy or recover the capacity for active choice, but his mind and awareness are infinitely expanded. And when sexual pleasure comes into play (not with the woman, but when she sends him off to a cruising area to "indulge" his "foul and unspeakable desires" as she has just indulged hers by beating him), again power and awareness bloom out of pleasure.[128] Thanks to the glove, this is now more thoroughly articulated: "With words whirling and falling in his head, the wonder, pulsing and pulsing from spine to genitals, settled slowly into the wordless memory of wonder."[129] For that moment, painful past and unpromising future become irrelevant in a moment of utopia that places Korga in the same world he will later occupy at the runs on Velm—the world of public sex's orgasmic futurity whose politics have mobilized much of Delany's nonfiction.

In the depictions of Velm's runs I discuss above, we can find a hopeful figure for interracial and interclass sexual contact here on Earth, overcoming oppression by a view of intercultural and interpersonal difference "that is not simply tolerated . . . but is actively *desired*, sought, and embraced."[130] Reid-Pharr, who is deeply suspicious of such liberal readings, has used his own experiences in sexual contact with others of radically different social and racial status to express a similar momentary utopian hope. In "Dinge," Reid-Pharr suggests that "something powerful" can happen in the orgasmic impulses of sex across race and class lines where participants "imagine, if only for a moment, a world transformed, a world so incredibly sexy and hot that the stupid, banal, and costly structures of racism, homophobia, poverty and disease that work to keep us apart become nothing more than dully painful memories from the past."[131] Of course, the pain of memory never will remain in the past, even in a world that is wholly imaginatively transformed; it cannot be separated from pleasure's production. Hartman, describing the incorporation of slaves' pleasures into masters' ends, writes that "it is impossible to separate the use of pleasure as a technique of discipline from pleasure as a figuration of social transformation."[132] Delany's speculations on sex, difference, and power are generative and complex in their capacity to figure pleasure as simultaneously transformative and disciplinary.

Narratives of power and subjection cluster around Korga and Marq's relation of mutual erotic perfection. The excess of pleasure that their mutual objectification allows is enabled by the impossibility of Korga's complete escape from the history of enslavement signaled by the title "Rat" that always remains part of his name, since the power differential between the lovers is an intrinsic part of their statistical erotic perfection. Marq acknowledges this when, as they lie in bed together, he reminds Korga that "if you had lived a more ordinary life on Rhyonon, you wouldn't *be* here."[133] Delany's work consistently demands that readers acknowledge the powerful pleasures that come from erotically inflecting power relationships that would be insupportable in the realm of the political. The figure of Gorgik in the *Nevèrÿon* series, the former slave turned liberator whose pleasure in sexualized master/slave relations enables his revolutionary work and "serves as an irritant to liberal fantasies of the easy transformation of the bonded to free labor" is the most obvious example of this, but Korga and Marq's relation follows the same model.[134]

In the moments of most pleasure Korga and Marq experience together we see that, even within structures of inequality, pleasure may have uses that are perversely transformative. Their sexual pleasure is described as "dizzying" and calls up a wealth of alien metaphors ("the line between my arm and his chest was the crevice of some sunken -wr"), which suggest an excess of joy beyond simple description; in public sexual encounters with others, they attain similar moments of transient bliss.[135] These moments of erotic perfection fulfilled are among those often taken to signify the utopian potential of the heterogeneous, multi-gendered, interspecies sexual acts in which Marq participates. And yet these sexual pleasures differ from the attempted erotic encounters that gave the enslaved Rat Korga some hope of transformative pleasure only because of their mutuality and success, not because of a fundamental difference in the structuring of desire between the contexts of enslavement and emancipation. Unequal power structures produce an eroticism whose fugitive pleasures provide an escape route for people subjected to those structures while they still remain within them. And the futures at which those pleasures hint could build a new world. Or, as we realize when the couple are forced to separate lest Cultural Fugue explode their planet, they could destroy one.

* * *

In the phrase from *Dhalgren* with which I opened this chapter, Delany has Kid say "it is not that I have no future. Rather it fragments on the insubstantial and indistinct ephemera of now."[136] Delany's queer science fictions recognize that living without a future is a commonplace experience. Yet he is committed to crafting and creating futures—it is *not*, after all, that Kid, or Korga, or Marq, have no future. Delany asserts that worlds can and do exist within which those marginalized by their desires will find life not only worth living but filled with pleasure. But his work maintains a critical relationship to the liberal progress narratives embodied by the well-intentioned "It Gets Better" campaign—insisting on the continual presence of racialization, violence, economic inequality, and other material differences that continually fragment the possibilities of futures. Sexual pleasure in his work links the past and present and lets a different future feel conceivable, even when it takes place within structuring limitations—for queer pleasure does not always mean the absence of violence, pain, and negativity.

Speculative fiction's potential role as an initiation into realms of possibility that are articulated by queer theory demonstrates that the two modes of writing link in the life narratives of their readers as well as by means of estrangements and futures in texts. Theory can offer contemporary readers detailed persuasion of the arbitrarily historical nature of sexual, racial and social structures; so can speculative fiction. But stories of estranged futures (and alternative pasts, presents, and other temporalities) can also offer passports for entry into queer worlds whose pleasures may provide fuel for political endeavor in mundane reality—or simply a way to think oneself out of it. Science-fictional, speculative sexual narrative offers worlds of sexual subjectivities that have not, yet, been lived, that misrepresent reality productively enough to queer our concepts of the future. Although Delany has moved away from large-scale science fiction world-building to continue his writing on sexuality and pleasure in other forms, his earlier works' old futures are still new for each reader who chooses to tentatively, joyfully, and transformatively step inside.

Try This at Home

Networked Public Sexual Fantasy

Bodies writhe together, naked, on the screen. Hands reach for bodies, bodies for mouths: men and men, women and women, women and men, gendered configurations not legible in the frame. Music beats out, and the background changes with each cut; we are in a swimming pool, a gym, a living room, on a bed, at a club, under the sun, by candlelight. Sometimes there are two bodies, often there are more. We continue to a point of climax . . . And gasping, sated faces are suddenly in the frame alone, some with a partner in the background, some not. What just happened? What was real and what was fantasy?

The first time Lana and Lilly Wachowski brought this queer future to our screens in their Netflix Original science fiction television series, *Sense8* (2015–2018), there were four bodies participating; by the January 2017 special, there were eight. Viewers familiar with the series will know that the sex is just one example of what can happen between and among the minds of the participants, who are connected as part of a "sensate cluster"—a group of eight people born at the exact same moment, anywhere in the world, whose telepathic link the show proposes as an evolutionary next step for humanity. Whatever one sensate is doing, the others experience, so they can simultaneously be alone and taking part in an orgy. The queer promiscuity of *Sense8*'s premise encourages an extensive reach for its tendrils of erotic connection: one unauthorized YouTube upload of the first sensate sex scene had, as of March 2017, more than 950,000 views.[1]

The scene of sensate sex fascinates me—not just because it is perhaps the queerest representation of a science fiction future yet to have found its way to popular media, but because of the material and speculative histories it evokes. Sensate sex is a potent metaphor, the hybrid progeny of two sometimes-utopian fantasies: the queer world of public sex (where bodies come together, which anyone can join) and the science fiction of intimate technological connectivity (where physical and spatial boundaries lose their meaning). Both are simultaneously real and imagined; both are structured by gendered and racialized exclusions that *Sense8* does not wholly succeed in overcoming. In "Sex in Public," Lauren Berlant and Michael Warner lament that the loss of public sexual spaces to restrictive zoning laws must drive those who used them into "the privatized virtual public of . . . the internet."[2] The digitally mediated connections that danah boyd names "networked publics" provide conduits for sexual world-making that are more than simply replacements for physical sexual activity, however.[3] The techno-erotic metaphors of *Sense8* and my own participation in the digitally mediated sensate clusters of online fan fiction lead me to consider how speculative fictions can enable images and imaginaries of queer sexual possibility to enter into spaces and bodies more often associated with private, domestic, feminized spheres. This section opens up a wormhole connection from the literary science-fictional pleasures I explore in part 2 to the screens and networks that mediate the visual and aural speculations in which part 3 engages. The wormhole passes through Samuel R. Delany's reflections on gay male public sex and into gendered spectatorship on its way to the queer possibilities of intimate media networks that come together around and through speculative fictions of sexual fantasy.

In Delany's 1974 science fiction novel *Dhalgren*, which chapter 4 discusses at greater length, an exchange between the protagonist (Kid) and his sometimes lover (Tak) calls attention to the gendered trouble with public sex. Tak asks Kid: "Show me a place where they tell women to stay out of at night because of all the nasty, evil men lurking there to do nasty, evil things; and you know what you'll find?" Kid responds with a statement of what seems to be obvious: "Queers."[4] It is clear to both of them that queer men's sexual expression in public space is policed through its construction as threatening to normative womanhood—even as the queers themselves are more interested in one another than in anyone of any gender who is just passing through. Delany's nonfiction and fiction alike are full of such spaces, documenting the history and persistence of what José Muñoz describes as the "vast, lost gay lifeworld that was seemingly devastated by the AIDS pandemic."[5] *Dhalgren* invites a shift to their gendered terms; its multi-gendered moments of cruising prefigure movements among sex radicals and queer feminist communities to open up public sex scenes to bodies not assumed to be cisgender and male.[6] But the terms remain in place outside the fiction, as we see in a passage of memoir, published twenty-five years later in *Times Square Red, Times Square Blue*, where Delany describes a visit to one of his regular sexual venues in the company of a woman friend.

Delany's elegiac descriptions of what went on between male viewers at the porn movie theaters of pre-gentrification Times Square have become touchstones of queer social theory. When his friend Ana joins him there, though, eager for a firsthand experience of the world he has described, she fails to perceive the sexual acts taking place in the dark until he carefully points them out. Out of her comfort zone, her eyes are drawn to and dazzled by the heterosexual porn playing on a screen at which Delany "hardly" glances.[7] Afterward, she tells him that she was "scared to death" throughout her time in the theater, though she cannot name a specific source for the fear.[8] Delany understands this discomfort as "fear of the outside that Ana brought within," produced by the narratives of gender that interpellate female bodies in public space as in constant danger of rape.[9] Reflecting on her experience, he writes that he does not "see any reason" why women could not take the same pleasure in the porn theaters that men did, save that to enable sufficient women to "consider such venues as a locus of possible pleasure" would do "unmitigated violence to the West's traditional concept of 'woman.'"[10] Such metaphorical violence would, he believes, "prevent actual violence against women's bodies and minds in the political, material world."[11]

I question whether conceptual and actual violence can so easily be separated. As Juana María Rodríguez reminds us, "The spaces of sexual exploration and expression so common in the narratives of urban gay male sexuality—sex clubs, bathhouses, public bathrooms, rest areas, and parks—are places that can prove deadly to female-bodied people, female-presenting people, and others perceived as physically vulnerable."[12] Misogynistic and transphobic forms of violence not only are realities but, through their centrality to the construction of masculinity, may be more integral to the formation of the porn theater than Delany hopes. Ana's wariness of certain spaces, though engendered by fear, is at least as much a survival strategy as it is a symptom of internalized oppression. Where, then, might she and others like her go to experience the pleasures, the worlds, that Delany found in public sex cultures?

In the porn theater, Ana stared at the screen. And it is that act of staring that I want to explore. For staring can be itself productive of pleasure, desire, and erotic connection. As filmmakers and as trans women who must live with the quotidian dangers of gendered public space, the Wachowski sisters are attentive to erotic operations other than physical contact among sexed/gendered bodies. In the first sensate orgy scene, a woman friend of two male lovers slips a hand into her underwear as she watches her own private piece of the action. She is a figure for the many viewers, watching on Netflix or on YouTube, who become their own network of shared sexual pleasure as they enjoy the scene. And not all those viewers will be content just to watch.

Networks that operate in the speculative realm of fantasy and narrative can, as Warner says, "make possible . . . active participation in collective world making through publics of sex and gender."[13] To say this is not to deny the persistent presence of women and gender nonconforming people in public space, to ignore the class privilege sometimes required to keep one's sexual activity private, or to supersede the urgent work that scholars like Rodríguez and LaMonda Horton-Stallings have recently undertaken of documenting the devalued "intimacies, logics, and politics" in porn, sex work, performance, and other spaces that explicitly enact racialized queer erotics.[14] It is simply to assert that one framework for the exploration and expansion of queer pleasures (which may or may not be accompanied by participation in physically embodied sexual cultures) is in the mode of the speculative, mediated by fictions and screens.

Speculative fictions mediate the ways we relate to, and through, our screens. In 1997, a famous advertisement for the internet, "Anthem," produced a powerful utopian narrative: "People can communicate mind to mind. There is no race. There are no genders. There is no age. There are no infirmities. There are only minds. Utopia? No . . . The internet. Where minds, doors, and lives open up."[15] The idea that structural inequalities of race, gender, and disability could be left behind by abandoning the bodies in which they were supposedly held has been thoroughly discredited; in the harassment-ridden, surveilled, algorithmic internet of the late

2010s, few can imagine that going online means entering a race-neutral, gender-neutral world.[16] Yet the debunking of this problematic idea risks losing what made parts of it appealing, and not just for corporations. *Sense8* suggests that the dream of mind-to-mind communication can be repackaged as a fantasy of sexual embodiment.

Whereas 1990s digital utopias posited an internet of textual connections where inequality would be overcome by the capacity for individuals to recognize one another as the same under the skin, the Wachowskis update the fantasy for the twenty-first-century internet of visual cultures and haptic interfaces. Bodies link without the benefit of visible technology, the characters' consciousnesses interfacing with diverse experiences of gender, race, and location. The show's sex scenes burst forth with the messiness and joy of queer embodiment, and it has been rightly celebrated for its casting of trans actress Jamie Clayton in a trans lead role that neither fetishizes nor desexualizes her gender. The failures of digital-utopian discourse have not disappeared, however, as the series' seemingly liberatory globalized vision fails to confront the contradictions of racism, sexism, and class exploitation that shape its protagonists' lives.[17] This is especially visible in the limited storylines granted to the only African, only black, and only poor sensate, Capheus (played by Aml Ameen in the first season and Toby Onwumere thereafter).[18] Yet it is Capheus who highlights both the limitations and the possibilities of *Sense8*'s network fantasy. At one point, Kala, a well-off Indian sensate, enters Capheus's home in a Nairobi slum and joins him in watching an action movie. Kala looks from the large TV to the rest of the one-room house and wonders why someone with so little would devote so much of his limited budget to media technology—rather than purchasing, say, a comfortable bed. Capheus's answer is that a bed keeps you in the slum, but a screen can take you out. His travels into the worlds of his clustermates are, like his TV viewing, a necessary but always and only speculative pleasure. Their failure to solve the problems of physical and social realities does not mean they are not transformative.

The convergence of digital connection, speculative pleasure, and sexual fantasy in *Sense8* is far from new. In *Queer Latinidad* (2003), Rodríguez describes her experiences of online sex. Insisting that, dominant fantasies to the contrary, she never leaves her body, her gender, or her race behind when she goes online, she writes that an "enchantment lies in the allure of possibilities, new ways to imagine the sensations of a seemingly familiar world."[19] In the chatrooms and private messages of the 1990s internet, she collaboratively performs textual sexual fantasies that contribute to her embodied and theoretical understanding of gender and desire, even as "the carnal reality" she lives in "refuses to be ignored."[20] Written a decade later, Rodríguez's 2014 *Sexual Futures* continues to explore how sexual fantasy makes possible new ways of imagining familiar sensations, through the connection of "intimate corporeal movements" to the "political force of . . . sexual fantasies, political fantasies, and utopian fantasies of futurity, survival, and pleasure."[21] Fantasies of futurity, survival, and pleasure, more and less utopian, are at the heart of parts 2 and 3 of this book, making worlds imaginable along with and despite the violences they sometimes evade and sometimes reproduce. For Rodríguez, as for Capheus, and as for many creators and consumers of speculative fiction, fantasy "functions not as an escape from the real-world materiality of living, breathing bodies, but as a way to conjure and inhabit an alternative world in which other forms of identification and social relations become imaginable."[22]

It is through collective speculation and the possibility of publics that sexual dreams and longings for connection articulate Judith Butler's expansive, political definition of fantasy: "Fantasy is what allows us to imagine ourselves and others otherwise. . . . When it is embodied, it brings the elsewhere home."[23] Science fiction reading provided me, and many other lonely teenage nerds, with elsewheres to imagine; Delany was a powerful gateway into the real world of queer possibility. I have never been to a pre-gentrification Times Square theater, nor have I participated in orgiastic sex with lizard-like sentient aliens.[24] But when I read Delany's words, when I entered his worlds, I felt as if I might someday live in those places. And when I found my way online and read my way through the fiction created in networked counterpublics of queer science fiction fans, I knew I would not travel there alone. Finding fandom online brought imagined elsewheres home; speculative fiction's centrality to my sense of self became part of the way I understood queerness as a set of possibilities that went beyond identification with one of a list of available sexual identities.[25]

It was in 2003 or thereabouts that I first read an article in a feminist magazine about slash fan fiction.[26] The author described a sprawling and diverse network, populated predominantly by women, in which fictional characters, most of whom seemed to be male, were imagined to be having queer sex.[27] I was immediately fascinated and began to search online. It took a few weeks to find the writers, stories, and fandoms that called forth my deepest and most inchoate longings, but soon I was hooked. At the same time, I was reading queer theory as I prepared to begin my graduate studies. The worlds of public sex that I read about in Warner, in Muñoz, and in Delany's nonfiction compelled me powerfully, despite their distance from my everyday experiences. They resonated with my fantasy life in science fiction and in fandom.

Muñoz writes in *Cruising Utopia* about the "ghosts of public sex" that persist for queer readers who engage with narratives of sexual cultures past, recalling the "experience of being 'shocked' by the prison that is heteronormativity" when writers shift between sex cultures and straight realities.[28] He describes what it is like to read explicit sexual descriptions "at some predominantly straight coffee shop near where I live, looking up after the experience, and feeling a similar shock effect."[29] I have spent many hours in coffee shops reading about queer sex, in fiction, theory, and memoir. But those lines in Muñoz call me back most of all to my self of fifteen years ago, when I read my first fan stories in a university computer lab as an undergraduate in Edinburgh. I recall glancing over my shoulder between extended sessions of awed pleasure to see if anyone was looking, feeling both anxious and exhilarated at the thought that they might be, while I downloaded *Harry Potter* fic on floppy disks to take home and reread on my non-networked PC.

By 2016, everything had changed in fan culture, technology, and my own life alike, but I continue to occupy that affective space. I sit on an Amtrak train with thingswithwings's epic *Known Associates*, a 300,000-word slash novel that uses the Marvel Comics mythos of Captain America to meditate on queer and trans historiography, open on my laptop.[30] I glance down the carriage to see if anyone notices the overwhelming pleasure I feel as a scene of sexual and archival connection unfolds, or the tears that come to my eyes when her telling of queer history is too much to bear. Perhaps I send out a tweet or a chat message; perhaps I just savor and memorize the moment. I am in public and in private and in networked collectivity all at once. Straighter worlds intrude, but it barely feels relevant; Muñoz's "shock effect" does not capture the pleasures that sometimes accompany the jar of transition. The shifts in consciousness of the characters on *Sense8* are the best metaphor I have seen for what it feels like.

In 2006, fairly soon after I began to not just lurk but occasionally make myself known in fannish online spaces as a graduate student doing queer cultural studies, I was invited by fan studies scholars Kristina Busse and Robin Reid to participate in organizing an online roundtable of fans who were discussing whether online fandom could or should be understood as a queer female space. The resulting discussions, selections from which were published as a scholarly article, showed that I was not alone in experiencing fandom as a formative erotic experience.[31] T. suggested that "the communal creation and consumption of sexual material, the gleefully masturbatory discussions of source texts and the ideas they inspire" could "constitute sexual acts even when they don't lead any participants to relate directly to each other in erotic ways."[32] Cat told stories of how she and others had moved from shared fantasy into offline sexual and romantic relationships, even while other participants described their offline lives as wholly straight.[33] In our analysis, we described how slash fandom had become "a place where a young urban dyke shares erotic space with a straight married mom in the American heartland, and where women whose identity markers suggest they would find few points of agreement have forged erotic, emotional, and political alliances," and posited that our network might be a site in which "the forms of radical intersubjective contact Samuel R. Delany has called for can take place."[34] That the connections occurred (at least initially) through "sexual fantasy rather than . . . erotic physicality" did not, we insisted, make the pleasures and the connections "less real."[35] These networked publics made space for sexual expression gendered as queer and female as queer theory's classic sex publics have been gay and male.

In his 1988 memoir, *The Motion of Light in Water*, Delany pauses after an extended description of group sex among men at the St. Mark's Bathhouse in 1960s New York to reflect on the value of writing in detail about queer sexual publics. He hopes that "the infiltration of clear and articulate language into the marginal areas of human sexual exploration" might contribute, "once the AIDS crisis is brought under control," to "a sexual revolution to make a laughing stock of any social movement that till now has borne the name," in which "heterosexuals and homosexuals, females and males" alike would find their way to "the marginal areas of human sexual exploration."[36] Delany's sexual revolution remains very, very far from the dominant US public sphere. But it still glimmers brightly, an ongoing unrealized possibility, in both fictive and physical spaces—as much amid fantasies and connections that pass through pixels and screens as in lines of text and touches of bodies.

I framed this section in the first person because I am quite aware that my sense of slash fandom as a queer sexual public is not remotely universal.[37] As Ika Willis writes, the "material, technological, sexual-political, gendered and conceptual landscapes within which slash is written, read and circulated" change rapidly.[38] The shifting structures of digitally mediated sociality might someday prove as dangerous to slash fandom's erotic publics as AIDS-era crackdowns and gentrification have been to the gay sexual publics Delany elegizes, or as the sinister Whispers is to the protagonists of *Sense8*. Whatever shapes they may take at different temporal and spatial locations, though, my own movements through these networks of speculative interchange (sexual and otherwise) have grounded the intellectual labor of this book's project. They have especially made possible the engagements with speculative media futures that I track in part 3.

While part 1 of *Old Futures* pursued the political imaginaries of negative possibility, the work of part 2 has been to articulate how speculative fiction creators build worlds, designing social and material infrastructures that allow for the imaginative engagement of queer possibilities in excess of everyday reality. Fantasy and fandom create ways to live inside those worlds—not as a grand revolution, but as an everyday opening of possibility within diverse personal realities. Part 3 shifts the focus away from the speculative redirection of narrative timelines and toward world-making media practices that produce and reproduce futures out of dominant time. We turn now to speculative queer futures lived on, in, and through screens.

PART III

It's the Future, but It Looks like the Present

Queer Speculations on Media Time

It is the future, but it looks like the present.
—Anne Friedberg describing Lizzie Borden's film
Born in Flames (1983)

All of this has happened before. And all of this will
happen again.
—*Battlestar Galactica* (2003–2009)

5

Queer Deviations from the Future on Screen

Speculative Moving Images

In conversations about my work during the early years of this project, I often heard the response: "You're writing about queer science fiction? But there isn't any queer science fiction, is there?" Having been immersed in literary science fiction's non-normative sexual imaginaries since my early teens, I found such statements perplexing—until I realized that they invariably came from people whose primary familiarity with speculative genres came from film. Science fiction blockbusters have taught us that the future looks like chrome-plated robots, post-catastrophe wildernesses, infinite expanses of space; that it sounds like laser guns, space battles, majestic musical soundtracks; and that there is little queer representation to be found there. Celebrated comics writer Gail Simone asked, in a June 2016 tweet, for examples of LGBTQ relationships in "the films considered the great canon of f/sf"; even the most avid fans who responded to her could not think of any.[1] Film scholars concur. In their 2006 history of American gay and lesbian film, Harry M. Benshoff and Sean Griffin posit a generic "Hollywood science fiction blockbuster" as the least queer genre they can imagine.[2] Patricia MacCormack's 2008 *Cinesexuality* describes the power of cinematic images to create queerly speculative desiring relationships with the spectator, but asserts that queer possibilities are unlikely to be found in science fiction film, which she finds uninterestingly reproductive of "paradigmatic . . . realities."[3] The consensus seems to be that science fiction films present futures that simplistically extrapolate from the present—granting dominant political and economic realities the potential to feel eternal.

Science fiction blockbusters are not as straight as they used to be. Lieutenant Sulu of the Starship Enterprise appeared with a same-sex partner in 2016's *Star Trek Beyond* (directed by Justin Lin); *Mad Max: Fury Road* (directed by George Miller, 2015) cites feminist critiques of patriarchal reproductive politics; and Kate McKinnon stars as the fabulously, if implicitly, queer Holtzmann in the 2016 remake of *Ghostbusters* (directed by Paul Feig).[4] And the visual tropes of science fiction film have long been open to appropriation in the service of what Benshoff and Griffin call "new and varied types of identities and sexualities."[5] Independent filmmakers have connected science fiction to queer politics, histories, and desires through such speculative and fantastical figures as ghosts (*Zero Patience*, directed by John Greyson, 1993), time travel (*The Sticky Fingers of Time*, directed by Hilary Brougher, 1997), or alien invasion (*Liquid Sky*, directed by Slava Tsukerman, 1982).[6] Beyond the use of LGBTQ bodies, perspectives, and politics to extend or divert the implications of existing franchises and tropes, though, there are few examples of what it might mean to envisage a queer future on the big screen. Yet, while the first *Star Wars* trilogy was dominating the box office with its science fantasy of a space age long ago in a galaxy far far away, while Steven Spielberg and Ridley Scott were creating aliens and robots to warm hearts and chill spines, queer filmmakers were developing different practices for speculating futures through image and sound. This chapter focuses on two speculative films whose genealogy in queer screen history is secure although they rarely appear in canons of science fiction media: Derek Jarman's 1978 *Jubilee* and Lizzie Borden's 1983 *Born in Flames*. Each queerly frames the future as a practice of worlding that begins on the screen and extends beyond it.

For reasons that owe much to economic necessity, Jarman's and Borden's images of the future look and feel like the present of their creation. They envision neither technological progress nor grand-scale destruction, but instead depict worlds that move only a little ahead of the possible. "It is the future, but it looks like the present," as Anne Friedberg said about Borden's film in 1985.[7] But whatever they may look like, these old futures are emphatically *not* the present. They teach viewers to inhabit a temporality whose futuristic orientation is marked not by technology but by an alternative mediation and reproduction of political and social life. And the futures they envisage, which look like the respective presents of London in 1977 and New York between 1978 and 1983, have continued to resonate for viewers who approach them from times and spaces the filmmakers did not seek to anticipate.

In screening the future, filmmakers in the twentieth century have taught audiences how to live in it by integrating content and form to represent and showcase technological development in the service of emerging economic possibilities. The first section of this chapter explores how science fiction film's futures on screen have projected temporal lines oriented to the reproduction of capitalism and white supremacy—upward to progress, down to degeneration, on through hetero-reproductivity to futures that preclude the humanity of some. I then turn to ways that *Jubilee* and *Born in Flames* bend, break, and reorient those lines by refusing the visual tropes of genre science fiction while making use of its imaginative methods. Their speculative images have endured not by becoming familiar or marketable but making themselves available for reconfiguration within futures they tried neither to predict nor to promote.

This chapter, the last part of *Old Futures* to be completed, was reconceptualized to center on these films during the political earthquakes of 2016, when old futures marched into the present with stomach-churning rapidity. I found myself urgently compelled by resonances with the present in the films' attention to capitalism, fascism, sexism, racism, homophobia, police brutality, music, art, and media distribution. While science fiction film's visual iconography often provokes nostalgia as it grows more dated, these images thrown forward out of past political imaginaries felt astonishingly current. Watching *Jubilee* brings the present to light as a dystopian future whose polite public face hides deep-seated violence; *Born in Flames* shows us how the politics of revolutionary transformation replicate the problems of the untransformed world through the failure to reckon with them.

Each film also resonates with different elements of the old futures unpacked in the first two parts of this book. *Jubilee* echoes the history of no future in part 1, its vision of a future for queer negativity imbricated with an ambiguous critique of whiteness and of British imperial legacies. *Born in Flames* connects to the queer of color imaginaries of part 2, its expansive opening of possibilities refusing single-issue political logics along with linear temporalities. Both posit futures without reliance on commonplace visual tropes of speculative film, on detailed extrapolative logics of science fiction world-building, or on narrative conventions of storytelling. Their stories and relationships meander and intertwine, opening possibilities without fully resolving them, hinting at relationalities between characters without fully giving them away, and demanding that viewers actively engage in order to make sense of what they are seeing. Screening the future queerly, they seek to reorient and recreate what might be possible, crafting images and sounds that invoke radically different worlds.

Straight Futures and Queer Screens

Many sounds and images of imagined futures have been described in this book's archive of queer speculations. Yet these futures have by and large been *told*: articulated in words. Works of art and media seeking to *show* what imagined futures might look and sound like have appeared only briefly. This book is as literarily focused as it is because, until very recently, written text has been the medium most available for those with limited resources to produce and archive narratives that speculate alternative futures in defiant appropriation of imposed temporalities. Visual and especially moving-image media forms require access to greater resources than the solitude, space, and time required for writing (often difficult enough to come by on their own, as feminist writers from Virginia Woolf to Audre Lorde have reminded us).[8] Circulating often as entertainment and cultural commentary rather than as high art, the old futures from twentieth-century print culture that I have examined nevertheless form something of an avant garde for popular fiction, in which strange and unsettling ideas get extrapolated to their logical and illogical conclusions. Yet visual culture has a reach and range that print fiction lacks, even when—like the two films on which this chapter centers—it may not reach mass audiences.

While written narrative invites abstraction, speculative futures created in non-print media necessarily foreground their materiality. From brush strokes to camera lenses to the timbre of sonic creation, the technologies, economics, and sensory capacities of production are necessarily perceptible in audiovisual content and style. Speculative film creates images that move both literally and figuratively as their creators index and induce the feeling of change, inviting viewers to sit not only with the idea that the future might be different from the present, but with visual, aural, and affective elements of how that future could manifest. Vivian Sobchack writes that science fiction film uses "the magic of design and special effects cinematography to show us things which do not exist," while techno-futurist Brian David Johnson praises "visions of the future so powerful they can last for decades."[9] Science fiction films set forth visual languages for speculative imaginaries; their images shape popular conceptions of the future and thereby influence the future itself. But we should not forget that the futures most films invite us to imagine are structured by the dominant needs of the interests that create and market them. The spectacular logics of the future on screen, whether portraying technological possibility or imagined disaster, connect the imperial and racial temporal logics of the histories I trace in parts 1 and 2 of this book to contemporary media industries and the flows of finance capital.

Visual invocations of technological futures have shaped economic aspects of film since its early days. Georges Méliès's 1902 *Trip to the Moon*, often described as the first science fiction film, launched the genre's visual culture of space colonization. His free-floating fantasia would pave the way for more realist modes of speculation with the development of visual effects technology.[10] Méliès claims in a 1907 talk to have enabled film to "sustain itself" economically, making the form profitable through his "tricks" of nonrealist representation.[11] In a 1915 treatise, the American poet Vachel Lindsay posits film as a technology that can "set before the world a new group of pictures of the future," bringing together art and industry through the new means of representation at their disposal and constructing a "tomorrow . . . rich in forecastings" for the glory and profit of the American nation and of private investors alike.[12] Méliès's embrace of visual novelty and Lindsay's evocation of a "rich" tomorrow both prefigure the speculative economics of the contemporary film industry, where studios produce vastly expensive visual spectacles in the hope that their worth will be recouped many times over in opening weekend ticket sales. The literal "pictures of the future" that science fiction films create, through props and design elements, are key to their profitability—whether through the toy and model market instigated by *Star Wars* (directed by George Lucas, 1977) or through direct and indirect connections to technology industries. The touch screen interfaces of *Minority Report* (directed by Steven Spielberg, 2002), for example, resonant with the gestural interfaces that have since become ubiquitous in smartphone and tablet design, are the most celebrated exemplars of the concept of science fiction prototyping. This method that now has its own corporate sponsors, employing engineers and science fiction writers to speculate profitably on the likelihood that filmmakers' expensive visions of things that do not exist will become advertisements for commodities that might exist soon.[13]

At least as popular as speculative commodities in Hollywood science fiction are visions of the end of the world. Iconic examples are easy to bring to mind, from scenes of terror invading from outer space to the many recent iterations of the zombie apocalypse. In her classic 1965 essay "The Imagination of Disaster," Susan Sontag writes of films like these that in them

> one can participate in the fantasy of living through . . . the destruction of humanity itself. . . . The science fiction film . . . is concerned with the aesthetics of destruction, with the peculiar beauties to be found in wreaking havoc, making a mess. . . . We may, if we are lucky, be treated to a panorama of melting tanks, flying bodies, crashing walls, awesome craters and fissures in the earth, plummeting spacecraft, colorful deadly rays; and to a symphony of screams, weird electronic signals, the noisiest military hardware going, and the leaden tones of the laconic denizens of alien planets and their subjugated earthlings.[14]

In critical and political dystopias, representations of violence and destruction can invite readers to recalibrate their understanding of their present. As I argue in chapter 2, the uncomfortable pleasures of negative imagining—speculating a future that is no future—can both disrupt and reinforce political narratives that rely on hope, progress, and redemption. To view destruction as a spectacle within a popular genre, though, is to invite pleasure in the details of its aesthetics. Sontag understands the panoramas to which we may, "if we are lucky," be treated by science fiction films as invitations to admire the technological expertise it took to create the tanks and spacecraft, to make them melt and plummet. Her articulation of audience enjoyment suggests that for speculators looking to invest in a film that is likely to make good money, images of disaster are a good bet.

Cinematic representations of the end of the world have a pedagogical aspect, teaching viewers which worst-case scenarios to worry about. Sontag argues that the repeated spectacle of ending worlds creates an overall effect of becoming accustomed to destruction, an "apathy" that tempers the "sense of otherness" with the "grossly familiar," placing the viewer in "complicity with the abhorrent."[15] The protagonist will live on, and so will the audience—but even as the technological ingenuity of the spectacle of disaster is admired, so does the disaster itself become familiar, its conditions of possibility perhaps a little less terrifying when they grow recognizable in the everyday world.

Sontag was writing during the Cold War, when nuclear holocaust was a fear that structured the public sphere, though popular narratives of alien invasion and dangerous alterity were also informed by the contexts of decolonization and the African American civil rights movement.[16] Now that global climate change is the likeliest, though far from the only, prospect of catastrophe, the argument that disaster imagery compels greater comfort with the ways in which the world has already ended is even stronger. The 2004 disaster movie *The Day after Tomorrow* (directed by Roland Emmerich), for example, included a scene in which the Statue of Liberty was buffeted by giant waves—an homage, along with the film's poster of the statue encased in ice, to *Planet of the Apes* (directed by Franklin J. Schaffner, 1968), where the statue lies cast down on a beach after the demise of human civilization. Emmerich's sequence invites viewers to enjoy a frisson of terror over the elemental and uncontrollable power of weather, even as the director's capacity to create a realistic image of this event calls forth admiration for a feat of technological prowess that implies even the weather can be controlled. During Hurricane Sandy, which struck the Mid-Atlantic states in 2012, footage of this scene circulated online and was taken for reality: it had become easy to believe that we were living in the future the film had imagined.[17] But the film is not simply portraying climate disaster—it is also contributing to it, given that capitalist economics are the driving force in ongoing ecological catastrophe. *The Day after Tomorrow* cost $125 million to make and made $544,272,402 over the course of its release.[18] Through the carbon impact of those dollars, the complicity of the spectacle with the "abhorrent" it represents becomes literal, embodying the aphorism that it is easier to imagine the end of the world than it is to imagine the end of capitalism.[19]

The clichéd futures of science fiction film are tied to heterosexual time. In its conventional narrative structure, the danger of the end of the world is turned aside through the resolution of a heterosexual family plot: a man and woman (or perhaps a woman and a child, or a man and a child) come together to suggest that they, and the human race as embodied by their progeny, will live on. (In *The Day after Tomorrow*, it is the struggle to reunify a father and son and save the life of the son's wife.) Children, and the possibility of children, allow a future for humanity in its current form to be salvaged from the world's ends. As Rebekah Sheldon writes, "From the vantage of eco-catastrophe . . . the child stands in the place of the species and coordinates its transit into the future."[20] Amid spectacles of disastrous futures, images of hopeful children divert attention from the ongoing realities of violence that continue to curtail the prospect of Hollywood-esque futures for the majority of the world's youth.

Even films whose speculative vision is structured by a critique of capitalist futurity reproduce this image. The 2013 film *Snowpiercer* (directed by Bong Joon-Ho) envisages a dark, satiric post-apocalypse in which violent conflict erupts between rich and poor survivors of a climate disaster that has destroyed all life save that on their perpetually-in-motion train. Yet it ends with a heterosexual origin story, albeit one whose plausibility is wearing thin. The film's Adam and Eve, two racialized children who do not embody the iconic white child of conservative political futurism, sit on the snowy mountainside of a new world, standing for humanity's last chance not to conquer the universe but simply to exist. Though the film's director has stated that the children's role is to "spread the human race," their chances of living are close to zero, with no institutions, no human or animal allies, and nothing but the naked hope of heterosexual reproductivity itself to sustain them.[21] It cannot possibly be enough. And it indexes the limits of even critical versions of the future as mediated by the visual and narrative conventions of science fiction film. What, then, might it take to create a screen future that deviates from these logics?

Just as science fiction film's futures have been straight, it seems, queer film has not been well suited to the futuristic. Much scholarly conversation about queer cinematic temporalities has taken place under the rubric of New Queer Cinema, the name given by B. Ruby Rich to identify an upsurge in queer filmmaking that took place alongside the academic emergence of queer theory in the early 1990s and led several queer filmmakers to mainstream success. Rich finds a common thread of New

Queer Cinema to be its focus on historiography: "The queer present negotiates with the past, knowing full well the queer future is at stake."[22] But, though Rich names the "girls" of New Queer Cinema as "alchemists" (the "boys" are "archaeologists") in their speculative orientation to lesbian histories, neither the 1990s films with which the movement is associated nor the ones it inspired have created many narratives devoted to imagining what that queer future might look like.[23] More typical is what Dustin Bradley Goltz identifies as a "queer temporal camp" in Gregg Araki's films of the 1990s. Araki, Goltz writes, punctures "the ongoing punch line of the totalizing and violent joke of heteronormative time" by offering a "temporal intervention through and against the queer foreclosures of straight time's momentum" that "reverses heteronormativity's sole claim to the future by declaring 'Ha! No future for *you.*'"[24] Queer temporality in film here means abandoning the future to its overdetermination by heteronormative reproduction and Hollywood science fiction cliché, approaching it through camp mockery if it must be approached at all.

Yet among the films that Rich names as key precursors to New Queer Cinema are two that make use of the future not as a point to gesture toward or evade but as a setting.[25] In divergent ways that intersect at many points, *Jubilee* and *Born in Flames* manifest visions of how the future could look, sound, and feel in ways that simultaneously refuse the totalizing violence of straight time and insist that the future is not solely heteronormativity's domain. If dominant science fiction film teaches us to live in the future, to become so familiar with prevailing discourses of technological and political temporality that they come to feel inevitable, one use for a queer screen future can be to viscerally and visually remind its viewers of continuities between past and present rebellions and refusals of temporal common sense.

No Future in England's Dreaming

No future no future no future for you
No future no future no future for me
No future no future no future for you
No future no future for me.
—The Sex Pistols, "God Save the Queen"

Near the end of Jarman's 1978 film *Jubilee*, the heteronormative future explodes. Crabs (Little Nell), the cheeriest and most sexually voracious of the film's coterie of protagonists, is in bed with an attractive blond policeman (Barney James) following a scene of mutual seduction that takes place while they both disrobe in an empty laundromat. After sex, the camera lingers on their faces, close-up and half-shadowed on the pillow, while Crabs languorously suggests that they get married and settle down together. The cop agrees, adding, "We could have kids." Crabs encourages: "Lots of boys like you." Before the fantasy can get too far advanced, the cop pauses to wonder what Crabs does for a living; she replies that she is an actress. Then the doorbell rings and the cop goes off to answer it. At the door are two women in overalls—Mad (Toyah Willcox) and Bod (Jenny Runacre), flatmates and co-conspirators with Crabs and instigators of many violent acts in the film—who have arrived on a motorbike, carrying a firebomb made from a champagne bottle. They light the fuse and throw the bottle hard into the doorway of the red-brick suburban home, yelling "NO FUTURE!" as it explodes.

A cry of "No future!" followed by the literal burning down of straight sex and hetero-familial hopes and dreams: it is difficult to imagine a more on-the-nose depiction of Lee Edelman's 2004 demand that queerness express itself in opposition to the politics of futurity.[26] A more immediate reference is the refrain from the Sex Pistols' 1977 "God Save the Queen," released the year *Jubilee* was filmed. In fact, Tavia Nyong'o describes the film as a "historically and theatrically erudite iteration" of the song.[27] The Sex Pistols' "no future" entered queer scholarly debates about futurity at a 2006 roundtable, where Jack Halberstam challenged Edelman for his lack of attention to the song with whose lyrics his book shares its title.[28] Edelman replied that punk's "no future," unlike the queer anti-futurism that unfolds in his work, is not so much anti-futurity as generational rebellion. As working-class rock upstarts declaiming "no future *for you*" to the conventional society that would get a thrill out of buying their records, the Sex Pistols offer just one more cycle of an endlessly repeated challenge to literal or symbolic parents, the basis of reformist politics.[29]

That the last line of the chorus is "no future for me" suggests that lyricist John Lydon might not be wholly on board with Edelman's interpretation. But in Lydon's snarl and *Jubilee*'s explosion alike, the cry of "no future" is performative. In symbolically casting out one future, it makes space for another, which may or may not belong to the person who speaks the words. In his 1992 book about the Sex Pistols, Jon Savage quotes a newspaper's remark that "simply by stating 'No Future' the Sex Pistols are creating one."[30] He associates the Pistols' future with English radical history and the "millennial" politics of the seventeenth-century Diggers and Ranters, placing their rebellious utterance into a history of "utopian heresies."[31] Savage hears "no future" as an ongoing refusal echoing down the generations. *Jubilee* builds a world from that refusal as it invokes, creates, and burns down the future of English national and British imperial imaginaries.[32]

In the late 1970s, Jarman—the gay artist and filmmaker whose merging of queer politics, formal experimentation, and English heritage would bring him international renown by the time of his death from AIDS-related illness in 1994—had just experienced modest success with his first film, the sexually explicit gay historical fantasy *Sebastiane* (1976). *Jubilee*, its successor, began as a super-8 capture of Jordan—style doyenne of London's punk scene—doing ballet.[33] The film, operating on a minimal budget, was shot with a cast of friends in and near Jarman's warehouse studio, in a space that would soon be rendered unrecognizable by waves of regeneration and gentrification. Savage writes that *Jubilee* is one of the few places where you can now see what London looked like in 1977.[34]

In the lexicon of science fiction cinema, 1977 is most associated with *Star Wars'* initiation of a new age in global box office success for Hollywood genre film.[35] In British cultural memory, it resonates with two key events: the silver jubilee (twenty-fifth anniversary) of Queen Elizabeth II's coronation, after which *Jubilee* is ironically named, and the surging rebellion of punk's youth culture, which it documents. Using few science fiction conventions to orient viewers to what we are seeing, the film exacerbates punk's *no future* to underscore the violence of the history celebrated and preserved by the national jubilee. In bucolic interludes that contrast seashore and garden to the urban wasteland of most scenes, Queen Elizabeth I wanders from the past, transported across time through the unexplained magic of her mystical courtier, John Dee. Her impassive gaze links the inception of England's imperial glories with a London crumbling after their end. The punk protagonists revel in the violence the queen mourns, spreading mayhem before they sell out their style to the corporate media empire of mogul Borgia Ginz and retire to a neofascist state in the rural English county of Dorset. In a planned sequel for which Jarman wrote a script in 1981, Ginz purchases all of England and rules it as a dictator, while a few musicians and artists remain in rebellion.[36]

To watch *Jubilee* now is to experience the 1970s London punk scene shorn of the overwhelmingly heteromasculine image that looms large in mainstream cultural memory—though not of that same scene's whiteness.[37] The characters whose actions the film's loose narrative tracks embody right-wing imagery of punk as a violent threat to national order, security, and comfort, offered up for the pleasure of those who were participating and to stoke the ire of those who disapproved. In contrast to the media spectacle of punk embodied by the Sex Pistols, it is mostly women who mete out destruction, especially Toyah Wilcox's pyromaniac Mad and Jenny Runacre's calculating Bod (who kills Queen Elizabeth II and steals her crown). The film was not particularly well received by the subculture it depicted. Vivienne Westwood, whose Chelsea clothing store Sex (also called Seditionaries) was the ground zero of London punk style, responded with a famous "open T shirt" that castigated Jarman's "homosexual" interpretation of the punk milieu: "You pointed your nose in the right direction then you wanked."[38] Westwood's critique of *Jubilee* for its art school snobbery takes aim at the film's insistence on aesthetically speculating about rather than representing a "reality" of the punk scene; she tells Jarman: "I am not interested in however interestingly you say nothing."[39] Evidently the film was too queerly literal in its affirmation of the references to sex between men with which the term "punk" originated, without being sufficiently affirmative of the London punk world itself.[40]

About the less than thrilled reactions to the first screening, Jarman writes: "For an audience who expected a punk music film, full of 'anarchy' and laughs at the end of the King's Road, it was difficult to swallow. They wanted action, not analysis."[41] What Westwood saw as masturbatorily "saying nothing," Jarman saw as analysis—crafting an even more uncomfortable vision from the least comfortable elements of punk politics and performance. Jim Ellis describes Jarman as having been "disappointed that the political critique offered by the film was overlooked in the largely negative reviews" and thinks that this may have been "because of the degree to which it [the film] embodied the anarchic, unpredictable, and hence uncomfortable nature of punk performance rather than the reassuring certainties of narrative cinema."[42] Yet, even as the film takes up certain performative aspects of punk, it also refuses to celebrate subcultural anarchy. *Jubilee* displays punk as "unglamorized" violence rather than noble rebellion, and highlights its complicity with the worst of English politics.[43]

The political landscape in which the film intervenes was a volatile one. Savage describes the mood of London in the late 1970s as "apocalyptic."[44] A familiar "political and social order seemed to be breaking up" now that "Britain was no longer a world power . . . merely a small island held in thrall by the USA."[45] Even as movements mobilized in support of decolonization, feminism, and labor unions, the affective landscape of dominant English culture created a sense of "wallowing in a not unpleasurable masochism and lashing out at scapegoats."[46] The scapegoats who suffered most from post-imperial British masochism were immigrants of color from formerly colonized countries. The neo-Nazi National Front whipped up racial tensions at marches, local elections, and punk gigs; police turned on antifascist protestors in the black neighborhood of Lewisham and at the 1976 Notting Hill Carnival.[47] Margaret Thatcher had just risen to leadership of the Conservative Party and her right-wing nationalist platform looked set to win power over a left political establishment in some disarray after conflicts between unions and Harold Wilson's Labour government. *Jubilee*'s chaotic narrative projected the moment of transition at which it was created into a future Jarman could later accurately describe as having been "prophetic."[48] Soon after *Jubilee*'s release, public sector strikes led Londoners to a visceral experience of what a breakdown in state services and organization might be like, with uncollected refuse mounting in the streets.[49] In 1979, Thatcher initiated nineteen years of Conservative government with an election campaign that "carefully synthesized the fears of the middle and working classes."[50] And the construction of British whiteness through "wallowing" in the aftermath of empire and "lashing out at scapegoats" was not about to lessen. Jarman wrote that "a bitter chill blows through" *Jubilee*.[51] That chill may be felt more acutely years after the film's release.

For many speculating about possible futures from the vantage of Britain in the 1970s, the dangers of state control were paramount.[52] Jarman's apocalyptic future takes the opposite form, envisioning an absolute withdrawal of state intervention and organization: "law and order has [sic] been abolished," leaving the violent impulses of both individuals and corporations to rampage unchecked. Old ladies in a bingo parlor lament the necessity of carrying a weapon in order to stay alive, but also appear sympathetic to the economic causes of violence's ubiquity, asking, "What do you expect with millions unemployed?" Meanwhile, the police have become independent militia, happily watching groups of men and woman smash up a car and torture a woman but stepping in with their own weapons raised at the first flirtatious glance from a queer man.

The film's ending challenges any viewer's desire to celebrate punk's anti-establishment impulses by aligning their rebellious violence directly with the violence that maintains the dominant economic and racial social order. For the punks become part of Borgia Ginz's media empire, retreating to a heartland from which "blacks, Jews, and homosexuals" are turned back at the border. Ginz is played by the queer blind performer Orlando, who gives a manically comic, unpredictable edge to the sinister figure's declarations that "they all sign up in the end." He owns every media institution as well as the county of Dorset, his annexation of cultural and political life enabled by quiescent suburban audiences who continue to watch TV while the world falls apart. Having attained dictatorial power through the force of money alone, Ginz explains that he has "bought them all": the "CIA, FBI, BBC, ITV, and C of E," making government, media, and religion as well as national distinctions equivalent and irrelevant in the face of purchase power. He has even purchased Buckingham Palace and turned it into a recording studio, transforming the site of imperial power into a home for the new kind of empire to which most of the rebels will have signed themselves up by the film's end. This narrative of selling out is so familiar that it is difficult to recall that *Jubilee* was scripted before punk's explosion into a mainstream market and before Dick Hebdige articulated the process of subcultural incorporation for the then-emerging academic field of cultural studies.[53] What we are seeing is not so much the end of the world as a prophesy of the neoliberal policies Thatcher would enact in the next decades: the coexistence of a cozy conservatism with post-industrial landscapes in which the day to day life, media consumption, and economic practices of middle-class suburban voters would be not only irrelevant but unimaginable.

I have been describing *Jubilee* as a future that looks like the present because it depicts a future world without any science fiction trappings of visual or technological futurity. Yet the film does engage in speculative world-building, crafting images that unpack the alternate future history it portrays.[54] Props, costumes, and set design are the main tools with which the world is built, with Amyl Nitrate (Jordan) as its primary on-screen architect. In the film's only explanatory moment, she creates her own textbook in a handwritten journal that visually resembles both a zine and a school exercise notepad, detailing English history in red felt pen with accompanying doodles (figure 5.1). Pyromaniac Mad soon snatches and burns the book, refusing the notion that anything about *Jubilee's* imaginary could pertain to a linear timeline. But Amyl's theory of history nevertheless provides a frame through which we can understand the film as a work of politicized speculation. Amyl tells English history as a story of violence, beginning with the Norman Conquest and expanding out to an imperial project of "fight[ing] the rest of the world." She goes on to narrate empire's end:

> One day when there was no one left to fight, it dawned on them that the real enemy was at home, and they should fight among themselves. Having grown greedy on the booty they had looted from the world they decided to fight with money, but by now this was made with paper and was pretty worthless, so when they discovered this they took to fighting with guns. The rest of the world sighed a sigh of relief to be rid of them and got on with their own business, and England slowly sunk into the sea.

Jubilee is England sunk under the sea, the "rest of the world" having vacated post-imperial England and left it to get on with its work of self-destruction. Amyl's DIY pedagogy situates the film as showing what happens when a metropole turns on itself.

Next to Amyl as she writes in her notebook sits a globe on which she has been mapping her worldview. Huge patches of black cover land masses, as the words "negative world status," "obsolete," and "no reason for existance [sic]" sprawl in white across continents. The image in

Figures 5.1 and 5.2. DIY speculations on imperial history and geography: Amyl's punk world-building in *Jubilee* (directed by Derek Jarman, 1978).

figure 5.2 shows the Soviet Union, Korea, Japan, Vietnam, and Egypt blacked out; as the globe spins, we also see that all of Europe (including Ireland) and all of North America are also obscured, with the exception of the British mainland. The globe mocks maps on which a British Empire colored pink could reassure its leaders-to-be and subjects alike that the sun would never set on its power, even as it enacts a violent erasure of realities beyond their usefulness in the view of the globe's maker. The contrast between "England . . . sunk into the sea" and the imperial presumption inherent in naming the "negative status" of half the world defines a contradictory politics that *Jubilee* continually evokes, rebelling against and reproducing dominant orders simultaneously. Jarman, the son of a military family, wrote of his privileged English childhood as having been shaped by a "feeling of guilt" that he and his were "living at the expense of others, of the planet itself."[55] *Jubilee*'s inchoate negation of empire seems rooted in a desire to expiate that guilt without much hope that something better could emerge in its place.

Zooming out from Amyl and her desk, the camera reveals the flat where the punks live to be likewise obsessed with the end of empire. At first glance, figures 5.3 and 5.4 might appear to show a riot of memorabilia entirely appropriate to the jubilee year. Walls covered in newspaper clippings are accompanied by Second World War posters, a statue of Britannia, a Winston Churchill mug; Union Jacks are draped and hung on a wall along with red, white, and blue bunting. These objects' conservative connotations are belied by the appearance of the people who inhabit the flat, however—queerly naked Angel (Ian Charleson), just up from the bed on which he has been sleeping with his brother, and Amyl Nitrate with her spiked hair and geometric makeup atop twin set and pearls. The writing on the walls spells out the situation. Graffiti, associated with the unruliness of punk, is a constant backdrop in *Jubilee*, and we can rarely make out full sentences. In figure 5.4, though, we see a fraction of a slogan: "Empire is no more and so the lion shall cease." The origin of this line is William Blake, and it appears in two of his works: "The Marriage of Heaven and Hell" (1790) and "America: A Prophesy" (1793). Blake's visionary critique came at a moment of British imperial and industrial expansion, whose brutality he opposed; the poet and artist has been a mainstay of an English radical literary tradition in which Jarman can also be situated.[56] Blake's words on the wall position *Jubilee*

Figures 5.3 and 5.4. Memorabilia after empire: Amyl Nitrate's desk and speculative punk interior design in *Jubilee* (directed by Derek Jarman, 1978).

as a reckoning with empire's real and imagined ends even as imperial images and symbols multiply, suggesting that the inhabitants of the flat are the ones keeping its memory alive.

Amyl, whose mantra is "Make your desires reality," occupies *Jubilee*'s post-imperial contradictions fully as she moves from chronicler to maker of history. By the end of the film, she performs as the embodiment of the lost British Empire in order to sell its image to former subjects whose consumption is now mobilized to maintain Borgia Ginz's media empire. Dressed in a sequined Union Jack dress and lip-syncing "Rule Britannia" for an audience of TV cameras, she goose-steps across the stage in lime green stockings and tall heels, wielding a plastic trident and a neon pink fan (figure 5.5). Having laid out her clear-sighted vision of history as the ending of imperial teleology, she takes the national kitsch of the punks' apartment to its logical conclusion, replaying history as for-profit farce by roleplaying a Britain that consumes and resells its own image to an ever-decreasing audience of buyers.

Jordan's ironic performance in imperial drag, one of the most memorable scenes in *Jubilee*, was a powerful satire on the patriotic fervor of 1977's Royal Jubilee. Decades later, though, with punk one of England's most popular heritage exports, Jarman's farce would repeat itself as history. In the 1990s, Spice Girl Geri Halliwell became famous for performing in a Union Jack minidress almost identical to Jordan's attire in *Jubilee* (figure 5.6). Borgia Ginz's declamation of "they all sign up in the end" came even more true than Jarman imagined.

Jubilee's ambiguous critique of empire highlights punk's relationship with white supremacy. Jayna Brown writes that punk was "primarily identified as the voice of white working class lads from the East London estates and the West London squats," the same demographic whose violent impulses the National Front sought to turn against the immigrant communities who had been invited to the United Kingdom from its former colonies to work after the Second World War.[57] Many white punks pursued political solidarity and cultural collaboration with black British people and subcultures, but those efforts were somewhat undermined by the high-profile visibility of racist symbols like swastikas worn for shock value.[58] Punk tended to be a musical genre from which the African American origins of rock had been whitewashed away, leaving it available for and vulnerable to white supremacist appropriation.[59] Yet it

Figures 5.5 and 5.6. Amyl Nitrate dresses as the Union Jack in *Jubilee* (directed by Derek Jarman, 1978); former Spice Girl Geri Halliwell wears a similar outfit to perform in 2008 (photograph taken on February 4, 2008 by emutree and licensed under Creative Commons).

was also a site where, as Brown's "woman of color's intervention into the white male history of punk" demonstrates, Poly Styrene, "the daughter of a Somali father and a white English mother from Brixton by way of Bromley," could sing "a high-pitched, driving, dystopian critique of capitalist consumption and sexist violence."[60]

Jubilee makes no space for a figure like Poly Styrene. Amyl's lessons about the British Empire—both its asserted ending and its marketability—assume and assert that the white English encounter racial and ethnic others only overseas or through the media, never in daily life. Another page from her notebook provides one of the film's two explicit mentions of race: "From the dull blank suburbs a generation of people who have grown up, not with book [sic] and not with the cinema but with the TV. Because of television we know about social problems, political problems, and racial problems." Television is a demon in Jarman's imaginary, the conduit through which Borgia Ginz has risen to power. To have "racial problems" appear only through this lens makes them seem imposed and irrelevant even without the presumptive whiteness of Amyl's "we." Amyl and her friends ironically embody the "social" and "political" problems suburbanites see on TV—but race, with or without "problems," is present only as a structuring absence, with every body visible on screen at least appearing to be white and English. Yet the London Jarman was representing is the origin of televisual representations of "racial problems." It is from there that broadcasts travel to the "dull blank suburbs" from which Amyl and the other real and fictional punks appear to hail.

The second mention of race in the film comes at the border checkpoint for Borgia Ginz's Dorset police state, from which "blacks, Jews, and homosexuals" are excluded. As she enters, safely accepted as none of the suspect groups, Amyl remarks blandly: "It used to just be the color of your skin." Racism slips into the past, seemingly normalized when antisemitism and homophobia appear alongside it. Jarman makes a similar comment in a memoir published in 1987 with reference to the virulent state-sponsored homophobia of Thatcher's government. He writes that the "sinister times" of the 1980s feel "very different from those far-off days when Enoch Powell's rivers-of-blood speech was so vilified."[61] Powell was a Conservative Member of Parliament whose famous 1968 speech argued that for Britain to allow immigration was tantamount to "watching a nation busily engaged in heaping up its own funeral pyre."[62] He lost his ministerial position for his inflammatory rhetoric. Nevertheless, to dismiss his ideas as "vilified" elides their very real impact. Such nationalist discourse was foundational to right wing power in the "sinister times" of the 1980s that Jarman predicted in *Jubilee* and critiqued in later work. Gilroy writes that Powell's ideas permeated Thatcherism by "making 'race' and nation the framework for a rhetoric of order through which modern conservatism could voice populist protest against Britain's post-imperial plight."[63]

In 2016, after the devastating triumph of anti-immigrant rhetoric that manifested in the United Kingdom's EU referendum result, I looked up Powell's speech on YouTube and found an avalanche of comments stating that he had been proven right.[64] The calls for immediate mass deportations used language that seemed entirely appropriate to Borgia Ginz's Dorset. Ironically, state support for the homophobia that affected Jarman more powerfully and personally than Powell's racism has dissipated in comparison.[65] *Jubilee*'s vision of an immigrant-free Britain eating itself in a frenzy of violence, capital, and kitsch began to feel like a poisonous warning of what post-Brexit England could become. Indeed, Savage tweeted in June 2016 that the result of the Brexit referendum left him feeling "like [he] did in 1976/77," calling up the relevance of this old future for a new present.[66] Hovering on the edge between critiquing and reproducing white English supremacy, the nihilism and violence of the film provide an example of what an England cleansed of both immigrants and the exploitation of former imperial subsidiaries would potentially look like. It looks, apparently, like an array of punks and capitalists enjoying cocktails on their sofa alongside an aged version of Hitler. Britishness after empire, corporate media, fascist politics, and the potentiality of punk become equivalent prospects in this queer and brutal possibility that the present seems in danger of approaching.

Jarman writes that "in *Jubilee* all the positives are negated, turned on their heads."[67] Yet his comments about the film also insist that its negativity should not be viewed as a dismissal of art or political action. In response to an assertion that his films contain "very little hope," his reply is that "the activity is the hope," for "if I were negative, I would have stopped, committed suicide."[68] The activity of hope is most visible in *Jubilee* through the scene of queer negativity with which I opened my discussion of the film. In fact, the scene with "no future" and a firebomb opens up the film's only escape route from its inexorable slide toward Borgia Ginz's Dorset—a route that feels all the more important when Dorset lurches ever closer to reality.

The "no future" firebomb is the only act of violence in the film from which much ethical, moral, or political meaning can be extracted. The film is full of murders—including one of Crabs's sexual partners, punished for premature ejaculation, and (in the most difficult-to-stomach scene in the film) a glamorous gender-nonconforming rock star (Jayne County) whose place at the top of the charts will be taken by Amyl. The bombing, though, is a direct reprisal for the police murder of two queer male characters: the incestuous brother lovers Sphinx (Karl Johnson) and Angel, who are in a triad relationship with a woman artist, Viv (Linda Spurrier). A few scenes earlier, the cop has shot the brothers, flying off the handle after one of them has made a flirtatious comment. Viv witnesses the death of her lovers and rushes off in shock to the punks' flat, where she is urged by Mad and Bod not to cry, but to help make a "firebomb instead." We as viewers are primed for retribution, and a brief scene of heteronormative hope is unlikely to convince us otherwise—especially after we see Crabs naively commenting that the blood on the cop's shirt looks terribly artistic. The firebomb satisfies.

Crabs survives the bombing; we see her in Borgia Ginz's car, cheerily entering fascist Dorset, in later scenes. But Viv disappears after this moment. On one level, this is one more example of the film's negativity. Just as we think some kind of justice might be being done, the murderer and lover of murderers is given safety while the righteous and wronged individual vanishes off the screen. Yet we might also perceive Viv's disappearance, her absence from Hitler's living room at the film's end, as an escape—a gesture toward some queerer possibility than the dead end of claustrophobic rural English nationalism.

Viv stands for such a possibility throughout *Jubilee*. Parallel to the main strands of the film, her scenes with Angel and Sphinx are distinct in tone and palette, her apartment's blank walls signaling calm amid chaos and violence.[69] In her one monologue, she situates herself amid futures and worlds different from the ones the film portrays. She names herself a "prophetic" artist, perhaps much like Jarman himself, and describes artists as a life force, driven "into corners" by "the people who control the world." "Our only hope," she says, speaking less to Angel and Sphinx and more to the viewers who might be turning to her as a respite from the chaos of the film or the world, "is to recreate ourselves as artists, or anarchists if you like, and liberate the energy for all." And so her absence from the art-less media empire with which the film finishes suggests that there is hope for England yet. Behind, within, around, or through Jarman's aggressive foreclosure of positive futures, another universe might be lurking. Another future might be possible: one not limited by the constraints of English whiteness, which lock *Jubilee* into its struggle with the empty future of nation and empire. When fascist Dorset grows too much, we can imagine Viv hiding out, planning to liberate the energy of the exploding firebomb and transform "no future" into new possibility.

It Looks like the Past, but It Feels like the Future

In Lizzie Borden's 1983 film *Born in Flames*, such creative, inchoate possibilities for transformation are front and center. Created amid what Lucas Hilderbrand calls the "nothing-to-lose cultural formations" of New York City prior to the gentrification of the 1980s, the film takes place "ten years after" a socialist revolution whose date is not specified.[70] *Born in Flames* and *Jubilee* have rarely been placed in conversation, but the films have many commonalities; Jon Davies calls *Jubilee* "an all-White, dystopian *Born in Flames*," a description I find compelling.[71] The films share a focus on violence, a profound suspicion of media industries, and an imbrication with punk art and music scenes. Each film takes a promise of futurity as progress and turns it on its head. *Jubilee* responds to the depressing present, oppressive past, and unpromising future of the Queen's Jubilee by charting a devastatingly negative tomorrow, completing the exclusionary work of empire by eliding the presence of the colonized even as it leaves open a small radical space for the potentiality of art. *Born in Flames* also highlights the exclusions of a dominant temporality, but it targets not the pressing political oppression of its moment but rather the limitations of leftist movements that default to straight masculinity. Setting its action in a proclaimed social-democratic society of a sort that activists in the 1980s and the 2010s alike have longed desperately for the United States to approach, *Born in Flames* insists that a revolution achieved by single-issue class struggle can still look like oppressive stasis when it is approached through an emerging collective consciousness led by queer women of color. The film has inspired a generation of feminist and queer filmmakers, from the performative political interventions of Eric Stanley and Chris Vargas's 2006 *Homotopia* and 2012 *Criminal Queers*, to Wu Tsang's 2012 queer of color documentary *Wildness*, to Jamie Babbit's 2007 feminist comedy *Itty Bitty Titty Committee*.[72]

Borden completed *Born in Flames* after several years spent filming in multiple communities of radical, lesbian, and feminist women in New York. Most actors who took part were not industry professionals (although Kathryn Bigelow, who would later become the first woman director to win an Academy Award, appears and is converted from state-sponsored intellectual to revolutionary over the course of the film). Much of the setting is simply where people happened to be, the dialogue drawn from conversations they were already having in their organizing, socializing, and creative work. Borden described the film as having been "born on the editing table," from footage whose final shape emerged from

Figure 5.7. *Born in Flames* (directed by Lizzie Borden, 1983) invites us into the future.

factors that included availability of actors, continuity of appearances over five years, and many other elements, none of which included a formal script.[73]

The closest character the film has to a protagonist, Adelaide Norris (Jeanne Satterfield) is the black lesbian leader of the Women's Army, a revolutionary organization that challenges white heteropatriarchal capital in the guise of democratic socialism while also organizing support services for working-class women. She decides to take up arms for the cause and travels to Western Sahara to acquire them from women revolutionaries there—a decision that leads to her imprisonment and death, which in turn inspires the Women's Army to rise up and form a coalition with other women's groups. Adelaide is mentored toward her revolutionary decision-making by a participant in the founding of the socialist revolution who is disillusioned at what it has become: black feminist revolutionary lawyer Zella Wylie, played by black feminist revolutionary lawyer Florynce Kennedy. Much of the film is taken up with meetings and discussions in which different feminist contingents argue, debate, and plan. Meanwhile, two DJs give the film its pirate radio soundtrack: white punk Isabel (played by Adele Bertei, a mainstay of the New York City punk scene at the time) and the eponymous Honey (Borden's partner at the time), a queer black woman whose image created the film's iconic poster.

Borden describes the film as agit prop, always oriented toward the world-making power of art as activism.[74] An early title of the film had been *The Guerillas*, after Monique Wittig's *Les Guérillères*, the influential 1969 work of French poetic speculation that imagined a world of women at war with patriarchy. The setting was the future because Borden observed women's issues as always being put off until then. If dominant left discourse assumes that women can become full people only after the revolution has been otherwise completed, or at least set well under way, then a narrative that assumes women's personhood and moves into complex politics from there can only begin in the future. A future where we begin signifies not the end point of a timeline that could be mapped from the present or past, but rather a demand to overleap constraints of temporal convention. The film's only concession to explanatory cause and effect is one caption in the title sequence, where the words "ten years after the social-democratic war of liberation" appear superimposed on a TV set featuring a blurry downtown New York scene (figure 5.3). The film is not interested in the circumstances of the "social democratic war," only the incompleteness of the progress it supposedly signified—an incompleteness we can detect from the absence of signifiers of futurity in the image on which the text is superimposed.

Beginning in the future in this way, the film becomes unmoored from its historical moment. When I have assigned *Born in Flames* to advanced undergraduates in feminist and queer studies, many have been astonished to discover, *after* viewing the film, that it is a speculative work. Some have read it as documentary, assuming the references to revolution were factual histories for which they lacked context; others have perceived fiction, but imagined that it tells a story far closer to the present than the 1980s. These temporal displacements would be easy to dismiss as inattentive viewing or inadequate knowledge of recent history, but they are also emblematic of the film's power as a speculative prototype for a queer feminist political future that refuses to be pinned down.

Borden discussed her film in early interviews as a work of "science fiction," but few critics have taken that delineation seriously.[75] The film has not entered the canon of texts beloved by the forty-year tradition of feminist science fiction theory and criticism, though in the 1980s it helped inspire L. Timmel Duchamp to write her majestic five-volume feminist science fiction meditation on the process of revolutionary change, *The Marq'ssan Cycle*.[76] *Born in Flames* incorporates little of the visual language of science fiction cinema: there are no special effects showing us things that do not yet exist. It does not even offer the artistic spectacle that Jarman's design, props, and costuming provide. Instead, the film overlays queer feminist speculation onto the streets, subways, apartments, kitchen tables, and U-Haul parking lots of the world its cast and crew inhabited.

For some spectators, science fiction is not a relevant category for viewing the film at all. Hilderbrand argues that it is named as such only because of an "impoverishment of ways to understand a work of sociopolitical fantasy" among critics and theorists.[77] Yet for Vivian Sobchack, whose 1987 book *Screening Space* shaped genre studies of science fiction film, the socio-political fantasy of *Born in Flames* is itself a challenge to impoverished understandings of science fiction. Sobchack lauds the film as a "new mode of representation for the SF film," which does not "regress to the past," "nostalgize," or "complacently accept the present as the only place to live."[78] While dominant science fiction film's intimacy with multinational capital leads Sobchack to critique the ways that it "either nostalgically locates the future in an imagined past and thus articulates it as 'over,' or . . . complacently locates the future in the present, celebrating it as 'here' and 'now,'" *Born in Flames* emerges as proof that "the science fiction film still has a future."[79] Though they come to opposing conclusions on its genre, Hilderbrand and Sobchack both identify *Born in Flames* as opening a novel relationship to the future as a site of political struggle and possibility. Its socio-political fantasy operates neither through literary science fiction's logic of extrapolation nor through cinematic science fiction's modality of spectacle, but by affectively embedding viewers in the feeling of what it might be like to live in a future speculated from the multiple marginal subjectivities of feminist coalition politics.[80]

To create coherence from footage gathered across multiple times and places, *Born in Flames* connects images and characters through music rather than scripted narrative. The sonic connective tissue of the film holds open the possibility of contradictory interpretations for any given sequence, as songs played by Isabel and Honey slip out of their purported context to shape the world the film invites us to occupy. Sound becomes an affective technology for producing and reproducing the feeling of a possible future in the minds and bodies of viewers and listeners. Then the world seeps out of the margins to become real as we come to recognize, in Stephen Dillon's words, that "the future within the film is not the future that awaits us, but the present and past we are and have been living."[81] The strength of the affects *Born in Flames* inspires can be seen in the ways that creative audience members have been inspired to work with its footage. In 2011, Kaisa Lassinaro made a graphic translation that transforms the film's sounds and images into a book, using creative typography and color to invoke and extend the experience of viewing it. And in 2012, I created a video remix response of the film, reveling in the intimate details of Borden's editing as I used music of my own choice to bring forth the characters and moments that most compelled me.[82]

The recurrent appearances of the film's theme song, The Red Krayola's "Born in Flames," call attention to the critical world-building in which *Born in Flames* engages at the level of sound and image. The lyrics seem to refer both to the social-democratic revolution whose failure to account for sex and race the film critiques, and to the intersectional revolutionary movement that rises against it. Introduced by Isabel in the film's opening as a song that listeners will be "hearing an awful lot of these days from the makers of our revolution," the lyrics offer a version of the story of the War of Liberation that the film otherwise refuses to tell:

> At a new life we took aim
> We set the vast conglomerates aflame
> The working class avowed its name
> Of America's mysteries none remain
> We broke the hidden tyrannies
> Of the reptilian joint-stock companies
> Nor did their armed brutality
> Ever bring us to our knees
> We are born in flames[83]

Yet what we see on screen in these first shots does not conform to a heroic narrative in which working-class revolution destroys capitalist power. Instead, as the song plays, we see women working at their jobs in secretarial, construction, and retail positions, the provenance of the shots in the film's emerging narrative unclear. Smiling, they may perhaps be the heroic revolutionaries—those who have "avowed" the name of the working class—posing for a propaganda video. But they may equally be showing us that much less has changed than the song would like us to believe.

Later, once we have seen Adelaide lose her job because the government prioritizes men over women, the same lyrics play over a montage of stereotypical women's work: feeding a baby, calculating accounts, preparing and serving food, providing sexual services, cutting hair. The lyric "of America's mysteries none remain" plays over an image of dark-skinned feminine hands wrapping raw chicken in cellophane; as the next line begins, we cut to light-skinned feminine hands wrapping a penis in a condom. Whatever revolution may have happened, the humorous juxtaposition implies, some things have not changed. Women's reproductive and affective labor continues to be exploited, the "hidden tyranny" of sexism still evidently a "mystery" to the new regime that perpetuates it.

Friedberg describes the temporality of *Born in Flames* in a line that gives part 3 of this book its title: "It is the future, but it looks like the present."[84] The phrase names Borden's lack of interest in the trappings of technofuturity—though it is also an accurate description of any work of speculative visual culture, which by necessity imagines futures using material that the present has on hand. Encountered thirty years after publication, it also describes the sense of presentness and urgency that the film continues to evoke from its viewers and critics.[85] *Born in Flames* has come most into its own in that very future whose visual details it refused to try to imagine.

In the 1980s, the film's representation of a possible future for feminism did not convince many in its audience, especially feminist film critics who "attacked it for its 'irresponsible' politics."[86] Feminist critiques of the film came largely from those who wished to imagine that their movement would lead to a future more tangibly different from the present than the version *Born in Flames* created. Reviewing in the film journal *AfterImage*, Kathleen Hulser thought the film offered "little in the way of strategies for political impact."[87] Karen Jaehne, in *Film Quarterly*, complained that "the women . . . cannot seem to rid their own movement of class distinctions and discriminations inherited from the white male-dominated structure. Nothing seems to have changed."[88] These respondents did not want to see the disagreements and critiques they perceived as the failures of the feminist movement transposed into its imaginable future. Instead, they wanted to imagine measurable "change" and "impact"—to bask in the visualized possibility of a moment when "distinctions and discriminations" would at last have passed away. The future they sought for feminist struggle would be a straight line, a progress narrative, an open view through which they could cast their line of sight and see a light at the end of the tunnel, which would provide something (even if not a full utopia) to push towards. But that is not what *Born in Flames* offers. Instead, the film insists on a point that has been a recurrent theme of the works this book has brought together: that straight lines and clear views become perceptible only when impractical bodies are set aside. *Born in Flames* not only refuses such erasures, it dramatizes and archives its process of refusal.

Thirty years after the film's release, the elements that were initially critiqued for their lack of political tangibility are precisely the ones that have kept its politics alive and vital for those who watch from the future the film both did and did not envision. That future, the present, is a radically different world from Borden's imaginary, but it is also one in which there is still no all-encompassing revolution, no universally agreed-upon definition of feminism, and plenty of "distinctions and discriminations" to be found around politicized categories. In their introduction to a 2013 special issue of *Women and Performance* dedicated to the film, Craig Willse and Dean Spade write of *Born in Flames* as an "unexploded bomb," whose presentation of multiplicity and coalition within the category of "women" "somehow shows us how no individual actor or group has a grasp of either the current conditions, the causes and effects of resistance, or the ultimate destination."[89] Within the issue, Christina Hanhardt calls the film a "future still in the making," which holds power to reroute the identity- and rights-focused scripts of gay and lesbian movement history that have become hegemonic since its release.[90] Borden states that she wanted *Born in Flames* to "move away from sexuality" because she did not want people to "use . . . their desire for transformation" in "battling for the right to be 'different' or to be autonomous within the structure that's available for sexual behavior at the time."[91] Instead, the queer central characters engage in political speeches and actions that render their genders and desires inseparable from their racialization and class position. Dillon argues that "by showing the continuity between the racialized and gendered violence of the past, present, and future, the film constructs an anticipatory queer politics of urgency and presentism."[92] *Born in Flames* needed the queer and queer of color politics and temporalities that emerged after it for its aesthetics and practices of open-ended speculation to become legible as a politics. The future looked like the present when it was created. It has become the past, but somehow it still feels like *the future in the present* now.[93]

In catching on to the vitality of the film's speculated future in the years since its release, feminist and queer thinkers have also been catching up to the women of color feminist thinkers whose writing has only recently begun to be taken seriously as theory within academic canons.[94] If *Born in Flames* was illegible to the feminist reviewers invested in visibility politics and psychoanalytic film theory whom I quoted above, it resonates powerfully with the work of other feminist thinkers active in the 1970s and 1980s: women of color who were, at the same time Borden was making her film, creating Kitchen Table Press to publish books like *This Bridge Called My Back* and *Home Girls: A Black Feminist Anthology*.[95] The film's world-building reinforces arguments made by the Combahee River Collective in their 1977 "Black Feminist Statement," which called for any "socialist revolution" to also be "feminist" and "anti-racist" and insisted that "if Black Women were free, it would mean that everyone else would have to be free since our freedom would necessitate the destruction of all the systems of oppression."[96] Echoing their words, Honey declares: "Black women . . . may be among a minority and be insignificant to many. But just like the fuse that ignites the whole bomb, we are important." Alicia Garza and the core organizers of Black Lives Matter have reaffirmed the necessity of this assertion for the 2010s, writing that "if Black people get free, everybody gets free" and marking the ongoing reproduction of racist violence in the face of ongoing claims of its amelioration.[97]

In *Born in Flames*, it is the denial of freedom and ultimately of life to a queer black woman, Adelaide Norris, that instigates the coalition that will successfully struggle against the incompleteness of the socialist revolution. Adelaide's death in prison, claimed by police to be a suicide, reminded Kathleen Hulser of the 1976 death of German revolutionary Ulrike Meinhof; Christina Hanhardt links it to the 1970 "contested murder/suicide of Young Lords member Julio Roldan."[98] For viewers watching after 2015, it is more likely to bring to mind Sandra Bland's death in police custody. Conversations in the film about publishing images of Adelaide's body recall arguments about social media posts of videos that capture the deaths of black people at the hands of police.[99] The film's placement of anti-black violence at the center of its movement also calls attention to the failure of cross-racial coalitions to stand up for and fight back against the ever-increasing toll of black lives lost to state violence since its release. The transformative future of black-led feminist coalition of which the film offers us an experience has, like its socialist revolution, yet to arrive.

While *Born in Flames* prefigures some formations of queer of color theory and makes the affective experience of women of color feminist coalition available to many who did not participate in such movements personally, it does not offer utopian political solutions. The one solution it does suggest—a coalition of antiracist feminist solidarity—is not without flaws. As Hanhardt writes, "The fantasy of *Born in Flames* is not only of an imagined activist struggle but also of black-white feminist harmony that uses black bodies to code revolutionary authenticity."[100] The film displays race more than discussing it. It does not shy away from mentioning "black women" nor from showing racial conflict within feminism, but it nevertheless continually returns to the image of an army united around *women*, unmodified, as an organizing category. Sharon Holland writes that the "black.female.queer" body has become a "vanguard" of queer/feminist politics in the age of queer of color critique.[101] She points out that, despite the best of intentions, this can be a gesture toward intersectional radicalism that ends up reducing blackness, queerness, femaleness to the body itself. In other words, "black.female.queer" *critique* is too easy to reduce to a politics of identity that cannot account for the nuanced, diverse, and contradictory analyses of black feminist thinkers whose perspectives, while informed by their embodied positionalities, cannot be predicted or assumed on that basis.

Indeed, Borden's statements about her decision to center on black women do not cite the feminist theory they were, at the time, producing. In her interview with Friedberg, she states that the "science fiction part of the film" was "taking people who usually do the least about oppression, black women in the ghetto (although they are very very powerful)" and "channeling their power into a larger frame."[102] Borden does not here acknowledge black women as theorists of their own lives and proponents of transformative politics. From whose perspective can those among the most oppressed be blithely assumed to "do the least about oppression," and how can a white filmmaker assume that science fiction is the only way to grant them political agency?

Yet Borden also insists that the film's politics rest in the "process" through which it was made, one in which her role as filmmaker was collaborative and filled with the "contradictions" she hoped the film would emphasize. Because of this, individual failings in her analysis or politics would not necessarily be reproduced in the film itself.[103] She did not seek to make a narrative that would portray individuals' stories from the inside, believing it impossible and inappropriate to speak for them in this way.[104] Instead, Borden recorded her collaborators speaking in their own words, theorizing their present through the premise of a failed revolution, a Women's Army, a future. She created the film, then tried—though doomed to failure, given the structures governing film distribution and funding—to give up control over its meaning to the women whose images and words it archives. *Born in Flames* documents both the conflicts and triumphs of the coalition politics it enacts: women of color's intellectual and political histories sit alongside the failures, unintentional reproductions of problematic dynamics, and contradictory investments that occur when we wrestle with privilege and complicity.

Born in Flames models its idea of a coalition-based future politics most urgently through its representation of media. Science fiction films are often, as Garrett Stewart writes, about "the future of movies," depicting possible developments of screen technologies.[105] *Born in Flames* sticks with technologies that existed in 1983, but meditates intensely on how media transmission affects political possibility. In the old media future it provides, radio, print, and television are methods for both revolution and counter-revolution. Much screen time is devoted to broadcasts, which provide backstory to tell us what the protagonists are rebelling against. Mayors and newscasters give speeches; talk show hosts and newspaper editors defend the actions of the government. We meet Adelaide through a nonconsensual media depiction in the form of FBI surveillance videos that capture her in bed with a lover, playing basketball, spending time with her siblings—her continual subjection to state surveillance highlighting the lack of change espoused by a supposedly revolutionary society. The surveillance cameras first observe and catalogue her black queer body for a white male gaze, then document her arrest and death. When images of Adelaide's body enter the media ecology, the film shifts gear and the Women's Army gains in power. White feminist newspaper editors debate the politics of reproducing the image, and when they finally do, it is as a decision to enter into coalition with the Women's Army; Honey, who has been hesitating to jump into the movement, sees the body of her former comrade at the newsstand and commits to revolution on the spot. In a climactic moment, the Women's Army takes over the news at gunpoint, appropriating airwaves to bring

Figure 5.8. The Women's Army takes over TV in *Born in Flames* (directed by Lizzie Borden, 1983).

their message directly into the homes of the women, and perhaps even men, they hope will support them.

Zella Wylie declares explicitly what Borden's editing implies: "The most important thing of all is media, our media. The most important thing is communication." In one of the most compelling shots in the film (figure 5.8), Zella's voice beams directly into Honey's home as she listens intently, verbally encouraging Zella to say more. Honey is already devoted to the cause, but it is easy to imagine Zella's broadcast transforming myriad other viewers into Women's Army activists. The Women's Army comes together around what activists would later come to call media justice, a framework developed in the 2000s by organizers in communities of color who were seeking to challenge exclusion and misrepresentation through the creation of "new relationships with media and a new vision for its control, access, and structure" with "systems that treat our airways and our communities as more than markets."[106] The film's explosive final shot serves this utopian project.

Born in Flames ends with a bang: a bomb at the top of the World Trade Center. An example of an old future that cannot not be interpreted in the light of the more recent past, the explosion of this bomb casts its shadow over the entire film. Having seen it for the first time in the mid-2000s, for a long time I viewed the ending as an eruption of pure revolutionary violence. I thought that the Women's Army had reached the end of the futures they believed it possible to access with their current tactics and were deciding to pursue *no future* instead: to have no truck with the state, setting off a queer explosion to end the possibility of incorporation into patriarchal socialism. Like Dillon, who analyzes the Women's Army through queer and black studies' frameworks of the future as a "horizon of death," I saw the end of the film as "the destruction of the present."[107] The explosion resonated viscerally for me with the "no future" firebomb in *Jubilee*: two iterations of speculative imaginations of disaster blowing up in the face of heteropatriarchal politics of hope at the institutional and personal level.

Yet neither film entirely refuses hope, though *Jubilee* is driven by a far more dystopian impulse.[108] The explosion in *Born in Flames* is not dystopian; it has just been irrevocably rewritten by real-world future events. For it is actually very clear in the film, if one is not rendered unable to see it by an overdetermined spectacle of destruction, that what the Twin Towers bomb was initiated to signify was the sabotage of a media transmitter. The explosion's meaning is not only its powerful symbolism, but also its pragmatic capacity to stop the mainstream signal so that the only media standing will be Phoenix Ragazza Radio, the Women's Army's pirate broadcasting coalition (figures 5.9 and 5.10). In 1983, the very small explosion did not stand in for destroying the world, nor did it brand the films' protagonists permanently as "terrorists" and force audiences to reinterpret the rest of the film in that light. It could register instead as a strategic act of political violence aimed at opening up a future closed down by the pretense of progress.

The Women's Army wants to get across a message not that the future stops here, but that a different future is coming—a new age of transformative media justice in which their very technical act of violence will mean that the top-down transmission of false socialism will be ended and feminist coalition enabled by peer to peer communication will be the new norm. Isabel lays out the film's ultimate hope while we watch a white Women's Army member in business attire stride into the World Trade Center and plant a bomb:

> We are all, women and men, the prophets of this new age. . . . This fight will not end in terrorism and violence. It will not end in a nuclear holocaust. It begins in the celebration of the rites of alchemy. The transformation of shit into gold. The illumination of dark chaotic night into light. This is the time of sweet, sweet change for us all.

* * *

"The rites of alchemy" describes the future on screen in both *Jubilee* and *Born in Flames*. Both produce visions of change and transformation through unexpected leaps of image, narrative, and music. *Jubilee* turns the gold of nostalgic imperial splendor into shit through a discomfiting encounter with punk's assimilability to the nihilist embrace of white supremacist capitalist fascism. *Born in Flames* shows that revolutionary transformations can fail in their alchemical aspirations, enacting conflicted possibilities that summon forth a sense of the possibility of revolution even as they open themselves to critique. Both films also create futures to challenge a corporate and state media industry perceived by the filmmakers as universal, unitary, and overwhelming—the instrument of a flattening future that hides difference and colonizes possibility. For all the films' many resonances with the present, their critique of media's homogenizing effects is one depiction of an old future that audiences accustomed to social media are likely to approach with a wry smile. Even in the context of the 1970s and 1980s, scholarship in cultural studies had long made it clear that audiences' responses to media are neither simplistic nor predictable. In the age of the internet, it seems naive indeed to imagine that access to media would be the greatest problem a revolutionary organization could face, as *Born in Flames* seems to do. It is, after all, at least in part because of the availability of direct access to media that the grassroots revolutionaries of the far Right have been so successfully in siphoning political power to figures who resemble *Jubilee*'s fascist tycoon, Borgia Ginz. *Jubilee* highlights the limits of oppositionality by showing how saleable it can be: "They all sign up in the end," after all, and even the film itself is most often now approached as part of the celebrated punk scene that it scathingly critiques. *Born in*

Figures 5.9 and 5.10. A map to the World Trade Center transmitter, and the explosion that altered the meaning of *Born in Flames* (directed by Lizzie Borden, 1983) forever on September 11, 2001.

Flames, on the other hand, insists on the possibility of revolution. It takes us from a project for radical transformation that failed because it claimed to be complete into a media landscape that has become part of every-day materiality, to the point where both utopian claims to radical media democracy and their debunking have become quotidian. Yet the film's popularity and resonance with new generations of radical activists and scholars show that its approach to futurity remains vivid for those craft-ing oppositional politics.

Born in Flames and *Jubilee* place the future not in a projection of prior narratives and teleologies forward in time, but in the act of reframing and refiguring the present. Their visions of futures are most powerful not in what is on the screen but what slips off it; not in the technological reproduction of visuals but in affects transmitted across time. They have provided raw material in the form of images, sounds, and icons that have been easy for viewers to take up, translate, and transform into other al-chemical possibilities, other imagined futures. The next and final chapter takes up the process of such transformations.

6

How to Remix the Future

Old New Media

In the recent past, one futuristic rhetoric has had a tendency to over-power all others: digital media technology. Media theory has been and continues to be a genre of speculative fiction, just as speculative fiction has been and continues to be a form of media theory. When speculative rhetorics are used to theorize changes in media for popular audiences, this has often taken the form of universalizing statements about media futures—from Marshall McLuhan's predictions of a global village to cur-rent panics about digital distraction.[1] Speculative fiction itself, as I have shown throughout this book, makes space for more nuanced and com-plex understandings of what the future might contain. The ease of online communication has seemed to fulfill previous moments' dreams and nightmares alike, retrospectively turning works from Edward Bellamy's 1888 vision of friction-free commerce to E. M. Forster's 1909 fear of the loss of all human contact into concrete predictions.[2] William Gibson's speculative term "cyberspace," coined in his 1982 short story "Burning Chrome" and popularized with 1984's influential *Neuromancer*, domi-nated analyses of the emergent medium of the internet in the 1990s and early 2000s, despite the disparity between the immersive experience Gib-son described and the screen-based, initially text-based structures of the actually existing internet.[3]

Less canonical answers to the questions posed by media change and the effects of mediated communication are everywhere in the futuris-tic fictions whose temporalities I have been unpacking in this book. In Elizabeth Burgoyne Corbett's 1889 *New Amazonia* (chapter 1), entertain-ment in the form of remote connectivity is technologically possible but shunned by a society whose leaders have calculated that their utopia will be better served by privileging in-person interaction. In Katharine Bur-dekin's 1937 *Swastika Night* (chapter 2), the book is a banned and dangerous archival technology. In Jewelle Gomez's 1991 Afrofuturist vampire fiction *The Gilda Stories* (chapter 3), telepathy is the wireless technology that enables decolonial collectivity among racialized women. Samuel R. Delany's 1984 *Stars in My Pocket like Grains of Sand* (chapter 4) prefigures a Web that enables liberating interconnection, terrifying surveillance, and pleasures imaginable only through a computational approach to desire. *Born in Flames* (directed by Lizzie Borden, 1983) and *Jubilee* (directed by Derek Jarman, 1978) (chapter 5) envisage mass media as the route to utopian and dystopian political futures respectively. And, as shifting technologies open up new possibilities for cultural production, the affordances of digital media have themselves opened spaces for new kinds of speculative cultural production. The speculative modes of cultural production and reception among science fiction media's feminist fans have taught me much about the queer possibilities that emerge from efforts to push back against the pressures of dominant media temporalities. Their creative methods are the focus of this chapter, which highlights a practice that has emerged from obscurity to some influence in the last ten years: the subcultural art form of fan-made music video, or vidding, of which I have been a scholar, participant, and informal archivist since 2008.

In the digital era, shifts in production and reception practices, as well as in the kind of content that rises to prominence, happen so fast that any cultural theorist hoping to analyze them will find herself breathlessly falling behind. The onslaught of increased communication speed, storage capacity, and convergence of diverse analogue signals into digital data streams has created a landscape in which existing media technologies (always unevenly distributed along familiar global, national, and local contours of economic inequality) quickly overtake even the futuristic representations that appear in speculative fiction. The framework of the old future allows me to bypass the impetus to keep up and to focus instead on the lingering repercussions of what may seem (falsely) to have passed into irrelevance. Within a media landscape saturated both with futurity and with anxieties about the future's loss, amateur digital interventions into industrially produced imaginaries bring together the critiques and concerns of the marginal speculative archive I have been building with the genre specificities of science fiction media.

Wendy Hui Kyong Chun describes computing technology as the "constantly inspiring yet disappointing medium of the future."[4] She writes that computers seem "capable of being the future because, based on past data, they shape and predict it"; they are cast by programmers and laypeople alike as "all-knowing" computational "intelligence that can comprehend the future by apprehending the past and present."[5] Digital media are defined by powerful calculating machines that seem to take the possibility out of speculation, shutting the future down into a capitalist global modernity where alternative modes of being will always already have been wiped out. Chun highlights not just the exclusions of this model but its impossibility, arguing that to go along with this presumption is to ignore the realities of life with computers in favor of an ideal version. For her, what makes digital and computational media interesting is "not what has been touted as its promise, but rather, what's been discarded or decried as its trash"—its old futures.[6] Elizabeth Freeman locates queer possibilities in precisely such trashy locations—in art that works with "the excess generated by capital," that can "collect and remobilize archaic or futuristic debris as signs of things that have been and could be otherwise."[7]

This book has collected archaic futuristic debris across a span of more than a hundred years, and has sought to remobilize them in an exploration of queer rhythms and affective historiographies lived in relationship to reproductive and technological futures. In company with Freeman, I have sought new and old ways of "moving through and with time, encountering pasts, speculating futures, and interpenetrating the two in ways that counter the common sense of the present tense."[8] Kara Keeling writes that the intersection of the queer and the digital "offers a way of making perceptible presently uncommon senses . . . [and] makes this formulation of *queer* function as an operating system" for more than our computers.[9] To understand the uncommon senses emerging at the margins of the digital future some of us appear to be inhabiting, we must look not only at what new technological artifacts are created and what it means to use them, but also at what people do with the archive of culture that surrounds them—how we rewrite and remake histories, even in forms and contexts rarely taken seriously.

The flourishing of diverse remix cultures is one place where both the promise and the threat of digital media seem to have been fulfilled.[10]

While the temporalities of cinema and television continue, even in the age of digital distribution, to be largely theorized through models of industrial production in which audiences receive the creations of professional creators, the user-focused structures of digital production have offered a sense of comparative freedom. As Lev Manovich writes, in our interactions with digital media, "the 'message' that the user 'receives' is not just actively 'constructed' by him/her (through a cognitive interpretation) but also actively managed" such that "it is easy to start playing/viewing media at an arbitrary point, and to leave at any point."[11] It is also easy to copy, download, edit, and publish text, sound, image, and video. This shift from the dominance of broadcast models to the transformational capacities of digital media has been held up as both a utopian and a dystopian promise. In 2001, Manovich wrote, with some apparent sadness, that "now anybody can become a creator by simply . . . making a new selection from the total corpus available."[12] He found the prospect of a cut and paste culture—where users manipulate content within the capacities of software about whose inner workings they may not be knowledgeable—to be something to regret. It signaled the advent of a closed world in which the sensation of freedom and creativity covers over the extent to which actions are mediated by what is technologically possible.

When we feel we are at our most original and creative, we may be most hemmed in by the technological structures of software as well as the ideological structures of culture and politics. Becoming aware of this requires attending to the advice of Tara McPherson, whose work on race and computing highlights the ideologies embedded in supposedly neutral operating systems and programming languages: "We cannot read the logics of . . . . systems and networks solely at the level of our screens."[13] In response to the limits of screen-based critique, McPherson calls for scholars of media and representation to dig down beneath the screen into the materialities of technological form. I agree wholeheartedly that this is necessary. Yet I want to insist that the uses we make of our screens' content—the ways we play with it, the alternatives we make even within the lines that software makes most available, the affective experiences our practices induce—matter, too.

Amy Villarejo has pointed out that the feminized medium of television often gets jumped over in narratives that speak of a transition in dominant media forms "from cinema to new media."[14] I place television at the center of my engagement with digital mediations of futurity because it has been a center around which media fan networks (likewise feminized, and composed primarily of women) have clustered and from which they have created forms that are often left out of new media histories.[15] In contrast to the collective viewing experiences that shaped the form of cinema, television has been, in Gary Needham's words, "a domestic media technology"; its representations are encountered through "experiences of intimacy, emotion, the familiar and the private"—making it a site that, for many scholars, has been particularly open to queer cathexis.[16] And while science fiction film has provided an audiovisual language for shared popular references to an imagined technocultural future, it is through television that such sounds and images gain the familiarity of habit.[17] Science fiction television cannot rely on the singularity of a spectacle that lasts an hour or two and is remembered for a lifetime. It must come up with new plots and new images for every episode (whether these will be watched week by week or all at once via streaming services), building a world that viewers will want to return to, and most likely doing so on a limited budget.[18] And the televisual affordance of seriality allows viewers to make creative use of the space between episodes, supplementing and challenging the world a series builds. Perhaps for this reason, televisual science fiction is recognized as a significant site for social and political speculation.[19]

The industrial structures through which television operates have, in the past few years, been transforming rapidly along with the rest of the media landscape. Television is no longer only a flow that one can access by tuning in to one of a multitude of channels; it is a "complicated, deliberate, and individualized" set of options accessed through multiple sites and devices.[20] Meanwhile, the entertainments we enjoy on our screens are as likely to be nonprofessionally as industrially created.[21] Nurtured in media fan communities since the 1980s, vidding predates both these shifts, but it invites us to see them from a different perspective. Vids' alternate visual and sonic versions of digital futures emerge from creatively recombinant orientations to the archives of cultural production that digital transformations have made more readily available for appropriation. I describe vidding as a way to remix the future because I have found in it the potential to craft alternate versions of media temporalities, producing works of speculative critique that repurpose gendered and racialized temporalities of reproduction and colonization. As creative engagements with televised speculative fiction, vids have the capacity both to reproduce and to challenge the clichés of technological futurity that circulate around the narratives to which they respond and the digital media they use to do so. The vids on which I focus here were made between 2005 and 2009—a period when the digital future was well under way, but still new enough that practitioners were keen to reflect on recent shifts and transitions.

This chapter is written with the goal of performing some of the processes and affects it discusses, combining image, description, and analysis to remix insights from the rest of the book. Familiar themes, tropes, and connections will recur, as futures from the older and more recent past touch across time through the repetitive imagery of serial television and the reproductive technology of digital media. I begin by exploring what it means to critically reconfigure the imagined future at the interface of television and the digital, considering the queer kinds of temporality that vidders create and laying out the affordances of this affect-centered form of remix. Then I look at fan responses that perform explicit critiques of television's speculative futures, briefly discussing one critical vid made in response to *Firefly* (2002–2003) before moving to engage vidders' analyses of the 2003–2009 TV series *Battlestar Galactica* at greater length. The temporal complexities of *Battlestar Galactica*— itself a remake, engaging its 1970s predecessor through retro production design and creating extensive analogies to early-2000s technologies and politics as well as to racial and imperial histories—make it especially apt as a final example for *Old Futures*.

The appropriation of *Battlestar Galactica*'s temporal weirdnesses and their reconfiguration in amateur art is testimony to the deviant futures and queer speculations that can blossom amid the contradictions and complications of newly mediated relationships to older forms and narratives. In creative work nurtured in digitally mediated worlds that are part of, yet rarely highly visible within, mainstream spheres of social media, online video, and new media studies, this chapter uncovers queer rhythms and affects lived in relationship to reproductive and technological futures. Such critically queer fan engagements with digital futurity are one form in which the histories—old futures with continuing possibilities—this book has traced can perpetuate themselves. The final section describes some of my own experiments using these techniques in speculative scholarly audiovisual production, methods that have had a shaping influence on the composition and development of the book itself. Through the processes of juxtaposition, repetition, and audiovisual suturing by which they make meaning within their subcultural community, vids have the capacity not only to comment on science fiction cultures but also to reinscribe, reimagine, and queer media histories and temporalities.

Digital Video and Queer Fannish Love

The creativity of media fans has become part of the everyday landscape of digital media. Fan-made music videos, in which clips from film and television are edited together to music, are likely to be among the first results for any search on YouTube for either video clips or musical performances; they have even been viewed as more lucrative for music rights holders than official music videos.[22] For scholars and critics thinking through particular aspects of a visual text, they can be a boon, as Villarejo discovers in analyzing the central lesbian narrative between Helen Mirren and Kyra Sedgwick in the 1996 film *Losing Chase* (directed by Kevin Bacon). She writes:

> It would have taken me some pages to generate a narrative of their encounter, but that has been done on YouTube by a fan who has assembled the Sedgwick-Mirren lovefest to the late Whitney Houston's "I Have Nothing." The exposition with the soundtrack is much better than I ever could have generated in prose! (The video was called "Losing Chase—I Have Nothing," by deltarose1, and it appears to have been deleted from You-Tube: such is the ethereality and ephemerality of our digital archive!) . . . [The video] cuts, as it were, right to the chase of lesbian desire, pulling shot-reverse-shot sequences out of *Losing Chase* and building others to drive home the point. . . . Before YouTube, in fact, I saw *Losing Chase* as an ode to loss, as a way of grieving lost forms of intimacy, creativity, and expression and dying visions of equity, intimacy, and connection that were articulated in the cultural-feminist and lesbian-feminist practices of the previous two decades (the 1970s and 1980s). But "deltarose1," who mashed

Losing Chase and Whitney Houston, reads the film as a baldly declarative love story: "I Have Nothing" begins 'Share my life / take me for what I am.' And she does, they do.[23]

Villarejo is excited to discover a video that places the currents of queer desire front and center, making the delights of a lesbian "lovefest" available to those who might not have seen the film or who might be less interested in its "ode to loss" than in its sexy encounter. Yet she also reads the video as interchangeable with a narrative that she might herself have composed in "some pages"; questions of how, for whom, or in what context it was crafted and shared are not relevant to her project. Villarejo acknowledges deltarose1's skill ("better than I ever could have generated in prose!") even as her introduction of the video makes its creator appear secondary to its vehicle of distribution ("done on YouTube by a fan"). The interpretive labor of remix is also rendered invisible when it appears that deltarose1 watched the film and simply saw a "baldly declarative love story" that she then naively reproduced on her own screen, rather than making an artistic decision to intensify the film's queer romantic pleasures through the medium of Whitney Houston.

I do not labor this point to castigate Villarejo. I was in fact delighted to see her engage with a fan music video at so much length, and I am certain that many scholars have been similarly influenced by such videos without citing them in their books. But I hope to point out how the very visibility of certain digital cultural forms elides their significance *as* forms, as well as the labor that produces them. As I have had brought home to me when I have screened vids to those trained in film production and critique, vidders' editing practices can be almost unbearably earnest—but so, after all, are some of our interpretations as cultural critics. Unsuturing video sequences in order to reformulate them according to a sonic temporality appropriated from somewhere else, as deltarose1 does, necessitates a creative and counterintuitive relationship to media flows, regardless of the content of the result. What if the creative labor of deltarose1 and her peers were taken as seriously as the work of critics and scholars, or for that matter the work of remix artists whose creations are screened in galleries?

The rest of this chapter makes an argument for doing so, through the history, practice, and speculated possibilities of the strand of fan culture in which this kind of remix has been nurtured and developed. In a digital world where the sheer volume of cultural production means that manipulating large volumes of so-called big data seems like the only way to analyze what is out there, I argue for the usefulness of close attention to the small, situated interventions vidders have made into the media futures they inhabit, challenge, and reorganize.

Despite the easy access to fan-made music videos on YouTube that viewers like Villarejo have come to expect, the existence of a self-conscious artistic community around the form is not well known—though some scholars have championed its representation. Francesca Coppa celebrates vidding as "an editing room of one's own" for women whose perspectives are rarely privileged in mainstream media, but whose creative practices were not instigated but only made easier by the advent of digital technologies.[24] As narrated by Coppa, the history of vidding begins in approximately 1975 when a *Star Trek* fan named Kandy Fong started making slide shows about Kirk and Spock, which were taped and shared on video at conventions. Later, fans created vids using multiple VCRs, gathering their resources in collectives for this labor-intensive and expensive operation, and sharing the results by mail.[25] Fans gradually turned to the digital as consumer video-editing software became available. Digital media's affordances both in terms of technological ease (nonrivalrous copying, video sharing) and of communication (linking localized audiences into global networks of grassroots production with diverse perspectives) have allowed vidding to branch out into more diverse forms, as well as enabling both cross-fertilization and conflict among remix artists and fans who have engaged in similar practices without necessarily being aware of, or interested in, fan traditions that preceded them.

In common with other kinds of remix, such as musical sampling, vids create meaning "through the selection, placement, and recontextualization of reused source text."[26] The particularity of vidding as a form is its juxtaposition of music and image, combining recognizable images with the sound, lyrics, and connotations of a particular song that does not sound—though in practice it often is—digitally altered. Josh Kun writes of the "audiotopias" that music can create when a song "is experienced not only as sound that goes into our ears and vibrates through our bones but as a space that we can enter into."[27] Vidders, like deltarose1 with Whitney Houston, take the affective power of music and use it to structure their cutting-together of image and movement such that the edits invite viewers into a world where their longings can feel, for a few minutes, like an alternate reality.

This form of retelling by re-editing connects to multiple histories of playing with, celebrating, and queering loved texts. Video remix has long been a playground for non-normative desires, drawing out the queer and perverse pleasures hidden in plain sight within mainstream media.[28] Exchanging these technologies among networks on- and offline has been a form of queer world-making that does more than make visual unspoken media narratives of same sex romance. In the media fan communities on which Coppa focuses, the lingering gazes on media products that created the conditions of possibility for working out new narratives were often in the service of slash fan fiction, which has been a way to recuperate relatively uncommon images of queer representation and to reframe them in a new context.[29] Under a different name, the queer art of vidding was invented by artist Cecilia Barriga, whose 1991 video Meeting Two Queens used the two-VCR technique to edit together a steamy affair between Marlene Dietrich and Greta Garbo. Mary Desjardins argues that "the significance of Meeting Two Queens . . . lies . . . in its interpellation of a spectator who identifies with the images as a fan and who responds to their strategies of affect."[30] The same description applies to vidding, in which creative practices of queer viewership in critical fan communities refuse the logics of heterosexual plots and normative endings and stay instead with the joys, troubles, and sexy moments through which both media and the world can be reimagined.

The 2005 vid "Walking on the Ground," by vidding dyad Flummery, uses fan video's queer methods to explore anxieties surrounding the future of media.[31] The vid, made for the fan convention Vividcon's celebration of thirty years of vidding history, brings together images from speculative film and television with a narrative that comments on the history of vidding itself. The year it premiered, YouTube—presumed by many to be the beginning and end of grassroots video creativity—first went live. Placing imagery of fan vid creation to the tune of a comic Sheldon Allman song about the temporality of technological progress, Flummery's vid writes subcultural history into an evolutionary narrative of technological obsolescence, angst, and renewal (figure 6.1). "Walking

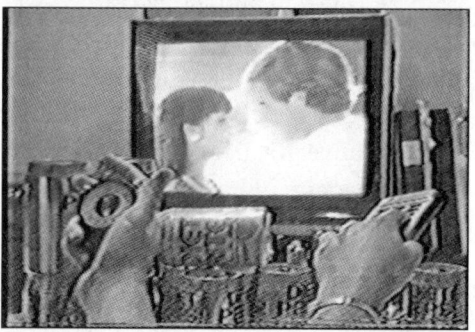

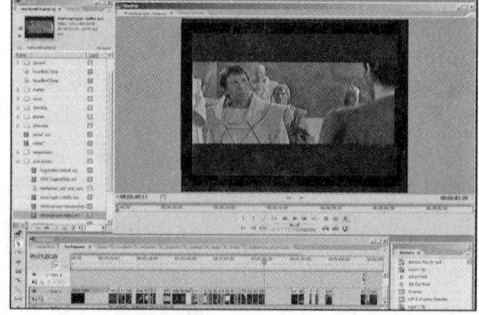

Figures 6.1–6.4. The evolution of fan-made remix music video, as depicted in Flummery's 2005 vid "Walking on the Ground."

on the Ground" brings together a collection of clips that may seem random but that have been carefully chosen for their meaning to the fan communities who established the pre-digital form of vidding. Drawing on images from many of the films and shows around which fan communities have gathered, the vid suggests that for as long as there have been media futures, fans have been remixing them.

Flummery's documentation of the pre-YouTube history of vidding begins with Kandy Fong's clips from the *Star Trek* cutting room floor (figure 6.2) and moves on to the dual-VCR duplication practiced by vidding collective California Crew (figure 6.3).[32] Digital video editing software (figure 6.4) appears one-third of the way into the vid, as the song's lyrics tell of a shift from trains and planes to spaceships. While some might prefer to hang on to older technology ("I'm going to fly in a plane like the good Lord intended"), and indeed some vidders did continue to create using VCRs after digital technology became available, the implication is that digital technology catapulted the art of video remix into the stratosphere.

The climax of "Walking on the Ground" takes a turn to the speculative when the song narrates a move from progress to apocalypse that is familiar from many a science fiction dystopia: "They're gone now, all those things at which the people used to scoff / and so are all the people, since that cobalt bomb went off." We see a world explode (figure 6.5); in the next shot, this becomes a symbol for the danger of digital rights management technologies, symbolized by Macrovision copy protection (figure 6.6). Such restrictions have often made it difficult for remix artists to create, but there are "a handful of us left" who will persist, the vid assures us with the image of a tough few at their computers (figure 6.7). Casting vidders as the potential germination of a resistant new media future, an old-fashioned projector next screens an egg and sperm as we are invited to "start the world anew" (figure 6.8). Finally, a sequence familiar to anyone who knows the work of genre television auteur Joss Whedon (likely most of the audience at a fan convention in 2005) invites the vid's viewers to imagine themselves as part of the story, as Buffy the vampire slayer calls on her high school classmates to fight the evil of demonic authority (figures 6.9–6.10).[33]

Flummery weaves anti-corporate, anti-copyright critique with science fiction television to tell a compelling story about recovering the

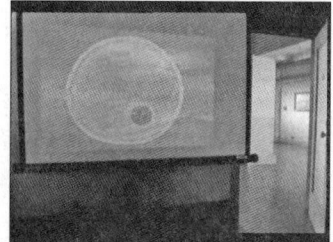

Figures 6.5–6.10. Telling a story of apocalypse, rebellion, and renewal in Flummery's 2005 vid "Walking on the Ground."

commons for subcultural art and building a politicized futurism out of fannish love and creativity. The vid's narrative resonates with the activism of groups like the Electronic Frontier Foundation, as well as with widespread challenges to intellectual property legislation that fails to account for the range of creative and critical ways ordinary people engage with digital media.[34] However, it is also important to complicate the logic of a sperm-and-egg revolution that casts vidding, or remix in general, as a newborn or reborn media future. In the years since "Walking on the Ground" premiered, it has become very clear that, while the changing media landscape has made video remix increasingly culturally central, the ways of viewing that vidding demands and invites are under threat, and not only because of the cat-and-mouse game of copyright protection that this vid documents. It takes an educated and patient gaze to recognize those specificities. The intense kind of viewing needed to fully appreciate a vid (repeated, focused, perhaps in company with friends who can provide contexts one watcher may lack) is out of sync with the rapid movement through sites, the multitasking and multiple tabs and windows, that characterize everyday engagements with the digital environment circa 2017.

Without knowledge of the history of vidding, Flummery's video would still tell a recognizable narrative about media evolution and the overreach of copyright law, but much would be confusing. With the addition of history and community, the vid invites viewers to an intimate relationship with the images it recontextualizes—one that assumes and requires multiple viewings to appreciate the nuance contained in every cut. Even while creating a narrative of progress, destruction, and reproductive renewal, Flummery reminds viewers to slow down and spend time with each clip, each moment, each remix of the past. The vidders insist that the aggregated moments of popular media, far from being transient or disposable, can remain current forever if their viewers only love them enough. Through labors of piracy, file-sharing, and informal education to teach the technical skills that make video remix possible, popular media becomes a shared archive, its images as cathected to personal lives as family photographs. The processes involved in vidding—both for the creator and for the watcher—are as important as the narratives they create.

Vidding as process is documented in one of the most widely screened vids, "Us" by Lim (2007), which has screened at the California Museum of Photography, featured in an influential educational video by anthropologist Michael Wesch, and appeared on the cover of *Cinema Journal*.[35] As in most vids, every choice of image, cut, and effect is overdetermined, dependent on the contextual knowledge and affective investment the viewer brings to the footage. "Us" makes this overdetermination its subject, utilizing visual effects to craft a meta-analysis of media fan culture rooted in the history of male/male slash.[36] Footage is taken from television shows and films that have large fan followings and have been dominant texts within some of the most vocal communities of slash fans in Anglo-American science fiction media fandom. Sources include *Star Trek, Blake's 7, The Professionals, The X Files, Stargate, Buffy, Lord of the Rings*, and many more.

Lim used a digital paint program to modify the footage used in the vid, shading over it with pencil-colored lines; the result is that the filmed images appear to be drawn by hand. This becomes a visual metaphor for the way fan creators understand their art as transforming commodities sold them by the culture industries into personal, handcrafted objects whose disposability they override. As Regina Spektor sings "They made a statue of us / and put it on a mountain top," Kirk and Spock appear on screen, their uniforms the only splash of color in a grey and white expanse (figure 6.11). The audio/visual juxtaposition suggests that fans work with the comparatively unexceptional and transform it into something monumental. In its significance for subcultural lives, popular culture's science fiction futures, forgettable and clichéd from many perspectives, have become statuesque. Later, to the refrain "We're living in a den of thieves," we see a reminder of the queer desires that shape these remix histories in a shot of Captain Kirk's face with Spock's hand against it, 1980s-style green computer text superimposed on the penciled-over image in a nod to the many fan fiction authors who have written their stories on to these two characters (figure 6.12). The image, canonically a "mind meld" but eroticized in fans' queer gaze, is one that has been used in many Kirk/Spock slash vids before; one such use is even reproduced by Henry Jenkins as part of his discussion of K.M.D.'s 1980s vid "I Needed You" in his foundational fan studies book, *Textual Poachers*.[37] Lim's use of this image indexes the communality of fans' appropriative art.

The next shots in the sequence underline the connections that my inclusion of a chapter on vidding in this book draws between histories of

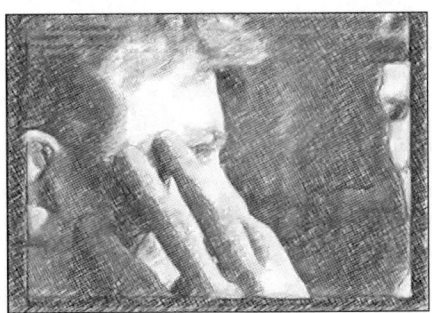

Figures 6.11–6.14. *Star Trek* and *V for Vendetta* reconfigured in Lim's vid "Us" (2007).

feminist and queer science fiction literature and media fandom. Images of books and DVDs—solicited by Lim from fellow fans—get superimposed on the *Star Trek* image, including Samuel R. Delany's *Stars in My Pocket like Grains of Sand*, whose queer world-building I discussed in chapter 4 (figure 6.13).[38] Lim's layered images make visible the interpretive and affective labor of a fandom that transforms its objects. They showcase vids' dense synchronization alongside their tendency to draw on gesture to create arguments that merge the obvious with subtleties visible only to those who share an obsessive familiarity with any given media image.

Another science fiction narrative with queer connections, the 2006 film *V for Vendetta* (directed by James McTeigue), gives "Us" its final, iconic image.[39] In it, a bespectacled young girl slips off a mask (figure 6.14). In 2009, I wrote about this shot:

> Images from . . . *V for Vendetta*, which portrays a masked revolutionary, V, instigating revolt against government oppression, punctuate the fannish history in "Us." In the film, V preaches popular democracy, reminding cowed citizens that "people shouldn't be afraid of their governments, governments should be afraid of their people." This is visualized when a crowd of ordinary people, given masks and incited to protest by V, show their faces at the film's close. Lim appropriates this scene to show that the V who is associated with creative destruction, piracy, and radical theft is the "us" of media fandom: her geeky woman is part of V's masked multitude, and she reminds us that if the world is changing, fans may have a hand in it.[40]

Since "Us" was released, the mask has grown significantly more iconic: first associated with the slippery and politically amorphous digital pranksters of Anonymous, it has been variously taken up by protest movements, particularly the Occupy movement of the early 2010s.[41] This retrospective view increases the vid's resonance with the antifascist message in *V for Vendetta*, whose climax sees the citizens of a future authoritarian dystopia take up the masks to take back power from their government. The sight of a young girl slipping off that mask suggests that the feminized activities of fandom, so often associated with teenage girlhood, have implications for more than subcultural pleasure. In the remainder of this chapter, I explore how the temporalities of vidding have been and can be mobilized for critical, politicized ends.

Critical Fandom: Remixing the Future of Race and Empire

"Fandom" is often taken, by casual observers as well as by media producers who hope to harness it, to denote an uncritical positivity. To be a fan is to be in a position of emotional excess, invested to the point of identifying oneself with an object, a community, a text, or a theory—offering up love and labor to build a world around it. To be critical, on the other hand, is what professional academic and intellectual practice requires of us: critical theory, critical distance, critical analysis, critical rigor. What might it mean to pursue *critical fandom*?[42]

The term "fandom" names a shared space as well as an affective relationship. To be *in fandom* can mean to participate in a collective conversation organized not around any given media text but through the practices of transformative engagement with cultural production. Jenkins, Camille Bacon-Smith, and other 1990s initiators of fan studies spoke of media fans' transformative creativity in terms of resistance to media industries' domination of popular pleasures and desires, suggesting that their practices had an implicitly critical element.[43] Later scholarship has pointed out that fan creativity often runs neatly along the lines laid out for it by industry, whether through cult television's reliance on non-normative sexualities to maintain its narrative or via producers' encouragement of fan works as a marketing strategy.[44] Yet not all fans have been willing to color within those lines.

Seeking to capture the idea of subcultural fandom as a space organized through logics different than those of media industries, Will Brooker describes subcultural media fandom as a "rogue green planet in an increasingly colonized system of shiny corporate worlds winking with advertising satellites and buzzing with traffic."[45] This science fiction metaphor, resonant with my own uses of Fred Moten's and Stefano Harney's language of the "undercommons," frames subcultural fandom as a decolonial space—perhaps a home base from which rebel missions could be sent out against corporate systems.[46] Other scholars have also used colonial metaphors to describe subcultural fannish communities. Suzanne Scott, writing about attempts to monetize the circulation of fan fiction in the late 2000s, compares fans' non-profit-oriented circulation of creative work to anthropologist Lewis Hyde's description of the ways that European colonizers in the Americas sought to enclose and commodify Native property systems, casting "online female fan communities as the Indians in the Hydean analogy."[47] These comparisons name a real difference between fan communities and dominant media systems, highlighting the ways that creative practices in the interstices of profit economies build communities and worlds.[48] Yet their use also risks erasing fans' status as complicit in or subject to the historical and ongoing violences of nonmetaphorical colonization.[49]

Fans are often acutely aware of the gendered and racialized power differentials in the media and among themselves alike—and suspicious of academic generalizations. Critical questions about race, gender, desire, and representation have been the subject of intense debate in fannish spaces for decades, and are addressed both explicitly and implicitly in some fans' creative works. This section seeks to move the conversation about fandom and colonization from the metaphorical to the material, focusing on specific works of critical fan production as they challenge science fiction television's reproduction of the temporalities of race and empire.

Subcultural science fiction media fandom is often assumed to be predominantly occupied by white people. The images from vidders' reflections on fannish practice in figures 6.1–6.14 support that view: every visible body that appears in them looks white, and while this is not wholly true for the full videos, it is close to it.[50] When images of fans appear in popular culture, as Mel Stanfill has shown, they are almost always white, and even "exceptions to the overall trend of fans as white serve to reinforce that whiteness is the expectation for fans."[51] The interdisciplinary field of fan studies has centered on gender and sexuality since its inception, but has only occasionally engaged with questions of race and racialization. In an important 2015 intervention, Rebecca Wanzo points out that "scholars sometimes lament the ubiquitous absence of race as an object of analysis," yet assume that the only way to incorporate it would be to seek out sociological studies of fans of color.[52] Wanzo goes on to highlight scholars' reluctance to explore the operations of whiteness in fan subcultures, suggesting that such an engagement would be likely to undermine desires for "a utopian understanding of fans in science fiction communities as being antiracist and progressive."[53] Her critique echoes comments made by fans of color, whose challenges to the racism they faced within predominantly white spaces have often been dismissed by white fans convinced of their own progressiveness.[54]

The critical analysis of race and empire is just beginning to become part of fan studies' interdisciplinary formation through the work of scholars like Wanzo, but it has been in the process of being enacted within fan communities for some time. Conversations about race within science fiction fandom reached critical mass in the late 2000s, when fans of color made a number of interventions aimed at challenging the normalization of white supremacy in their community.[55] Thanks to subcultural intersections and social media connections as well as to offline overlap, geek cultures formed around science fiction media began to converge with radical critiques of race and gender in ways that reflected national and transnational concerns with uneven distributions of power in the digital age. Out of these encounters have come fan works that traffic in and through networked knowledges around race, gender, sex, and transnational feminism, areas that are rarely considered to be part of media fan culture even in the most utopian depictions of its resistances. While they have never been a dominant group, participants in these networks—a group in which I include myself—have sought to mobilize the practices of fan creativity in order to demand more from the futures that speculative pop-culture production makes available.

As this chapter demonstrates, vids create affective continuities in ways that are similar to those of queer artistic forms, which Freeman describes as finding new means of "moving through and with time, encountering pasts, speculating futures, and interpenetrating the two in ways that counter the common sense of the present tense."[56] The common senses they counter might be the meanings attributed to the ending of a familiar story, or the idea that we should invest only a limited amount of our emotional and intellectual energy in popular culture. But they can also intervene in the political common senses that govern the construction of racial, gendered, national futurity along with the temporalities of media technology. Like the feminist utopians of this book's first chapter, who worked with received imagery of patriarchal futures and imagined their own possibilities within and against it, vidders may not break wholly with the conventions of media time, but they turn and twist them in ways that matter.

A powerful example of a remixed speculative future is the 2008 vid "How Much Is that Geisha in the Window?" (hereafter "Geisha") by Lierdumoa, which uses cuts, connotations, and affective connections to critique the racial and national lines along which popular culture, science fiction, and cultural rhetorics of global futures tend to flow.[57] The vid is a response to Joss Whedon's *Firefly* (Fox, 2002–2003), a short-lived science fiction TV series that depicts a future wherein much-loved rebel "Browncoats" try to hold on to independence in a world of corporate dominion by the "Alliance." *Firefly* fans calling themselves Browncoats organized after the show's cancellation in a successful activist campaign that culminated in the film *Serenity* (directed by Joss Whedon, 2005).[58] Challenging then-commonplace characterizations of Whedon as a feminist auteur and progressive force in mass media, Lierdumoa's vid offers a reading lesson in global race and gender politics for science fiction TV fans.

Firefly takes up a narrative of resistance that fans and other members of creative subcultures have long been fond of telling one another. For American fans in particular, to identify with resistance to imperial overlords is a contradictory yet familiar proposal. Mumia Abu-Jamal's contribution to the 2015 anthology *Octavia's Brood* analyzes this tendency through *Star Wars*, describing the film franchise as a system of fantasy by which citizens of a global superpower whose nationhood is rooted in slavery and genocide can imagine themselves as "oppressed, fighting for freedom" through the image of "a ragtag bunch of rebels . . . fighting against a fearsome, militarily invincible empire" even as they are being groomed to take up the imperial mantle.[59] *Firefly* updates this narrative for twenty-first century concerns, framing its rebels as marginalized descendants of American culture within a future dominated by Chinese technological, cultural, and military power. Lierdumoa brings things resoundingly back to the present by calling up the violences, rhetorical and material, that must be enacted in order to create the dubious pleasures of this fantasy marginalization.

"Geisha" skewers the frequently unacknowledged racial and cultural privilege on which US popular culture's imagined futures rely, zooming in instead on the implications of Whedon's decision to set his space-age version of the western genre in a Chinese world yet to cast no Asian actors in central roles. To an atmospheric instrumental

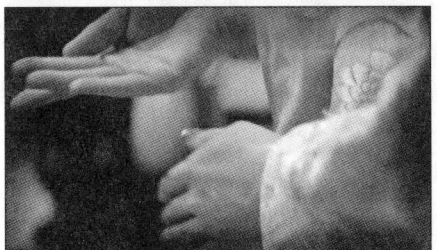

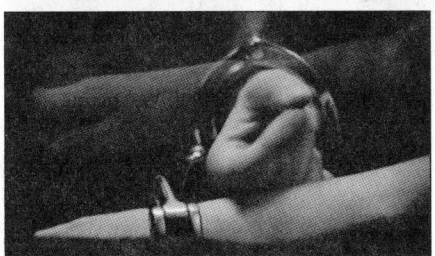

Figures 6.15–6.20. Asian bodies' labor, oppression, and vanishing: critique by juxtaposition in Lierdumoa's 2008 vid "How Much Is that Geisha in the Window?"

soundtrack of Damon Albarn's composition "Boyd's Journey," the vid makes its points by focusing on *Firefly*'s background imagery—on the design of the show's world rather than characters or plot. Lierdumoa's use of detail is such that the vid was used in 2009 as an exemplar in copyright hearings at the Library of Congress, which led to the granting of an exemption to Digital Millennium Copyright Act restrictions for remix artists, because it proved the need for high-quality capture of video footage.[60] Stereotyped images flicker in time with the twanging banjo and combine with small amounts of external film footage, whose juxtaposition with *Firefly* clips drives the critique. Footage of Chinese railroad workers from the western *3:10 to Yuma* (directed by James Mangold, 2007), along with one brief shot of a confederate flag, from *Gone with the Wind* (directed by Victor Fleming, 1939), intensify the vidder's focus on the multiple kinds of racialized labor that underlie the images of scrappy American independence employed by the science fiction western. A few shots from *Memoirs of a Geisha* (directed by Rob Marshall, 2005) highlight *Firefly*'s orientalist representation of Asian cultures as interchangeable, fetishized images appearing as background for the primary story of plucky rebels challenging interplanetary hegemony.

"Geisha" offers—unusually, given the understated meaning-making in which vids typically engage—a final message in on-screen text at its end. Red letters on a black background state that "there is one Asian actor in all of *Firefly*" and "she plays a whore." Through this statement, fans and others are invited to think about the matter of representation in imagined futures. Which kinds of racialized bodies get to star on American television in general and science fiction in particular, and why? Yet this punchline may also reduce the potential meanings of the vid. Taking the message as the meaning risks closing in on a reformist narrative where more or more diverse Asian bodies in Western TV would be the most desirable future media activism could possibly ask for. If we let go of this explicit claim and allow the vid to stand as an evocative speculative narrative in its own right, though, "Geisha" offers something more. It becomes an effective takedown of US-centric futurisms that fear a replacement of American empire with Chinese domination, paying lip service to multiculturalism while erasing the transnational flows of racialized and gendered labor.

In a key sequence, unnamed, undifferentiated Asian female bodies are made to literally disappear into the orientalized production design, highlighting their status as objects for consumption analogous to food and media (figures 6.15–6.16). As the vid goes on, we are repeatedly reminded of the bodies that build the things we use to create possible futures. As they did in the historical US West, edited-in Chinese laborers build a railroad (figure 6.17) that will be an important plot device in a key episode, "The Train Job" (figure 6.18). The history of race and settler colonialism on American soil is also invoked, though more briefly. A flash of the Confederate flag, a reminder of the history of the plucky rebel stories *Firefly* invokes, signals the erased labor of enslaved black people that built much of America. Not marked directly in the vid are the Native people whose murder, on Earth if not on the speculated colonized planets, constituted the precondition for the western genre, and on whom *Firefly*'s mindlessly violent Reavers were based.[61] The laboring bodies and hands that Lierdumoa carefully extracted from background scenery and forgettable moments are constant reminders that the future, like the present, takes work to build—and that this labor is often carried out by marginalized people who will not get to live in the futures that would not exist without them.

As the science fiction future is remixed to show how it reproduces the erasures of the United States' racial past and present, we might also come to think about the labor and the violence that are hidden in our production and consumption of the digital future itself. After all, our digital media future, including the remix cultures it makes possible, has been built from much of the same material as Whedon's space western. Who makes the devices of the digital future? As Lisa Nakamura reminds us in her work on transnational racialized and gendered labor in the production of digital hardware, almost all of the devices we are likely to use to type, tweet, watch TV, or vid have been touched by the hands of an Asian woman whose labor, along with the conditions in which that labor took place, vanishes from our understanding of the final product.[62] Lierdumoa shows many Asian hands in the vid, doing service labor or in chains; the vid demands that we see the labor and the oppression as two sides of a coin (figures 6.19–6.20). What to do once we have looked and seen is an open question, for the common consumer response of becoming paralyzed with guilt is scarcely a useful one. The creative work of vidding is not an answer, but it does open a possible conversation about how to mobilize the convergences of fannish and critical affect, futures dreamed and futures denied.

The possibilities of critical fandom were intensively realized in responses to *Battlestar Galactica* (SciFi, 2003–2009), where vidding became a technology to unpack the queer potentiality of the show's speculative future. Deeply engaged in emergent processes of television/ digital convergence through its webisodes, sponsored fan activity, and active online communities, *Battlestar Galactica* offered a prime example of contemporary anxieties surrounding media's industrial futures, or what Julie Levin Russo describes as "the reproduction of television itself."[63] While I do not give a fully detailed analysis of the series' conditions of production, strategies of representation, and complexities of reception here, it is a rich case study for the ways that diverse and deviant futures are continually produced, erased, rediscovered, and recombined through marginal subjects' and networks' speculative negotiations with dominant media.

Aired simultaneously on the SciFi (now SyFy) Channel in the United States and on Sky One in the United Kingdom between 2003 and 2009, the series was structured as an old future made new again. The plot, adapted from a 1978 space opera about human/lizard warfare, was about searching for a future: the last remnant of the human race floats adrift on a fleet of spaceships, trying to stay alive while at war with the cyborg robots who destroyed them and seeking a mythical home called Earth. The series, and the range of responses fans made to it both while it was airing and afterward, resonate with futural forms I have gone back in time to uncover throughout *Old Futures*—from speculative eugenics and the gendered burden of responsibility for the future of the human (and not so human) race, to the consequences of authoritarian efforts to wrest control of political futures, to alternative modes of biological and technological reproduction.

Key both to the future that *Battlestar Galactica* speculates and to the ways that fans would reimagine it are the Cylons: cyborg figures, existing as twelve human-appearing models as well as in chrome-plated robot and spacecraft form, who instigate the action of the series by annihilating the humans' twelve home planets. The succinct explanatory phrases of the first season's opening sequence give a sense of the multiplicity of connotations these figures carry:

> The Cylons were created by man.
> They rebelled.
> They evolved.
> They look and feel human.
> Some are programmed to think they are human.
> There are many copies.
> And they have a plan.[64]

The Cylons are rebels, interchangeable machinelike laborers, slaves, terrorists; they refuse to know their place. In an allegorical narrative common to science fiction robot stories, the cyborgs were created to do humanity's manual labor, but turned out to have too much in common with the dehumanized yet rebellious downtrodden subjects who had been relegated to subordinate roles before them.[65] Product and symbol of the technological future that humans created, their evolution went unnoticed because it did not benefit their creator-captors; taken to be machines, they were enslaved because their consciousness could not be recognized. Like technological creations since Mary Shelley's Frankenstein, the Cylons were made by those whom they came to terrorize, reckless creators reaping what they sowed.

In a series that sought to promote liberal ideas of a post-racial future with allegedly colorblind casting, the Cylons stood in for race in the tradition of white science fiction, offering a multipurpose racial allegory that Jinny Huh describes as "a code word for otherness."[66] Their upstart belief that they are worthy of personhood, "programmed to think they are human," harks to the discourses that justified European colonization, especially given that the humans name their own society as Colonial. Their enslavement links them to blackness (though just one model, who appears rarely, is played by a black actor). Tavia Nyong'o writes that the Cylons activate "an ur-conflict between masters and slaves, the outcome of which, in proper Hegelian fashion, could leave neither position untransformed," although placing their rebellion "outside the main storyline kept *Battlestar* from resonating with the long history of slave and plebeian insurrection."[67] Their affinity with/identity as technology links them to Asian-ness through discourses of techno-orientalism that figure Asians as robot-like.[68] And their sexual and reproductive practices, as demonstrated by myriad shots of naked newborn adult bodies emerging from pods into the arms of their waiting clone siblings, are decidedly queer.

The Cylons had a key feature that hooked them in to the technological future viewers were living through: they communicated through wireless networks. While its representations of digital futurity were figured through Cylons' dangerous alterity, *Battlestar Galactica*'s creators and marketers were much heralded for their uses of digital media, especially in the transmedia strategies that aimed to increase fans' investment. Webisodes brought viewers online; competitions encouraged creative use of the show's material; even five years after the last episode aired, the rebranded SyFy website hosted a *Battlestar*-themed massively multiplayer online game.[69] As Russo and Scott have written, however, such invitations to fan creativity encouraged quite narrow forms of engagement, and those forms were largely gendered male.[70] In unlicensed online realms, however, *Battlestar Galactica* had an incredibly active fan fiction and vidding community that built on subcultural practices of audience creativity to realize prospects of critically queer futurity at which the show could only hint. While the series often operated through reductive racial analogies, clichéd techno-anxieties, and heterosexual male gazes, transformative fan production liberated its unrealized possibilities for queer and decolonial futures.

For vidders embedded in counterpublics connected through digital networks that reverberated with desire, critique, and possibility, the Cylons offered a feast of creative potential.[71] A vibrant vidding culture developed around the show as it aired, and many vids explored intersections of reproduction, technology, violence, and sexuality. While the show asked us most often to identify with humans, the Cylon perspective—from which humanity is, at least in the earlier seasons, far from appealing—was often more seductive. Some followed the show's perspective quite closely, simply shifting their sympathies: Luminosity's 2006 vid "More Human than Human" used a White Zombie track to map the convergence of Cylon sexuality and destruction, splicing explosions and seductions with an even closer interweaving than the show offered.[72] Others sought more insistently to invite identification with Cylon alterity, including my 2008 vid "Love Is the Plan the Plan Is Death (Sons and Daughters)."[73] Citing James Tiptree Jr's 1973 science fiction story about alien reproductive drives, I reframed a song by the Decemberists, whose lyrics tell of post-apocalyptic rebuilding, to narrate the conjoined perspective of Cylon metal robots and humanistic cyborgs. Through the juxtaposition of the song's melancholically inflected hope ("When we arise, sons and daughters / we'll build our homes on the waters . . . . all the bombs fade away"), with the Cylons' disturbing experiments in antihumanist reproductive futurism, I hoped to frame their genocidal actions as directly related to their enslavement, whether as the rebellion of people driven past clemency or as acts of world-building gone wrong.

Vidders also used their creative work to highlight critical awareness of the historical narratives *Battlestar Galactica* invoked. In "Unnatural Selection," a 2009 crossover vid between *Battlestar Galactica*, the *Terminator* spinoff series *Sarah Connor Chronicles*, and Darwin's *Origin of Species*, Charmax highlighted the temporalities of evolution and eugenics within both techno-apocalypse narratives.[74] Pulling no punches in her commemoration of science fiction futures in which human-made technology destroys humankind, the vid cuts shots of human and cyborg skulls together and flashes up the caption, "Whom we have made our slaves / we do not like to consider our equal." In figure 6.21, a quota-

Figure 6.21. Darwinism revised into Cylon genetic experimentation in Charmax's 2009 vid "Unnatural Selection."

tion from Charles Darwin—"the preservation of favoured races in the struggle for life"—appears superimposed on an image from *Battlestar Galactica*, a flashback of human prisoners being experimented on as the Cylons turned the tables on their makers. The implication is that Darwin's "favoured races" have had their comeuppance, ousted by the evolutionary prowess of their own creations. In the superimposition of Darwin's text on images of violence carried out in the name of science, we might also see a reinscription of the damage done by those who appropriated Darwin's ideas to impose evolutionary temporalities onto human difference.[75] Anne Kustritz describes *Battlestar Galactica*'s focus on species futurity as a form of "eugenic pastiche," which presents narratives about the survival of the species as "wholly new" through a systematic "forgetting" of eugenic histories, including "colonialism and its sciences of racial superiority."[76] "Unnatural Selection," driving its Darwinian citations home over a pounding beat from DJ Lobsterdust's mashup of the Pixies' "This Monkey's Gone to Heaven," points toward the recollection of those histories, even if it does not take us all the way there.

The serial temporalities of television place creative fandom's interventions into continual obsolescence—at least until shows end and all new creation becomes equally unauthorized. Even as vidders explored multiple interpretations of Cylon metaphors, the next installment of the authorized narrative would always be there to cause trouble. Watching many of the vids described above, for those who have seen the show's finale, will be confusing: one is forced to travel back in time to a moment before narrative closure emerged. The final season's events led many fans to reinterpret their relationship to their show's temporalities, and I end this chapter by looking at how the series' futures were speculatively remixed by angry queer fan critics.

The plot of *Battlestar Galactica* was structured around teleologies wherein the past became the present and the future. Over five post-apocalyptic years, the relationship between humans and their cyborg enemy kin traced multiple analogies for post-9/11 American power relations, refracted through the influence of the Cold War–era original show.[77] Its "rigorous, messy, emotional exploration of important questions" even brought its stars, including veteran Latino actor Edward James Olmos, an invitation to discuss its themes at the United Nations.[78] Finally, in 2009, the show's overarching plot of the search for an "Earth" nobody thought existed was complete. And what had seemed, through all its genre trappings, to be a futuristic story, folded back on itself as the Colonial and Cylon fleets arrived on Earth—20,000 years in the viewers' past.

In the *Battlestar Galactica* finale, humans and Cylons come together to colonize the planet, setting aside their differences to form a new, hybrid humanity. In preparation to be our ancestors, the convergent Cylon/human colonists throw away their technology, abandoning the non-humaniform Cylons along with all other trappings of the science fiction future in favor of a fantasy pre-technological past. On discovering that there are already people on the planet (first observed in a shot that invites the viewer to look, with the settlers, through the colonial gaze of military-issue binoculars), they immediately make plans to teach the indigenous population to be human their way. The series' closure models Jodi Byrd's description of the ways that indigeneity becomes a "transit . . . through which US empire orients and replicates itself"[79] The contradictions of US empire that the series showcased through its metaphorical and literal depictions of race are suddenly resolved through the convenient appearance of an indigenous Other whose presence grants a fresh slate for the (re)construction of a colonial state.

A recurrent phrase throughout the series, "All of this has happened before and all of this will happen again," related the struggles of the human refugee fleet, which constantly wrestled with questions of national inclusion, military ethics, and liberal diversity, to US national politics in the era of the second US-Iraq War.[80] But in the finale, with the emergence of a new planet, the Colonial humans and their Cylon kin become "our" past by beating and breeding out the future of Earth's indigenous inhabitants. This restaging of settler colonialism was a depressingly perfect example of the dynamic whose limitations and oppositions this book was written to track: the ways that straight, colonizing forms of time shut down openings to different histories or queerer futures.

In the tired old future that the last episodes of *Battlestar Galactica* made new again, evolution became an alibi for the use of heterosexual reproduction to straighten out the queer technological possibilities the show had opened up. Lee Edelman, whose critiques of reproductive futurism have fueled this project, describes the heteronormative politics of "saving the children" as an excuse for avoiding the dangers of real change, resulting in a guarantee that projections of futurity will be "just as lethal as the past."[81] *Battlestar Galactica* both reproduced and complicated that narrative through a baby whose birth and childhood are key plot points. Hera is half Cylon and half Asian: science-fictional and real-world racializations overlap, since her mother is the Cylon sleeper agent turned informer, Sharon Valerii, played by Korean-Canadian actor Grace Park.[82] The child begins her life as a symbol for reproductive monogamous heterosexual love, which the Cylon community is obsessed with developing (despite the absence of any coherent reason for this quest). Hera ends up with her futuristic symbolism transposed into the past when she is identified in the last episode as "mitochondrial Eve," the hypothetical ancestor of the present-day human species.[83] Hera's transferral into everyone's matrilineal origin clarifies and exemplifies the conservative politics Nyong'o has identified as the racialization of reproductive futurism, wherein "heterosexuality has been a preeminent metaphor through which a heterogeneous, mongrel past is recuperated as both a stable racial binary in the present and a possible hybrid utopia in the future."[84] Her figuration, as manifestation of her parents' love story, defuses any radical power the Cylons might hold as metaphors for racial alterity. It suggests that post-human connections are valuable only insofar as they can translate into possibilities for an already achieved eugenic future. And speculative fiction's suggestive futurity becomes just another iteration of heteronormative cliché, in which liberal multiculturalism serves as an alibi for colonial white supremacy.

As Hera and her parents settled down for a short life on earth, the humans sent the technology that had brought them there into the sun. And a queer fan collective decided that enough was enough. Cylon Vidding Machine (CVM) was a loose collective of fan artists and theorists with whom I sometimes collaborated; the group made and shared queer art with and from the resources that *Battlestar Galactica* provided. Alert to the show's queer possibilities, the group's artworks developed an expanded notion of critical Cylonicity to play through possibilities for gendered and racialized narratives that would deviate from the future the show suggested. Asserting, in Russo's words, "the authority of diversified fan production over univocal industrial production," CVM attempted to revise the show's finale entirely in *Battlestar Redactica: A Fan-Edited Mutiny and Resurrection*, which refashioned the ending in a fashion fit for a queer and decolonial Cylon future.[85] The fan-edited finale, posted in May 2009 (the series finale aired in March of that year), closes with sweeping music and a montage of earth, sky, and robots: less an alternative than an insistence that the viewer continue the work of imagination. On a DVD-commentary track that the creators of *Redactica* made available, they stated that they wanted "the ending to be open, not bland, reductive, and unempowering for women," that viewers should finish on "the edge of something big"—something that is not the recolonization of an earthly past toward which the show had arguably been marching since its very beginning, something that would build another time and space out of the archives of that industrially produced future.[86] Yet it is difficult to watch *Redactica* without wishing for more and thereby seeing the extent to which its narrative is determined by the lack of resources available to critical fans in comparison to the media industries. The short, playful form of fan video, though relying on insider knowledge for full appreciation of the allusive connections on which it is based, works more ably within these limitations.

As *Battlestar Galactica* marched toward its close, women, queers, and most of the racially marked humans were killed off one by one. The Cylon Vidding Machine's comic video "The Enemy Within" (figures 6.22–6.25), created as a gift from four collective members to a fifth, rerouted the show's reliance on reproductive and colonial temporalities by digitally casting a queer fandom that lives on as a threat to the Colonial hierarchy that eventually wins.[87] Linking to contexts and histories well beyond the show it remixes, the vid has a fictional diegetic context as a warning video, riffing off the warnings against dangerous radical futures created by Cold War–era US propaganda. Depicting the Cylon women, who are eye candy for a straight male target audience in the original show, as queer female figures who "recruit"—and splicing in some explicit lesbian sex to get the point across (figure 6.22)—the vid moves from images of desire and seduction to violence and death, editing such that shots of the walking wounded appear after death and bring lost female characters back to life as lesbian zombies (figure 6.23). In case the editing was not enough for viewers to get the point, a title card declares: "These monstrous women pay a price for cheating death."[88] Announcing that "No one is safe," the vid comically reanimates the violence that *Battlestar Galactica*'s patriarchal, heteronormative, colonial conclusion

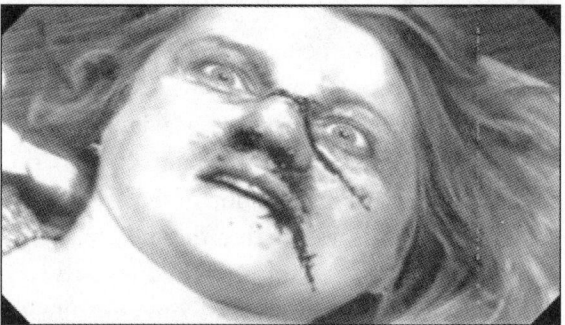

Figures 6.22–6.25.
Queerly remixing
Battlestar Galactica in
Cylon Vidding
Machine's 2009 vid
"The Enemy Within."

enacted on the bodies of women, making it explicit and suggesting a counternarrative (figure 6.24).

Among the last shots of "The Enemy Within" (figure 6.25) is a scene that appeared in the opening credits of the show, with multiple images of Cylon Number Eight, one of whose iterations is Sharon "Athena" Valerii, the mother of Hera and thereby of the hybrid colonial future.[89] In its season 1 iteration, this shot was the point where Sharon "Boomer" Valerii realized she was not human after all, when she arrived on a military mission to destroy a Cylon ship and discovered multiple naked versions of herself. Eve Bennett describes it as a classic stereotypical representation of Asian women's bodies as interchangeable, sexualized, and robotic.[90] In "The Enemy Within," the image marks an opening of nonhuman possibility: What if queer Cylonic multiplicity did not become part of the old colonial future but instead built a world with its own pleasures and possibilities? What if the naked Eights were not objects but subjects, and Sharon's encounter with them a reunion rather than a refusal?

The interpretations of the Cylon Vidding Machine do not make critiques of *Battlestar Galactica*'s heteronormativity and coloniality less true, but they allow moments of affective engagement to open up possibilities in which the show becomes a pretext for connectivity and world-making beyond its screens. Nodding to a viewer who will enjoy identifying with this "enemy within" and regarding the cyborg femmes fatales through what Russo has called "girlslash goggles," the vid interjects queer pleasures into what was a grindingly oppressive, and grindingly familiar, set of storylines for any viewer invested in queer female possibility.[91] It is a potentiality that leaves plenty to be desired—the representation of actual queer women and women of color staying alive, for a start. But it was never supposed to be a final say. It is simply one example of opening a future that seems otherwise unalterably closed.

Scholarly Vidding as Queer Methodology

Vidding began as an object of study for me, but it has become a methodology. I have come to research futurity, speculation, and media temporality not only by writing but also by remixing. In 2008, as I began to explore the ideas about reproduction and eugenics that would be central to this project, I was also becoming immersed in vidding culture for the first time. This was partly, as I discuss above, in the context of *Battlestar Galactica*'s critical fandom. But vidding would also become a central part of the research process that culminated in this book.

While writing early versions of what would become the third chapter of *Old Futures*, I created a remix video that edited images of *Children of Men*'s main character, Kee—the young black woman pregnant with the first child to be born in eighteen years—with female figures who represent futurity in other science fiction films: Evey in *V for Vendetta* and Selena in *28 Days Later* (directed by Danny Boyle, 2002). The song choice was from UNKLE's 1998 album *Psyence Fiction*: a collaboration with Thom Yorke titled "Rabbit in Your Headlights." Its lyrical allusions to surveillance, violence, and obsession are open to interpretation; I used them to gather together the ways that gendered and racialized bodies labor to make collective futures possible while having their individual futures curtailed. Calling attention to a moment in *Children of Men* that appears to cite Edelman's anti-futurist queer theory, I titled the vid "The Future Stops Here."[92] I sought to explore what it would mean to break down the narrative temporalities and reproductive orders in which these characters were variously encoded, to make visible the ways their images traffic beyond their original context: how a queer or feminist or antiracist audience fascinated against its better judgment might take problematic images and run with them.

Delving into and cutting through the film footage led me to develop the reading of Kee I elaborate in the wormhole between parts 1 and 2, in which I highlight that, though she is not a queer character in any obvious way, there is something queer about the way she fails to synchronize with the narrative in which she is situated. Making the vid shaped the way my argument about Kee and her precursors (who include Stella in *Woman Alive*, Edith in *Swastika Night*, and the unnamed black woman in Du Bois's "The Comet") developed, giving me a sense that I could move queerly through time into archives to touch them. I wrote annotations around it for a multimodal scholarly work in which I first began to make connections between remix, temporality, and queerness.

Vidding and multimodal writing gave me the space to explore scholarly ideas in diverse registers. As Kristina Busse and I write in a 2011 essay, the dense interpretive labor that vids perform means that they can become "connections between the world of academic digital humanities and the emerging digital critical and creative practices that thrive outside traditional institutional contexts."[93] Yet "ultimately different emotional and intellectual investments and rewards" structure the spaces through which vids can move.[94] "The Future Stops Here," as a standalone video or with its now dated annotated frame, has had a wider reach than my scholarship can usually hope to achieve and has been screened at fan and remix conventions as well as taught in classes. Yet it travels in those spaces without my interpretive control: a moment of my thinking captured for posterity, an old future speculating about work in progress that is now out of date yet still has ripples of influence.

In 2011, as I began to compose what would become chapter 5, I vidded *Born in Flames*.[95] I was compelled to write about the film but did not know yet how my argument would take shape; I wanted to get inside the film as a way to understand it better. As I re-watched the film and worked my way through the implications of its old future, Trayvon Martin was being mourned and the Black Lives Matter movement was beginning. I had spent the summer of 2011 in London, and my mind had been full of the riots exploding there from a cauldron of unemployment and institutionalized racism—sparked by the death of Mark Duggan, another young black man, at the hands of police. It felt desperately necessary to connect Adelaide Norris's and other women of color's oppression in the imagined future with structural anti-black racism in the present and the past.

Seeking to make this connection through music, I chose Tricky's 1995 cover of Public Enemy's "Black Steel in the Hour of Chaos," with vocals by Martina Topley-Bird. The song is about incarceration, the speaker a black man choosing to break out no matter the cost—knowing that he has been shut out of citizenship, of humanity as defined by white supremacy, since before his birth. Topley-Bird's vocals turn the original rap into a softer melody, dropping the song's explicitly violent storyline and giving it the feeling more of a question than of a challenge. Using this music brings in in hip-hop's remix genealogies to the white-women-dominated art form of vidding and highlights Adelaide's status as a racialized body subjected to state violence. Topley-Bird's voice, singing lyrics gendered male, encourages viewers to attend to the gender trouble of Adelaide's butch appearance.

Remixing the film this way frames it as a story about race, premature death, and post-mortem political power that has grown only more urgent since 2011. It also brings out the post-2001 resonances of the film's closing image (figure 5.10), which I used to invite viewers to consider whether the Women's Army's bomb should be seen as necessary revolutionary violence or mourned as a step too far. I expected that such questions of violence would form a larger part of my eventual argument about the film than they did; as I discuss in the previous chapter, I came to understand the bomb as a targeted intervention to communication networks rather than an act of sheer destruction. A vid, though, is an excellent venue in which to explore the ways that context can indelibly shift what an image means.

"Black Steel" was completed in time to premiere at the feminist science fiction convention WisCon in May 2012. I hoped to invite the feminist science fiction community in which the vid premiered, a community engaged in reckoning with the kinds of conflicts for which the film dramatizes a resolution, to write the film into a canon from which it has been surprisingly absent. My vid was well received at WisCon and after, and yet I continued to wonder about what it meant to have made it. Was I widening the reach of Borden's film, reimagining it, critiquing it, or altering it beyond recognition? In vidding *Born in Flames*, I was declaring myself a fan of it in a way that I was not when I used the same methodology to reinterpret the meaning of reproductive bodies in more mainstream science fiction films. When I vidded the film, I took it out of its originating rhythms and temporalities, replacing Borden's carefully constructed flow with an urgent, staccato rapidity. I extracted Adelaide's scripted story and made it a primary narrative, taking other elements from the film and flashing them in as interstices. Even as I brought her queer body front and center, in some ways I was straightening the story. I thought often of *Born in Flames*'s queer refusal to follow the conventions of either Hollywood narrative or science fiction spectacle, and about whether I was narrating it back toward those restrictive rhythms. My vid traffics exclusively in nonprofit spaces, but does it sell Borden's film back in to the capitalist media structures it evades and symbolically destroys all the same? Or does the existence of this vid on YouTube and Vimeo potentially bring Borden to unexpected audiences, like the all too brief appearance of *Born in Flames* streaming on Netflix?

I would eventually receive affirmation from an unexpected source, when Lizzie Borden herself reached out to me via social media to tell me that she had seen the vid and enjoyed it. Our correspondence led to my meeting her in Los Angeles for coffee and an intense, profound conversation in which she shared insights into the production and reception of the film that would shape the arguments I make about it in chapter 5 of this book. Borden affirmed my hopes for what vidding can be when the form is placed in conversation with social justice movements and critiques: a way of turning images, and our responses to them, into a mode of transformative communication that extends and expands their reach and their significance. Further possibilities for what the methodology of vidding might become are signaled by the work of Roxanne Samer, who has joined me in the project of scholarly vidding with her 2014 vid "Gold Rush," which uses images from *Orphan Black* alongside citations from feminist theory in order to craft "a transfeminist media archaeology of radical feminism's futures."[96]

When I began to share my project of scholarly vidding in digital humanities contexts, fellow scholars would ask me why I had chosen such a specific genealogy rather than drawing from other, more radical traditions of appropriative art and critique. I hope that this discussion has shown why vidding's affective histories mean, for me, that there is something about the form of the music video that makes a difference. Like the sugar-coated speculations of popular science fiction, vids are simple to watch, once you have learned the genre's conventions. But they demand ways of seeing and hearing that go against the flow. Vidding can teach us how to attend to the affective and material labor that shapes our audiovisual landscapes, even when it seems as if all that is happening is that somebody is unthoughtfully putting together preexisting media objects.

My practice as a vidder also makes me uncertain of these answers—especially as I use the techniques of vidding to engage with the work of independent media artists, who may not all be as welcoming of creative appropriation as Borden proved to be. The comparative ease with which we can now come by media files and remix them might mean a risk of losing context, letting go of cultural and subcultural specificities. All the same, vidding has brought me to recognize that to look for what might be said when others' words and images come together under your control is not to know what might come out. There is an alchemy to the timeline that is sometimes different and sometimes similar to the alchemy of the blank page. There is something deceptively easy about following the lines software makes available, and much that is unpredictable about the results.

To explore the possibilities of remixing the future and to experiment with them for myself was to learn methodology from unexpected places. It took me from theory-rich analyses of narrative and image into thinking about how media temporalities have been shifting and changing as digital technologies make it easier to mix up and mash up media production and consumption. Since I first began to vid, I have found the process to be experientially similar to the labor of producing scholarship in cultural theory. In both cases, finding one's archive and articulating connections between the creative and/or scholarly work of others is central. I have often wished to use the juxtapositional logic of a vid, rather than the explanatory and linear flow of textual argument, to demonstrate how imaginary futures created at particular historical moments both consolidate and undermine the ways power structures are embedded in temporal narratives. So far as it is possible in textual form, that is what I have sought to do in this book. Although the temporal and spatial journeys it has taken emerge from issues whose historical and material significance I could not have recognized without my scholarly training, it is with a vidder's instinct that I have brought the pieces together.

Epilogue

Queer Geek Politics after the Future

Is the future ancient history? Italian autonomist Marxist Franco "Bifo" Berardi argues that we are living in a "post-future" now that the twentieth century, "the century that trusted in the future," with its dominant narratives of capitalist expansion and technological development, has ended. [1] In place of the former future, his 2011 book calls for recognition of "the infinity of the present."[2] The idea of a post-capitalist post-future is an appealing speculative fiction, even as its capacity to become real must be unevenly distributed by race, gender, class, and location. The creators of the fictions I have traced in this book know that the infinite possibilities of past and present can also be contemplated from the perspective of a future we might seek to occupy even while knowing it to be untrustworthy.

In the decade-plus of work that has gone into this project, I have often thought that the future might well be over. Moving to the United States from Scotland soon after George W. Bush was re-elected, I girded myself with hope and cynicism as I set off to start working on a PhD—an amorphous project on the connections between science fiction and queer theory in mind. In the wake of the Second Gulf War, my optimistic, anarchistic fascination with transformative change and radical political futures seemed faintly naive and embarrassing even to me. I settled into a critical pessimism when I commenced my dissertation in the first flush of Obama's presidency, keen to counter the narratives of liberal, normative hope he put forward when it was so evident that the future he promised offered more of the same. I worked on the project for the full eight years of the Obama administration, submitting chapters and then the dissertation, revising, subtracting, and adding through my first years as an assistant professor (an institutional timeline both normative and rare in higher education's present economy). As I received my contract and began to revise for publication, I watched the meteoric rise of Donald Trump and felt my archival research on speculative responses to European fascism rise up to touch the present. Meanwhile, in my home country, austerity and Brexit crushed the progressive narratives of welfare state security with which I had been raised; a new social democratic nationalism with what I hoped might be anti-imperial tinges arose to entice me with the speculative possibilities of a Scotland disarticulated from the United Kingdom.

As I have unpacked the histories of complicated futures, the public political currency of hope and speculation has continually outpaced my attempts to understand where it all might be coming from. Conservative policymakers on both sides of the Atlantic have set out to eradicate the public educational and welfare systems that gave people like me the access and capacity to write scholarly work; the ravages of speculative capital are everywhere evident in the permanent, ubiquitous, and expanding presence of crisis. But futures for radical and queer alternate worlds are also continually becoming real—beyond just a few marginal communities and the pages of science fiction. When I left off writing it was to dive into news of anti-cuts protests and student occupations in the United Kingdom, California, and beyond; of the movements that became known as the Arab Spring; of the setting up and eviction of Occupy camps; of uprisings in London, Oakland, Baltimore; of a growing public attention to the racialized curtailment of individual collective futures thanks to the Movement for Black Lives; of challenges to the repeated, whitewashing assertion that queer and trans futures had fully emerged into the present.

As I finish writing in 2017, borders are slamming closed on both the nations I call home, protest actions are proliferating, and the institutions and infrastructures of government look ever more malevolent and less reliable. I have wondered what the point of coming back to science fiction and its cultures, to the small-scale contestations of pages and screens, might be, when worlds and futures away from those protected zones have been constantly falling apart and occasionally coming together. If I have found any answers in the process of writing, it is that speculative fiction, like queer critique, is a world-making practice that promotes speculative organizing, radical possibility, and queer love—even as it may have equally often worked against such impossible prospects.

Living in and with the futures of the past cautions against the temptation to exceptionalize the present. The imagined futures I unpack here, especially their conflicts and failures, provide me with terms and frameworks to understand the importance of hopes and dreams impossible within conventional political frames. Walidah Imarisha writes that "once the imagination is unshackled, liberation is limitless," and that speculative fiction is key to that unshackling.[3] The histories of speculative imagination I have traced here are not always liberatory; they often demonstrate how shackles we think have disappeared can nevertheless persist in minds and bodies. And yet, within and around queer and speculative temporalities that may be retrogressive, futuristic, transformative, or all three and more, there are possibilities that remix, reorient, and re-envisage futures both in the world and in shared imaginations.

On one hand, queer speculative fictions, like other histories of speculative futurity, are the projects of dreamers against power who are struggling for—and sometimes against—different futures now: in digital mode, on the street, in classrooms, in lasting ephemeral pleasures of dancing, loving, sex. On the other, they and we will inevitably end up reproducing old troubles while holding out for the transformative realization of new and not-so-new longings. I have tried to better comprehend the history of hoped-for, daydreamed, and warned-against futures by delving into some specific examples: by lingering with the compromised pleasures and critical possibilities they involve. I have explored marginal, quiet moments in conversations about technological and political possibility that are often overlooked but that suggest alternative speculative engagements with the present. We may not find an outside to systems of colonialism, capitalism, and racialized gender, but in working with and through their old futures, we can produce divergent and deviant alternatives, territories, and temporalities. In the speculative queer remixes of dominant time that this book has explored, the future becomes as immediate as the present, the present as inaccessible as the past, the past as unpredictable as the future. As one textual configuration of the continuing history of queer speculation, *Old Futures* stands as a reminder that no matter how dystopian the future seems, somebody somewhere will be trying to remake it. There are always new ways to live in the old future.

ACKNOWLEDGMENTS

Over the decade and a half in which it grew from daydream to manuscript, this book has been shaped by myriad individuals across multiple worlds. To name them all would be impossible; I apologize to those I have inadvertently omitted.

This project's seeds were sown while I was a part of the Sexual Dissidence and Cultural Change MA program at the University of Sussex, where Vincent Quinn, Esther Saxey, Alan Sinfield, and many participants in Queory seminars showed me the kind of world-making queer academia can, at its best, unfold. It grew to fruition while I was in graduate school at the University of Southern California in the Department of English and Program in Gender Studies, where an interdisciplinary atmosphere and flexible requirements enabled my engagement with faculty and students in American Studies and Ethnicity, Interactive Media Arts and Practice, and Critical Studies in Cinematic Arts. My thinking and writing were deepened by the work of the Center for Feminist Research, including the financial support of the Diana Meehan Award for feminist communication studies, and I was lucky to have the material and administrative aspects of my graduate school experience coordinated by Flora Ruiz (whose generosity in picking me up at LAX on my prospective student visit was just a small preview of things to come) and Jeanne Weiss.

The project has benefited from generous invitations to share my work at Northwestern University, University of Wisconsin Milwaukee, University of Sussex, University of Oregon, Maryland Institute for Technology in the Humanities, University of Illinois Urbana-Champaign, University of California San Diego, University of California Riverside, Durham University, and Pennsylvania State University, as well as the engagement of panelists and audiences at the Science Fiction Research Association, American Studies Association, National Women's Studies Association, Society for Cinema and Media

Studies, Modern Language Association, and the International Association for the Fantastic in the Arts. Portions of the manuscript have appeared in previous publications for which the editorial process also helped move my ideas forward. A short section of chapter 4 was published online as "Speculating Queerer Worlds" in *Social Text Periscope*, January 4, 2012, https://socialtextjournal.org. Parts of chapter 2 were published as "A Speculative History of No Future: Feminist Negativity and the Queer Dystopian Impulses of Katharine Burdekin's *Swastika Night*," *Poetics Today* 37, no. 3 (2016): 443–72. They are included here by permission of the publisher, Duke University Press. Parts of chapter 6 were previously published as "*Sense8* and Utopian Connectivity," *Science Fiction Film and Television* 9, no. 1 (2016): 93–95. They are included here by permission of the publisher, Liverpool University Press.

At New York University Press, my dream publisher from very early on, I am deeply grateful to Eric Zinner for longstanding support, patience, and the final title; to series editors Karen Tongson and Henry Jenkins for their unwavering excitement about the project; and to Alicia Nadkarni, Dolma Ombadykow, and Alexia Traganas for guidance through the publishing process. Many thanks also to the two reviewers whose thought and care has made this work infinitely better. A subvention award from the College of Arts and Humanities, University of Maryland enabled reproduction of the many images contained in these pages.

Many less formal discussions have also improved the work; most surprising and exciting have been my interactions with Lizzie Borden, whose excitement about the book has warmed my fangirl heart. L. Timmel Duchamp helped me to think about Elizabeth Burgoyne Corbett and brought her work back into print. I am indebted to Lierdumoa, Lim, Seah and Margie, Charmax, and the Cylon Vidding Machine for their work and their willingness to have me write about it.

Academic life is an isolating experience for many, but I have been part of intellectual communities that rarely left me feeling alone. At USC, my advisors had incredible faith in the expansive project I proposed; encouraging my transdisciplinary and creative ambitions, they pushed me to be bold, complex, and grounded in my thinking. Thanks to Jack Halberstam for modeling what it means to be a queer subcultural scholar and placing subversion and anarchy at the heart of academic life; to Karen Tongson, a savvy and inspirational mentor and guide whose 2006 seminar on queer of color critique shaped everything I've written since; to Kara Keeling, whose work on speculation, futurity, and technology has pushed me to aspire to greater depth and complexity; to Alice Gambrell for showing and teaching me how to think by making; and to Tara McPherson, inspirational instigator in critical new media studies, whose geeky excitement for this project was consistently sustaining. The book also bears the traces of transformative courses taken with Fred Moten, David Lloyd, Ruth Wilson Gilmore, and Tania Modleski, of class discussions and reading groups, and of my journeys through the less scholarly dimensions of life in Los Angeles and beyond alongside Patty Ahn, Deborah Al-Najjar, Jen Ansley, Jillian Burcar, Matt Carrillo-Vincent, Jih-Feh Cheng, Gino Conti, April Davidauskis, Mary Ann Davis, Penny Geng, Nora Gilbert, Raeanna Gleason, Kai M. Green, Silvie Grossmann, Raquel Gutierrez, Emily Hobson, Yetta Howard, Shayna Kessel, Sharon Luk, José Navarro, Arunima Paul, Annemarie Perez, Saba Razvi, Tom Sapsford, Suraj Shankar, Charlie Shipley, J. C. Sibara, Josie Sigler Sibara, Margarita Smith, Stefanie Snider, Sriya Shrestha, Sam Solomon, Virginia Solomon, Trisha Tucker, Erika Wenstrom, and Alex Wescott.

At conferences, on social media, and in print, my engagements with peers, mentors, collaborators, and co-conspirators in the fields to which this work contributes have enriched and inspired my thinking. The always incomplete list must include Aren Aizura, Aimee Bahng, Moya Bailey, Fiona Barnett, Zach Blas, Will Brooker, adrienne maree brown, Jayna Brown, micha cárdenas, Anne Cong-Huyen, Abigail De Kosnik, Grace Dillon, Ramzi Fawaz, Megan Graham, Jonathan Gray, Joan Haran, Ayana Jamison, Jessica Marie Johnson, Ronak Kapadia, Adeline Koh, Melanie Kohnen, Katie Morrissey, Lisa Nakamura, Tavia Nyong'o, Amanda Phillips, Margaret Rhee, Juana María Rodríguez, Roxanne Samer, Sami Schalk, Suzanne Scott, Shanté Paradigm Smalls, Rebekah Sheldon, Tuesday Smillie, Mel Stanfill, Louisa Stein, Shelley Streeby, K. J. Surkan, and Anna Wilson. Juliet Jacques and Kaite Welsh took divergent paths from our shared starting points, and I've been buoyed by their rise.

Since 2014, I have found space to build infinite worlds in collaboration with colleagues and students at the University of Maryland. In the Department of Women's Studies, faculty life alongside Elsa Barkley Brown, LaMonda Horton-Stallings, Seung-Kyung Kim, Katie King,

Robyn Muncy, Michelle Rowley, Iván Ramos, Catherine Schuler, Carol Stabile, Ashwini Tambe, and Ruth Zambrana has shown me how radical intellectual practice can be imbued into (or at least not completely leeched from) the most mundane of institutional tasks. Cliffornia Royals Pryor and Catalina Toala make administrative survival a pleasure, and JV Sapinoso's organizational superpowers give me life. In the creative interdisciplinary universe of Design Cultures and Creativity, it is a joy and a privilege to work with Jason Farman, Krista Caballero, and Jarah Moesch. Conversations with my UMD colleagues in many departments enriched my thinking in the final stretches of writing: Mercedes Baillargeon, La Marr Jurelle Bruce, Christina Hanhardt, Matt Kirschenbaum, Marilee Lindemann, and Martha Nell Smith have made Maryland home in the first three years, and I look to the future with excitement when I think how many brilliant colleagues I have yet to get to know. Before joining UMD, I worked for two years at Indiana University of Pennsylvania, where I learned much from Susan Comfort, David Downing, Bryna Siegel Finer, Tanya Heflin, Todd Thompson, and Veronica Watson.

Working with graduate students has taught me to recognize academic life as a world-building practice. At IUP, Lauren Shoemaker (whose research assistance helped lay the foundations for chapter 5) and Gregory Luke Chwala helped me learn to be a mentor; I'm proud to call both of them "Doctor." At UMD, my thinking has been enriched by the projects of DB Bauer, Avery Dame, Damien Hagen, Eva Peskin, Melissa Rogers, Anna Storti, Jessica Vooris, and the students in my graduate seminar, Producing Feminist Knowledge.

Alongside my institutional academic life, I have participated in the intellectual and affective worlds of fandom during all my years of writing. Crossing the aca/fan divide with me over and over again have been Kristina Busse—my co-writer, one-time adviser in the undercommons, and not infrequently the other half of my brain—and Julie Levin Russo. Melissa Getreu, Sandy Olson, thingswithwings, and Gretchen Treu have been permanent sources of inspiration and camaraderie. Through feminist science fiction and media fandom, I've been honored to know and learn from Jess Adams, alchemia, Anne, anoel, beccatoria, Bronwyn Bjorkman, Chesya Burke, chaila, Katherine Cross, Moondancer Drake, eruthros, Laurie Fuller, Jaymee Goh, Jeanne Gomoll, Jackie Gross, kiki_miserychic, Sumana Harihareswara, Karen Joy Fowler, Marianne Kirby, Lauren Lacey, Jackie Lee, S. Qiouyi Lu, Allison Morris, Pat Murphy, Debbie Notkin, oyceter, Laura Shapiro, Jeff Smith, Julia Starkey, Micole Sudberg, wrdnrd, and many more. This book owes at least as much to the feminist science fiction convention WisCon as it does to my academic affiliations.

None of it would be possible without my family of origin, who have never encouraged submission to the regimes of the normal: Anne Lothian, Eleanor Smith, Leslie Smith, Merryl Drakard, David Lothian, Annick Guidez, Kirsty Lothian, Anthony Cummins, Tom Lothian, and the next generation—Noa, Gordon, and Jean Lothian—to whom I couldn't be a prouder auntie. I wish Ellen Brush, Alan Lothian, Agnes Lothian, Alexander Lothian, and Pat McCusker could have seen it in print. And I thank my UK friends who have kept our connections alive despite years of miles of distance and who certainly qualify by now as family: Alice Bell, Liz Berry, Alex Dove, Catherine Foley, Linda Howie, Darren Irwin, Jennifer Waring.

Finally, my greatest acknowledgment must go to the beings who co-create my mundane world with me. I am grateful to Frida for wet-nosed, wagging-tailed reminders of mammal embodiment and for persuading me to go outside in all weathers. And over the last five years, in four cities and six apartments, my partner, Kathryn Wagner, has read multiple drafts of each chapter—dissuading me from my attachments to incomprehensible sentences, offering new insights on affect, ethics, and social justice, and reminding me that there are also worlds that exist outside of books and computers. With her, each day of my present is as exciting as a speculative future.

NOTES

INTRODUCTION

1 See Luckhurst, *Science Fiction*; Rieder, *Colonialism and the Emergence of Science Fiction*.

2 See Chakrabarty, *Provincializing Europe*; Lim, *Translating Time*; Keeling, "Looking for M—."

3 The conservatism of the future is Edelman's argument in *No Future*, while Muñoz's *Cruising Utopia* makes the case for ephemerality and Freeman's *Time Binds* for backwardness.

4 I am thinking of work such as Jameson's *Archaeologies of the Future* and Paik's *From Utopia to Apocalypse*.

5 Recent books emerging from those shared conversations include Sheldon, *The Child to Come*; Bahng, *Migrant Futures*; and Imarisha and brown, *Octavia's Brood*.

6 On speculative capital, see Pryke and Allen, "Monetized Time-Space Derivatives." An example of solutionism is Stephenson, "Innovation Starvation"; of abandonment, Engelhardt, "Ending the World the Human Way."

7 Gibson has used variations of this phrase in several interviews; see Morrow, "The Future Catches Up with Novelist William Gibson."

8 Halley and Parker, Introduction, 8.

9 Foucault is not often considered a utopian. But he closes the first volume of *The History of Sexuality* with a turn to the future, writing that "perhaps one day people will wonder" at the nineteenth and twentieth century's presumptions around sex and power (157). In an interview with Duccio Trombadori, he insists on his project's transformative potential: "I think that there are a thousand things to do, to invent, to forge, on the part of those who, recognizing the relations of power in which they're implicated, have decided to resist or escape them. . . . I do not conduct my analyses in order to say: this is how things are, look how trapped you are. I say certain things only to the extent to which I see them as permitting the transformation of reality" (Foucault, *Remarks on Marx*, 174).

10 de Lauretis, "Queer Theory," x.

11 Butler, *Gender Trouble*, 189–90.

12 Berlant and Warner, "What Does Queer Theory Teach Us About X?" 344.

13 Hall, *Queer Theories*, 11–12; emphasis in original.

14 Duggan, *The Twilight of Equality*, 50.

15 Cohen, "Punks, Bulldaggers, and Welfare Queens," 50.

16 See Conrad, *Against Equality*, which includes sections on marriage, military inclusion, and hate crimes laws.

17 Spade, *Normal Life*, 16.

18 Halberstam, *In a Queer Time and Place*, 1.

19 Edelman, *No Future*, 1–3.

20 Ibid., 31.

21 Ibid., 30.

22 Ibid., 165.

23 Firestone, *The Dialectic of Sex*, 85.

24 Ibid., 65.

25 See Spillers, "Interstices" for an important critique of the racism inherent in Firestone's association of the unmarked category woman with white womanhood. My analyses of feminist utopian and dystopian thought in chapters 1 and 2 likewise focus on ways that re-imaginings of reproduction have been complicit with imperial imaginaries.

26 Love, *Feeling Backward*, 10.

27 Freeman, *Time Binds*, xiii.

28 Ibid., xvi.

29 Ibid., 3.

30 Ibid., xi.

31 Ahmed, *Queer Phenomenology*, 175.

32 Ibid., 174.

33 See Hong, *Death beyond Disavowal*, for discussion of "impossibility" as a political strategy used by women of color feminist theorists to intervene in neoliberal temporalities that reinforce white supremacy by falsely marking racial violence as a thing of the past.

34 Cohen, "Punks, Bulldaggers, and Welfare Queens"; Ferguson, *Aberrations in Black*.

35 Somerville, *Queering the Color Line*, 24.

36 Rohy, *Anachronism and Its Others*, xv.

37 Keeling, "Looking for M—," 565.

38 Suvin, *Metamorphoses of Science Fiction*.

39 Jameson, *Archaeologies of the Future*, 66.

40 Luckhurst, *Science Fiction*, 3.

41 Sontag, "Imagination of Disaster," 44.

42 Schneider, *101 Sci-Fi Movies*, 7.

43 Stewart, "The 'Videology' of Science Fiction," 159.

44 Knight, *In Search of Wonder*, 1.

45 Freedman, *Critical Theory and Science Fiction*, xvi.

46 See Lefanu, *In the Chinks of the World Machine*; Barr, *Feminist Fabulation*; Melzer, *Alien Constructions*. On academic feminist science fiction scholarship as

a cultural formation, see Merrick, *The Secret Feminist Cabal*. For thorough and incisive analysis of 1970s feminist science fiction fandom, see Samer, *Receiving Feminisms*.

47 Haraway, "A Cyborg Manifesto."
48 Melzer, *Alien Constructions*, has chapters on *Alien* and *The Matrix*; see also Penley et al., *Close Encounters*.
49 Kilgore, "Queering the Coming Race."
50 Hollinger, "Something like a Fiction."
51 Pearson, "Towards a Queer Genealogy of SF."
52 Delany, "The Second Science-Fiction Studies Interview," 346.
53 "Speculative Fiction," TV Tropes, http://tvtropes.org (accessed March 14, 2017). I cite this fan-created wiki despite its textual instability because it is an effective index of popular knowledge in a subculture whose intensely active online presence is legendary.
54 For an example of the conservative element in science fiction culture, see Heer, "Science Fiction's White Boys' Club Strikes Back," The catalogue of the feminist science fiction publisher Aqueduct Press is an excellent source for speculative and science fiction that challenges hegemonic understandings of science and technology; Nisi Shawl's award-winning short story collection *Filter House*, for example, includes ghosts and orishas alongside clones and spaceships.
55 Bersani, "Is the Rectum a Grave?"
56 Muñoz, *Disidentifications*, 25.
57 Rieder, *Colonialism and the Emergence of Science Fiction*.
58 Eshun, "Further Considerations of Afrofuturism," 291.
59 Johnson, *Science Fiction Prototyping*, v.
60 See Kilgore, *Astrofuturism*.
61 See Imarisha and brown, *Octavia's Brood*, an anthology that can productively be understood as a set of politically radical science fiction prototypes.
62 Griffith and Pagel, *Bending the Landscape*.
63 Larbalestier, *Daughters of Earth*.
64 Hopkinson and Meehan, *So Long Been Dreaming*.
65 Dillon, *Walking the Clouds*.
66 See Chakrabarty, *Provincializing Europe*.
67 Lim, *Translating Time*.
68 Gordon, *Ghostly Matters*.
69 See Haiven, "Finance as Capital's Imagination?"; Shaviro, "Hyperbolic Futures."
70 Brown and Lothian, "Speculative Life."
71 Dorsey, "Sexuality and SF," 390.
72 Espiritu, *Body Counts*, 21. I thank Shelley Streeby for bringing my attention to this methodological correspondence.
73 Womack, *Afrofuturism*.

74 Dillon, "Indigenous Scientific Literacies"; Bahng, *Migrant Futures*; Marez, *Farm Worker Futurism*; cárdenas, "Shifting Futures"; Streeby, "Speculative Archives": Kafer, *Feminist, Queer, Crip*.

75 Delany, *Dhalgren*, 76; emphasis in original.

CHAPTER 1. UTOPIAN INTERVENTIONS TO THE REPRODUCTION OF EMPIRE

1 Ahmed, *Queer Phenomenology*, 178.

2 On heteronormative life narratives, see Halberstam, *In a Queer Time and Place*; on development and progress as straight temporalities, see Freeman, *Time Binds*.

3 Caserio et al., "The Antisocial Thesis in Queer Theory."

4 See Sinfield, "Review of Lee Edelman's *No Future*," on Edelman's national context.

5 Edelman, *No Future*, 15.

6 Ibid., 16.

7 See Muñoz, *Cruising Utopia*; Keeling, "Looking for M—"; Giffney, "Queer Apocal(o)ptic/ism" for a range of the many responses that critique Edelman's engagements with racialization and gender by focusing on how reproductive futurisms can be evaded rather than looked at them directly. A notable exception is Fraiman, *Cool Men and the Second Sex*, 130.

8 For a discussion of how the structural inequalities of reproductive labor persist even where the gender of reproducing bodies is trans and queer, see Aizura, "Communizing Care."

9 In *Radiant Motherhood* (1921), for example, which I discuss further in chapter 2, British women's rights activist Marie Stopes argued for prenatal care, birth control, and the sterilization of the unfit. On Margaret Sanger's similar US-based work and the overlap between pro-eugenics, pro-abortion, and white supremacist politics in the history of American feminism, see Ordover, *American Eugenics*, and Davis, "Racism, Birth Control, and Reproductive Rights."

10 Benjamin, "Theses," 257. See Ferguson, "The Relevance of Race for the Study of Sexuality" on Benjamin's importance for critical sexuality and race studies.

11 Benjamin, "Theses" 262.

12 Freeman discusses Jephcott's 1978 translation of Benjamin's *gesättigen* (saturated) as "pregnant" (*Time Binds* 155); Redmond's 2001 translation of Benjamin's essay as "On the Concept of History" translates the German word as "overflowing" (np). I have chosen to center the earlier translation because of the immense influence this rendition of Benjamin has had in English-language criticism.

13 Benjamin, "Theses," 262. In the Redmond translation, this passage is rendered "Historicism depicts the 'eternal' picture of the past; the historical materialist, an experience with it, which stands alone. He leaves it to others to give themselves to the whore called 'Once upon a time' in the bordello of historicism. He remains master of his powers: man enough, to explode the continuum of history" (n.p.).

14 This moment in Benjamin is reminiscent of Marx's "use of the prostitute as the apocalyptic symbol of capital's emergence," which Ferguson critiques in *Aberrations in Black* (9).

15 Benjamin, "Theses," 260.

16 See Hewitt, *Fascist Modernism* for discussion of the politics of the modernist avant-garde.

17 Kristeva, "Women's Time," 16.

18 See Wegner, *Imaginary Communities*; Luckhurst, *Science Fiction*.

19 For a broad overview of shifts in the everyday experience of temporality at the turn of the twentieth century, see the introduction to Doane, *The Emergence of Cinematic Time*.

20 Wegner, *Imaginary Communities*, 62.

21 Ahmad, *Landscapes of Hope*, 19.

22 Bellamy, *Looking Backward*, 36.

23 Ibid., 62.

24 Ahmad, *Landscapes of Hope*, 27.

25 See ibid., and Gandhi, *Affective Communities*, which analyzes an "antiimperialism" made available through "small, defiant" "utopic flights from imperial similitude" that challenged the distinctions between "West" and "non-West" (7).

26 Murphy, *Time Is of the Essence*, 4.

27 Bellamy, *Looking Backward*, 185.

28 Ahmad, *Landscapes of Hope*, 20.

29 Ledger, *The New Woman*, 5.

30 Murphy, *Time is of the Essence*, 6.

31 Lewes, *Dream Revisionaries*, 1.

32 Galton, *Hereditary Genius*, 362.

33 Freud, *Civilization and Its Discontents*, 97.

34 Galton, *Hereditary Genius*, 348.

35 Mazumdar, *Eugenics*, 17.

36 Dollimore, "Perversion, Degeneration, and the Death Drive," 96.99.

37 Foucault, *The Will to Knowledge*.

38 Ibid., 26.

39 Ibid., 54.

40 Ibid., 188.

41 Ibid., 54.

42 Stoler, *Race and the Education of Desire*, 178.

43 See Kessler, *Daring to Dream*; Lewes, *Dream Revisionaries*.

44 See Larbalestier, *The Battle of the Sexes in Science Fiction*.

45 Weinbaum, *Wayward Reproductions*, 104.

46 Galton, *Hereditary Genius*, 205.

47 Gilman, *Herland*, 205.

48 Gilman, "With Her in Ourland," 387.

49 Lane, *Mizora*, 92.

50 Ahmad, *Landscapes of Hope*, 59.

51 See Nadkarni, *Eugenic Feminism*.

52 Hossain, "Sultana's Dream," 8.

53 In 2011, lionpyh wrote a wonderful fan fiction response extending Hossain's story: see lionpyh, "Fifty Years in the Virtuous City."

54 Lothian, "A Foretaste of the Future," 2.

55 Duchamp, "Elizabeth Burgoyne Corbett."

56 Corbett, *New Amazonia*, 26–29.

57 Ibid., 30.

58 Ibid., 44–45.

59 Ibid., 48–67. Ireland, whose anticolonial movements are depicted with some sympathy, is remembered as a country "subjugated by the warlike English," which "suffered for centuries from want and oppression" (49). Of the indigenous Irish in New Amazonia, she writes: "It was many years . . . before the last flickerings of discontent were extinguished, and before they could be induced to take kindly to the mode of living universally enforced throughout the country. This end being finally attained, the mingled races became amalgamated, and were henceforth alike devoted to their country and its constitutional laws. It was well for New Amazonia in the end that a good many Irish women had survived, for the arts of linen-making and lace-making, which they perpetuated and improved, are among the most valuable sources of revenue in the country" (70).

60 Ibid., 113–14. The contrast with Gilman's elevation of motherhood is striking. Lewes notes that British women utopians often shied away from the total elevation of motherhood and domesticity that was common among their settler American contemporaries, preferring to idealize women's participation in the public sphere (58–59).

61 Robb, "The Way of All Flesh," 6.

62 Corbett, *New Amazonia*, 115.

63 Ibid., 74.

64 Ibid., 70.

65 Hasian, *The Rhetoric of Eugenics*, 73; 78.

66 Caird, *The Morality of Marriage*, 183.

67 Corbett, *New Amazonia*, 115.

68 Ibid., 34.

69 Ibid., 181.

70 Ibid., 181–85.

71 Beaumont, *Utopia Ltd.*, 13.

72 Ertz, *Woman Alive*, 34.

73 Maslen, *Political and Social Issues*, 7.

74 Pares came from an upper-class English military family and drew campaign maps during the Second World War as well as illustrating and designing for commercial publishers. Her most abstract illustration for *Woman Alive* provided the cover image for this book. See Connelly, "Bibliography—Bip Pares," and "Bip Pares 2."

75 Ertz, *Woman Alive*, 100.

76 Ibid., 33.

77 Ibid., 82.

78 Ibid., 34.

79 Ibid., 39, 27.

80 Ibid., 143.

81 Ibid., 42.

82 Ibid., 90.

83 Ibid., 99.

84 Ibid., 64.

85 Female masculinity has often been fostered within nationalist and military projects: see Halberstam, *Female Masculinity*.

86 Ertz, *Woman Alive*, 42.

87 Ibid., 100.

88 Ibid.

89 Ibid.

90 Forty years after the publication of *Woman Alive*, Russ wrote *We Who Are About To . . .* about another white woman who refuses to give up her reproductive autonomy for the sake of the human species. Russ's narrator must resort to murder and suicide to avoid being reduced to a reproductive vessel, a contrast that highlights the respect Stella's personal autonomy is granted by the men around her.

91 Ertz, *Woman Alive*, 181.

92 Ibid., 160.

93 Ibid., 162.

94 Ibid., 173.

CHAPTER 2. DYSTOPIAN IMPULSES, FEMINIST NEGATIVITY, AND THE FASCISM OF THE BABY'S FACE

1 Orwell, *Nineteen Eighty-Four*, 280.

2 For example, the statement that "every one belongs to everyone else" seems designed to make an implied reader draw back in horror. Huxley, *Brave New World*, 47.

3 Haldane reviewed Huxley's novel on its appearance, making perhaps a sidelong reference to her earlier, less successful work in her opening statement: "The writing of 'Utopias' is far more entertaining than reading them" (Haldane, "Dr. Huxley and Mr. Arnold," 597).

4 See Patai, "Orwell's Despair, Burdekin's Hope"; McManus, "*Swastika Night*: *Nineteen Eighty-Four*'s Lost Twin."

5 *Nineteen Eighty-Four* topped the bestseller charts immediately after the election of Donald Trump, with Sinclair Lewis's 1935 *It Can't Happen Here* also gaining in sales; see Gilbert, "*1984* Isn't the Only Book Enjoying a Revival." This chapter was, however, conceived and largely completed before the rise of Trumpism.

6 See Cohen, "Punks, Bulldaggers, and Welfare Queens"; Puar, *Terrorist Assemblages*; Reddy, *Freedom with Violence*.

7 Haldane, *Man's World*, 282, 8.

8 Claeys, "Origins of Dystopia," 307.

9 See chapter 1 for discussion of the ambiguous continuity of Enlightenment optimisms in the 1930s.

10 Benjamin, "Theses," 262.

11 Ibid., 260.

12 da Silva, *Toward a Global Idea of Race*, xii.

13 I discuss blackness and futurity further in chapter 3.

14 Baccolini and Moylan, "Dystopia and Histories," 7.

15 Bloch, *The Possibility of Hope*, 196. I discuss utopian impulses further in chapter 4.

16 Hocquenghem, *Homosexual Desire*; Bersani, "Is the Rectum a Grave?" and *Homos*; Edelman, *No Future*.

17 Hocquenghem, *Homosexual Desire*, 148.

18 Ibid., 148–50.

19 Bersani, "Rectum," 220–22.

20 Bersani, *Homos*, 180.

21 Edelman, *No Future*, 21. I engage these arguments further in the introduction and chapter 1.

22 Ibid., 151.

23 Benjamin, "Conversations with Brecht," 218.

24 Ibid.

25 Edelman, *No Future*, 151.

26 US right-wing rhetoric accusing Obama, feminists, or anyone with an investment in the welfare state of being simultaneously fascist and socialist suggests that, for many, the term has lost all meaning save a vague dystopian threat (see Slane, *A Not So Foreign Affair*). Even where "fascism" accurately describes political movements, this remains true; white nationalist Richard Spencer, for example, was punched by an antifascist protester at Donald Trump's inauguration in January 2017 while denying that he was a "Neo-Nazi." See Burris, "WATCH: White Nationalist Richard Spencer Sucker-Punched in the Face during Trump Inauguration."

27 Edelman, *No Future*, 165.

28 See Hall, *Outspoken Women*, for examples of Stopes's writings on sexuality.

29 Stopes, *Radiant Motherhood*, 244.

30 Ibid., 245.

31 See Adamson, *Charlotte Haldane*, 26.

32 Ibid., 21.

33 Squier, *Babies in Bottles*, 108.

34 Haldane, *Motherhood*, 152.

35 Ibid., 235.

36 See Adamson, *Charlotte Haldane*, 65.

37 Stopes, *Radiant Motherhood*, 208.

38 Haldane's vision of a scientific state has much in common with Wells, *A Modern Utopia*.

39 Haldane, *Man's World*, 8.

40 Ibid., 64.

41 Ibid.

42 Mbembe, "Necropolitics," 18.

43 Haldane, *Man's World*, 184.

44 Gamble, "Gender and Science," 5.

45 Adamson, *Charlotte Haldane*, 92–98. The status of Jewishness in this novel deserves sustained examination: one Jewish man (Mensch) instigates the scientific revolution and encourages the extermination of most of humanity, while another (Arcous Weil) sparks a conspiracy against the state and makes several soliloquies on the Jewish "race" that recall anti-Semitic ideas about Jewish conspiracies. Haldane, *Man's World*, 154–55.

46 Russell, "The Loss of the Feminine Principle," 16.

47 Gamble, "Gender and Science," 13.

48 Haldane, *Man's World*, 51.

49 Squier, "Conflicting Scientific Feminisms," 183.

50 Haldane, *Man's World*, 51–54.

51 Ibid., 54.

52 Ibid., 130.

53 Ibid.

54 Ibid., 296; Stopes, *Radiant Motherhood*, 157.

55 Haldane, *Man's World*, 237.

56 Ibid., 298.

57 Ibid., 282.

58 Ibid., 298–99.

59 Ibid., 188.

60 Ibid., 260.

61 Ibid., 292.

62 Ibid., 260.

63 See for example Seed, "Aldous Huxley, *Brave New World*," 484.

64 Huxley, *Brave New World*, 9; 102.

65 Huxley, *Brave New World Revisited*, 6.

66 Edelman, *No Future*, 165.

67 Huxley, *Brave New World*, 3.

68 Ibid., 38.

69 Ibid., 159.

70 Ahmed, *The Promise of Happiness*, 50.

71 Halberstam, *The Queer Art of Failure*, 123.

72 Burdekin, *Proud Man*, 226.

73 Ibid., 227.

74 Burdekin's novels under her full name or Kay Burdekin were *Anna Colquhoun* (1922); *The Reasonable Hope* (1924); *The Burning Ring* (1927). *The Children's Country* (1929); *The Rebel Passion* (1929); and *Quiet Ways* (1930). As Murray Constantine, she published *Proud Man* (1934); *The Devil, Poor Devil* (1934); *Swastika Night* (1937); and *Venus in Scorpio* (co-written with Margaret Goldsmith, 1940). *The End of This Day's Business* was posthumously published in 1989. Where not otherwise specified, biographical and bibliographic information is taken from Patai's introductions and afterwords to the reissued novels.

75 "Her friends and admirers did though include Radclyffe Hall, H.D., Margaret Goldsmith, and Frederick Voight, as well as the Woolfs and Bertrand and Dora Russell" (McKay, "Katharine Burdekin," 187).

76 This novel's sympathetic presentation of the monk and his sister draws on the discourse of inversion without falling into the tragic narrative exemplified by Hall's *The Well of Loneliness*, published a year earlier. As is common in encounters with old futures, contemporary readers in search of affirmative histories for our political allegiances are likely to experience affective whiplash as we shift from Burdekin's gentle affirmation of nonheteronormative gender to the virulent racism in her depiction of slavery as necessary to the development of black Americans and annihilation as the destiny of "the yellow races" (Burdekin, *The Rebel Passion*, 244). It is easy to see why this novel has not been reissued by feminist presses.

77 In *The End of This Day's Business*, Burdekin views the power of empire, white supremacy, and religious fundamentalism as all being tied to masculinity, inverting the male-reason/woman-emotion dyad to argue that the "silliness" of masculine domination renders it unfit for power (61). This faith is not maintained in *Swastika Night*: evidently, the rapid pace of political events in 1930s Europe cured Burdekin of her belief in the reasonableness of women and its capacity to prevail.

78 The most famous is Dick's 1962 *The Man in the High Castle*, now a successful Amazon Original series.

79 Croft, "Worlds without End," 209.

80 Williams, "Back from the Future," 152. On Nazism as a cult of masculinity, see Theweleit, *Male Fantasies*.

81 Burdekin, *Swastika Night*, 79.

82 Ibid.

83 The idea of reproduction without "the stinking complicity and help of the female womb" was also seductive for Italian futurists such as F. T. Marinetti, whose support of fascism is well documented. See Orban, "Mothers of Invention," 57.

84 Burdekin, *Swastika Night*, 14.

85 Weininger also insists that maleness and femaleness cannot be defined through biology alone, that "female men" and "male women" and any number of "sexually indeterminate types" exist, and that their deviations from a heterosexual norm must be considered fully natural. His critique of the biological basis of gender replaces biology with Platonic models of man and woman that allow him to casually

dismiss all counterexamples to his arguments as the result of "sexual indeterminacy." Weininger, *Sex and Character*, 9.

86 Sengoopta, *Otto Weininger*, 11.
87 Burdekin, *Swastika Night*, 70.
88 Weininger, *Sex and Character*, 216.
89 Woolf, *Three Guineas*, 129.
90 On Woolf and fascism, see Gättens, "*Three Guineas*."
91 Burdekin, *Swastika Night*, 82.
92 Ibid.
93 Koonz, *Mothers in the Fatherland*, xx.
94 Ibid. On old feminist futurity, see chapter 1.
95 Both of these are quoted in Theweleit, *Male Fantasies*, 54–55.
96 Spurlin, *Lost Intimacies*, 73.
97 Jensen, "The Pink Triangle," 322.
98 Marshall, "The Contemporary Political Use of Gay History."
99 Bersani, *Homos*, 171.
100 Ibid.
101 Ibid.
102 Ibid., 183.
103 Ibid., 171.
104 Carlson, *Thinking Fascism*, 180.
105 Ibid., 181.
106 Burdekin, *Swastika Night*, 120.
107 Ibid., 33–34.
108 Ibid., 166.
109 Joannou, "*Ladies, Please Don't Smash These Windows*," 182.
110 Sedgwick, *Between Men*.
111 Burdekin, *Swastika Night*, 157.
112 Ibid., 15.
113 For an antifascist dystopia contemporary with *Swastika Night* where old women do spearhead resistance, see Jameson, *Then We Shall Hear Singing*.
114 Burdekin, *Swastika Night*, 70; 12.
115 Ibid., 70; 14.
116 McKay, "Katharine Burdekin," 198.
117 Claeys, "Origins of Dystopia," 126.
118 Patai, "Orwell's Despair, Burdekin's Hope."
119 Crossley, "Dystopian Nights," 98.
120 Constantine, *Swastika Night*, n.p.; emphasis in original.
121 Brighouse, "Three Novels and a Nightmare," 7.
122 Burdekin, *Swastika Night*, 23.
123 Ibid., 67.
124 Ibid., 77.
125 Ibid., 69.

126 Ibid., 78. On indifferent British responses to Nazism's early rise, see Brothers, "British Women Write the Story of the Nazis," 259.

127 Burdekin, *Swastika Night*, 106.

128 I am thinking of examples such as Winston's longing for Julia in Orwell's *Nineteen Eighty-Four*.

129 Stec, "Dystopian Modernism vs Utopian Feminism," 184–85.

130 Burdekin, *Swastika Night*, 160–65.

131 Nast, "Queer Patriarchies," 895–96.

THE FUTURE STOPS HERE

1 Butler, *Undoing Gender*, 39.

2 For additional perspectives on *Children of Men*, see Shaw, *The Three Amigos*, on transnational aspects, and Udden, "Child of the Long Take," on cinematic style.

3 Edelman, *No Future*, 12.

4 Ibid.; emphasis in original.

5 See chapters 1, 2, and 3 for extended discussion of eugenics.

6 James, *The Children of Men*, 7–8; emphasis added.

7 Cuarón quoted in Riesman, "Future Shock."

8 James, *The Children of Men*, 188.

9 Ibid., 58.

10 *Sleep Dealer* (dir. Alex Rivera, 2008), in which Mexican factory workers control robots that send their labor to the United States while their bodies remain south of the border, offers a powerful speculative commentary on this.

11 See Ahmed, *The Promise of Happiness*, 160–99, on Theo.

12 The writers evidently do not think that her lack of recollection needs an explanation, relying perhaps on racialized gender stereotyping that will lead viewers to fill in their own backstory.

13 Bahng, "Speculative Acts," 113.

14 Spillers, "Mama's Baby, Papa's Maybe," 208.

15 Brown, "The Human Project," 123.

16 See Hodapp, "The Specter of the Postcolonial Child," 177.

17 Lothian, "The Future Stops Here (2008)," *Queer Geek Theory*, September 1, 2012, www.queergeektheory.org. I discuss this video further in chapter 6.

18 See sabrina_il, "After Tomorrow," and sophinisba, "Sick."

CHAPTER 3. AFROFUTURIST ENTANGLEMENTS OF GENDER, EUGENICS, AND QUEER POSSIBILITY

1 Lorde, *Collected Poems*, 255.

2 See Patterson, *Slavery and Social Death*; Mbembe, "Necropolitics."

3 "The history of blackness is testament to the fact that objects can and do resist" (Moten, *In the Break*, 1).

4 See, for example, Fox and Older, *Long Hidden*, an anthology funded through a wildly successful Kickstarter campaign.

5   See Taylor, *From #BlackLivesMatter to Black Liberation.*

6   See Reddy, *Freedom with Violence.*

7   "We are the dreams of enslaved Black folks, who were told it was 'unrealistic' to imagine a day when they were not called property. Those Black people refused to confine their dreams to realism, and instead they dreamed us up. Then they bent reality, reshaped the world, to create us" (Imarisha, "Rewriting the Future," n.p.).

8   Gumbs, "We Can Learn to Mother Ourselves," 12. See Gumbs, "Speculative Poetics" for further engagement with Lorde as a creator of speculative poetic visions in relation to the black feminist vampire connections I discuss in the second half of this chapter.

9   Dery, "Black to the Future," 180.

10 Ibid., 179. See Marika Rose, "The Uncomfortable Origins of 'Afrofuturism.'" An Und Fur Sich, November 18, 2014. https://itself.blog.

11 See Womack, *Afrofuturism.*

12 Kelley, *Freedom Dreams*, 5.

13 Phillips, "Black Quantum Futurism," 16.

14 Ellison, *Invisible Man*, 8. See Yaszek, "An Afrofuturist Reading of Ellison's *Invisible Man.*"

15 Kara Keeling, "Black Futures," presented at the Los Angeles Queer Studies Conference, UCLA, May 5, 2010.

16 See Puar, *Terrorist Assemblages*, and part 1 of this book.

17 See Carrington, *Speculative Blackness.*

18 Csicsery-Ronay Jr., "Science Fiction and Empire," 231.

19 da Silva, *Toward a Global Theory of Race.*

20 Gilroy, *The Black Atlantic.*

21 Thomas, *Dark Matter*, x.

22 Rutledge, "Futurist Fiction and Fantasy," 237.

23 Mosley, "Black to the Future," 405.

24 Page references to "The Comet" are to its publication in *Dark Matter.*

25 Thomas, *Dark Matter*, xii.

26 Du Bois, "The Comet," 251.

27 The mundanity of apocalypse is a defining premise of black science fiction. See Bould, "The Ships Landed Long Ago"; Smith, "Droppin' Science Fiction."

28 Du Bois, *Darkwater*, 63.

29 Du Bois, "The Comet," 254. See Rabaka, "W. E. B. Du Bois's 'The Comet' and Contributions to Critical Race Theory," 26; Kaplan, *The Anarchy of Empire*, 209.

30 "Death wasn't a goal of its own but just a by-product of commerce, which has had the lasting effect of making negligible all the millions of lives lost. Incidental death occurs when life has no normative value, when no humans are involved, when the population is, in effect, seen as already dead" (Hartman, *Lose Your Mother*, 31).

31 On slavery as the basis for racial capitalism, see Robinson, *Black Marxism.*

32 Du Bois, "The Comet," 252.

33 Kaplan, *The Anarchy of Empire*, 207.

34 Du Bois, "The Comet," 251.

35 Ibid., 255.

36 The other early twentieth-century work that entered the emergent canon of black science fiction through *Dark Matter*, George Schuyler's 1931 *Black No More*, considers racial futurity even more explicitly as a capital investment. In that satirical novel, the future of racialization looks set to disappear when whiteness goes up for sale. But it is the black protagonists (all heterosexual men) who profit, giving up on racial history to buy up a future of access to whiteness in which color will be fetishized.

37 See Weinbaum, "Interracial Romance and Black Internationalism," 101.

38 Du Bois, "The Comet," 264–65.

39 Ibid., 264.

40 Ibid.

41 See Ordover, *American Eugenics*; Stern, *Eugenic Nation*.

42 English, *Unnatural Selections*, 29; 17.

43 Ibid., 16.

44 Quoted in ibid., 43.

45 Du Bois, "The Comet," 268.

46 Ibid.

47 Du Bois, *Darkwater*, 189.

48 Quoted in Rohy, *Anachronism and Its Others*, 94.

49 Stavney, "Mothers of Tomorrow," 543–44.

50 Ibid., 544.

51 Larsen, *Quicksand and Passing*.

52 Spillers, "Mama's Baby, Papa's Maybe," 214.

53 Ibid., 203.

54 Morrison, *Beloved*, 275.

55 Gordon, *Ghostly Matters*, 22.

56 Keeling, "Looking for M——," 578.

57 Ibid., 567. See part 1 for extended discussion of Edelman.

58 Weheliye, *Habeas Viscus*, 8.

59 Rodriguez, *Sexual Futures*, 184.

60 Freeman, "Time Binds, or, Erotohistoriography," 58.

61 My approach in bringing these texts together owes much to my work in remix; see chapter 6.

62 On lesbian vampire figurations, see Case, "Tracking the Vampire"; on the vampire as gay man, see Hansen, "Undead."

63 Marx, *Capital*, 367.

64 Haraway, *Modest Witness*, 215.

65 Vora, *Life Support*, 3.

66 Ibid., 13.

67 Gomez, *The Gilda Stories*, x.

68 See Lorde, "Uses of the Erotic: The Erotic as Power"; Freeman, *Time Binds*.

69 Gomez, *The Gilda Stories*, xi. On Butler's import, see Streeby, *Imagining the Future of Climate Change*.

70 Shawl, "The Third Parable," 208.

71 Gomez, *The Gilda Stories*, 11–12.

72 Winnubst, "Vampires, Anxieties, and Dreams," 9.

73 Gomez, *The Gilda Stories*, 10–11.

74 Butler, *Fledgling*, 8.

75 Ibid., 69.

76 Ibid., 79.

77 Ibid., 69.

78 Gomez, *The Gilda Stories*, 10.

79 Morgensen, *Spaces between Us*, 26.

80 Smith, "Queer Theory and Native Studies," 50.

81 Gomez, *The Gilda Stories*, 177.

82 Ibid., 196.

83 Gomez, *The Gilda Stories*, 44.

84 Tinsley, "Black Atlantic, Queer Atlantic," 199.

85 Butler, *Fledgling*, 72.

86 Ibid., 218.

87 For more on histories of gender, eugenics, and speculative futurity in Europe at this period, see part 1.

88 Butler, *Fledgling*, 233.

89 Ibid., 154.

90 Ibid., 305–7.

91 Gomez, *The Gilda Stories*, 235.

92 Ibid., 234.

93 Ibid., 251.

94 Nyong'o, *The Amalgamation Waltz*, 5.

95 See Greer, "Yes We Can."

96 See Vint, "Only by Experience"; Knabe and Pearson, "Gambling against History."

CHAPTER 4. SCIENCE FICTION WORLDING AND SPECULATIVE SEX

1 Delany, *Dhalgren*, 10.

2 Ibid., 76; emphasis in original.

3 Ibid., 699–700.

4 See Chisholm, *Queer Constellations*; Warner, *Publics and Counterpublics*.

5 Delany, *Times Square Red*, 90.

6 See Delany, "The Politics of Paraliterary Criticism."

7 Nelson, "Making the Impossible Possible," 110.

8 Tucker, *A Sense of Wonder*, 55.

9 "What Is the It Gets Better Project?," It Gets Better, www.itgetsbetter.org (accessed March 9, 2017).

10 Lim, "Queer Suicide"; Puar, "In the Wake of It Gets Better."

11 Sedgwick, "Queer and Now," 1.

12 Ahmed, *The Promise of Happiness*, 59.

13 Warner, *Fear of a Queer Planet*, vxi.

14 Berlant and Warner, "Sex in Public," 558.

15 Ahmed, *The Promise of Happiness*, 223.

16 Muñoz, *Disidentifications*, 23.

17 Ibid., 100.

18 Muñoz, *Cruising Utopia*, 49.

19 Ibid., 147–68; 83–96.

20 Dolan, *Utopia in Performance*, 7. Part 1 of this book suggests cautions to Dolan's utopia, showing ways that this kind of intense feeling can also serve imperialism, fascism, and racism.

21 Bloch, *The Principle of Hope*, 196.

22 Ibid., 4.

23 Ibid., 144–45. See Levitas, *The Concept of Utopia*, 67.

24 Muñoz, *Cruising Utopia*, 5.

25 Bloch, *The Principle of Hope*, 64.

26 Ibid., 5.

27 See part 1 for discussion of Edelman.

28 Bloch, *The Principle of Hope*, 18.

29 Suvin, *Metamorphoses*, 63; emphasis in original.

30 Ibid., 61.

31 Jameson, *Archaeologies of the Future*, 7.

32 Suvin, *Metamorphoses*, 64.

33 Delany, "The Necessity of Tomorrows," 35.

34 Delany, "Starboard Wine: An Introduction," 15.

35 Delany, "About 5,750 Words," 44; emphasis in original.

36 Delany, "The Necessity of Tomorrows," 30.

37 Ibid., 31.

38 See Jerng, "A World of Difference," 256.

39 In the same essay, Delany describes his reading of politicized African American fiction at the same age, when realist descriptions of American racism made him feel that change was hopeless. See Tucker, *A Sense of Wonder*, on the relationship of Delany's work to African American literary studies.

40 See the introduction for discussion of this book's terminological decisions.

41 Delany, "Second Science-Fiction Studies Interview," 317.

42 Pearson, "Alien Cryptographies."

43 Sallis, Introduction, xiii.

44 Nyong'o, "Do You Want Queer Theory?" 105.

45 Ibid., 103. For more on punk futurities in the 1970s, see chapter 5.

46 Ibid., 106.

47 On *Dhalgren* and urban space, see Bianco, "Queer Urban Composites."

48 Gibson, "The Recombinant City," xiii.

49 Califia, "The City of Desire," 213.

50 Ingram, "Strategies for (Re)Constructing Queer Communities," 461.

51 On critic Algis Budrys's challenge to *Dhalgren*'s science fiction status, see Jerng, "A World of Difference," 264.

52 Delany, *Dhalgren*, 4.

53 Ibid., 372.

54 John P. Mitchell, "Dhalgren," Dhalgren MOO, 2003, http://mentallandscape.com /Dhalgren.htm.

55 Delany, *Dhalgren*, 376–77.

56 Ibid., 414.

57 Ibid., 801, 1.

58 Weedman, *Samuel R. Delany*, 63; Bray, "Rites of Reversal."

59 Butler, "Heteronormative Futures."

60 Delany, *Dhalgren*, 307.

61 Ibid., 674.

62 Delany, "Of Sex, Objects," 40.

63 Delany, *Dhalgren*, 123–53.

64 Delany, *Dhalgren*, 676.

65 Jerng, "A World of Difference," 270.

66 Delany, *Dhalgren*, 675–77.

67 Ibid., 672.

68 Delany, *Dhalgren*, 684–85.

69 Nash, *The Black Body in Ecstasy*, 3. Racialized gender and questions of consent are further explored in the relationship between George and June, a black man and young white woman whose interactions are linked both to the ruin of Bellona and to speculative transformations such as the appearance of a new moon in the sky. See Tucker, *A Sense of Wonder*, 70–78. I discuss gender in Delany further in the wormhole section between parts 2 and 3.

70 Ibid., 480.

71 Allison, "Puritans, Perverts, and Feminists," 100.

72 Online encounters might be more likely these days, but science fiction's texts and fandoms still offer lifelines to weird kids and adults who need more narratives of sexual and gender identity than their immediate worlds can offer. See the second wormhole and chapter 6.

73 Weinstone, "Science Fiction," 43.

74 Ibid., 47.

75 Delany, *Dhalgren*, 720.

76 Delany, "Second Science-Fiction Studies Interview," 343.

77 Berlant and Warner, "Sex in Public," 548.

78 Ibid.

79 Freedman, *Critical Theory and Science Fiction*, 150.

80 See Rosenberg and Rusert, "Framing Finance," which focuses on Delany's work in the fantasy genre but quotes his assertion that "science fiction represents what can

most safely be imagined about the transition from a money economy to a credit economy" (67).

81 Delany, *Stars in My Pocket like Grains of Sand*, 166.
82 Ibid., 73.
83 Rogan, "Alien Sex Acts," 450.
84 Califia, *Sex Changes*, 277.
85 See Stone, *The War of Desire and Technology at the Close of the Mechanical Age.* I discuss digital media futures further in chapter 6.
86 See Tucker, "The Necessity of Models," 253.
87 Delany, *Stars in My Pocket like Grains of Sand*, 90.
88 Ibid., 79.
89 Ibid., 79; my emphasis.
90 Reid-Pharr, "Clean."
91 Delany's 1976 *Trouble on Triton* addresses gender transition directly. Its representations of a trans woman who transitions out of a desire to create the woman she would have most desired when she was a man, as well as of a black trans man who has transitioned both racially and sexually, have elicited many and contradictory analyses. See Snorton, "Gender Trouble in *Triton*."
92 Delany, "Second Science-Fiction Studies Interview," 323.
93 Delany, *The Motion of Light in Water*, 268. I return to this assertion and its implications in the wormhole section that follows this chapter.
94 Delany, *Times Square Red*, xv.
95 Delany, *Stars in My Pocket like Grains of Sand*, 225.
96 Ibid., 278.
97 Ibid., 276.
98 Ibid., 213–14.
99 Reid-Pharr, "Clean," 401.
100 Morgensen, *Spaces between Us*, 25.
101 Delany, *The Motion of Light in Water*, 202.
102 Chisholm, *Queer Constellations*, 45.
103 Halberstam, *In a Queer Time and Place*, 2.
104 *Through the Valley of the Nest of Spiders* (2012) is an exception whose 800-page length may explain where Delany's speculative energies were directed in the 1990s and 2000s, although its modest depiction of technological and social change in the background of a sexual and familial relationship firmly located at the margins is a style of world-building very different from his science fiction of the 1970s and 1980s.
105 On *Neveryon*, see Rosenberg and Rusert, "Framing Finance."
106 Delany, "The Tale of Plagues and Carnivals," 476; emphasis in original.
107 Reid-Pharr, "Clean," positions *Stars* as a prescient critique of gay male respectability politics. My observations about the timing of Delany's work are based on publication dates and are not claims to any knowledge about his actual writing process.
108 See Crimp, "How to Have Promiscuity in an Epidemic," 262–63.
109 Lehr, *Queer Family Values*, 98.

110 Delany, *Stars in My Pocket like Grains of Sand*, 117–18.

111 Ibid., 120.

112 Ibid., 301.

113 Ibid., 340.

114 Ibid., 342.

115 Reid-Pharr, "Clean," 401.

116 Delany, *Stars in My Pocket like Grains of Sand*, 66.

117 Bray, "To See What Condition Our Condition Is In," 19.

118 Freedman, *Critical Theory and Science Fiction*, 157–9.

119 Hartman, *Scenes of Subjection*, 33.

120 Delany, *Stars in My Pocket like Grains of Sand*, 3.

121 Ibid.

122 "Racism is the state-sanctioned and/or extralegal production and exploitation of group-differentiated vulnerability to premature death" (Gilmore, *Golden Gulag*, 28).

123 Compare the opening of da Silva, *Toward a Global Theory of Race*, with the official's address to soon-to-be-Rat Korga:

> No tomorrow. . . . You are black and young; you are in jail or on probation. . . . You are the underclass: people without a future, people who do not know how to behave properly because the institutions—families, businesses, churches, and so on—have left the ghettos with the middle class, who took advantage of affirmative action to take better jobs and find better places to live. You deal drugs. You are a rapist. You are a criminal. You may even be a terrorist. We will keep you off the streets. If we do not arrest you, we will fire at you, as many bullets as necessary. (xii)

124 Hartman, *Scenes of Subjection*, 116.

125 Ibid., 48.

126 Delany, *Stars in My Pocket like Grains of Sand*, 23.

127 Ibid., 31.

128 Ibid., 49.

129 Ibid., 50.

130 Freedman, *Critical Theory and Science Fiction*, 158.

131 Reid-Pharr, "Dinge," 11.

132 Hartman, *Scenes of Subjection*, 78.

133 Delany, *Stars in My Pocket like Grains of Sand*, 200; emphasis in original.

134 Rosenberg and Rusert, "Framing Finance," 82.

135 Delany, *Stars in My Pocket like Grains of Sand*, 197; 278.

136 Delany, *Dhalgren*, 10.

TRY THIS AT HOME

1 Groovy Movies, "Sense8—1x06—Orgy Scene," December 30, 2015, https://www.youtube.com/watch?v=sE9XpfJYyMY. The upload is the most popular video on this Portuguese-language YouTube channel by an order of magnitude.

2 Berlant and Warner, "Sex in Public," 551.

3 Boyd, "Social Network Sites as Networked Publics."

4 Delany, *Dhalgren*, 21.

5 Muñoz, *Cruising Utopia*, 33.

6 See Califia, *Public Sex*.

7 Delany, *Times Square Red*, 27.

8 Ibid., 30.

9 Ibid., 31.

10 Ibid., 31–32.

11 Ibid., 32.

12 Rodríguez, *Sexual Futures*, 14.

13 Warner, *Publics and Counterpublics*, 57.

14 Rodríguez, *Sexual Futures*, 14; Horton-Stallings, *Funk the Erotic*.

15 "MCI TV Ad 1997," posted by Steven Jones, October 12, 2010, https://www.youtube .com/watch?v=ioVMoeCbrig.

16 For critiques of the early digital discourses "Anthem" represents, see Nakamura, *Cybertypes*, 14; Chun, *Control and Freedom*, 144.

17 See Bailey et al., "*Sense8* Roundtable."

18 Ameen "left the show amid rumors that he did not want to kiss a man as scripted and that he resented taking direction from Lana and Lilly Wachowski," though "another theory cites Lana Wachowski's anti-Black racism as Ameen's motivation" (ibid., 82).

19 Rodríguez, *Queer Latinidad*, 117.

20 Ibid., 120.

21 Rodríguez, *Sexual Futures*, 183, 26.

22 Ibid., 26.

23 Butler, *Undoing Gender*, 29.

24 See chapter 4's discussion of Delany's *Stars in My Pocket like Grains of Sand*.

25 A recent oral history project in which I was a participant found this transformative encounter with fan fiction archives to be a widely shared experience. See De Kosnik, *Rogue Archives*, 135.

26 I think it was Noy Thrupkaew, "Fan/Tastic Voyage: A Journey into the Wide, Wild World of Slash Fan Fiction," Bitch Media, April 1, 2003, https://bitchmedia.org/.

27 On slash fandom and gender identifications, see Willis, "Writing the Fables of Sexual Difference."

28 Muñoz, *Cruising Utopia*, 39.

29 Ibid.

30 thingswithwings, "Known Associates."

31 Lothian, Busse, and Reid, "Yearning Void and Infinite Potential."

32 This quotation is not in the published article but can be found at its accompanying online archive: http://slashroundtable.livejournal.com.

33 Lothian, Busse, and Reid, "Yearning Void and Infinite Potential," 104, 107.

34 Ibid., 104. I supplied the young dyke, as well as the Delany reference.

35 Ibid., 105.

36 Delany, *The Motion of Light in Water*, 268.

37 See Lothian, "Sex, Utopia, and the Queer Temporalities of Fannish Love."

38 Willis, "Writing the Fables of Sexual Difference," 293. See also Busse and Lothian, "A History of Slash Sexualities."

CHAPTER 5. QUEER DEVIATIONS FROM THE FUTURE ON SCREEN

1 Gail Simone, Twitter post, June 26, 2016, 8:26 a.m., https://twitter.com/Gail Simone/status/747088670692278274. Numerous respondents did give examples, but all were from literature, comics, or television.

2 Benshoff and Griffin, *Queer Images*, 10.

3 MacCormack, *Cinesexuality*, 7.

4 Science fiction television has moved more quickly to incorporate LGBTQ identities, notably in the *Doctor Who* spin-off *Torchwood* (BBC/Starz, 2006–2011), which starred out gay actor John Barrowman as Captain Jack Harkness, an immortal pansexual from the future. See Wälivaara, "Dreams of a Subversive Future."

5 Benshoff and Griffin, *Queer Images*, 11.

6 On these films' speculative elements, see Knabe and Pearson, *Zero Patience*; Freeman, *Time Binds*, 111–23; Howard, "Alien/ating Lesbianism."

7 Friedberg, "An Interview with Filmmaker Lizzie Borden," 37.

8 Woolf, *A Room of One's Own*; Lorde, "Poetry Is Not a Luxury."

9 Sobchack, *Screening Space*, 91; Johnson, *Science Fiction Prototyping*, 60.

10 On the imagined and real stakes of space travel in science fiction, see Kilgore, *Astrofuturism*.

11 Méliès, "Trick Effects," 2.

12 Lindsay, *The Art of the Moving Picture*, 283, 288.

13 See Kirby, *Lab Coats in Hollywood*, 199–201; Johnson, *Science Fiction Prototyping*.

14 Sontag, "The Imagination of Disaster," 44.

15 Ibid., 42.

16 See Grewell, "Colonizing the Universe"; Nama, *Black Space*.

17 Abramovitch, "Disaster Movie Stills Masquerade as Hurricane Sandy on Social Media."

18 Box Office Mojo, "The Day after Tomorrow," www.boxofficemojo.com (accessed March 9, 2017).

19 This phrase is attributed to both Fredric Jameson and Slavoj Žižek. See Fisher, *Capitalist Realism*, 2. I hope that this book offers an array of examples of the diverse, contradictory ways in which ends of capitalism have been and are being continuously imagined—albeit in contexts that major Marxist theorists might disregard.

20 Sheldon, *The Child to Come*, vii.

21 Ibid.

22 Rich, *New Queer Cinema*, 29.

23 Ibid. Thanks to Roxanne Samer for calling my attention to this passage in Rich.

24 Goltz, "Love(sick) Aliens in the Wasteland," 110.

25 Rich, *New Queer Cinema*, 49 (on Jarman), 7 (on Borden).

26 Edelman, *No Future*. See part 1 for extensive engagement with his work.

27 Nyong'o, "Do You Want Queer Theory," 111.

28 Caserio et al., "The Antisocial Thesis in Queer Theory," 824.

29 Ibid., 822.

30 Savage, *England's Dreaming*, 355.

31 Ibid., 356; 541.

32 A Scot born and raised, I am acutely aware of what is erased when "England" is used as a synonym for the United Kingdom of Great Britain and Northern Ireland. To call Jarman's work "British," though, would elide his career-long exploration of local and national English histories and imaginaries that, while they may be familiar to most citizens due to the dominance of English culture, do not carry the same weight across Scotland, Wales, and (Northern) Ireland. I use "England/English" throughout this chapter to refer to these, while "Britain" names the expansionist imperial imaginaries that subsume and incorporate the non-English parts of the British Isles.

33 Jarman, *Dancing Ledge*, 168.

34 Savage, *England's Dreaming*, 377.

35 The popular understanding of *Star Wars* as a watershed film is demonstrated by the separation of "pre–*Star Wars*" and "post–*Star Wars*" eras at a fan site I discovered while googling my prospective book title. See "OldFutures.com: Where Futures of the Past Meet the Present," http://www.oldfutures.com (accessed March 9, 2017).

36 Jarman, "B Movie: Little England / A Time of Hope," in *Jubilee: Six Film Scripts*. These collected scripts include two other works of dystopian science fiction: "Neutron" (1980), in which armed militia hunt down a David Bowie-esque prophetic performer; and "Sod 'Em" (1986), which depicts a privatized police force, mass quarantine for the HIV-positive, and the criminalization of homosexuality. Though these films were never made, Jarman's 1987 film *The Last of England* is rich in imagery that draws from them.

37 On the early punk scene as having been "unusually accommodating to women and gay men," see Ellis, *Derek Jarman's Angelic Conversations*, xx.

38 Vivienne Westwood, "Open T Shirt to Derek Jarman from Vivienne Westwood," V and A Collections, http://collections.vam.ac.uk (accessed February 16, 2017).

39 Ibid.

40 On implications and histories of the term "punk," see Nyong'o, "Do You Want Queer Theory."

41 Jarman, *Dancing Ledge*, 171.

42 Ellis, *Derek Jarman's Angelic Conversations*, 49; 51.

43 Jarman, *The Last of England*, 109.

44 Savage, *England's Dreaming*, 430.

45 Ibid., 320, 108.

46 Ibid., 229.

47 Ibid., 392–93. See Gilroy, *There Ain't No Black in the Union Jack*.

48 Jarman, *Dancing Ledge*, 171.

49 Savage, *England's Dreaming*, 520.

50 Ibid., 540.

51 Jarman, *Dancing Ledge*, 171.

52 See for example Fairbairns, *Benefits*, a 1979 novel about government control over women's bodies by way of social welfare.

53 Hebdige, *Subculture*.

54 Chapter 4 discusses world-building in more depth.

55 Jarman, *The Last of England*, 109.

56 O'Pray, *Derek Jarman*, 8.

57 Brown, "Brown Girl in the Ring," 460.

58 Ibid., 463; Savage, *England's Dreaming*, 237.

59 Savage, *England's Dreaming*, 242.

60 Brown, "Brown Girl in the Ring," 456.

61 Jarman, *The Last of England*, 82.

62 The full text of the speech can be viewed at "Enoch Powell's 'Rivers of Blood' Speech."

63 Gilroy, *There Ain't No Black* in the Union Jack, 47.

64 Anonimus di Anonimi, "Enoch Powell's Rivers of Blood Speech," 2013, https://www.youtube.com/watch?v=mw4vMZDItQo.

65 Section 28, the legislation banning "promotion" of homosexuality in schools, which was passed in 1988, was repealed in Scotland in 2000 and in England in 2003. In 2009, Conservative Prime Minister David Cameron made a public apology for it. Andrew Pierce, "David Cameron Says Sorry over Section 28 Gay Law," *Telegraph*, July 1, 2009, www.telegraph.co.uk.

66 Jon Savage, Twitter post, June 24, 2016, 12:34 a.m., https://twitter.com/Jon Savage1966/status/746244721048227840.

67 Jarman, *Dancing Ledge*, 170.

68 Jarman, *The Last of England*, 109.

69 See Ellis, *Derek Jarman's Angelic Conversations*, 64.

70 Hilderbrand, "In the Heat of the Moment," 7.

71 Davies, "Surfaces, History, and Noise."

72 See Stanley, Tsang, and Vargas, "Queer Love Economies"; Rich, *New Queer Cinema*, 202–3.

73 Jaehne, "Born in Flames," 24; Friedberg, "An Interview with Filmmaker Lizzie Borden."

74 I was able to meet with Borden in Los Angeles in June 2016—a serendipitous encounter that she in fact initiated after seeing my video remix of her film, as

I discuss in chapter 6 below. Where Borden's insights are described in this chapter without citation of a written text, I am drawing on our conversation.

75 Friedberg, "An Interview with Filmmaker Lizzie Borden," 39.

76 Duchamp, personal communication. See Duchamp, *Alanya to Alanya*, *Renegade*, *Tsunami*, *Blood in the Fruit*, and *Stretto*. The novels were written in the 1980s and eventually published between 2005 and 2008.

77 Hilderbrand, "In the Heat of the Moment," 9.

78 Sobchack, *Screening Space*, 305.

79 Ibid., 300, 305.

80 On literary science fiction, see chapter 4.

81 Dillon, "'It's Here, It's that Time,'" 39.

82 I discuss my video "Black Steel" in chapter 6.

83 The lyrics are not easy to hear, but are printed in Lassinaro, Born in Flames, 2.

84 Friedberg, "An Interview with Filmmaker Lizzie Borden," 37.

85 My own first introduction to the film is a good example: I was at a performance by the feminist pop band Le Tigre in the early 2000s, and Kathleen Hanna scrawled the name of the film on a poster I asked her to sign.

86 Friedberg, "An Interview with Filmmaker Lizzie Borden," 37.

87 Hulser, "Les Guerilleres," 14.

88 Jaehne, "Born in Flames," 22.

89 Willse and Spade, "We Are Born in Flames," 3.

90 Hanhardt, "LAUREL and Harvey," 31.

91 Friedberg, "An Interview with Filmmaker Lizzie Borden," 39.

92 Dillon, "'It's Here, It's that Time,'" 38.

93 The phrase "the future in the present" originates with to C. L. R. James and is used extensively by Muñoz, for whom it signals the politicized affective longing of/for queer futurity. Munõz, *Cruising Utopia*, 49–64.

94 See Hong, *Death beyond Disavowal*, 74.

95 See Smith, "A Press of Our Own."

96 Combahee River Collective, "Black Feminist Statement," 270. That this statement appeared the same year as British punk's explosion and Queen Elizabeth II's jubilee should not go unnoticed. See Brown, "Brown Girl in the Ring," 460.

97 Garza, "A Herstory of the #BlackLivesMatter Movement."

98 Hulser, "Les Guerilleres," 14; Hanhardt, "LAUREL and Harvey," 30.

99 See Beckford, "Stop Posting Videos of Black Folks Dying."

100 Hanhardt, "LAUREL and Harvey," 27.

101 Holland, *The Erotic Life of Racism*, 77–8.

102 Friedberg, "An Interview with Filmmaker Lizzie Borden," 39.

103 Ibid., 43–44.

104 Borden made this point during our conversation in 2016.

105 Stewart, "The 'Videology' of Science Fiction," 159.

106 "Media Justice," Reclaim the Media, www.reclaimthemedia.org (accessed April 19, 2013).

107 Dillon, "'It's Here, It's that Time,'" 48.

108 On dystopian impulses, see chapter 2.

CHAPTER 6. HOW TO REMIX THE FUTURE

1 McLuhan, *Understanding Media*.

2 On early twentieth-century utopias, see chapter 1.

3 See Chun, *Control and Freedom*, 37–76.

4 Chun, *Programmed Visions*, 1.

5 Ibid.

6 Chun and Rhody, "Working the Digital Humanities," 4.

7 Freeman, *Time Binds*, xvi.

8 Ibid., xv.

9 Keeling, "Queer OS," 153. See Barnett et al, "QueerOS: A User's Manual," for a speculative elaboration of Keeling's ideas that resonates with the arguments of this section.

10 Hip-hop cultures have been especially crucial to the shaping of digital remix and the ways it has intersected with copyright law. See Miller, *Rhythm Science*.

11 Manovich, *Software Takes Command*, 31.

12 Manovich, *The Language of New Media*, 127.

13 McPherson, "U.S. Operating Systems at Midcentury," 34.

14 Villarejo, *Ethereal Queer*, 9.

15 See Coppa and Tushnet, "How to Suppress Women's Remix." Predominantly female media fan communities have been quite successful in writing themselves into media studies' histories of digital creativity, but they remain largely absent in the histories digital humanities scholars tell about transformations in knowledge production and dissemination.

16 Needham, "Scheduling Normativity," 153. On queer televisual formations, see Doty, *Making Things Perfectly Queer*; Joyrich, "Epistemology of the Console."

17 On science fiction film, see chapter 5.

18 On production processes in science fiction television, see Chow-White, Deveau, and Adams, "Media Encoding in Science Fiction Television."

19 See J. P. Telotte, *Science Fiction TV*, 82–105.

20 Lotz, *The Television Will Be Revolutionized*, 2.

21 See Burgess and Green, *YouTube*.

22 See Eastwood, "Recording Industry Earns More from Fan Videos than from Official Music Videos."

23 Villarejo, *Ethereal Queer*, 155–157.

24 Coppa, "An Editing Room of One's Own."

25 Coppa, "Women, *Star Trek*, and the Early Development of Fannish Vidding."

26 Stanfill, "Spinning Yarn with Borrowed Cotton," 134.

27 Kun, *Audiotopia*, 2.

28 See McIntosh, "A History of Subversive Remix Video before YouTube"; Kreisinger, "Queer Video Remix and LGBTQ Online Communities."

29 On fan fiction, see the second wormhole section.

30 Desjardins, *Meeting Two Queens*, 26.

31 Flummery, "[VID] Walking on the Ground."

32 See Coppa, "Pressure."

33 This was the climax to season 3 of *Buffy the Vampire Slayer* (*Mutant Enemy*, 1997–2003) which aired in 1998–1999: the evil Buffy fought was embodied in the Mayor, who ascended to demon status during the assembly.

34 See Tehranian, "Infringement Nation"; Tushnet, "Payment in Credit."

35 Lim, "Us | Multifandom"; Wesch, "An Anthropological Introduction to YouTube"; Lothian, "Living in a Den of Thieves."

36 On the history of this fan subculture, see Busse and Hellekson, "Introduction: Work in Progress"; Coppa, "A Brief History of Media Fandom."

37 Jenkins, *Textual Poachers*, 241.

38 Books depicted in the following images include feminist science fiction by Ursula K. Le Guin and a variety of cultural studies scholarship. I learned about the solicitation through personal communication with fans whose images were included.

39 The screenplay for *V for Vendetta* was written by the Wachowski sisters, both trans women, and its plot hinges on a lesbian relationship between two women who are persecuted for their love by a fascist state.

40 Lothian, "Living in a Den of Thieves," 134.

41 See Nickelsburg, "A Brief History of the Guy Fawkes Mask."

42 For a slightly different answer to this question, which focuses on how critical fandom, defined as the participatory convergence of affective engagement and critical thinking, can be deployed pedagogically within and against the neoliberal university, see Booth, "Fandom."

43 Jenkins, *Textual Poachers*; Bacon-Smith, *Enterprising Women*.

44 See Jones, "The Sex Lives of Cult Television Characters"; Russo, "User-Penetrated Content."

45 Brooker, "Going Pro," 94. On the use of "subculture" to refer to fandom, see Lothian, "Archival Anarchies."

46 Lothian, "A Different Kind of Love Song," 139.

47 Scott, "Repackaging Fan Culture."

48 See Gibson-Graham, *The End of Capitalism* on noncapitalist modes within global capitalism; Hellekson's "A Fannish Field of Value" on fandom as noncapitalist; and De Kosnik, "Fandom as Free Labor" for important cautions.

49 While my use of "undercommons" is an effort to capture this doubleness, I include myself in the critique I make here inasmuch as I am taking a term developed to refer to radical black politics and applying it within a community where—though radical black politics are not absent—critical understandings of settler colonialism and white supremacy are very far indeed from universal.

50 The effects in "Us" make it difficult to identify every character, but none looks visibly racialized to my eye; in "Walking on the Ground" I notice one black character. This absence is not reproduced in more recent vids that represent and

celebrate fan communities, such as the 2012 "A Different Kind of Love Song" that I discuss in my essay of the same name. I understand this shift as partly one of available images and partly a direct result of the activism by fans of color I discuss below, which has led to increased expectations that subcultural fans actively push against dominant tides of racial representation in popular culture.

51 Stanfill, "Doing Fandom, Misdoing Whiteness."
52 Wanzo, "African American Acafandom and Other Strangers."
53 Ibid.
54 See TWC Editor, "Pattern Recognition."
55 See ibid.; Carrington, *Speculative Blackness*, 195–237; Reid, "'The Wild Unicorn Herd Check-In'"; De Kosnik, *Rogue Archives*, 161–186.
56 Freeman, *Time Binds*, xv.
57 Lierdumoa. "How Much Is That Geisha in the Window?"
58 See Cochran, "The Browncoats are Coming!"
59 Abu-Jamal, "*Star Wars* and the American Imagination," 256–58.
60 Rebecca Tushnet wrote: "Low-quality doesn't let you see what you need to see, which is . . . the constant references to Asian cultures, and the fact that nonetheless there aren't any Asian characters except in deep background—the critique is meaningless if you can't tell why the artist is complaining because one pixelated person looks pretty much like another." ("Copyright Office DMCA Hearings: Noncommercial Remix," Rebecca Tushnet's 43(B)log, May 5, 2009, http://tushnet .blogspot.com/).
61 Amy Pascale's biography of Joss Whedon includes the information that the murderous Reaver characters were based on the "looming threat of the Apache" to American settlers. See Charlie Jane Anders, "The Real Reason Why Joss Whedon Named His Space Western Show *Firefly*," io9, July 7, 2014, http://io9.gizmodo.com.
62 Nakamura, "Economies of Digital Production in East Asia," and "Indigenous Circuits."
63 Russo, "Indiscrete Media," 99.
64 *Battlestar Galactica*, season 1 credits.
65 See Hairston, "Romance of the Robot."
66 Huh, "Race in Progress," 327.
67 Nyong'o, "So Say We All." See also Knight, "Black Markets and Black Mystics."
68 See Bennett, "Techno-Butterfly"; Rhee, "In Search of My Robot."
69 Selznick, "Branding the Future."
70 Scott's "Is Fan Production Frakked?"; Russo, "User-Penetrated Content."
71 On networked fan counterpublics, see the second wormhole section.
72 Luminosity, "More Human than Human."
73 Lothian, "Love Is the Plan the Plan Is Death / Sons and Daughters (*Battlestar Galactica*) (2008)," *Queer Geek Theory*, September 1, 2012, www.queergeektheory .org.
74 Charmax, "Unnatural Selection—*Battlestar Galactica / Terminator: Sarah Connor*."

75 See the discussion of Francis Galton in chapter 1.

76 Kustritz, "Breeding Unity," 3.

77 See Pegues, "Miss Cylon"; Nishime, "Aliens"; Dillon, "Diaspora Narrative in *Battlestar Galactica.*"

78 Lara Pellegrinelli, "At the U.N., 'Battlestar' Troops Talk Ethics of War," National Public Radio, March 20, 2009, www.npr.org.

79 Byrd, *The Transit of Empire*, xiii.

80 See Randell, "Now the Gloves Come Off."

81 Edelman, *No Future*, 31. See part 1 for extended discussion of Edelman's work.

82 For discussion of the character from Asian American Studies perspectives see Huh, "Race in Progress"; Pegues, "Miss Cylon"; Nishime, "Aliens."

83 See Lewin, "The Unmasking of Mitochondrial Eve."

84 Nyong'o, *The Amalgamation Waltz*, 172.

85 Russo, "Battlestar Redactica."

86 CVM Productions, "Battlestar Redactica: A Fan-Edited Mutiny and Resurrection."

87 Cylon Vidding Machine, "The Enemy Within."

88 The unreasonably short lifespans of queer women on TV have long been the subject of fan critique. In 2016 this perspective went mainstream when a storyline of consummated love between two women on *The 100* (The CW, 2014–) was cut short with the immediate death of one member of the couple. Fans responded by researching the history of fictional lesbian death, boycotting the show, and speculatively casting the couple in a different series. See Cava, "When the Fandom Gets Creative." I am grateful to Jasmine Whims for introducing me to the creative breadth of Clexa fandom.

89 My 2011 vid "Metal Heart" explores relationships between multiple iterations of Sharon's Cylon model.

90 Bennett, "Techno-Butterfly," 31.

91 Russo, "Hera Has Six Mommies."

92 Lothian, "The Future Stops Here (2008)," *Queer Geek Theory*, September 1, 2012. www.queergeektheory.org.

93 Busse and Lothian, "Scholarly Critiques and Critiques of Scholarship," 142.

94 Ibid.

95 Lothian, "Black Steel (Born in Flames) (2012)," *Queer Geek Theory*, September 1, 2012, www.queergeektheory.org.

96 Samer, "Transfeminist Orphan Black Vid."

EPILOGUE

1 Berardi, *After the Future*, 25.

2 Ibid., 165.

3 Imarisha, *Octavia's Brood*, 4.

BIBLIOGRAPHY

Abramovitch, Seth. "Disaster Movie Stills Masquerade as Hurricane Sandy on Social Media." *Hollywood Reporter*, October 10, 2012. www.hollywoodreporter.com.

Abu-Jamal, Mumia. "*Star Wars* and the American Imagination." In *Octavia's Brood: Science Fiction Stories from Social Justice Movements*, edited by Walidah Imarisha and adrienne maree brown, 255–58. Oakland, CA: AK Press, 2015.

Adamson, Judith. *Charlotte Haldane: Woman Writer in a Man's World*. Basingstoke: Macmillan, 1998.

Ahmad, Dohra. *Landscapes of Hope: Anti-Colonial Utopianism in America*. Oxford: Oxford University Press, 2009.

Ahmed, Sara. *The Promise of Happiness*. Durham, NC: Duke University Press, 2010.

———. *Queer Phenomenology: Orientations, Objects, Others*. Durham, NC: Duke University Press, 2006.

Aizura, Aren. "Communizing Care in the Left Hand of Darkness." *Ada: A Journal of Gender, New Media, and Technology* 12 (November 2017). https://doi.org/10.13016/M2RB6W385.

Allison, Dorothy. "Puritans, Perverts, and Feminists." In *Skin: Talking about Sex, Class and Literature*, 93–119. Ithaca, NY: Firebrand, 1994.

Baccolini, Raffaella, and Tom Moylan. "Introduction: Dystopia and Histories." In *Dark Horizons: Science Fiction and the Dystopian Imagination*, edited by Raffaella Baccolini and Tom Moylan, 1–12. New York: Routledge, 2003.

Bacon-Smith, Camille. *Enterprising Women: Television Fandom and the Creation of Popular Myth*. Philadelphia: University of Pennsylvania Press, 1992.

Bahng, Aimee. *Migrant Futures: Decolonizing Speculation in Financial Times*. Durham, NC: Duke University Press, 2018.

———. "Speculative Acts: The Cultural Labors of Science, Fiction, and Empire." PhD diss., University of California, San Diego, 2009.

Bailey, Moya, micha cárdenas, Laura Horak, Lokeilani Kaimana, Cáel M. Keegan, Geneveive Newman, Roxanne Samer, and Raffi Sarkissian. "*Sense8* Roundtable." *Spectator* 37, no. 2 (2017): 74–88.

Barnett, Fiona, Zach Blas, micha cárdenas, Jacob Gaboury, Jessica Marie Johnson, and Margaret Rhee. "QueerOS: A User's Manual." In *Debates in the Digital Humanities 2016*, edited by Matthew K. Gold and Lauren Klein. Minneapolis: University of Minnesota Press, 2016.

Barr, Marleen. *Feminist Fabulation: Space/Postmodern Fiction*. Iowa City: University of Iowa Press, 1992.

Beaumont, Matthew. *Utopia Ltd: Ideologies of Social Dreaming in England 1870–1900.* Leiden: Brill, 2005.

Beckford, Kerry L. "Stop Posting Videos of Black Folks Dying." *Hartford Courant,* July 7, 2016. www.courant.com.

Bellamy, Edward. *Looking Backward 2000–1887* [1888]. New York: Penguin, 1982.

Benjamin, Walter. "Conversations with Brecht." In *Reflections: Essays, Aphorisms, Autobiographical Writings,* 203–19. New York: Schocken Books, 2007.

———. "On the Concept of History." Translated by Dennis Redmond, 2001. http://members.efn.org.

———. "Theses on the Philosophy of History." In *Illuminations: Essays and Reflections,* edited by Hannah Arendt, translated by Edmund Jephcott, 253–64. New York: Schocken Books, 1968.

Bennett, Eve. "Techno-Butterfly: Orientalism Old and New in *Battlestar Galactica.*" *Science Fiction Film and Television* 5, no. 1 (2012): 23–46.

Benshoff, Harry M., and Sean Griffin. *Queer Images: A History of Gay and Lesbian Film in America.* Lanham, MD: Rowman & Littlefield, 2006.

Berardi, Franco "Bifo." *After the Future,* edited by Nicholas Thorburn and Gary Genosko. Oakland, CA: AK Press, 2011.

Berlant, Lauren, and Michael Warner. "Sex in Public." *Critical Inquiry* 24 (December 1998): 547–66.

———. "What Does Queer Theory Teach Us About X?" *PMLA* 110, no. 3 (1995): 343–49.

Bersani, Leo. *Homos.* Cambridge, MA: Harvard University Press, 1995.

———. "Is the Rectum a Grave?" *October* 43 (Winter 1987): 197–222.

Bianco, Jamie "Skye." "Queer Urban Composites: Any City or 'Bellona (after Samuel R. Delany).'" *Ada: A Journal of Gender, New Media and Technology* 3 (November 2013). https://doi.org/10.7264/N33F4MH2.

Bloch, Ernst. *The Principle of Hope.* Cambridge, MA: MIT Press, 1986.

Booth, Paul J. "Fandom: The Classroom of the Future." *Transformative Works and Cultures* 19 (December 2015). https://doi.org/10.3983/twc.2015.0650.

Bould, Mark. "The Ships Landed Long Ago: Afrofuturism and Black SF." *Science Fiction Studies* 34 (July 2007).

boyd, danah. "Social Network Sites as Networked Publics: Affordances, Dynamics, and Implications." In *A Networked Self: Identity, Community, and Culture on Social Network Sites,* edited by Zizi Papacharissi. New York: Taylor & Francis, 2010.

Bray, Mary Kay. "To See What Condition Our Condition Is In: Trial by Language in *Stars in My Pocket like Grains of Sand.*" In *Ash of Stars: On the Writing of Samuel R. Delany,* edited by James Sallis, 17–25. Jackson: University Press of Mississippi, 1996.

———. "Rites of Reversal: Double Consciousness in Delany's Dhalgren." *Black American Literature Forum* 18, no. 2 (1984): 57–61.

Brighouse, Harold. "Three Novels and a Nightmare." *Manchester Guardian,* June 6, 1937.

Brooker, Will. "Going Pro: Gendered Responses to the Incorporation of Fan Labor as User-Generated Content." In *Wired TV: Laboring Over an Interactive Future,* edited by Denise Mann, 72–97. New Brunswick, NJ: Rutgers University Press, 2014.

Brothers, Barbara. "British Women Write the Story of the Nazis: A Conspiracy of Silence." In *Rediscovering Forgotten Radicals: British Women Writers, 1889–1939*, edited by Angela Ingram and Daphne Patai, 244–64. Chapel Hill: University of North Carolina Press, 1993.

Brown, Jayna. "The Human Project: Utopia, Dystopia, and the Black Heroine in *Children of Men* and *28 Days Later*." *Transition* 110 (2013): 120–35.

———. "'Brown Girl in the Ring': Poly Styrene, Annabella Lwin, and the Politics of Anger." *Journal of Popular Music Studies* 23, no. 4 (2011): 455–78.

Brown, Jayna, and Alexis Lothian. "Speculative Life: An Introduction." *Social Text Periscope*, January 4, 2012. https://socialtextjournal.org.

Burdekin, Katharine. *Proud Man* [1934]. New York: Feminist Press, 1993.

———. *The End of This Day's Business*. New York: The Feminist Press, 1989.

———. *Swastika Night* [1937]. New York: Feminist Press, 1985.

Burdekin, Kay. *The Rebel Passion*. New York: William Morrow & Company, 1929.

Burgess, Jean, and Joshua Green. *YouTube: Online Video and Participatory Culture*. Cambridge, UK: Polity Press, 2009.

Burris, Sarah. "WATCH: White Nationalist Richard Spencer Sucker-Punched in the Face during Trump Inauguration," *RawStory*, January 20, 2017, www.rawstory.com.

Busse, Kristina, and Karen Hellekson. "Introduction: Work in Progress." In *Fan Fiction and Fan Communities in the Age of the Internet*, edited by Karen Hellekson and Kristina Busse, 5–32. Jefferson, NC: McFarland, 2006.

Busse, Kristina, and Alexis Lothian. "A History of Slash Sexualities: Debating Queer Sex, Gay Politics, and Media Fan Cultures." In *The Routledge Companion to Media, Sex and Sexuality*, edited by Feona Attwood, Danielle Egan, Brian McNair, and Clarissa Smith, 117–29. New York: Routledge, 2017.

———. "Scholarly Critiques and Critiques of Scholarship: The Uses of Remix Video." *Camera Obscura* 26, no. 2 (2011): 139–46.

Butler, Andrew M. "Heteronormative Futures." *Science Fiction Studies 36, no. 3* (2009): 388–89.

Butler, Judith. *Undoing Gender*. New York: Routledge, 2004.

———. *Gender Trouble: Feminism and the Subversion of Identity*, 2nd ed. New York: Routledge, 1999.

Butler, Octavia E. *Fledgling*. New York: Warner Books, 2005.

———. *Kindred* [1979]. Boston: Beacon Press, 2003.

Byrd, Jodi A. *The Transit of Empire: Indigenous Critiques of Colonialism*. Minneapolis: University of Minnesota Press, 2011.

Caird, Mona. *The Morality of Marriage and Other Essays on the Status and Destiny of Women*. London: George Redway, 1897.

Califia, Pat. *Public Sex: The Culture of Radical Sex*. Jersey City, NJ: Cleis Press, 2000.

———. "The City of Desire: Its Anatomy and Destiny." In *Public Sex: The Culture of Radical Sex*, 205–13. Jersey City, NJ: Cleis Press, 1994.

Califia, Patrick. *Sex Changes: Transgender Politics*, 2nd ed. Jersey City, NJ: Cleis Press, 2003.

cárdenas, micha. "Shifting Futures: Digital Trans of Color Praxis." *Ada: A Journal of Gender, New Media, and Technology* 6 (January 2015). http://dx.doi.org/10.7264/N3WH2N8D.

Carlson, Erin G. *Thinking Fascism: Sapphic Modernism and Fascist Modernity.* Stanford, CA: Stanford University Press, 1998.

Carrington, André M. *Speculative Blackness: The Future of Race in Science Fiction.* Minneapolis: University of Minnesota Press, 2016.

Case, Sue-Ellen. "Tracking the Vampire." *Differences: A Journal of Feminist Cultural Studies* 3, no. 2 (1991): 1–20.

Caserio, Robert L., Lee Edelman, Judith Halberstam, José Esteban Muñoz, and Tim Dean. "The Antisocial Thesis in Queer Theory." *PMLA* 121, no. 3 (2006): 819–27.

Cava, Jin Jet. "When the Fandom Gets Creative: Who Is Elyza Lex and Why Does She Matter?" *Huffington Post*, March 22, 2016. www.huffingtonpost.com.

Charmax. "Unnatural Selection—*Battlestar Galactica / Terminator: Sarah Connor.*" March 2, 2009. www.youtube.com.

Chakrabarty, Dipesh. *Provincializing Europe: Postcolonial Thought and Historical Difference.* Princeton, NJ: Princeton University Press, 2000.

Chisholm, Dianne. *Queer Constellations: Subcultural Space in the Wake of the City.* Minneapolis: University of Minnesota Press, 2005.

Chow-White, Peter A., Danielle Deveau, and Philippa Adams. "Media Encoding in Science Fiction Television: *Battlestar Galactica* as a Site of Critical Cultural Production." *Media, Culture & Society* 37, no. 8 (2015): 1210–25.

Chun, Wendy Hui Kyong. *Programmed Visions: Software and Memory.* Cambridge, MA: MIT Press, 2011.

———. *Control and Freedom: Power and Paranoia in the Age of Fiber Optics.* Cambridge, MA: MIT Press, 2006.

Chun, Wendy Hui Kyong, and Lisa Marie Rhody. "Working the Digital Humanities: Uncovering Shadows between the Dark and the Light." *Differences* 25, no. 1 (2014): 1–25.

Claeys, Gregory. "The Origins of Dystopia: Wells, Huxley and Orwell." In *The Cambridge Companion to Utopian Literature*, edited by Gregory Claeys, 107–34. Cambridge: Cambridge University Press, 2010.

Cochran, Tanya R. "'The Browncoats Are Coming!': *Firefly*, *Serenity*, and Fan Activism." In *Investigating Firefly and Serenity: Science Fiction on the Frontier*, edited by Rhonda V. Wilcox and Tanya R. Cochran, 239–49. New York: I. B. Tauris, 2008.

Cohen, Cathy. "Punks, Bulldaggers, and Welfare Queens: The Radical Potential of Queer Politics?" *GLQ* 3, no. 4 (1997): 437–65.

Combahee River Collective. "A Black Feminist Statement." *WSQ: Women's Studies Quarterly* 42, nos. 3–4 (2014): 271–80.

Connelly, Bill. "Bip Pares 2." *Studies in Illustration* 30 (2005): 6–15.

———. "Bibliography—Bip Pares." *Studies in Illustration* 21 (2002): 32–42.

Conrad, Ryan, ed. *Against Equality: Queer Revolution, Not Mere Inclusion.* Oakland, CA: AK Press, 2014.

Constantine, Murray. *Swastika Night*. London: Victor Gollancz, 1940.

Coppa, Francesca. "An Editing Room of One's Own: Vidding as Women's Work." *Camera Obscura* 26, no. 2 (2011): 123–30.

———. "'Pressure': A Metavid by the California Crew." *In Media Res*, January 28, 2008. http://mediacommons.futureofthebook.org/.

———. "Women, *Star Trek*, and the Early Development of Fannish Vidding." *Transformative Works and Cultures* 1 (September 2008). http://dx.doi.org/10.3983 /twc.2008.0044.

———. "A Brief History of Media Fandom." In *Fan Fiction and Fan Communities in the Age of the Internet*, edited by Kristina Busse and Karen Hellekson, 41–60. Jefferson, NC: McFarland, 2006.

Coppa, Francesca, and Rebecca Tushnet. "How to Suppress Women's Remix." *Camera Obscura* 26, no. 2 (2011): 131–38.

Corbett, Elizabeth Burgoyne. *New Amazonia: A Foretaste of the Future* [1889]. Seattle: Aqueduct Press, 2013.

Crimp, Douglas. "How to Have Promiscuity in an Epidemic." *October* 43 (Winter 1987): 237–71.

Croft, Andy. "Worlds without End Foisted onto the Future—Some Antecedents of *Nineteen Eighty-Four*." In *Inside the Myth: Orwell: Views from the Left*, edited by Christopher Norris, 183–286. London: Lawrence & Wishart, 1984.

Crossley, Robert. "Dystopian Nights: Review of Katharine Burdekin, *Swastika Night*, and Joseph O'Neill, *Land under England*." *Science Fiction Studies* 14, no. 1 (1987): 93–98.

Csicsery-Ronay Jr, Istvan. "Science Fiction and Empire." *Science Fiction Studies* 30, no. 2 (2003): 231–45.

CVM Productions. "Battlestar Redactica: A Fan-Edited Mutiny and Resurrection." July 2009. http://cvm-productions.livejournal.com.

Cylon Vidding Machine. "The Enemy Within" [2009]. February 25, 2010. www.you tube.com.

da Silva, Denise Ferreira. *Toward a Global Theory of Race*. Minneapolis: University of Minnesota Press, 2007.

Davies, Jon. "Surfaces, History and 'Noise' in Derek Jarman's *Jubilee*." *Kersplebedeb*, 2003. www.kersplebedeb.com.

Davis, Angela Y. "Racism, Birth Control, and Reproductive Rights." In *Women, Race and Class*, 202–21. New York: Vintage, 1983.

De Kosnik, Abigail. *Rogue Archives: Digital Cultural Memory and Media Fandom*. Cambridge, MA: MIT Press, 2016.

———. "Fandom as Free Labor." In *Digital Labor: The Internet as Playground and Factory*, edited by Trebor Scholz, 98–111. New York: Routledge, 2013.

Delany, Samuel R. *Through the Valley of the Nest of Spiders*. New York: Magnus Books, 2012.

———. *Stars in My Pocket like Grains of Sand* [1984]. Middletown, CT: Wesleyan University Press, 2004.

———. "The Politics of Paraliterary Criticism." In *Shorter Views: Queer Thoughts and the Politics of the Paraliterary*, 218–70. Middletown, CT: Wesleyan University Press, 1999.

———. "The Second Science-Fiction Studies Interview: Of *Trouble on Triton* and Other Matters." In *Shorter Views: Queer Thoughts and the Politics of the Paraliterary*, 315–52. Middletown, CT: Wesleyan University Press, 1999.

———. *Times Square Red, Times Square Blue*. New York: New York University Press, 1999.

———. *Trouble on Triton: An Ambiguous Heterotopia*. Middletown, CT: Wesleyan University Press, 1996.

———. *Dhalgren*. Middletown, CT: Wesleyan University Press, 1996.

———. "Of Sex, Objects, Signs, Systems, Sales, SF." In *The Straits of Messina*, 33–55. Seattle: Serconia, 1989.

———. "The Tale of Plagues and Carnivals, or: Some Informal Remarks toward the Modular Calculus, Part Five." In *Flight from Nevèrÿon*, 237–480. London: Grafton, 1989.

———. *The Motion of Light in Water*. London: Paladin, 1988.

———. "Introduction." In *Starboard Wine*. Pleasantville, NY: Dragon Press, 1984.

———. "The Necessity of Tomorrows." In *Starboard Wine*, 23–36. Pleasantville, NY: Dragon Press, 1984.

———. "About 5,750 Words." In *The Jewel-Hinged Jaw: Notes on the Language of Science Fiction*, 33–50 [1971]. New York: Berkley, 1977.

Dery, Mark. "Black to the Future: Interviews with Samuel R. Delany, Greg Tate, and Tricia Rose." In *Flame Wars: The Discourse of Cyberculture*, 179–222. Durham, NC: Duke University Press, 1994.

Desjardins, Mary. "*Meeting Two Queens*: Feminist Film-Making, Identity Politics, and the Melodramatic Fantasy." *Film Quarterly* 48, no. 3 (1995): 26–33.

Dick, Philip K. *The Man in the High Castle* [1962]. Boston: Mariner Books, 2012.

Dillon, Grace L. "Diaspora Narrative in *Battlestar Galactica*." *Science Fiction Film and Television* 5, no. 1 (2012): 1–21.

———. "Indigenous Scientific Literacies in Nalo Hopkinson's *Ceremonial Worlds*." *Journal of the Fantastic in the Arts* 18, no. 1 (2007): 23.

———, ed. *Walking the Clouds: An Anthology of Indigenous Science Fiction*. Tucson: University of Arizona Press, 2012.

Dillon, Stephen. "'It's Here, It's That Time': Race, Queer Futurity, and the Temporality of Violence in *Born in Flames*." *Women & Performance: A Journal of Feminist Theory* 23, no.1 (2013): 38–51.

Dixie, Lady Florence. *Gloriana, or, The Revolution of 1900*. London: Henry and Company, 1890.

Doane, Mary Anne. *The Emergence of Cinematic Time: Modernity, Contingency, the Archive*. Cambridge, MA: Harvard University Press, 2002.

Dolan, Jill. *Utopia in Performance: Finding Hope at the Theater*. Ann Arbor: University of Michigan Press, 2005.

Dollimore, Jonathan. "Perversion, Degeneration, and the Death Drive." In *Sexualities in Victorian Britain*, edited by Andrew H. Miller and James Eli Adams, 96–117. Bloomington: Indiana University Press, 1996.

Dorsey, Candas Jane. "Some Notes on the Failure of Sex and Gender Inquiry in SF." *Science Fiction Studies* 36, no. 3 (2009): 389–90.

Doty, Alexander. *Making Things Perfectly Queer: Interpreting Mass Culture*. Minneapolis: University of Minnesota Press, 1993.

Du Bois, W. E. B. *Darkwater: Voices from Within the Veil*. Amherst, NY: Humanity Books, 2003.

———. "The Comet." In *Dark Matter: A Century of Speculative Fiction from the African Diaspora*, edited by Sheree R. Thomas, 5–18. New York: Aspect, 2000.

Duchamp, L. Timmel. "Elizabeth Burgoyne Corbett." In *Missing Links and Secret Histories: A Selection of Wikipedia Entries from across the Known Multiverse*, edited by L. Timmel Duchamp, 184–201. Seattle: Aqueduct Press, 2013.

———. *Stretto*. Seattle: Aqueduct Press, 2008.

———. *Blood in the Fruit*. Seattle: Aqueduct Press, 2008.

———. *Tsunami*. Seattle: Aqueduct Press, 2007.

———. *Renegade*. Seattle: Aqueduct Press, 2006.

———. *Alanya to Alanya*. Seattle: Aqueduct Press, 2005.

Duggan, Lisa. *The Twilight of Equality? Neoliberalism, Cultural Politics, and the Attack on Democracy*. Boston: Beacon Press, 2003.

Eastwood, Joel. "Recording Industry Earns More from Fan Videos than from Official Music Videos." *Toronto Star*, March 3, 2014. www.thestar.com.

Edelman, Lee. *No Future: Queer Theory and the Death Drive*. Durham, NC: Duke University Press, 2004.

Ellis, Jim. *Derek Jarman's Angelic Conversations*. Minneapolis: University of Minnesota Press, 2009.

Ellison, Ralph. *Invisible Man*. New York: Vintage, 1990.

Engelhardt, Tom. "Ending the World the Human Way." *Nation*, February 3, 2014. www.thenation.com.

English, Daylanne K. *Unnatural Selections: Eugenics in American Modernism and the Harlem Renaissance*. Chapel Hill: University of North Carolina Press, 2004.

"Enoch Powell's 'Rivers of Blood' Speech." *Telegraph*, November 6, 2007. www.telegraph.co.uk.

Ertz, Susan. *Woman Alive*. New York: D. Appleton-Century, 1936.

Eshun, Kodwo. "Further Considerations of Afrofuturism." *CR: The New Centennial Review* 3 (July 2003): 287–302.

Espiritu, Yên Lê. *Body Counts: The Vietnam War and Militarized Refugees*. Berkeley: University of California Press, 2014.

Fairbairns, Zoë. *Benefits*. London: Virago, 1979.

Ferguson, Roderick A. "The Relevance of Race for the Study of Sexuality." In *A Companion to Lesbian, Gay, Bisexual, Transgender, and Queer Studies*, edited by Molly McGarry and George A. Haggerty, 109–23. Oxford, UK: Blackwell, 2008.

———. *Aberrations in Black: Toward a Queer of Color Critique*. Minneapolis: University of Minnesota Press, 2004.

Firestone, Shulamith. *The Dialectic of Sex: The Case for Feminist Revolution*. New York: Farrar, Strauss & Giroux, 2003.

Fisher, Mark. *Capitalist Realism: Is There No Alternative?* London: Zero Books, 2009.

Forster, E. M. "The Machine Stops." In *The Machine Stops and Other Stories* [1908], 87–118. London: Andre Deutsch, 1997.

Flummery. "[VID] Walking on the Ground" [2005]. *Archive of Our Own*, August 30, 2015. https://archiveofourown.org.

Foucault, Michel. *The Will to Knowledge: The History of Sexuality Volume 1* [1976]. London: Penguin, 1998.

———. *Remarks on Marx: Conversations with Duccio Trombadori*. Translated by R. James Goldstein and James Cascaito. New York: Semiotext(e), 1991.

Fox, Rose, and Daniel José Older, eds. *Long Hidden: Speculative Fiction from the Margins of History*. Framingham, MA: Crossed Genres Publications, 2014.

Fraiman, Susan. *Cool Men and the Second Sex*. New York: Columbia University Press, 2003.

Freedman, Carl. *Critical Theory and Science Fiction*. Hanover, NH: Wesleyan University Press, 2000.

Freeman, Elizabeth. *Time Binds: Queer Temporalities, Queer Histories*. Durham, NC: Duke University Press, 2010.

———. "Time Binds, or, Erotohistoriography." *Social Text* 23, nos. 3–4 (2005): 57–68.

Freud, Sigmund. *Civilization and Its Discontents*. In *The Standard Edition of the Complete Psychological Works of Sigmund Freud*, edited by James Strachey, 21:59–148. 1930. London: The Hogarth Press, 1961.

Friedberg, Anne. "An Interview with Filmmaker Lizzie Borden." *Women & Performance: A Journal of Feminist Theory* 1, no. 2 (1984): 37–45.

Galton, Francis. *Hereditary Genius: An Inquiry into Its Laws and Consequences*, 2nd ed. London: Macmillan, 1892.

Gamble, Sarah. "Gender and Science in Haldane's *Man's World*." *Journal of Gender Studies* 13, no. 1 (2004): 3–13.

Gandhi, Leela. *Affective Communities: Anticolonial Thought, Fin-de-Siècle Radicalism, and the Politics of Friendship*. Durham, NC: Duke University Press, 2006.

Garza, Alicia. "A Herstory of the #BlackLivesMatter Movement." *Feminist Wire*, October 7, 2014. www.thefeministwire.com.

Gättens, Marie-Luise. "*Three Guineas*, Fascism, and the Construction of Gender." In *Virginia Woolf and Fascism: Resisting the Dictators' Seduction*, edited by Merry Pawlowski, 21–38. Basingstoke: Palgrave, 2001.

Gibson, William. "The Recombinant City: A Foreword to *Dhalgren* by Samuel R. Delany." In *Dhalgren*, by Samuel R. Delany. Hanover, NH: Wesleyan University Press, 1996.

———. *Neuromancer* [1984]. New York: Ace Books, 1993.

Gibson-Graham, J. K. *The End of Capitalism (as We Knew It)*. Cambridge, MA: Blackwell, 1996.

Giffney, Noreen. "Queer Apocal(o)ptic/Ism: The Death Drive and the Human." In *Queering the Non/Human*, edited by Noreen Giffney and Myra J. Hird, 55–78. Burlington, VT: Ashgate, 2008.

Gilbert, Sophie. "*1984* Isn't the Only Book Enjoying a Revival." *Atlantic*, January 25, 2017. www.theatlantic.com.

Gilman, Charlotte Perkins. "With Her in Ourland" [1916]. In *Charlotte Perkins Gilman's Utopian Novels: Moving the Mountain, Herland, and With Her in Ourland*, edited by Minna Doskow, 270–387. Cranbury, NJ: Associated University Presses, 1999.

———. *Herland*. 1915. New York: Pantheon, 1979.

Gilmore, Ruth Wilson. *Golden Gulag: Prisons, Surplus, Crisis, and Opposition in Globalizing California*. Berkeley: University of California Press, 2007.

Gilroy, Paul. *The Black Atlantic: Modernity and Double Consciousness*. Cambridge, MA: Harvard University Press, 1993.

———. *"There Ain't No Black in the Union Jack": The Cultural Politics of Race and Nation*. Chicago: University of Chicago Press, 1991.

Goltz, Dustin Bradley. "Love(sick) Aliens in the Wasteland: Queer Temporal Camp in Araki's Teen Apocalyptic Trilogy." *Critical Studies in Media Communication* 29, no. 2 (2012): 97–112.

Gomez, Jewelle. *The Gilda Stories and Bones & Ash* [1991]. New York: Quality Paperback Book Club, 2001.

Gordon, Avery. *Ghostly Matters: Haunting and the Sociological Imagination*. Minneapolis: University of Minnesota Press, 1997.

Greer, Olivia J. "Yes We Can: (President) Barack Obama and Afrofuturism." *Anamesa* 7 (Fall 2009): 34–42.

Grewell, Greg. "Colonizing the Universe: Science Fictions Then, Now, and in the (Imagined) Future." *Rocky Mountain Review of Language and Literature* 55, no. 2 (2001): 25–47.

Griffith, Nicola, and Stephen Pagel, eds. *Bending the Landscape: Original Gay and Lesbian Writing: Science Fiction*. New York: Overlook Press, 1998.

Gumbs, Alexis Pauline. "Speculative Poetics: Audre Lorde as Prologue for Queer Black Futurism." In *The Black Imagination: Science Fiction, Futurism and the Speculative*, edited by Sandra Jackson and Julie E. Moody-Freeman, 130–45. New York: Peter Lang, 2011.

———. "'We Can Learn to Mother Ourselves: The Queer Survival of Black Feminism, 1968–1996." PhD diss. Duke University, 2010.

Hairston, Andrea. "Romance of the Robot: From RUR and Metropolis to Wall-E." In *The WisCon Chronicles 4*, edited by Sylvia Kelso, 60–75. Seattle: Aqueduct Press, 2010.

Haiven, Max. "Finance as Capital's Imagination? Reimagining Value and Culture in an Age of Fictitious Capital and Crisis." *Social Text* 29, no. 3 (2011): 93–124.

Halberstam, Judith. *The Queer Art of Failure*. Durham, NC: Duke University Press, 2011

———. *In a Queer Time and Place: Transgender Bodies, Subcultural Lives*. New York: New York University Press, 2005.

———. *Female Masculinity*. Durham, NC: Duke University Press, 1998.

Haldane, Charlotte. "Dr. Huxley and Mr. Arnold." *Nature* 129 (April 4, 1932).

———. *Motherhood and Its Enemies*. Garden City, NY: Doubleday, Doran, 1928.

———. *Man's World*. London: Chatto & Windus, 1926.

Hall, Donald E. *Queer Theories*. Basingstoke: Palgrave Macmillan, 2003.

Hall, Lesley A., ed. *Outspoken Women: An Anthology of Women's Writing on Sex, 1870–1969*. New York: Routledge, 2005.

Halley, Janet, and Andrew Parker. Introduction. In *After Sex: On Writing since Queer Theory*, edited by Janet Halley and Andrew Parker, 1–16. Durham, NC: Duke University Press, 2011.

Hanhardt, Christina B. "LAUREL and Harvey: Screening Militant Gay Liberalism and Lesbian Feminist Radicalism circa 1980." *Women & Performance: A Journal of Feminist Theory* 23, no. 1 (2013): 17–37.

Hansen, Ellis. "Undead." In *Inside/Out: Lesbian Theories, Gay Theories*, edited by Diana Fuss, 324–40. New York: Routledge, 1991.

Haraway, Donna. *Modest Witness@Second Millenium. FemaleMan Meets OncoMouse: Feminism and Technoscience*. New York: Routledge, 1997.

———. "A Cyborg Manifesto: Science, Technology, and Socialist-Feminism in the Late Twentieth Century." In *Simians, Cyborgs and Women: The Reinvention of Nature*, 149–81. New York: Routledge, 1991.

Hartman, Saidiya V. *Lose Your Mother: A Journey along the Atlantic Slave Route*. New York: Farrar, Strauss & Giroux, 2007.

———. *Scenes of Subjection: Terror, Slavery, and Self-Making in Nineteenth-Century America*. New York: Oxford University Press, 1997.

Hasian, Marouf Arif Jr. *The Rhetoric of Eugenics in Anglo-American Thought*. Athens: University of Georgia Press, 1996.

Heer, Jeet. "Science Fiction's White Boys' Club Strikes Back." *New Republic*, April 17, 2015. www.newrepublic.com.

Hebdige, Dick. *Subculture: The Meaning of Style*. New York: Methuen, 1979.

Hellekson, Karen. "A Fannish Field of Value: Online Fan Gift Culture." *Cinema Journal* 48, no. 4 (2009): 113–18.

Herring, Scott. *Another Country: Queer Anti-Urbanism*. New York: New York University Press, 2010.

Hewitt, Andrew. *Fascist Modernism: Aesthetics, Politics, and the Avant-Garde*. Stanford, CA: Stanford University Press, 1993.

Hilderbrand, Lucas. "In the Heat of the Moment: Notes on the Past, Present, and Future of *Born in Flames*." *Women & Performance: A Journal of Feminist Theory* 23, no. 1 (2013): 6–16.

Hocquenghem, Guy. *Homosexual Desire* [1972]. Translated by Daniella Dangoor. Durham, NC: Duke University Press, 1993.

Hodapp, James. "The Specter of the Postcolonial Child and Faux Long Takes in Cuarón's *Children of Men*." In *The Child in Post-Apocalyptic Cinema*, edited by Debbie Olson, 171–84. Lanham, MD: Lexington Books, 2015.

Holland, Sharon Patricia. *The Erotic Life of Racism*. Durham, NC: Duke University Press, 2012.

Hollinger, Veronica. "'Something like a Fiction': Speculative Intersections of Sexuality and Technology." In *Queer Universes: Sexualities in Science Fiction*, edited by Wendy Gay Pearson, 140–60. Liverpool, UK: Liverpool University Press, 2008.

Hong, Grace Kyungwon. *Death beyond Disavowal: The Impossible Politics of Difference*. Minneapolis: University of Minnesota Press, 2015.

Hopkinson, Nalo, and Uppinder Meehan, eds. *So Long Been Dreaming: Postcolonial Science Fiction*. Vancouver: Arsenal Pulp Press, 2004.

Horton-Stallings, LaMonda. *Funk the Erotic: Transaesthetics and Black Sexual Cultures*. Champaign: University of Illinois Press, 2015.

Hossain, Rokeya Sakhawat. "Sultana's Dream" [1905]. In *Sultana's Dream and Selections from The Secluded Ones*, edited by Roushan Jahan, 7–18. New York: Feminist Press, 1988.

Howard, Yetta. "Alien/ating Lesbianism: Ugly Sex and Postpunk Feminist Dystopia in Liquid Sky." *Women & Performance: A Journal of Feminist Theory* 21, no. 1 (2011): 41–61.

Huh, Jinny. "Race in Progress, No Passing Zone: *Battlestar Galactica*, Colorblindness, and the Maintenance of Racial Order." In *The Colorblind Screen: Television in Post-Racial America*, edited by Sarah Nilsen and Sarah E. Turner, 320–44. New York: New York University Press, 2014.

Hulser, Kathleen. "Les Guerilleres." *Afterimage* 11 (January 1984): 14–15.

Huxley, Aldous. *Brave New World* [1932]. New York: Rosetta Books, 2010.

———. *Brave New World Revisited* [1958]. New York: Rosetta Books, 2000.

Imarisha, Walidah. "Rewriting the Future: Using Science Fiction to Re-Envision Justice." *Bitch Magazine*, February 11, 2015. https://bitchmedia.org.

Imarisha, Walidah, and adrienne maree brown, eds. *Octavia's Brood: Science Fiction Stories from Social Justice Movements*. Oakland, CA: AK Press, 2015.

Ingram, Gordon Brent. "Strategies for (Re)Constructing Queer Communities." In *Queers in Space*, edited by Gordon Brent Ingram, Anne-Marie Bouthiellette, and Yolanda Retter, 447–58. Seattle: Bay Press, 1997.

Jaehne, Karen. "Born in Flames." *Film Quarterly* 37, no. 4 (1984): 22–24.

James, P. D. *The Children of Men* [1992]. New York: Vintage, 2006.

Jameson, Fredric. *Archaeologies of the Future: The Desire Called Utopia and Other Science Fictions*. New York: Verso, 2005.

Jameson, Storm. *Then We Shall Hear Singing, a Fantasy in C Major*. London: Macmillan, 1942.

Jarman, Derek. *Jubilee: Six Film Scripts*. Minneapolis: University of Minnesota Press, 2011.

———. *The Last of England*. London: Constable, 1987.

———. *Dancing Ledge*. London: Quartet Books, 1984.

Jenkins, Henry. *Convergence Culture: Where Old and New Media Collide*. New York: New York University Press, 2006.

———. "'Out of the Closet and into the Universe': Queers and *Star Trek*." In *Science Fiction Audiences: Watching Doctor Who and Star Trek*, edited by John Tulloch and Henry Jenkins, 237–66. New York: Routledge, 1995.

———. *Textual Poachers: Television Fans and Participatory Culture*. New York: Routledge, 1992.

Jensen, Erik N. "The Pink Triangle and Political Consciousness: Gays, Lesbians, and the Memory of Nazi Persecution." *Journal of the History of Sexuality* 11, nos. 1–2 (2002): 319–49.

Jerng, Mark Chia-Yon. "A World of Difference: Samuel R. Delany's *Dhalgren* and the Protocols of Racial Reading." *American Literature* 83, no. 2 (2011): 251–78.

Joannou, Maroula. *"Ladies, Please Don't Smash These Windows": Women's Writing, Feminist Consciousness and Social Change 1918–38*. Providence, RI: Berg, 1995.

Johnson, Brian David. *Science Fiction Prototyping: Designing the Future with Science Fiction*. San Francisco, CA: Morgan and Claypool, 2011.

Jones, Sarah Gwenllian. "The Sex Lives of Cult Television Characters." *Screen* 43, no. 1 (2002): 79–90.

Joyrich, Lynne. "Epistemology of the Console." *Critical Inquiry* 27, no. 3 (2001): 439–67.

Kafer, Alison. *Feminist, Queer, Crip*. Bloomington: Indiana University Press, 2013.

Kaplan, Amy. *The Anarchy of Empire in the Making of U.S. Culture*. Cambridge, MA: Harvard University Press, 2005.

Keeling, Kara. "Queer OS." *Cinema Journal* 53, no. 2 (2014): 152–57.

———. "Looking for M—: Queer Temporality, Black Political Possibility, and Poetry from the Future." *GLQ* 15, no. 4 (2009): 565–82.

Kelley, Robin. *Freedom Dreams: The Black Radical Imagination*. Boston: Beacon Press, 2002.

Kessler, Carol Farley. *Daring to Dream: Utopian Fiction by United States Women: 1836–1919*. Syracuse, NY: Syracuse University Press, 1984.

Kilgore, De Witt Douglas. "Queering the Coming Race? A Utopian Historical Imperative." In *Queer Universes: Sexualities in Science Fiction*, edited by Wendy Gay Pearson, 233–51. Liverpool, UK: Liverpool University Press, 2008.

———. *Astrofuturism: Science, Race, and Visions of Utopia in Space*. Philadelphia: University of Pennsylvania Press, 2003.

Kirby, David A. *Lab Coats in Hollywood: Science, Scientists, and Cinema*. Cambridge, MA: MIT Press, 2011.

Knabe, Susan, and Wendy Gay Pearson. "Gambling against History: Cruel Optimism and Queer Kinship in Octavia Butler's *Kindred*." In *Strange Matings: Science Fiction, Feminism, African American Voices, and Octavia E. Butler*, edited by Rebecca J. Holden and Nisi Shawl, 51–78. Seattle: Aqueduct Press, 2013.

Knabe, Susan Margaret, and Wendy Gay Pearson. *Zero Patience: A Queer Film Classic*. Vancouver, BC: Arsenal Pulp Press, 2011.

Knight, Damon. *In Search of Wonder: Essays on Modern Science Fiction*. Chicago: Advent Publications, 1967.

Knight, Nadine M. "Black Markets and Black Mystics: Racial Shorthand in *Battlestar Galactica*." *Science Fiction Film and Television* 5, no. 1 (2012): 47–66.

Koonz, Claudie. *Mothers in the Fatherland: Women, the Family, and Nazi Politics*. New York: St. Martin's Press, 1987.

Kreisinger, Elisa. "Queer Video Remix and LGBTQ Online Communities." *Transformative Works and Cultures* 9 (March 2012). http://dx.doi.org/10.3983/twc.2012.0395.

Kristeva, Julia. "Women's Time." Translated by Alice Jardine and Harry Blake. *Signs* 7, no. 1 (1981): 13–35.

Kun, Josh. *Audiotopia: Music, Race, and America*. Berkeley: University of California Press, 2005.

Kustritz, Anne. "Breeding Unity: *Battlestar Galactica*'s Biracial Reproductive Futurity." *Camera Obscura: Feminism, Culture, and Media Studies* 27, no. 3 (2012): 1–37.

Lane, Mary Bradley. *Mizora* [1890]. Lincoln: University of Nebraska Press, 1999.

Larbalestier, Justine. *Daughters of Earth: Feminist Science Fiction in the Twentieth Century*. Middletown, CT: Wesleyan University Press, 2006.

———. *The Battle of the Sexes in Science Fiction*. Middletown, CT: Wesleyan University Press, 2002.

Larsen, Nella. *Quicksand and Passing* [1928]. New Brunswick, NJ: Rutgers University Press, 1986.

Lassinaro, Kaisa. *Born in Flames*. London: Occasional Papers, 2011.

Lauretis, Teresa de. "Queer Theory: Lesbian and Gay Sexualities: An Introduction." *Differences: A Journal of Feminist Cultural Studies* 3, no. 2 (1992): iii–xviii.

Ledger, Sally. *The New Woman: Fiction and Feminism at the Fin de Siècle*. Manchester, UK: Manchester University Press, 1997.

Lefanu, Sarah. *In the Chinks of the World Machine: Feminism and Science Fiction*. London: Women's Press, 1988.

Lehr, Valerie. *Queer Family Values: Debunking the Myth of the Nuclear Family*. Philadelphia: Temple University Press, 1999.

Levitas, Ruth. *The Concept of Utopia*. Syracuse, NY: Syracuse University Press, 1990.

Lewes, Darby. *Dream Revisionaries: Gender and Genre in Women's Utopian Fiction 1870–1920*. Tuscaloosa: University of Alabama Press, 1995.

Lewin, Roger. "The Unmasking of Mitochondrial Eve." *Science* 238, no. 4823 (1987): 24–26.

Lierdumoa. "How Much Is That Geisha in the Window?" [2008]. July 24, 2009. www.youtube.com.

Lim, "Us | Multifandom." June 2, 2007. www.youtube.com.

Lim, Bliss Cua. *Translating Time: Cinema, the Fantastic, and Temporal Critique*. Durham, NC: Duke University Press, 2009.

Lim, Eng-Beng. "Queer Suicide: An Introduction to the Teach-In." *Social Text Periscope*, November 22, 2010. https://socialtextjournal.org.

lionpyh. "Fifty Years in the Virtuous City." *Archive of Our Own*, November 12, 2011. https://archiveofourown.org.

Lindsay, Vachel. *The Art of the Moving Picture*. New York: McMillan, 1915.

Lorde, Audre. *The Collected Poems of Audre Lorde*. New York: W. W. Norton, 2000.

———. "Poetry Is Not a Luxury." In *Sister Outsider: Essays and Speeches*, 36–39. Freedom, CA: Crossing Press, 1984.

Lothian, Alexis. "Sex, Utopia, and the Queer Temporalities of Fannish Love." In *Fandom: Identities and Communities in a Mediated World*, edited by Jonathan Gray, C. Lee Harrington, and Cornel Sandvoss, 2nd ed., 238–52. New York: New York University Press, 2017.

———. "A Different Kind of Love Song: Vidding Fandom's Undercommons." *Cinema Journal* 53, no. 3 (2015): 138–45.

———. "A Foretaste of the Future, a Caution from the Past: New Amazonia's Feminist Dream." In *New Amazonia: A Foretaste of the Future by Elizabeth Burgoyne Corbett*, 1–23. Seattle: Aqueduct Press, 2013.

———. "Archival Anarchies: Online Fandom, Subcultural Conservation, and the Transformative Work of Digital Ephemera." *International Journal of Cultural Studies* 16 (2013): 541–56.

———. "Living in a Den of Thieves: Fan Video and Digital Challenges to Ownership." *Cinema Journal* 48, no. 4 (2009): 130–36.

Lothian, Alexis, Kristina Busse, and Robin Anne Reid. "Yearning Void and Infinite Potential: Online Slash Fandom as Queer Female Space." *English Language Notes* 45, no. 2 (2007): 103–12.

Lotz, Amanda D. *The Television Will Be Revolutionized*. New York: New York University Press, 2007.

Love, Heather. *Feeling Backward: Loss and the Politics of Queer Life*. Cambridge, MA: Harvard University Press, 2007.

Luciano, Dana. *Arranging Grief: Sacred Time and the Body in Nineteenth-Century America*. New York: New York University Press, 2007.

Luckhurst, Roger. *Science Fiction*. Cambridge, UK: Polity Press, 2005.

Luminosity, "More Human than Human." December 2005. www.lumsvids.com.

MacCormack, Patricia. *Cinesexuality*. Burlington, VT: Ashgate, 2008.

Manovich, Lev. *Software Takes Command*. New York: Bloomsbury, 2013.

———. *The Language of New Media*. Cambridge, MA: MIT Press, 2001.

Marez, Curtis. *Farm Worker Futurism: Speculative Technologies of Resistance*. Minneapolis: University of Minnesota Press, 2016.

Marshall, Stuart. "The Contemporary Political Use of Gay History: The Third Reich." In *How Do I Look? Queer Film and Video*, edited by Bad Object Choices, 65–102. Seattle: Bay Press, 1991.

Marx, Karl. *Capital* [1867]. London: Penguin, 1990.

Maslen, Elizabeth. *Political and Social Issues in British Women's Fiction, 1928–1968*. New York: Palgrave, 2001.

Mazumdar, Pauline M. H. *Eugenics, Human Genetics and Human Failings*. New York: Routledge, 1992.

Mbembe, Achille. "Necropolitics." *Public Culture* 15, no. 1 (2003): 11–40.

McIntosh, Jonathan. "A History of Subversive Remix Video before YouTube: Thirty Political Video Mashups Made between World War II and 2005." *Transformative Works and Cultures* 9 (March 2012). http://dx.doi.org/10.3983/twc.2012.0371.

McKay, George. "Katharine Burdekin: An Alien Presence in Her Own Time." In *Recharting the Thirties*, edited by Patrick J. Quinn, 187–200. Cranbury, NJ: Associated University Presses, 1996.

McLuhan, Marshall. *Understanding Media: The Extensions of Man*. New York: McGraw-Hill, 1964.

McManus, Darragh. "*Swastika Night*: *Nineteen Eighty-Four*'s Lost Twin." *Guardian*, November 11, 2009. www.theguardian.com.

McPherson, Tara. "U.S. Operating Systems at Midcentury: The Intertwining of Race and UNIX." In *Race after the Internet*, edited by Lisa Nakamura and Peter Chow-White, 21–37. New York: Routledge, 2012.

Méliès, Georges. "Trick Effects." In *The Science Fiction Film Reader*, edited by Gregg Rickman, 2–4. Milwaukee, WI: Limelight Editions, 2004.

Melzer, Patricia. *Alien Constructions: Science Fiction and Feminist Thought*. Austin: University of Texas Press, 2006.

Merrick, Helen. *The Secret Feminist Cabal: A Cultural History of Science Fiction Feminisms*. Seattle: Aqueduct Press, 2009.

Miller, Paul D. *Rhythm Science*. Cambridge, MA: Mediawork/MIT Press, 2004.

Morgensen, Scott Lauria. *Spaces between Us: Queer Settler Colonialism and Indigenous Decolonization*. Minneapolis: University of Minnesota Press, 2011.

Morrison, Toni. *Beloved* [1987]. London: Picador, 1988.

Morrow, Fiona. "The Future Catches Up with Novelist William Gibson." *Globe and Mail*, October 3, 2007. www.theglobeandmail.com.

Mosley, Walter. "Black to the Future." In *Dark Matter: A Century of Speculative Fiction from the African Diaspora*, edited by Sheree R. Thomas, 405–7. New York: Aspect, 2000.

Moten, Fred. *In the Break: The Aesthetics of the Black Radical Tradition*. Minneapolis: University of Minnesota Press, 2003.

Muñoz, José. *Cruising Utopia: The Then and There of Queer Futurity*. New York: New York University Press, 2009.

———. *Disidentifications: Queers of Color and the Performance of Politics*. Minneapolis: University of Minnesota Press, 1999.

Murphy, Patricia. *Time Is of the Essence: Temporality, Gender, and the New Woman*. Albany: State University of New York Press, 2001.

Nadkarni, Asha. *Eugenic Feminism: Reproductive Nationalism in the United States and India*. Minneapolis: University of Minnesota Press, 2014.

Nakamura, Lisa. "Indigenous Circuits: Navajo Women and the Racialization of Early Electronic Manufacture." *American Quarterly* 66, no. 4 (2014): 919–41.

———. "Economies of Digital Production in East Asia: iPhone Girls and the Transnational Circuits of Cool." *Media Fields Journal* 2 (2011).www.mediafieldsjournal.org.

———. *Cybertypes: Race, Ethnicity, and Identity on the Internet.* New York: Routledge, 2002.

Nama, Adilifu. *Black Space: Imagining Race in Science Fiction Film.* Austin: University of Texas Press, 2010.

Nash, Jennifer. *The Black Body in Ecstasy: Reading Race, Reading Pornography.* Durham, NC: Duke University Press, 2014.

Nast, Heidi J. "Queer Patriarchies, Queer Racisms, International." *Antipode* 34, no. 5 (2002): 874–909.

Needham, Gary. "Scheduling Normativity: Television, the Family, and Queer Temporality." In *Queer TV: Theories, Histories, Politics,* edited by Glyn Davis and Gary Needham, 143–58. New York: Routledge, 2008.

Nelson, Alondra. "Making the Impossible Possible: An Interview with Nalo Hopkinson." *Social Text* 20, no. 2 (2002): 97–113.

Nickelsburg, Monica. "A Brief History of the Guy Fawkes Mask." *Week,* July 3, 2013. http://theweek.com.

Nishime, LeiLani. "Aliens: Narrating U.S. Global Identity through Transnational Adoption and Interracial Marriage in *Battlestar Galactica.*" *Critical Studies in Media Communication* 28, no. 5 (2011): 450–65.

Nyong'o, Tavia. "So Say We All." *Social Text: Periscope,* January 1, 2012. https://socialtextjournal.org.

———. *The Amalgamation Waltz: Race, Performance, and the Ruses of Memory.* Minneapolis: University of Minnesota Press, 2009.

———. "Do You Want Queer Theory (or Do You Want the Truth)? Intersections of Punk and Queer in the 1970s." *Radical History Review* 100 (Winter 2008): 102–19.

O'Pray, Michael. *Derek Jarman: Dreams of England.* London: BFI Publishing, 1996.

Orban, Clara. "Women, Futurism, and Fascism." In *Mothers of Invention: Women, Italian Fascism, and Culture,* edited by Robin Pickering-Iazzi, 52–75. Minneapolis: University of Minnesota Press, 1995.

Ordover, Nancy. *American Eugenics: Race, Queer Anatomy, and the Science of Nationalism.* Minneapolis: University of Minnesota Press, 2003.

Orwell, George. *Nineteen Eighty-Four* [1949]. London: Penguin, 1989.

Paik, Peter Y. *From Utopia to Apocalypse: Science Fiction and the Politics of Catastrophe.* Minneapolis: University of Minnesota Press, 2010.

Patai, Daphne. "Imagining Reality: The Utopian Fiction of Katherine Burdekin." In *Rediscovering Forgotten Radicals: British Women Writers, 1889–1939,* edited by Angela Ingram and Daphne Patai, 226–43. Chapel Hill: University of North Carolina Press, 1993.

———. Afterword. In *Proud Man,* by Katharine Burdekin, 319–50. New York: The Feminist Press, 1993.

———. Afterword. In *The End of This Day's Business,* by Katharine Burdekin, 159–90. New York: The Feminist Press, 1989.

———. Introduction. In *Swastika Night*, by Katharine Burdekin, iii–xv. New York: The Feminist Press, 1985.

———. "Orwell's Despair, Burdekin's Hope: Gender and Power in Dystopia." *Women's Studies International Forum* 7, no. 2 (1984): 85–95.

Patterson, Orlando. *Slavery and Social Death: A Comparative Study.* Cambridge, MA: Harvard University Press, 1982.

Pearson, Wendy. "Alien Cryptographies: The View from Queer." *Science Fiction Studies* 26, no. 1 (1999): 1–22.

Pearson, Wendy Gay. "Towards a Queer Genealogy of SF." In *Queer Universes: Sexualities in Science Fiction*, edited by Wendy Gay Pearson, 71–100. Liverpool, UK: Liverpool University Press, 2008.

Pegues, Juliana Hu. "Miss Cylon: Empire and Adoption in *Battlestar Galactica*." *MELUS* 33, no. 4 (2008): 189–209.

Penley, Constance, Elisabeth Lyon, Lynn Spigel, and Janet Bergstrom, eds. *Close Encounters: Film, Feminism, and Science Fiction.* Minneapolis: University of Minnesota Press, 1991.

Phillips, Rasheedah. "Black Quantum Futurism: Theory & Practice, Vol. 1." In *Black Quantum Futurism: Theory & Practice, Vol. 1*, edited by Rasheedah Phillips, 11–30. Philadelphia: Afrofuturist Affair / House of Future Sciences Books, 2015.

Pierce, Andrew. "David Cameron Says Sorry over Section 28 Gay Law." *Telegraph*, July 1, 2009. www.telegraph.co.uk.

Pryke, Michael, and John Allen. "Monetized Time-Space Derivatives—Money's 'New Imaginary'?" *Economy and Society* 29, no. 2 (2000): 264–84.

Puar, Jasbir. "In the Wake of It Gets Better." *Guardian*, November 11, 2010. www.theguardian.com.

———. *Terrorist Assemblages: Homonationalism in Queer Times.* Durham, NC: Duke University Press, 2007.

Rabaka, Reiland. "W. E. B. Du Bois's 'The Comet' and Contributions to Critical Race Theory: An Essay on Black Radical Politics and Anti-Racist Social Ethics." *Ethnic Studies Review* 29, no. 1 (2006): 22–50.

Ramirez, Catherine S. "Afrofuturism/Chicanafuturism: Fictive Kin." *Aztlan* 33, no. 1 (2008): 185–92.

Randell, Karen. "'Now the Gloves Come Off': The Problematic of 'Enhanced Interrogation Techniques' in *Battlestar Galactica*." *Cinema Journal* 51, no. 1 (2012): 168–73.

Reddy, Chandan. *Freedom with Violence: Race, Sexuality, and the US State.* Durham, NC: Duke University Press, 2011.

Reid, Robin Anne. "'The Wild Unicorn Herd Check-In': The Politics of Race in Science Fiction Fandom." In *Black and Brown Planets: The Politics of Race in Science Fiction*, edited by Isaiah Lavender III, 225–40. Jackson: University of Mississippi Press, 2014.

Reid-Pharr, Robert. "Clean: Death and Desire in Samuel R. Delany's *Stars in My Pocket like Grains of Sand*." *American Literature* 83, no. 2 (2011): 389–411.

———. "Dinge." In *Black Gay Man: Essays*, 85–97. New York: New York University Press, 2001.

Rhee, Margaret. "In Search of My Robot: Race, Technology, and the Asian American Body." *Scholar & Feminist Online* 13, no. 3 (2016). http://sfonline.barnard.edu.

Rich, B. Ruby. *New Queer Cinema: The Director's Cut*. Durham, NC: Duke University Press, 2013.

Rieder, John. *Colonialism and the Emergence of Science Fiction*. Middletown, CT: Wesleyan University Press, 2008.

Riesman, Abraham. "Future Shock: Director Alfonso Cuarón Revisits Children of Men." *Vulture*, December 26, 2016. www.vulture.com.

Robb, George. "The Way of All Flesh: Degeneration, Eugenics, and the Gospel of Free Love." *Journal of the History of Sexuality* 6, no. 4 (1996): 589–603.

Robinson, Cedric. *Black Marxism: The Making of the Black Radical Tradition*, 2nd ed. Chapel Hill: University of North Carolina Press, 2000.

Rodríguez, Juana María. *Sexual Futures, Queer Gestures, and Other Latina Longings*. New York: New York University Press, 2014.

———. *Queer Latinidad: Identity Practices, Discursive Spaces*. New York: New York University Press, 2003.

Rogan, Alcena Madeline Davis. "Alien Sex Acts in Feminist Science Fiction: Heuristic Models for Thinking a Feminist Future of Desire." *PMLA* 119, no. 3 (2004): 442–56.

Rohy, Valerie. *Anachronism and Its Others: Sexuality, Race, Temporality*. Albany: State University of New York Press, 2009.

Rosenberg, Jordana, and Britt Rusert. "Framing Finance: Rebellion, Dispossession, and the Geopolitics of Enclosure in Samuel Delany's Nevèrÿon Series." *Radical History Review* 2014, no. 118 (2014): 64–91.

Russ, Joanna. *We Who Are About To . . .* [1976]. Middletown, CT: Wesleyan University Press, 2005.

Russell, Elizabeth. "The Loss of the Feminine Principle in Charlotte Haldane's *Man's World* and Katherine Burdekin's *Swastika Night*." In *Where No Man Has Gone Before: Women and Science Fiction*, edited by Lucie Armitt, 15–28. New York: Routledge, 1991.

Russo, Julie Levin. "Indiscrete Media: Television/Digital Convergence and Economies of Online Lesbian Fan Communities." PhD diss., Brown University, 2010.

———. "Battlestar Redactica: Visual Revision of Narrative Error." *Media Commons*, November 11, 2009. http://mediacommons.futureofthebook.org.

———. "User-Penetrated Content: Fan Video in the Age of Convergence." *Cinema Journal* 48, no. 4 (2009): 125–30.

———. "Hera Has Six Mommies: A Transmedia Love Story." *Flow* 7 (December 12, 2007). www.flowjournal.org.

Rutledge, Gregory E. "Futurist Fiction and Fantasy: The Racial Establishment." *Callaloo* 24, no. 1 (2001): 236–52.

sabrina_il, "After Tomorrow." *Archive of Our Own*, December 12, 2009. http://archiveofourown.org.

Sallis, James. Introduction. In *Ash of Stars: On the Writing of Samuel R. Delany*, edited by James Sallis, ix–xviii. Jackson: University Press of Mississippi, 1996.

Samer, Roxanne. "Receiving Feminisms: Media Cultures and Lesbian Potentiality in the 1970s." PhD diss., University of Southern California, 2016.

Savage, Jon. *England's Dreaming: Anarchy, Sex Pistols, Punk Rock, and Beyond*. New York: St. Martin's, 1992.

Schneider, Steven Jay. *101 Sci-Fi Movies You Must See before You Die*. London: Octopus Publishing, 2009.

Schuyler, George S. *Black No More*. New York: Modern Library, 1999.

Scott, Suzanne. "Repackaging Fan Culture: The Regifting Economy of Ancillary Content Models." *Transformative Works and Cultures* 3 (September 2009). http://dx.doi.org/10.3983/twc.2009.0150.

———. "Authorized Resistance: Is Fan Production Frakked?" In *Cylons in America: Critical Studies in Battlestar Galactica*, edited by Tiffany Potter and T. W. Marshall, 210–23. New York: Continuum, 2008.

Sedgwick, Eve Kosofsky. "Queer and Now." In *Tendencies*, 1–22. New York, NY: Routledge, 1994.

———. *Between Men: English Literature and Male Homosocial Desire*. New York: Columbia University Press, 1985.

Seed, David. "Aldous Huxley, *Brave New World*." In *A Companion to Science Fiction*, edited by David Seed, 477–88. Oxford, UK: Blackwell, 2005.

Selznick, Barbara. "Branding the Future: Syfy in the Post-Network Era." *Science Fiction Film and Television* 2, no. 2 (2009): 177–203.

Sengoopta, Chandak. *Otto Weininger: Sex, Science, and Self in Imperial Vienna*. Chicago: University of Chicago Press, 2000.

Shaviro, Stephen. "Hyperbolic Futures: Speculative Finance and Speculative Fiction." *Cascadia Subduction Zone: A Literary Quarterly* 1 (April 2011): 3–6.

Shaw, Deborah. *The Three Amigos: The Transnational Filmmaking of Guillermo Del Toro, Alejandro Gonzalez Inarritu, and Alfonso Cuarón*. Oxford: Oxford University Press, 2016.

Shawl, Nisi. "The Third Parable." In *Strange Matings: Science Fiction, Feminism, African American Voices, and Octavia E. Butler*, edited by Rebecca J. Holden and Nisi Shawl, 208–13. Seattle: Aqueduct Press, 2013.

———. *Filter House*. Seattle: Aqueduct Press, 2008.

Sheldon, Rebekah. *The Child to Come: Life after the Human Catastrophe*. Minneapolis: University of Minnesota Press, 2016.

Sinfield, Alan. "Review of Lee Edelman's *No Future: Queer Theory and the Death Drive*." *Radical Philosophy* 134 (November/December 2005): 49–51.

Slane, Andrea. *A Not So Foreign Affair: Fascism, Sexuality, and the Cultural Rhetoric of American Democracy*. Durham, NC: Duke University Press, 2001.

Smith, Andrea. "Queer Theory and Native Studies: The Heteronormativity of Settler Colonialism." *GLQ* 16, nos. 1–2 (2010): 42–68.

Smith, Barbara. "A Press of Our Own Kitchen Table: Women of Color Press." *Frontiers: A Journal of Women Studies* 10, no. 3 (1989): 11–13.

Smith, Darryl A. "Droppin' Science Fiction: Signification and Singularity in the Metapocalypse of Du Bois, Baraka, and Bell." *Science Fiction Studies* 34, no. 2 (2007): 201–19.

Snorton, C. Riley. "Gender Trouble in *Triton*." In *No Tea, No Shade: New Writings in Black Queer Studies*, edited by E. Patrick Johnson, 83–94. Durham, NC: Duke University Press, 2016.

Sobchack, Vivian. *Screening Space: The American Science Fiction Film*, 2nd ed. New Brunswick, NJ: Rutgers University Press, 1987.

Somerville, Siobhan P. *Queering the Color Line: Race and the Invention of Homosexuality in American Culture*. Durham, NC: Duke University Press, 2000.

Sontag, Susan. "The Imagination of Disaster." *Commentary*, October 1965, 42–48.

sophinisba, "Sick." *Archive of Our Own*, December 12, 2009. http://archiveofourown .org.

Spade, Dean. *Normal Life: Administrative Violence, Critical Trans Politics, and the Limits of Law*. Brooklyn, NY: South End Press, 2011.

Spillers, Hortense J. "Interstices: A Small Drama of Words." In *Black, White, and in Color: Essays on American Literature and Culture*, 152–75. Chicago: University of Chicago Press, 2003.

———. "Mama's Baby, Papa's Maybe: An American Grammar Book." In *Black, White and in Color: Essays on American Literature and Culture*, 203–29. Chicago: University of Chicago Press, 2003.

Spurlin, William J. *Lost Intimacies: Rethinking Homosexuality under National Socialism*. New York: Peter Lang, 2009.

Squier, Susan. "Conflicting Scientific Feminisms: Charlotte Haldane and Naomi Mitchison." In *Natural Eloquence: Women Reinscribe Science*, edited by Barbara T. Gates and Ann B. Shteir, 179–95. Madison: University of Wisconsin Press, 1997.

———. *Babies in Bottles: Twentieth-Century Visions of Reproductive Technology*. New Brunswick, NJ: Rutgers University Press, 1994.

Stanfill, Mel. "Spinning Yarn with Borrowed Cotton: Lessons for Fandom from Sampling." *Cinema Journal* 54, no. 3 (2015): 131–37.

———. "Doing Fandom, (Mis)doing Whiteness: Heteronormativity, Racialization, and the Discursive Construction of Fandom." *Transformative Works and Cultures* 8 (November 2011). http://dx.doi.org/10.3983/twc.2011.0256.

Stanley, Eric, Wu Tsang, and Chris Vargas. "Queer Love Economies: Making Trans/ Feminist Film in Precarious Times." *Women & Performance: A Journal of Feminist Theory* 23, no. 1 (2013): 66–82.

Stavney, Anne. "'Mothers of Tomorrow': The New Negro Renaissance and the Politics of Maternal Representation." *African American Review* 32, no. 4 (1998): 533–61.

Stec, Lauretta. "Dystopian Modernism vs. Utopian Feminism: Burdekin, Woolf, and West Respond to the Rise of Fascism." In *Virginia Woolf and Fascism: Resisting the Dictators' Seduction*, edited by Merry M. Pawlowski, 178–93. Basingstoke, UK: Palgrave, 2001.

Stephenson, Neal. "Innovation Starvation." *World Policy Journal* 28, no. 3 (2011): 11–16.

Stern, Alexandra Minna. *Eugenic Nation: Faults and Frontiers of Better Breeding in Modern America*. Berkeley: University of California Press, 2005.

Stewart, Garrett. "The 'Videology' of Science Fiction." In *Shadows of the Magic Lamp*, edited by George E. Slusser and Eric S. Rabkin, 159–207. Carbondale: Southern Illinois University Press, 1985.

Stoler, Ann L. *Race and the Education of Desire: Foucault's History of Sexuality and the Colonial Order of Things*. Durham, NC: Duke University Press, 1995.

Stone, Allucquere Rosanne. *The War of Desire and Technology at the Close of the Mechanical Age*. Cambridge, MA: MIT Press, 1995.

Stopes, Marie. *Radiant Motherhood: A Book for Those Who Are Creating the Future*. London: G. P. Putnam & Sons, 1921.

Streeby, Shelley. *Imagining the Future of Climate Change*. Berkeley: University of California Press, 2017.

———. "Speculative Archives: Histories of the Future of Education." *Pacific Coast Philology* 49, no. 1 (2014): 25–40.

Suvin, Darko. *Metamorphoses of Science Fiction: On the Poetics and History of a Literary Genre*. New Haven, CT: Yale University Press, 1979.

Taylor, Keeanga-Yamahtta. *From #BlackLivesMatter to Black Liberation*. Chicago: Haymarket Books, 2016.

Tehranian, John. "Infringement Nation: Copyright Reform and the Law/Norm Gap." *Utah Law Review* (2007): 537–49.

Telotte, J. P. *Science Fiction TV*. New York: Routledge, 2014.

Theweleit, Klaus. *Male Fantasies, 1. Women, Floods, Bodies, History*. Minneapolis: University of Minnesota Press, 1987.

thingswithwings, "Known Associates." *Archive of Our Own*, March 25, 2016. http://archiveofourown.org.

Thomas, Sheree R., "Introduction: Looking for the Invisible." In *Dark Matter: A Century of Speculative Fiction from the African Diaspora*, edited by Sheree R. Thomas, ix–xiv. New York: Aspect, 2000.

Tinsley, Omise'eke Natasha. "Black Atlantic, Queer Atlantic: Queer Imaginings of the Middle Passage." *GLQ* 14, nos. 2–3 (2008): 191–215.

Tongson, Karen. *Relocations: Queer Suburban Imaginaries*. New York: New York University Press, 2011.

Tucker, Jeffrey Allen. "The Necessity of Models, of Alternatives: Samuel R. Delany's *Stars in My Pocket like Grains of Sand*." *South Atlantic Quarterly* 109, no. 2 (2010): 249–78.

———. *A Sense of Wonder: Samuel R. Delany, Race, Identity, and Difference*. Middletown, CT: Wesleyan University Press, 2004.

Tushnet, Rebecca. "Payment in Credit: Copyright Law and Subcultural Creativity." *Law & Contemporary Problems* 70, no. 10 (2007): 135–75.

TWC Editor. "Pattern Recognition: A Dialogue on Racism in Fan Communities." *Transformative Works and Cultures* 3 (September 2009). http://dx.doi .org/10.3983/twc.2009.0172.

Udden, James. "Child of the Long Take: Alfonso Cuaron's Film Aesthetics in the Shadow of Globalization." *Style* 43, no. 1 (2009): 26–44.

Villarejo, Amy. *Ethereal Queer: Television, Historicity, Desire.* Durham, NC: Duke University Press, 2014.

Vint, Sherryl. "'Only by Experience': Embodiment and the Limitations of Realism in Neo-Slave Narratives." *Science Fiction Studies* 34, no. 2 (2007): 241–61.

Vora, Kalindi. *Life Support: Biocapital and the New History of Outsourced Labor.* Minneapolis: University of Minnesota Press, 2015.

Wälivaara, Josefine. "Dreams of a Subversive Future: Sexuality, (Hetero)normativity, and Queer Potential in Science Fiction Film and Television." PhD diss., Umea University, 2016.

Wanzo, Rebecca. "African American Acafandom and Other Strangers: New Genealogies of Fan Studies." *Transformative Works and Cultures* 20 (September 2015). http://dx.doi.org/10.3983/twc.2015.0699.

Warner, Michael. *Publics and Counterpublics.* New York: Zone Books, 2002.

———. Introduction. In *Fear of a Queer Planet: Queer Politics and Social Theory*, edited by Michael Warner, vi–xxxi. Minneapolis: University of Minnesota Press, 1994.

Weedman, Jane Branham. *Samuel R. Delany.* Mercer Island, WA: Starmont House, 1982.

Wegner, Phillip E. *Imaginary Communities: Utopia, the Nation, and the Spatial Histories of Modernity.* Berkeley: University of California Press, 2002.

Weheliye, Alexander G. *Habeas Viscus: Racializing Assemblages, Biopolitics, and Black Feminist Theories of the Human.* Durham, NC: Duke University Press, 2014.

Weinbaum, Alys Eve. "Interracial Romance and Black Internationalism." In *Next to the Color Line: Gender, Sexuality, and W. E. B. Du Bois*, edited by Susan Kay Gillman and Alys Eve Weinbaum, 96–123. Minneapolis: University of Minnesota Press, 2007.

———. *Wayward Reproductions: Genealogies of Race and Nation in Transatlantic Modern Thought.* Durham, NC: Duke University Press, 2004.

Weininger, Otto. *Sex and Character.* London: Heinemann, 1906.

Weinstone, Ann. "Science Fiction as a Young Person's First Queer Theory." *Science Fiction Studies* 26, no. 1 (1999): 41–48.

Wells, H. G. *A Modern Utopia* [1905]. Lincoln: University of Nebraska Press, 1969.

Wesch, Michael. "An Anthropological Introduction to YouTube." July 7, 2008. www.youtube.com.

Williams, Keith. "Back from the Future: Katharine Burdekin and Science Fiction in the 1930s." In *Women Writers of the 1930s: Gender, Politics and History*, edited by Maroula Joannou, 151–64. Edinburgh: Edinburgh University Press, 1999.

Willis, Ika. "Writing the Fables of Sexual Difference: Slash Fiction as Technology of Gender." *Parallax* 22, no. 3 (2016): 290–311.

Willse, Craig, and Dean Spade. "We Are Born in Flames." *Women & Performance: A Journal of Feminist Theory* 23, no. 1 (2013): 1–5.

Winnubst, Shannon. "Vampires, Anxieties, and Dreams: Race and Sex in the Contemporary United States." *Hypatia* 18, no. 3 (2003): 1–20.

Wojnarowicz, David. *Close to the Knives: A Memoir of Disintegration*. New York: Vintage, 1992.

Womack, Ytasha. *Afrofuturism: The World of Black Sci-Fi and Fantasy Culture*. Chicago: Lawrence Hill Books, 2013.

Woolf, Virginia. *Three Guineas* [1938]. Orlando, FL: Harcourt, 2006.

———. *A Room of One's Own* [1929]. Orlando, FL: Harcourt, 2005.

Yaszek, Lisa. "Afrofuturism, Science Fiction, and the History of the Future." *Socialism and Democracy* 20, no. 3 (2006): 41–60.

———. "An Afrofuturist Reading of Ellison's *Invisible Man*." *Rethinking History* 9, nos. 2–3 (2005): 297–313.

INDEX

3:10 to Yuma, 236

9/11, 91, 210, 212, 242, 250

28 Days Later, 248

1977, 185, 193, 196, 286n96

2016, 177, 196, 254

abortion, 34, 266n9

Abu-Jamal, Mumia, 234

academia: fandom and, 170–171, 220–221, 231, 248–249; queer studies in, 5–6, 182; science fiction in, 14, 15–17; temporality of, 13–14, 22, 215, 249, 252; vidding in, 247–252; women of color feminist theory in, 205

adolescence, 33, 68, 133, 148–149

affect: and digital media, 169–170, 217, 219; of dystopia, 59, 61, 187, 196; of fandom, 169–170, 223, 227–229, 230, 238, 244–245, 247; of feminist coalition, 202, 205; queer, 10–11, 135, 141, 147, 170, 213, 233; of science fiction, 140–141, 148–149; as speculative critical engagement, 23, 24, 233–237, 244–247; of speculative film, 178; of utopia, 135–137, 139, 160, 278n20; of vidding, 223, 227–229, 233, 238, 251

African Americans, 101–103, 106–115, 119, 123, 125, 127, 159, 278n39. *See also* blackness

African diaspora, 102, 105–107, 115, 159. *See also* blackness

Afrofuturism, 19, 26, 102–107, 127–128, 159; Black Quantum Futurism. 103;

and gender, 104, 113, 127–128; origin of term, 102

Ahmed, Sara, 12, 33, 72, 134, 274n11

Albarn, Damon, 236

aliens: as colonial metaphor, 19; immigrants as, 66; in James Tiptree, Jr., 241; in Samuel R. Delany, 150, 153–154, 155–156, 161, 169; in science fiction film, 16, 176, 180–181

Allison, Dorothy, 148

Allman, Sheldon, 223

alternate history, 74, 106, 189

Amyl Nitrate (*Jubilee*), 189–195, 197

androgyny, 52, 55, 69–70, 73, 151, 272n85

animals, 54, 84–85, 101, 121; people described as, 40, 46–47, 72, 85, 156

Anonymous, 230

"Anthem" (MCI TV ad), 167–168

antiblackness: as foundation of colonial temporalities, 13, 61, 65, 67, 71, 92, 105–108, 115, 239; in contemporary US, 100, 206, 249

antihumanism, 115–116, 241

antisemitism, 68, 83, 120, 188, 195, 271n45

antisocial thesis. *See under* queer theory

apocalypse: colonial history as, 107–109, 275n27; ecological 93, 181–182; fictional representations of, 51, 90, 125, 145, 157, 162; rhetoric of, 4, 267n14; visual depictions of 91, 95, 180–182, 187–188, 210, 225, 241–242. *See also* end of the world

Aqueduct Press, 45, 265n54

Araki, Gregg, 183

ABOUT THE AUTHOR

Alexis Lothian is Assistant Professor of Women's Studies and Core Faculty in the Design Cultures & Creativity Program at the University of Maryland, College Park. She is a member of the James Tiptree, Jr, Literary Award motherboard and is on the organizing committee for the feminist science fiction convention WisCon.